SIN

6
our price

THE BIRDS OF
CALIFORNIA

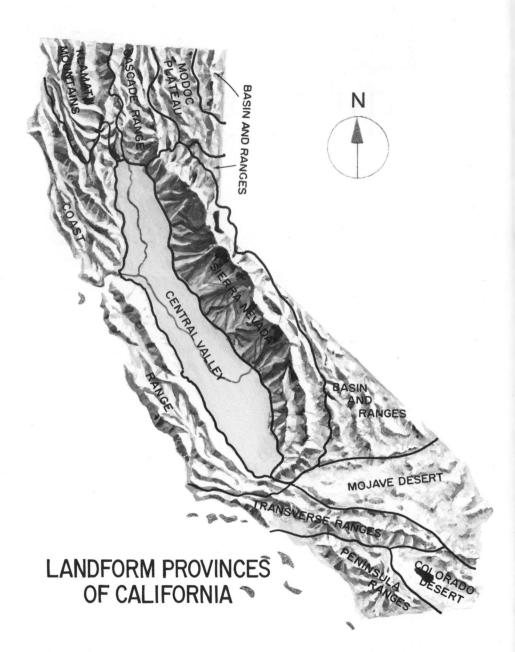

N

KLAMATH MOUNTAINS

CASCADE RANGE

MODOC PLATEAU

BASIN AND RANGES

COAST

SIERRA NEVADA

CENTRAL VALLEY

RANGE

BASIN AND RANGES

MOJAVE DESERT

TRANSVERSE RANGES

PENINSULA RANGES

COLORADO DESERT

LANDFORM PROVINCES
OF CALIFORNIA

THE BIRDS OF CALIFORNIA

by Arnold Small

with photographs by the author
and maps by Robert Sandmeyer & Keith Axelson

WINCHESTER PRESS • New York

To Mimi, Donalee, and Brian

Library of Congress Catalog Card Number: 73-78829
ISBN: 0-87691-119-X

Design by Dennis J. Grastorf

Second printing 1975

WINCHESTER PRESS
205 East 42nd Street
New York, N.Y. 10017

Printed in the United States of America

Contents

Checklist of the Birds of California   vii

Preface   xxiii

Introduction   1

1 California and Its Bird Life   5

    Land Regions and Climate of California   5

    Distribution of California Birds   11

2 Birds and Bird Study   22

3 Annotated List of the Birds of California   33

4 California's Habitats for Birds   139

    The Sea and the Seacoast   141

      The Open Sea   142

      The Offshore Islands and Coastal Sea Cliffs   149

      The Sea Beaches, Reefs, and Coastal Waters   156

      The Lagoons, Bays, and Estuaries   163

      The Tidal Flats and Salt-Water Marshes   169

    Fresh-Water Habitats   176

      The Fresh-Water Marshes   177

      Lakes, Rivers, and Streams   183

    Brushland   190

      Chaparral   190

    Grassland and Savannah   198

      Grassland   198

      Savannah   202

Woodlands 204

    Oak Woodland 205

    Riparian Woodlands and Oases 210

The California Deserts 220

    The San Joaquin Valley Desert 225

    The Sonoran Desert 228

    The Colorado Desert 231

    The Mojave Desert 236

The Great Basin 242

The Mountains and Mountain Forests 249

    Piñon-Juniper Woodland 252

    Montane Forest 257

    Subalpine Forest 265

    Alpine Zone 271

The Coastal Coniferous Forests 276

Man-Created Habitats 281

    Farms, Ranches, and Refuges 283

    Cities, Towns, and Suburbs 289

    The Salton Sea 294

Index 303

CHECKLIST OF
THE BIRDS OF CALIFORNIA

The following checklist of the birds of California is arranged in standard tax-onomic order. Of these 518* species, 304 species (plus two additional subspecies) are illustrated in photographs, for which page numbers are given. The number within the parentheses following the family name represents the total number of species within that family which have been recorded in California between 1900 and 1973. The checkbox preceding the species name may be used for tallying your state list.

Illustrated
on page

ORDER: Gaviiformes (Loons)
  FAMILY: Gaviidae (Loons; 4)
    SPECIES: ☐ COMMON LOON *(Gavia immer)* 164
             ☐ YELLOW-BILLED LOON *(Gavia adamsii)* 36
             ☐ PACIFIC LOON *(Gavia pacifica)* 157
               (classified by AOU Checklist as
               Arctic Loon *Gavia arctica*)
             ☐ RED-THROATED LOON *(Gavia stellata)* 157

ORDER: Podicipediformes (Grebes)
  FAMILY: Podicipedidae (Grebes; 6)
    SPECIES: ☐ RED-NECKED GREBE *(Podiceps grisegena)* .... −
             ☐ HORNED GREBE *(Podiceps auritus)* 164
             ☐ EARED GREBE *(Podiceps nigricollis)* 186
             ☐ LEAST GREBE *(Podiceps dominicus)* .... −
             ☐ WESTERN GREBE *(Aechmophorus occidentalis)* 37
             ☐ PIED-BILLED GREBE *(Podilymbus podiceps)* 179

*Note—In 1974, seven new species were added to the state list, bringing the state total to 525. These birds are not listed in their proper places in the checklist, but are listed on p. xxii, following the check-list.

ORDER: Procellariiformes (Tubenoses)
   FAMILY: Diomedeidae (Albatrosses; 4)
      SPECIES: ☐ WANDERING ALBATROSS *(Diomedea exulans)* .... −
                ☐ SHORT-TAILED ALBATROSS *(Diomedea albatrus)* .... −
                ☐ BLACK-FOOTED ALBATROSS *(Diomedea nigripes)* 38, 146
                ☐ LAYSAN ALBATROSS *(Diomedea immutabilis)* .... −

   FAMILY: Procellariidae (Fulmars, Shearwaters, and Petrels; 8)
      SPECIES: ☐ CAPE PETREL *(Daption capense)* .... −
                ☐ NORTHERN FULMAR *(Fulmarus glacialis)* 39, 146
                ☐ PINK-FOOTED SHEARWATER *(Puffinus creatopus)* 39, 146
                ☐ FLESH-FOOTED SHEARWATER *(Puffinus carneipes)* .... −
                ☐ NEW ZEALAND SHEARWATER *(Puffinus bulleri)* 147
                ☐ SOOTY SHEARWATER *(Puffinus griseus)* 146
                ☐ SHORT-TAILED SHEARWATER *(Puffinus tenuirostris)* .... −
                ☐ MANX SHEARWATER *(Puffinus puffinus)* .... −

   FAMILY: Hydrobatidae (Storm-Petrels; 8)
      SPECIES: ☐ FORK-TAILED STORM-PETREL *(Oceanodroma furcata)* .... −
                ☐ LEACH'S STORM-PETREL *(Oceanodroma leucorhoa)* .... −
                ☐ ASHY STORM-PETREL *(Oceanodroma homochroa)* .... −
                ☐ GALAPAGOS STORM-PETREL *(Oceanodroma tethys)* .... −
                ☐ HARCOURT'S STORM-PETREL *(Oceanodroma castro)* .... −
                ☐ BLACK STORM-PETREL *(Oceanodroma melania)* .... −
                ☐ LEAST STORM-PETREL *(Halocyptena microsoma)* .... −
                ☐ WILSON'S STORM-PETREL *(Oceanites oceanicus)* 41

ORDER: Pelecaniformes (Pelicans and Allies)
   FAMILY: Phaethontidae (Tropicbirds; 2)
      SPECIES: ☐ RED-BILLED TROPICBIRD *(Phaethon aethereus)* 42
                ☐ WHITE-TAILED TROPICBIRD *(Phaethon lepturus)* .... −

   FAMILY: Pelecanidae (Pelicans; 2)
      SPECIES: ☐ WHITE PELICAN *(Pelecanus erythrorhynchos)* 42
                ☐ BROWN PELICAN *(Pelecanus occidentalis)* 150, 151

   FAMILY: Sulidae (Boobies; 2)
      SPECIES: ☐ BLUE-FOOTED BOOBY *(Sula nebouxii)* 43, 298
                ☐ BROWN BOOBY *(Sula leucogaster)* 298

   FAMILY: Phalacrocoracidae (Cormorants; 4)
      SPECIES: ☐ DOUBLE-CRESTED CORMORANT *(Phalacrocorax auritus)* 44
                ☐ OLIVACEOUS CORMORANT *(Phalacrocorax olivaceus)* .... −
                ☐ BRANDT'S CORMORANT *(Phalacrocorax penicillatus)* 151
                ☐ PELAGIC CORMORANT *(Phalacrocorax pelagicus)* 152

   FAMILY: Fregatidae (Frigatebirds; 1)
      SPECIES: ☐ MAGNIFICENT FRIGATEBIRD *(Fregata magnificens)* 45

ORDER: Ciconiiformes (Herons and Allies)
　FAMILY: Ardeidae (Herons and Bitterns; 12)
　　SPECIES: ☐ GREAT BLUE HERON *(Ardea herodias)* 46
　　　　　　☐ GREEN HERON *(Butorides virescens)* 179
　　　　　　☐ LITTLE BLUE HERON *(Florida caerulea)* 173
　　　　　　☐ CATTLE EGRET *(Bubulcus ibis)* 298
　　　　　　☐ REDDISH EGRET *(Dichromonassa rufescens)* 172
　　　　　　☐ GREAT EGRET *(Casmerodius albus)* 179
　　　　　　☐ SNOWY EGRET *(Egretta thula)* 298
　　　　　　☐ LOUISIANA HERON *(Hydranassa tricolor)* 174
　　　　　　☐ BLACK-CROWNED NIGHT HERON *(Nycticorax nycticorax)* 186
　　　　　　☐ YELLOW-CROWNED NIGHT HERON *(Nyctanassa violacea)* . . . −
　　　　　　☐ LEAST BITTERN *(Ixobrychus exilis)* 180
　　　　　　☐ AMERICAN BITTERN *(Botaurus lentiginosus)* 179

　FAMILY: Ciconiidae (Storks; 1)
　　SPECIES: ☐ WOOD STORK *(Mycteria americana)* 47

　FAMILY: Threskiornithidae (Ibises and Spoonbills; 3)
　　SPECIES: ☐ WHITE-FACED IBIS *(Plegadis chihi)* 299
　　　　　　☐ WHITE IBIS *(Eudocimus albus)* 48
　　　　　　☐ ROSEATE SPOONBILL *(Ajaia ajaja)* 299

ORDER: Anseriformes (Waterfowl)
　FAMILY: Anatidae (Swans, Geese, and Ducks; 40)
　　SPECIES: ☐ WHISTLING SWAN *(Olor columbianus)* 49
　　　　　　☐ TRUMPETER SWAN *(Olor buccinator)* . . . . −
　　　　　　☐ CANADA GOOSE *(Branta canadensis)* 180, 286
　　　　　　☐ BRANT *(Branta bernicla)* 164
　　　　　　　　(classified by AOU Checklist as two species,
　　　　　　　　Brant and Black Brant *Branta nigricans)*
　　　　　　☐ EMPEROR GOOSE *(Philacte canagica)* . . . . −
　　　　　　☐ WHITE-FRONTED GOOSE *(Anser albifrons))* 50
　　　　　　☐ SNOW GOOSE *(Chen caerulescens)* 299
　　　　　　☐ ROSS' GOOSE *(Chen rossii)* 299
　　　　　　☐ BLACK-BELLIED TREE DUCK *(Dendrocygna autumnalis)* . . . . −
　　　　　　☐ FULVOUS TREE DUCK *(Dendrocygna bicolor)* . . . . −
　　　　　　☐ MALLARD *(Anas platyrhynchos)* 186
　　　　　　☐ BLACK DUCK *(Anas rubripes)* . . . . −
　　　　　　☐ GADWALL *(Anas strepera)* . . . . −
　　　　　　☐ PINTAIL *(Anas acuta)* 52
　　　　　　☐ GREEN-WINGED TEAL *(Anas crecca)* 181
　　　　　　☐ BLUE-WINGED TEAL *(Anas discors)* . . . . −
　　　　　　☐ CINNAMON TEAL *(Anas cyanoptera)* 181
　　　　　　☐ EUROPEAN WIGEON *(Anas penelope)* . . . . −
　　　　　　☐ AMERICAN WIGEON *(Anas americana)* 186
　　　　　　☐ NORTHERN SHOVELER *(Anas clypeata)* 182
　　　　　　☐ WOOD DUCK *(Aix sponsa)* 186

☐ REDHEAD *(Aythya americana)* . . . . –
☐ RING-NECKED DUCK *(Aythya collaris)* 186
☐ CANVASBACK *(Aythya valisneria)* 53
☐ GREATER SCAUP *(Aythya marila)* . . . . –
☐ LESSER SCAUP *(Aythya affinis)* 164
☐ TUFTED DUCK *(Aythya fuligula)* 187
☐ COMMON GOLDENEYE *(Bucephala clangula)* 164
☐ BARROW'S GOLDENEYE *(Bucephala islandica)* 164
☐ BUFFLEHEAD *(Bucephala albeola)* 165
☐ OLDSQUAW *(Clangula hyemalis)* . . . . –
☐ HARLEQUIN DUCK *(Histrionicus histrionicus)* 160
☐ KING EIDER *(Somateria spectabilis)* . . . . –
☐ WHITE-WINGED SCOTER *(Melanitta deglandi)* 165
☐ SURF SCOTER *(Melanitta perspicillata)* 160
☐ BLACK SCOTER *(Melanitta nigra)* 160
☐ RUDDY DUCK *(Oxyura jamaicensis)* 186
☐ HOODED MERGANSER *(Lophodytes cucullatus)* 187
☐ COMMON MERGANSER *(Mergus merganser)* . . . . –
☐ RED-BREASTED MERGANSER *(Mergus serrator)* 55, 168

ORDER: Falconiformes (Vultures, Hawks, Ospreys, and Falcons)
   FAMILY: Cathartidae (American Vultures; 2)
      SPECIES: ☐ TURKEY VULTURE *(Cathartes aura)* 56, 203
              ☐ CALIFORNIA CONDOR *(Gymnogyps californianus)* 57

   FAMILY: Accipitridae (Kites, Hawks, Eagles, and Harriers; 16)
      SPECIES: ☐ WHITE-TAILED KITE *(Elanus leucurus)* 58, 286
              ☐ MISSISSIPPI KITE *(Ictinia mississippiensis)* . . . . –
              ☐ GOSHAWK *(Accipiter gentilis)* . . . . –
              ☐ SHARP-SHINNED HAWK *(Accipiter striatus)* . . . . –
              ☐ COOPER'S HAWK *(Accipiter cooperii)* 212
              ☐ RED-TAILED HAWK *(Buteo jamaicensis)* 59
              ☐ RED-SHOULDERED HAWK *(Buteo lineatus)* . . . . –
              ☐ BROAD-WINGED HAWK *(Buteo platypterus)* . . . . –
              ☐ SWAINSON'S HAWK *(Buteo swainsoni)* 203
              ☐ ZONE-TAILED HAWK *(Buteo albonotatus)* . . . . –
              ☐ ROUGH-LEGGED HAWK *(Buteo lagopus)* . . . . –
              ☐ FERRUGINOUS HAWK *(Buteo regalis)* . . . . –
              ☐ HARRIS' HAWK *(Parabuteo unicinctus)* 229
              ☐ GOLDEN EAGLE *(Aquila chrysaëtos)* 203
              ☐ BALD EAGLE *(Haliaeetus leucocephalus)* . . . . –
              ☐ MARSH HAWK *(Circus cyaneus)* 60

   FAMILY: Pandionidae (Osprey; 1)
      SPECIES: ☐ OSPREY *(Pandion haliaetus)* 61, 187

FAMILY: Falconidae (Falcons; 5)

    SPECIES: ☐ GYRFALCON *(Falco rusticolus)* .... –

                 ☐ PRAIRIE FALCON *(Falco mexicanus)* 62

                 ☐ PEREGRINE FALCON *(Falco peregrinus)* .... –

                 ☐ MERLIN *(Falco columbarius)* .... –

                 ☐ AMERICAN KESTREL *(Falco sparverius)* 287

ORDER: Galliformes (Gallinaceous Birds)

  FAMILY: Tetraonidae (Grouse; 4)

    SPECIES: ☐ BLUE GROUSE *(Dendragapus obscurus)* 258

                 ☐ RUFFED GROUSE *(Bonasa umbellus)* .... –

                 ☐ SHARP-TAILED GROUSE *(Pedioecetes phasianellus)* .... –

                 ☐ SAGE GROUSE *(Centrocercus urophasianus)* 63, 244

  FAMILY: Phasianidae (Quail, Pheasants, and Partridges; 6)

    SPECIES: ☐ CALIFORNIA QUAIL *(Lophortyx californicus)* 64

                 ☐ GAMBEL'S QUAIL *(Lophortyx gambelii)* 237

                 ☐ MOUNTAIN QUAIL *(Oreortyx pictus)* 194

                 ☐ RING-NECKED PHEASANT *(Phasianus colchicus)* .... –

                 ☐ CHUKAR *(Alectoris chukar)* .... –

                 ☐ GRAY PARTRIDGE *(Perdix perdix)* .... –

  FAMILY: Meleagrididae (Turkeys; 1)

    SPECIES: ☐ TURKEY *(Meleagris gallopavo)* 65

ORDER: Gruiformes (Cranes, Rails, Gallinules, and Coots)

  FAMILY: Gruidae (Cranes; 1)

    SPECIES: ☐ SANDHILL CRANE *(Grus canadensis)* 66

  FAMILY: Rallidae (Rails, Gallinules, and Coots; 8)

    SPECIES: ☐ CLAPPER RAIL *(Rallus longirostris)* 171

                 ☐ VIRGINIA RAIL *(Rallus limicola)* 180

                 ☐ SORA *(Porzana carolina)* 67

                 ☐ YELLOW RAIL *(Coturnicops noveboracensis)* .... –

                 ☐ BLACK RAIL *(Laterallus jamaicensis)* .... –

                 ☐ PURPLE GALLINULE *(Porphyrula martinica)* .... –

                 ☐ COMMON GALLINULE *(Gallinula chloropus)* 67

                 ☐ AMERICAN COOT *(Fulica americana)* 68, 187

ORDER: Charadriiformes (Shorebirds, Gulls, and Alcids)

  FAMILY: Haematopodidae (Oystercatchers; 2)

    SPECIES: ☐ AMERICAN OYSTERCATCHER *(Haematopus palliatus)* 69

                 ☐ BLACK OYSTERCATCHER *(Haematopus bachmani)* 152

  FAMILY: Charadriidae (Plovers; 8)

    SPECIES: ☐ SEMIPALMATED PLOVER *(Charadrius semipalmatus)* 171

                 ☐ PIPING PLOVER *(Charadrius melodus)* .... –

☐ SNOWY PLOVER *(Charadrius alexandrinus)* 160
☐ WILSON'S PLOVER *(Charadrius wilsonia)* .... –
☐ KILLDEER *(Charadrius vociferus)* 70
☐ MOUNTAIN PLOVER *(Charadrius montanus)* 200
☐ AMERICAN GOLDEN PLOVER *(Pluvialis dominica)* .... –
☐ BLACK-BELLIED PLOVER *(Pluvialis squatarola)* 171

FAMILY: Scolopacidae (Sandpipers and Allies; 34)
  SPECIES: ☐ RUDDY TURNSTONE *(Arenaria interpres)* 171
☐ BLACK TURNSTONE *(Arenaria melanocephala)* 157
☐ COMMON SNIPE *(Capella gallinago)* 180
☐ EUROPEAN JACKSNIPE *(Lymnocryptes minimus)* .... –
☐ LONG-BILLED CURLEW *(Numenius americanus)* 172
☐ WHIMBREL *(Numenius phaeopus)* 71, 172
☐ UPLAND SANDPIPER *(Bartramia longicauda)* .... –
☐ SPOTTED SANDPIPER *(Actitis macularia)* .... –
☐ SOLITARY SANDPIPER *(Tringa solitaria)* .... –
☐ GREATER YELLOWLEGS *(Tringa melanoleuca)*......................173
☐ LESSER YELLOWLEGS *(Tringa flavipes)* .... –
☐ WANDERING TATTLER *(Heteroscelus incanus)* 153
☐ WILLET *(Catoptrophorus semipalmatus)* 172
☐ SURFBIRD *(Aphriza virgata)* 161
☐ RED KNOT *(Calidris canutus)* 174
☐ ROCK SANDPIPER *(Calidris ptilocnemis)* 161
☐ SHARP-TAILED SANDPIPER *(Calidris acuminata)* .... –
☐ PECTORAL SANDPIPER *(Calidris melanotos)* 171
☐ WHITE-RUMPED SANDPIPER *(Calidris fuscicollis)* .... –
☐ BAIRD'S SANDPIPER *(Calidris bairdii)* .... –
☐ LEAST SANDPIPER *(Calidris minutilla)* 172
☐ CURLEW SANDPIPER *(Calidris ferruginea)* .... –
☐ DUNLIN *(Calidris alpina)* 173
☐ SEMIPALMATED SANDPIPER *(Calidris pusillus)* .... –
☐ WESTERN SANDPIPER *(Calidris mauri)* 74
☐ SANDERLING *(Calidris alba)* 160
☐ SHORT-BILLED DOWITCHER *(Limnodromus griseus)* .... –
☐ LONG-BILLED DOWITCHER *(Limnodromus scolopaceus)* 172
☐ STILT SANDPIPER *(Micropalama himantopus)* .... –
☐ BUFF-BREASTED SANDPIPER *(Tryngites subruficollis)* .... –
☐ MARBLED GODWIT *(Limosa fedoa)* 75, 161, 172
☐ HUDSONIAN GODWIT *(Limosa haemastica)* .... –
☐ BAR-TAILED GODWIT *(Limosa lapponica)* .... –
☐ RUFF *(Philomachus pugnax)* .... –

FAMILY: Recurvirostridae (Avocets and Stilts; 2)
  SPECIES: ☐ AMERICAN AVOCET *(Recurvirostra americana)* 77, 299
☐ BLACK-NECKED STILT *(Himantopus mexicanus)* 76, 299

FAMILY: Phalaropodidae (Phalaropes; 3)
SPECIES: ☐ RED PHALAROPE *(Phalaropus fulicarius)* 147
☐ WILSON'S PHALAROPE *(Steganopus tricolor)* 78
☐ NORTHERN PHALAROPE *(Lobipes lobatus)* 161

FAMILY: Stercorariidae (Jaegers and Skuas; 4)
SPECIES: ☐ POMARINE JAEGER *(Stercorarius pomarinus)* 79, 147
☐ PARASITIC JAEGER *(Stercorarius parasiticus)* .... –
☐ LONG-TAILED JAEGER *(Stercorarius longicaudus)* .... –
☐ SKUA *(Catharacta skua)* .... –

FAMILY: Laridae (Gulls and Terns; 26)
SPECIES: ☐ GLAUCOUS GULL *(Larus hyperboreus)* .... –
☐ GLAUCOUS-WINGED GULL *(Larus glaucescens)* 161
☐ WESTERN GULL *(Larus occidentalis)* 80, 154
☐ HERRING GULL *(Larus argentatus)* 161
☐ THAYER'S GULL *(Larus thayeri)* 165
☐ CALIFORNIA GULL *(Larus californicus)* 165
☐ RING-BILLED GULL *(Larus delawarensis)* 187
☐ BLACK-TAILED GULL *(Larus crassirostris)* .... –
☐ MEW GULL *(Larus canus)* 161
☐ BLACK-HEADED GULL *(Larus ridibundus)* .... –
☐ LAUGHING GULL *(Larus atricilla)* 301
☐ FRANKLIN'S GULL *(Larus pipixcan)* 173
☐ BONAPARTE'S GULL *(Larus philadelphia)* 166
☐ LITTLE GULL *(Larus minutus)* 299
☐ HEERMANN'S GULL *(Larus heermanni)* 162
☐ BLACK-LEGGED KITTIWAKE *(Rissa tridactyla)* 147
☐ SABINE'S GULL *(Xema sabinii)* 147
☐ GULL-BILLED TERN *(Gelochelidon nilotica)* 301
☐ FORSTER'S TERN *(Sterna forsteri)* 167
☐ COMMON TERN *(Sterna hirundo)* 167
☐ ARCTIC TERN *(Sterna paradisaea)* .... –
☐ LEAST TERN *(Sterna albifrons)* 162
☐ ROYAL TERN *(Thalasseus maximus)* .... –
☐ ELEGANT TERN *(Thalasseus elegans)* 173
☐ CASPIAN TERN *(Hydroprogne caspia)* 83, 181
☐ BLACK TERN *(Chlidonias niger)* 180

FAMILY: Rynchopidae (Skimmers; 1)
SPECIES: ☐ BLACK SKIMMER *(Rynchops niger)* 84

FAMILY: Alcidae (Auks, Murres, and Puffins; 13)
SPECIES: ☐ COMMON MURRE *(Uria aalge)* 155
☐ THICK-BILLED MURRE *(Uria lomvia)* 85
☐ PIGEON GUILLEMOT *(Cepphus columba)* 155
☐ MARBLED MURRELET *(Brachyramphus marmoratus)* .... –

☐ KITTLITZ'S MURRELET *(Brachyramphus brevirostris)* .... −
☐ XANTUS' MURRELET *(Endomychura hypoleuca)* .... −
☐ CRAVERI'S MURRELET *(Endomychura craveri)* .... −
☐ ANCIENT MURRELET *(Synthliboramphus antiquus)* .... −
☐ CASSIN'S AUKLET *(Ptychoramphus aleuticus)* .... −
☐ PARAKEET AUKLET *(Cyclorrhynchus psittacula)* .... −
☐ RHINOCEROS AUKLET *(Cerorhinca monocerata)* 147
☐ HORNED PUFFIN *(Fratercula corniculata)* .... −
☐ TUFTED PUFFIN *(Lunda cirrhata)* .... −

ORDER: Columbiformes (Pigeons and Doves)
  FAMILY: Columbidae (Pigeons and Doves; 8)
    SPECIES: ☐ BAND-TAILED PIGEON *(Columba fasciata)* 208
             ☐ ROCK DOVE *(Columba livia)* 292
             ☐ WHITE-WINGED DOVE *(Zenaida asiatica)* 232
             ☐ MOURNING DOVE *(Zenaida macroura)* 87, 203
             ☐ SPOTTED DOVE *(Streptopelia chinensis)* 292
             ☐ RINGED TURTLE DOVE *(Streptopelia risoria)* 292
             ☐ GROUND DOVE *(Columbina passerina)* 212
             ☐ INCA DOVE *(Scardafella inca)* .... −

ORDER: Cuculiformes (Cuckoos and Roadrunners)
  FAMILY: Cuculidae (Cuckoos and Roadrunners; 3)
    SPECIES: ☐ YELLOW-BILLED CUCKOO *(Coccyzus americanus)* .... −
             ☐ BLACK-BILLED CUCKOO *(Coccyzus erythrophthalmus)* 88
             ☐ ROADRUNNER *(Geococcyx californianus)* 227

ORDER: Strigiformes (Owls)
  FAMILY: Tytonidae (Barn Owls; 1)
    SPECIES: ☐ BARN OWL *(Tyto alba)* 89, 226

  FAMILY: Strigidae (Typical Owls; 12)
    SPECIES: ☐ SCREECH OWL *(Otus asio)* .... −
             ☐ FLAMMULATED OWL *(Otus flammeolus)* .... −
             ☐ GREAT HORNED OWL *(Bubo virginianus)* 208
             ☐ SNOWY OWL *(Nyctea scandiaca)* .... −
             ☐ PYGMY OWL *(Glaucidium gnoma)* 278
             ☐ ELF OWL *(Micrathene whitneyi)* 233
             ☐ BURROWING OWL *(Speotyto cunicularia)* 200
             ☐ SPOTTED OWL *(Strix occidentalis)* 278
             ☐ GREAT GRAY OWL *(Strix nebulosa)* 268
             ☐ LONG-EARED OWL *(Asio otus)* 90, 213
             ☐ SHORT-EARED OWL *(Asio flammeus)* 173
             ☐ SAW-WHET OWL *(Aegolius acadicus)* 259

ORDER: Caprimulgiformes (Goatsuckers)
  FAMILY: Caprimulgidae (Goatsuckers; 4)
    SPECIES: ☐ WHIP-POOR-WILL *(Caprimulgus vociferus)* . . . . –
             ☐ POOR-WILL *(Phalaenoptilus nuttallii)* 245
             ☐ COMMON NIGHTHAWK *(Chordeiles minor)* 91
             ☐ LESSER NIGHTHAWK *(Chordeiles acutipennis)* 226

ORDER: Apodiformes (Swifts and Hummingbirds)
  FAMILY: Apodidae (Swifts; 4)
    SPECIES: ☐ BLACK SWIFT *(Cypseloides niger)* . . . . –
             ☐ CHIMNEY SWIFT *(Chaetura pelagica)* . . . . –
             ☐ VAUX'S SWIFT *(Chaetura vauxi)* . . . . –
             ☐ WHITE-THROATED SWIFT *(Aeronautes saxatalis)* 92

  FAMILY: Trochilidae (Hummingbirds; 8)
    SPECIES: ☐ BLACK-CHINNED HUMMINGBIRD *(Archilochus alexandri)* . 93, 214
             ☐ COSTA'S HUMMINGBIRD *(Calypte costae)* 235
             ☐ ANNA'S HUMMINGBIRD *(Calypte anna)* 193
             ☐ BROAD-TAILED HUMMINGBIRD *(Selasphorus platycercus)* 254
             ☐ RUFOUS HUMMINGBIRD *(Selasphorus rufus)* 278
             ☐ ALLEN'S HUMMINGBIRD *(Selasphorus sasin)* 278
             ☐ CALLIOPE HUMMINGBIRD *(Stellula calliope)* 268
             ☐ BROAD-BILLED HUMMINGBIRD *(Cyanthus latirostris)* 209

ORDER: Coraciiformes (Kingfishers and Allies)
  FAMILY: Alcedinidae (Kingfishers; 1)
    SPECIES: ☐ BELTED KINGFISHER *(Megaceryle alcyon)* 95

ORDER: Piciformes (Woodpeckers and Allies)
  FAMILY: Picidae (Woodpeckers; 16)
    SPECIES: ☐ COMMON FLICKER *(Colaptes auratus)* 208, 229
             ☐ PILEATED WOODPECKER *(Dryocopus pileatus)* . . . . –
             ☐ GILA WOODPECKER *(Centurus uropygialis)* 230
             ☐ RED-HEADED WOODPECKER *(Melanerpes erythrocephalus)* . . . . . –
             ☐ ACORN WOODPECKER *(Melanerpes formiocivorus)* 208
             ☐ LEWIS' WOODPECKER *(Asyndesmus lewis)*
             ☐ YELLOW-BELLIED SAPSUCKER *(Sphyrapicus varius)* . . . . –
             ☐ RED-NAPED SAPSUCKER *(Sphyrapicus nuchalis)* 97
                 (classified by AOU Checklist as a
                 subspecies of Yellow-bellied Sapsucker)
             ☐ RED-BREASTED SAPSUCKER *(Sphyrapicus ruber)* 260
                 (classified by AOU Checklist as a
                 subspecies of Yellow-bellied Sapsucker)
             ☐ WILLIAMSON'S SAPSUCKER *(Sphyrapicus thyroideus)* . . . . –
             ☐ HAIRY WOODPECKER *(Dendrocopos villosus)* 260
             ☐ DOWNY WOODPECKER *(Dendrocopos pubescens)* 214
             ☐ LADDER-BACKED WOODPECKER *(Dendrocopos scalaris)* 233

☐ NUTTALL'S WOODPECKER *(Dendrocopos nuttallii)* 208
☐ WHITE-HEADED WOODPECKER *(Dendrocopos albolarvatus)* . . . 261
☐ BLACK-BACKED THREE-TOED WOODPECKER
   (Picoides articus) . . . . –

ORDER: Passeriformes (Perching Birds)
FAMILY: Tyrannidae (Tyrant Flycatchers; 23)
SPECIES: ☐ EASTERN KINGBIRD *(Tyrannus tyrannus)* . . . . –
☐ THICK-BILLED KINGBIRD *(Tyrannus crassirostris)* . . . . –
☐ TROPICAL KINGBIRD *(Tyrannus melancholicus)* . . . . –
☐ WESTERN KINGBIRD *(Tyrannus verticalis)* 286
☐ CASSIN'S KINGBIRD *(Tyrannus vociferans)* . . . . –
☐ SCISSOR-TAILED FLYCATCHER *(Muscivora forficata)* 99
☐ GREAT CRESTED FLYCATCHER *(Myiarchus crinitus)* . . . . –
☐ WIED'S CRESTED FLYCATCHER *(Myiarchus tyrannulus)* . . . . –
☐ ASH-THROATED FLYCATCHER *(Myiarchus cinerascens)* 256
☐ OLIVACEOUS FLYCATCHER *(Myiarchus tuberculifer)* . . . . –
☐ EASTERN PHOEBE *(Sayornis phoebe)* 214
☐ BLACK PHOEBE *(Sayornis nigricans)* 187
☐ SAY'S PHOEBE *(Sayornis saya)* 246
☐ WILLOW FLYCATCHER *(Empidonax traillii)* . . . . –
☐ LEAST FLYCATCHER *(Empidonax minimus)* . . . . –
☐ HAMMOND'S FLYCATCHER *(Empidonax hammondii)* . . . . –
☐ DUSKY FLYCATCHER *(Empidonax oberholseri)* 195
☐ GRAY FLYCATCHER *(Empidonax wrightii)* . . . . –
☐ WESTERN FLYCATCHER *(Empidonax difficilis)* 278
☐ COUES' FLYCATCHER *(Contopus pertinax)* . . . . –
☐ WESTERN WOOD PEWEE *(Contopus sordidulus)* 262
☐ OLIVE-SIDED FLYCATCHER *(Nuttallornis borealis)* 262
☐ VERMILION FLYCATCHER *(Pyrocephalus rubinus)* 214

FAMILY: Alaudidae (Larks; 1)
SPECIES: ☐ HORNED LARK *(Eremophila alpestris)* 102

FAMILY: Hirundinidae (Swallows; 7)
SPECIES: ☐ VIOLET-GREEN SWALLOW *(Tachycinetta thalassina)* 262
☐ TREE SWALLOW *(Iridioprocne bicolor)* 215
☐ BANK SWALLOW *(Riparia riparia)* . . . . –
☐ ROUGH-WINGED SWALLOW *(Stelgidopteryx ruficollis)* 188
☐ BARN SWALLOW *(Hirundo rustica)* 287
☐ CLIFF SWALLOW *(Petrochelidon pyrrhonota)* 287
☐ PURPLE MARTIN *(Progne subis)* 103

FAMILY: Corvidae (Jays, Magpies, and Crows; 10)
SPECIES: ☐ GRAY JAY *(Perisoreus canadensis)* . . . . –
☐ STELLER'S JAY *(Cyanocitta stelleri)* 262
☐ BLUE JAY *(Cyanocitta cristata)* . . . . –

☐ SCRUB JAY *(Aphelocoma coerulescens)* 104, 208
☐ BLACK-BILLED MAGPIE *(Pica pica)* .... −
☐ YELLOW-BILLED MAGPIE *(Pica nuttalli)* 203
☐ COMMON RAVEN *(Corvus corax)* 238
☐ COMMON CROW *(Corvus brachyrhynchos)* 105
☐ PINYON JAY *(Gymnorhinus cyanocephalus)* 256
☐ CLARK'S NUTCRACKER *(Nucifraga columbiana)* 275

FAMILY: Paridae (Titmice, Verdin, and Bushtit; 6)
SPECIES: ☐ BLACK-CAPPED CHICKADEE *(Parus atricapillus)* .... −
☐ MOUNTAIN CHICKADEE *(Parus gambeli)* 263
☐ CHESTNUT-BACKED CHICKADEE *(Parus rufescens)* 278
☐ PLAIN TITMOUSE *(Parus inornatus)* 106
☐ VERDIN *(Auriparus flaviceps)* 234
☐ BUSHTIT *(Psaltriparus minimus)* 209

FAMILY: Sittidae (Nuthatches; 3)
SPECIES: ☐ WHITE-BREASTED NUTHATCH *(Sitta carolinensis)* 107
☐ RED-BREASTED NUTHATCH *(Sitta canadensis)* 268
☐ PYGMY NUTHATCH *(Sitta pygmaea)* 262

FAMILY: Certhiidae (Creepers; 1)
SPECIES: ☐ BROWN CREEPER *(Certhia familiaris)* 108

FAMILY: Chamaeidae (Wrentit; 1)
SPECIES: ☐ WRENTIT *(Chamaea fasciata)* 108, 193

FAMILY: Cinclidae (Dippers; 1)
SPECIES: ☐ DIPPER *(Cinclus mexicanus)* 109, 189

FAMILY: Troglodytidae (Wrens; 7)
SPECIES: ☐ HOUSE WREN *(Troglodytes aedon)* 209
☐ WINTER WREN *(Troglodytes troglodytes)* .... −
☐ BEWICK'S WREN *(Thryomanes bewickii)* 193
☐ CACTUS WREN *(Campylorhynchus brunneicapillus)* 238
☐ LONG-BILLED MARSH WREN *(Telmatodytes palustris)* 181
☐ CANYON WREN *(Catherpes mexicanus)* 110
☐ ROCK WREN *(Salpinctes obsoletus)* 227

FAMILY: Mimidae (Mockingbirds and Thrashers; 9)
SPECIES: ☐ MOCKINGBIRD *(Mimus polyglottos)* 111, 292
☐ GRAY CATBIRD *(Dumetella carolinensis)* .... −
☐ BROWN THRASHER *(Toxostoma rufum)* .... −
☐ BENDIRE'S THRASHER *(Toxostoma bendirei)* .... −
☐ CURVE-BILLED THRASHER *(Toxostoma curvirostre)* 112
☐ CALIFORNIA THRASHER *(Toxostoma redivivum)* 193
☐ LE CONTE'S THRASHER *(Toxostoma lecontei)* 228

☐ CRISSAL THRASHER *(Toxostoma dorsale)* .... −
☐ SAGE THRASHER *(Oreoscoptes montanus)* .... −

FAMILY: Turdidae (Thrushes, Bluebirds, and Solitaires; 11)
SPECIES: ☐ AMERICAN ROBIN *(Turdus migratorius)* 262
☐ RUFOUS-BACKED ROBIN *(Turdus rufopalliatus)* .... −
☐ VARIED THRUSH *(Ixoreus naevius)* .... −
☐ WOOD THRUSH *(Hylocichla mustelina)* .... −
☐ HERMIT THRUSH *(Catharus guttatus)* 113, 268
☐ SWAINSON'S THRUSH *(Catharus ustulatus)* 279
☐ GRAY-CHEEKED THRUSH *(Catharus minimus)* .... −
☐ WESTERN BLUEBIRD *(Sialia mexicana)* 209
☐ MOUNTAIN BLUEBIRD *(Sialia currucoides)* 274
☐ WHEATEAR *(Oenanthe oenanthe)* .... −
☐ TOWNSEND'S SOLITAIRE *(Myadestes townsendi)* 114

FAMILY: Sylviidae (Gnatcatchers and Kinglets; 4)
SPECIES: ☐ BLUE-GRAY GNATCATCHER *(Polioptila caerulea)* 115
☐ BLACK-TAILED GNATCATCHER *(Polioptila melanura)* 230
☐ GOLDEN-CROWNED KINGLET *(Regulus satrapa)* .... −
☐ RUBY-CROWNED KINGLET *(Regulus calendula)* 116

FAMILY: Motacillidae (Pipits and Wagtails; 2)
SPECIES: ☐ WATER PIPIT *(Anthus spinoletta)* 116
☐ RED-THROATED PIPIT *(Anthus cervinus)* .... −

FAMILY: Bombycillidae (Waxwings; 2)
SPECIES: ☐ CEDAR WAXWING *(Bombycilla cedrorum)* 117
☐ BOHEMIAN WAXWING *(Bombycilla garrulus)* .... −

FAMILY: Ptilogonatidae (Silky Flycatchers; 1)
SPECIES: ☐ PHAINOPEPLA *(Phainopepla nitens)* 117, 239

FAMILY: Laniidae (Shrikes; 2)
SPECIES: ☐ NORTHERN SHRIKE *(Lanius excubitor)* .... −
☐ LOGGERHEAD SHRIKE *(Lanius ludovicianus)* 118, 203

FAMILY: Family: Sturnidae (Starlings; 1)
SPECIES: ☐ STARLING *(Sturnus vulgaris)* 118

FAMILY: Vireonidae (Vireos; 10)
SPECIES: ☐ WHITE-EYED VIREO *(Vireo griseus)* .... −
☐ HUTTON'S VIREO *(Vireo huttoni)* .... −
☐ BELL'S VIREO *(Vireo bellii)* 215
☐ GRAY VIREO *(Vireo vicinior)* .... −
☐ YELLOW-THROATED VIREO *(Vireo flavifrons)* .... −
☐ SOLITARY VIREO *(Vireo solitarius)* 263
☐ YELLOW-GREEN VIREO *(Vireo flavoviridis)* .... −

☐ RED-EYED VIREO *(Vireo olivaceus)* .... −
☐ PHILADELPHIA VIREO *(Vireo philadelphicus)* .... −
☐ WARBLING VIREO *(Vireo gilvus)* 120

FAMILY: Parulidae (Wood Warblers; 46)
SPECIES: ☐ BLACK AND WHITE WARBLER *(Miniotilta varia)* .... −
☐ PROTHONOTARY WARBLER *(Protonotaria citrea)* .... −
☐ WORM-EATING WARBLER *(Helmintheros vermivorus)* .... −
☐ GOLDEN-WINGED WARBLER *(Vermivora chrysoptera)* .... −
☐ BLUE-WINGED WARBLER *(Vermivora pinus)* .... −
☐ TENNESSEE WARBLER *(Vermivora peregrina)* .... −
☐ ORANGE-CROWNED WARBLER *(Vermivora celata)* 193
☐ NASHVILLE WARBLER *(Vermivora ruficapilla)* 263
☐ VIRGINIA'S WARBLER *(Vermivora virginiae)* .... −
☐ LUCY'S WARBLER *(Vermivora luciae)* .... −
☐ NORTHERN PARULA *(Parula americana)* .... −
☐ YELLOW WARBLER *(Dendroica petechia)* 123, 215
☐ MAGNOLIA WARBLER *(Dendroica magnolia)* .... −
☐ CAPE MAY WARBLER *(Dendroica tigrina)* .... −
☐ BLACK-THROATED BLUE WARBLER *(Dendroica caerulescens)* .. −
☐ YELLOW-RUMPED WARBLER *(Dendroica coronata)* 268
☐ BLACK-THROATED GRAY WARBLER *(Dendroica nigrescens)* ... 255
☐ TOWNSEND'S WARBLER *(Dendroica townsendi)* 123
☐ BLACK-THROATED GREEN WARBLER *(Dendroica virens)* .... −
☐ GOLDEN-CHEEKED WARBLER *(Dendroica chrysoparia)* .... −
☐ HERMIT WARBLER *(Dendroica occidentalis)* 263
☐ CERULEAN WARBLER *(Dendroica caerulea)* .... −
☐ BLACKBURNIAN WARBLER *(Dendroica fusca)* .... −
☐ YELLOW-THROATED WARBLER *(Dendroica dominica)* .... −
☐ GRACE'S WARBLER *(Dendroica graciae)* .... −
☐ CHESTNUT-SIDED WARBLER *(Dendroica pensylvanica)* ...... −
☐ BAY-BREASTED WARBLER *(Dendroica castanea)* .... −
☐ BLACKPOLL WARBLER *(Dendroica striata)* .... −
☐ PINE WARBLER *(Dendroica pinus)* .... −
☐ PRAIRIE WARBLER *(Dendroica discolor)* .... −
☐ PALM WARBLER *(Dendroica palmarum)* .... −
☐ OVENBIRD *(Seiurus aurocapillus)* .... −
☐ NORTHERN WATERTHRUSH *(Seirus noveboracensis)* .... −
☐ LOUISIANA WATERTHRUSH *(Seirus motacilla)* .... −
☐ KENTUCKY WARBLER *(Oporornis formosus)* .... −
☐ CONNECTICUT WARBLER *(Oporornis agilis)* .... −
☐ MOURNING WARBLER *(Oporornis philadelphia)* .... −
☐ MACGILLIVRAY'S WARBLER *(Oporornis tolmiei)* 194
☐ COMMON YELLOWTHROAT *(Geothlypis trichas)* 181
☐ YELLOW-BREASTED CHAT *(Icteria virens)* 214
☐ RED-FACED WARBLER *(Cardellina rubrifrons)* .... −
☐ HOODED WARBLER *(Wilsonia citrina)* .... −
☐ WILSON'S WARBLER *(Wilsonia pusilla)* 279

☐ CANADA WARBLER *(Wilsonia canadensis)* . . . .   –
☐ AMERICAN REDSTART *(Setophaga ruticilla)* . . . .   –
☐ PAINTED REDSTART *(Myioborus pictus)* . . . .   –

FAMILY: Ploceidae (Weaver Finches; 1)
   SPECIES: ☐ HOUSE SPARROW *(Passer domesticus)* 126, 292

FAMILY: Icteridae (Blackbirds and Orioles; 15)
   SPECIES: ☐ BOBOLINK *(Dolichonyx oryzivorus)* 201
            ☐ WESTERN MEADOWLARK *(Sturnella neglecta)* 201
            ☐ YELLOW-HEADED BLACKBIRD *(Xanthocephalus xanthocephalus)* 127
            ☐ RED-WINGED BLACKBIRD *(Agelaius phoeniceus)* 181
            ☐ TRICOLORED BLACKBIRD *(Agelaius tricolor)* 180
            ☐ ORCHARD ORIOLE *(Icterus spurius)* . . . .   –
            ☐ HOODED ORIOLE *(Icterus cucullatus)* 128
            ☐ SCARLET-HEADED ORIOLE *(Icterus pustulatus)* . . . .   –
            ☐ SCOTT'S ORIOLE *(Icterus parisorum)* 240
            ☐ NORTHERN ORIOLE *(Icterus galbula)* 215
            ☐ RUSTY BLACKBIRD *(Euphagus carolinus)* . . . .   –
            ☐ BREWER'S BLACKBIRD *(Euphagus cyanocephalus)* 292
            ☐ GREAT-TAILED CRACKLE *(Cassidix mexicanus)* 287
            ☐ BROWN-HEADED COWBIRD *(Molothrus ater)* 215, 287
            ☐ BRONZED COWBIRD *(Tangavius aeneus)* . . . .   –

FAMILY: Thraupidae (Tanagers; 4)
   SPECIES: ☐ WESTERN TANAGER *(Piranga ludoviciana)* 129, 263
            ☐ SCARLET TANAGER *(Piranga olivacea)* . . . .   –
            ☐ HEPATIC TANAGER *(Piranga flava)* 263
            ☐ SUMMER TANAGER *(Piranga rubra)* . . . .   –

FAMILY: Fringillidae (Grosbeaks, Finches, Sparrows, and Longspurs; 59)
   SPECIES: ☐ CARDINAL *(Cardinalis cardinalis)* 217
            ☐ PYRRHULOXIA *(Pyrrhuloxia sinuata)* 234
            ☐ ROSE-BREASTED GROSBEAK *(Pheucticus ludovicianus)* . . . .   –
            ☐ BLACK-HEADED GROSBEAK *(Pheucticus melanocephalus)* . . . 130, 209
            ☐ BLUE GROSBEAK *(Guiraca caerulea)* 216
            ☐ INDIGO BUNTING *(Passerina cyanea)* . . . .   –
            ☐ LAZULI BUNTING *(Passerina amoena)* 195
            ☐ VARIED BUNTING *(Passerina versicolor)* . . . .
            ☐ PAINTED BUNTING *(Passerina ciris)* . . . .   –
            ☐ DICKCISSEL *(Spiza americana)* . . . .   –
            ☐ EVENING GROSBEAK *(Hesperiphona vespertina)* . . . .   –
            ☐ PURPLE FINCH *(Carpodacus purpureus)* 279
            ☐ CASSIN'S FINCH *(Carpodacus cassinii)* 269
            ☐ HOUSE FINCH *(Carpodacus mexicanus)* 293
            ☐ PINE GROSBEAK *(Pinicola enucleator)* . . . .   –
            ☐ GRAY-CROWNED ROSY FINCH *(Leucosticte tephrocotis)* 274

☐ BLACK ROSY FINCH *(Leucosticte ater)* .... –
☐ COMMON REDPOLL *(Acanthis flammea)* .... –
☐ PINE SISKIN *(Spinus pinus)* 269
☐ AMERICAN GOLDFINCH *(Spinus tristis)* .... –
☐ LESSER GOLDFINCH *(Spinus psaltria)* 287
☐ LAWRENCE'S GOLDFINCH *(Spinus lawrencei)* 209
☐ RED CROSSBILL *(Loxia curvirostra)* 269
☐ GREEN-TAILED TOWHEE *(Chlorura chlorura)* 194
☐ RUFOUS-SIDED TOWHEE *(Pipilo erythrophthalmus)* 193
☐ BROWN TOWHEE *(Pipilo fuscus)* 195
☐ ABERT'S TOWHEE *(Pipilo aberti)* .... –
☐ LARK BUNTING *(Calamospiza melanocorys)* .... –
☐ SAVANNAH SPARROW *(Passerculus sandwichensis)* 173
☐ GRASSHOPPER SPARROW *(Ammodramus savannarum)* .... –
☐ BAIRD'S SPARROW *(Ammodramus bairdii)* .... –
☐ LE CONTE'S SPARROW *(Ammospiza leconteii)* .... –
☐ SHARP-TAILED SPARROW *(Ammospiza caudacuta)* .... –
☐ VESPER SPARROW *(Pooecetes gramineus)* .... –
☐ LARK SPARROW *(Chondestes grammacus)* 203
☐ RUFOUS-CROWNED SPARROW *(Aimophila ruficeps)* .... –
☐ CASSIN'S SPARROW *(Aimophila cassinii)* .... –
☐ BLACK-THROATED SPARROW *(Amphispiza bilineata)* 240
☐ SAGE SPARROW *(Amphispiza belli)* 247
☐ DARK-EYED JUNCO *(Junco hyemalis)* 269
☐ GRAY-HEADED JUNCO *(Junco caniceps)* .... –
☐ TREE SPARROW *(Spizella arborea)* .... –
☐ CHIPPING SPARROW *(Spizella passerina)* 264
☐ CLAY-COLORED SPARROW *(Spizella pallida)* .... –
☐ BREWER'S SPARROW *(Spizella breweri)* 248
☐ FIELD SPARROW *(Spizella pusilla)* .... –
☐ BLACK-CHINNED SPARROW *(Spizella atrogularis)* 194
☐ HARRIS' SPARROW *(Zonotrichia querula)* .... –
☐ WHITE-CROWNED SPARROW *(Zonotrichia leucophrys)* 275
☐ GOLDEN-CROWNED SPARROW *(Zonotrichia atricapilla)* 137
☐ WHITE-THROATED SPARROW *(Zonotrichia albicollis)* .... –
☐ FOX SPARROW *(Passerella iliaca)* 195
☐ LINCOLN'S SPARROW *(Melospiza lincolnii)* 269
☐ SWAMP SPARROW *(Melospiza georgiana)* .... –
☐ SONG SPARROW *(Melospiza melodia)* 219
☐ McCOWN'S LONGSPUR *(Calcarius mccownii)* .... –
☐ LAPLAND LONGSPUR *(Calcarius lapponicus)* ....
☐ CHESTNUT-COLLARED LONGSPUR *(Calcarius ornatus)* .... –
☐ SNOW BUNTING *(Plectrophenax nivalis)* ....

ADDITIONS, 1974

The following birds were added to the California state list during 1974, thus raising the state list to 525 species:

FAMILY: Charadriidae (Plovers)

    SPECIES: ☐ DOTTEREL *(Eudromias morinellus)*
        Seasonal status–accidental; note–one record: one bird at Farallon Islands, Marin County, Sept. 12–20, 1974. Photograph.

FAMILY: Scolopacidae (Sandpipers and Allies)

    SPECIES: ☐ RUFOUS-NECKED SANDPIPER *(Calidris ruficollis)*
        Seasonal status–accidental; *note*–two records: one bird at Arcata, Humboldt County, June 17, 1974 (photograph) and another at the south end of the Salton Sea, Imperial County, Aug. 17, 1974. Specimen.

FAMILY: Cuculidae (Cuckoos and Roadrunners)

    SPECIES: ☐ GROOVE-BILLED ANI *(Crotophaga sulcirostris)*
        Seasonal status–accidental; *note*–one record: one bird near Pastime Lake, Riverside County, Nov. 4–10, 1974. Photograph.

FAMILY: Tyrannidae (Tyrant Flycatchers)

    SPECIES: ☐ SULPHUR-BELLIED FLYCATCHER *(Myiodynastes luteiventris)*
        Seasonal status–accidental; *note*–one record: one bird at Sycamore Canyon, Point Mugu State Park, Ventura County, Sept. 22–Oct. 2, 1974. Sight record.

FAMILY: Turdidae (Thrushes, Bluebirds, and Solitaires)

    SPECIES: ☐ VEERY *(Catharus fuscescens)*
        Seasonal status–accidental; *note*–one record: one bird at Sycamore Canyon, Point Mugu State Park, Ventura County, Oct. 12–13, 1974. Photograph.

FAMILY: Motacillidae (Pipits and Wagtails)

    SPECIES: ☐ WHITE WAGTAIL *(Motacilla alba)*
        Seasonal status–accidental; *note*–one record: one bird at McGrath State Park, Ventura County, Oct. 18–20, 1972. Sight record.

    SPECIES: ☐ SPRAGUE'S PIPIT *(Anthus spragueii)*
        Seasonal status–accidental; *note*–one record: at least three birds near Imperial Beach, San Diego County, Oct. 19–23, 1974. Specimen.

Additional notes:

The skuas appearing along the Pacific coast of California are now recognized as being South Polar or McCormick's Skuas *(Catharacta maccormicki),* a species widely accepted as being distinct from the Skua *(Catharacta skua).*

The elusive nest of the Marbled Murrelet *(Brachyramphus marmoratus)* was located for the first time in North America on Aug. 8, 1974. A California State Park Service tree trimmer found the nest high up in a Coast Redwood tree in Big Basin Redwood State Park, Santa Cruz County.

PREFACE

Ornithology—the study of birds—was once a select and esoteric endeavor engaged in by a small group of intense scientists devoted to the study of dead specimens housed in antiseptic cabinets and accessible only to a few specialists. It has metamorphosed to a vibrant dynamic pursuit whose objectives include knowledge of the living birds themselves. Within this framework are millions of people, both professionals and amateurs, who study living birds in their natural habitats. Today's amateur and professional ornithologists no longer accumulate sets of birds' eggs and study skins merely to enlarge their collections. What necessary specimens are taken from the wild are utilized for essential studies in taxonomy, evolution, physiology, anatomy, and pollution. However, more and more ornithologists are turning their attention to the living bird and its relation to its environment.

In addition to the professional and semi-professional ornithologists, there are millions of amateur ornithologists who enjoy the hobby and sport of "birding." Some of these people have risen to international prominence as bird artists, wildlife photographers, ecologists, conservationists, writers, and lecturers. Others have undertaken important and worthwhile studies that have resulted in real contributions to scientific ornithology. The reams of notes and other data accumulated by amateur ornithologists over the years have formed the bases for important population and distributional studies.

This book should prove useful to both amateur and professional alike. California's environment and avifauna have undergone many significant changes since 1944 when the classic *The Distribution of the Birds of California* by Joseph Grinnell and Alden H. Miller was published by the Cooper Ornithological Society. This book does not purport to revise or supplant that essential work, as its emphasis and thrust are different. However, there have been real changes in the intervening years and some of these changes have been the results of environmental as well as biological factors. Moreover, a very significant change has taken place in amateur ornithology in California as well as everywhere else in the United States. There are more amateur ornithologists or "birders" today than ever before, and "birding" is one of the fastest growing hobbies or sports in the country. This new breed of birder, armed with better optical and sound-recording equipment, better field guides and more complete distributional lists, and employing better and more skillful field techniques, has forever changed the complexion of field ornithology in California. Virtually all of the distributional changes and additions to the California state bird list since 1944 have been contributed by amateurs. It is primarily the amateurs who spend thousands of man-hours at mist nets and in the field hoping to fill in some of the great gaps in chronology and distribution of California's migrant birds. Other amateurs devote most of their waking hours during the nesting season to studying breeding biology of so many of the native birds whose nesting behavior and processes are imperfectly known even today. Censuses of all kinds—Christmas, strip, breeding-bird, winter-bird population, migrational, endangered species, and others—are undertaken by amateurs and professionals alike and working together.

Gratefully I should like to acknowledge the help and advice received from many people in the formulation and completion of this book. In particular I should like to mention Guy McCaskie, who provided me with many of the records of casual and accidental species and who deserves belated credit for "fathering" a new breed of field birder in California and for contributing so much to a new and better understanding of bird distribution and identification in this state. Olga Clarke typed the original manuscript and in doing so made numerous valuable comments and corrections. I am grateful to Herb Clarke and Gerald Maisel for the use of some of their photographs. The maps were painstakingly done by Robert Sandmeyer and Keith Axelson, to whom I am deeply indebted. Thomas R. Howell was kind enough to read the manuscript and offered important comments and suggestions for which I am deeply grateful.

—ARNOLD SMALL
Beverly Hills, California
June 1973

THE BIRDS OF
CALIFORNIA

INTRODUCTION

California is the most populous and the most popular state. And for good reason. Nowhere else in the United States has nature blessed the land with more beauty and such bounty. This is attested to by the establishment within the state of no less than six national parks (more than in any other state), seven national nature monuments, and numerous state parks. Californians are probably the most outdoor-oriented people in the nation and California's natural beauty and agreeable climate attract more visitors than any other state.

California is a state of contrasts—from the verdant and humid northwest corner to the parched, brown, and starkly beautiful deserts of its southeastern portion; from its lush golden valleys to its sparkling alpine lakes and meadows; from the strange and lonely lava and sagebrush flats of its sparsely inhabited Modoc Plateau in the northeastern corner to the incomparable beaches and bays of San Diego County; from the incredible blue of the surging Pacific, through the rolling green and gold of its foothills, up through the dense forests of pine and fir, past glaciated gorges and tumbling waterfalls, to the polished granite and glaciers of the high Sierra peaks.

Only in California (near the summit of Mt. Pinos in southern Kern County) can one view the largest flying land bird in North America—the California Condor with a wingspread of 10 feet, and the smallest bird in the United States—the diminutive Calliope Hummingbird, on the same afternoon. Only in California can an energetic birdwatcher execute a trip from the ocean, through the river valleys, across the foothills, and into the desert, and find more than 200 species of birds during a single day in the spring. Only in southern California can an energetic and knowledgeable birder find more than 100 kinds of birds in a single day, any day of the year.

To date, at least 518 species of birds have occurred in California in modern times (since 1900), of which 301 breed or may have bred, and 276 are regular nesters. Two species of birds—the California Condor and the Yellow-billed Magpie—are not know to breed anywhere else in the world. Indeed, the Yellow-billed Magpie is the only American bird that has never been recorded anywhere but its native state. Another four species—Ashy Storm-Petrel, Elegant Tern, Xantus' Murrelet, and California Thrasher—are not known to breed in any other state of the United States. Sixty-five families of birds occur in California and this is exceeded (by one family) only by Texas. Some bird species from 59 of these 65 families nest or have nested within the state.

Only in California have any birdwatchers succeeded in finding more than 400 kinds of birds within the borders of their state in a single calendar year. California's intricate physiography, varied climate, and diversity of habitats have in large measure molded California's uniquely rich bird life. One of the objectives of this book is to relate the geography, climate, and natural environments of California to its avifauna.

This book will serve as an introduction to the hobby and sport of bird study as well as provide a comprehensive overview of the spatial and temporal distribution of the birds of California. In this last regard, one section of the book includes a complete and annotated list of all species of birds recorded from California since 1900 as well as some remarks regarding their status and general distribution within the specific habitat preferences for the different species.

The numerous photographs of representative birds, all of which were photographed by the author unless otherwise specified, are of wild birds in their natural habitats. They will serve to acquaint the beginning student of birds with many of the more common and easily seen California forms as well as some of the rarer ones. All of the families of birds occurring in California are illustrated. That portion of the book concerning natural habitats contains numerous photographs, including many of the most typical species to be found regularly in those habitats.

Birdwatching, or preferably birding, is a fast-growing hobby and sport. This is understandable in the light of increasing public awareness of and concern for the natural environment. Birding offers a new dimension to outdoor recreation and requires a minimum of equipment. A section of this book is devoted to the techniques of studying and enjoying the birds of California on the subprofessional level. Indeed, virtually all professional ornithologists of today began their careers as amateurs and still pursue the pleasures of simple birding whenever they can. Because of this common interest and background, both professional and amateur ornithologists enjoy an amicable relationship seldom found in any other field.

Unfortunately, California's role as the most populous and most popular state has exacted a high price in the destruction and deterioration of much of its natural environment. Some of these environmental problems are unique to this state and the book contains information about some of the effects of environmental alteration and deterioration on California's bird life.

The nomenclature and classification followed in this book are essentially based upon the taxonomy of the American Ornithologists Union *Checklist of North American Birds* (1957) and the Thirty-second Supplement to the A.O.U. *Checklist of North American Birds* as published in The Auk 90:411-419, April 1973. However, due to the fact that this original checklist is now somewhat out of date and additional taxonomic changes will be forthcoming, some other taxonomic modifications have been included which partially agree with *A Checklist of the Birds of California*, McCaskie *et al.,* published in Vol. 1, No. 1, January, 1970, of *California Birds* and subsequently published as the *C.F.O.* (California Field Ornithologists) *Field List of the Birds of California,* compiled by Guy McCaskie, January 1, 1972. The nomenclature adopted therein generally agrees with the scheme recommended in *Species Taxa of North American Birds* (1970), by Ernst Mayr and Lester L. Short.

CHAPTER 1

California and Its Bird Life

Land Regions and Climate of California

CALIFORNIA'S STATE BIRD list, which exceeds 500 species, is second only to that of Texas, a vastly larger state. The wealth and diversity of the California avifauna is accounted for by many factors, not the least of which is the size of the state. California's northern boundary at the Oregon border is the 42° parallel of north latitude and its common border with Mexico roughly coincides with about 32° 30′ north latitude. Its southernmost point, just a few miles south of Imperial Beach, San Diego County, is at 32° 34′ north latitude. Its westernmost point at Cape Mendocino, Humboldt County, is 124° 22′ west longitude and its easternmost point at Parker Dam, San Bernardino County, is 114° 08′ west longitude. The coordinates of its right-angular northeastern corner are exactly at 42° north latitude and 120° west longitude. In its north-south axis then, California extends through almost ten degrees of latitude or almost 700 miles, and its climatic types range from subtropical to arctic and from desert to temperate rain forest. With an area of 158,693 square miles, it is surpassed in size only by Alaska and Texas. Its largest county, San Bernardino, covers over 20,000 square miles—almost as much area as that of Connecticut, Massachusetts, and New Jersey combined. Within its borders, California harbors more distinct and unique types of natural environments or habitats for birds and other forms of wildlife than any other of the fifty United States. No less than twenty-nine major vegetation types and plant communities have been defined, and while these in part reflect certain climatic and soil factors, they result in an unparalleled assortment of habitats for birds. This variety of habitats includes a number of types such as the redwood forest and the chaparral, which are found virtually nowhere else in the world. The large array of natural habitats also includes such diverse forms as several types of marine habitat, deserts of at least five distinctive types, glaciers and alpine fell-fields, and vast mountain forests, to name but a few.

This diversity of natural habitats is a partial consequence of the uniqueness of the California flora which consists of a large number of plants to be found growing in no other area of the world. Of the more than 4,000 species listed in Jepson's *A Manual of the Flowering Plants of California,* 1951, over 1,400 are found only in California. These plants, known as endemics, thus form more than one-third of the entire flora of the state.

The California coastline stretches for 1,190 miles or roughly two-thirds of the west coast of the contiguous United States. Added to this are an additional 287 miles of coastline for numerous offshore islands. In conjunction with the coastline and its beaches, sandbars, reefs, and rocky headlands are numerous tidal estuaries and salt marshes. Little wonder then that California has the richest and most varied marine and water bird faunas of any state.

California has some of the hottest, coldest, wettest, and driest areas of the United States. In altitude it extends from below sea level (–282 feet in Death Valley) to the top of the highest mountain (Mt. Whitney, 14,495 feet) in the contiguous United States. Eleven major land regions have been described for the state. Most northwesterly is the Klamath Mountains Region, consisting of several small heavily forested ranges with numerous peaks towering from 6,000 to 9,000 feet. The rugged and picturesque Salmon Mountains are carved by deep canyons and gorges which are the result of uplifting, folding, faulting, erosion, and some glaciation. East of the Klamath Mountains is the heavily timbered volcanic Cascade Mountains Region crowned by the extinct volcano Mt. Shasta rising to 14,162 feet. Nearby Lassen Peak (10,466 feet) is an active volcano. The Modoc Lava Plateau Region, one of the largest lava fields in the world, and with an average elevation of about 4,500 feet, lies to the east of the Cascade Mountains. It is an extension of the Columbian Lava Plateau into northeastern California and it defines the northern limit of that vast expanse of desert and semi-desert country lying to the east of the Sierra Nevada-Cascade axis of mountains. Much of eastern California, north of the Mojave Desert, is included in the Basin and Ranges Region. This dry eastern portion of the state is marked by desert valleys and bleak desert ranges which trend in a north-south direction. Death Valley is one such area. These desert ranges—the Inyo-White Mountains and the Panamint, Funeral, and Grapevine Mountains—are quite high. White Mountain Peak stands 14,242 feet above sea level and numerous other peaks exceed 10,000 feet. Open forests of Bristlecone and Limber Pines occur at 8,500 to 11,500 feet. Because of the desert location, annual precipitation is low with an average of only 15 inches. The middle slopes contain extensive stands of piñon pine and juniper which give way to great expanses of sagebrush lower down. The Basin and Range Region is actually part of the Great Basin area that extends into Nevada, Utah, Idaho, and Oregon and terminates at the western foothills of the Rocky Mountains.

Along California's Pacific Coast lies the Coast Range Region, extending south from Oregon to the San Rafael Mountains in Santa Barbara County. This low intermittent range composed chiefly of sedimentary rocks is dissected by grassy valleys. In places it is heavily forested with Coast Redwoods, pines, oaks, and other large trees. Elsewhere it is verdant with northern coastal scrub and coastal sage scrub. The Great Valley or Central Valley Region is a large alluvial plain filled with sediments and extends more than 450 miles from northwest to southeast. It lies in a trough as much as eighty miles wide in places between the Sierra Nevada on the east and the Coast Range to the west. The Great Valley is really two valleys. To the north, the Sacramento River drains the Sacramento Valley and the San Joaquin River system drains the San Joaquin Valley in the southern part. Most of the state's drainage then passes through a mile-wide gap in the Coast Range where both of these great rivers empty into San Francisco Bay. Three-fifths of California's farmland occurs in the Valley which, in the southern portion especially, is intensively irrigated. Prior to human settlement the natural habitats of the Valley included extensive fresh-water marshes, grasslands and savannah, dense riverine (riparian) forests, large lakes and rivers, and even true desert. Irrigation and agriculture have altered much of this natural environment and there has been a concomitant change in the populations of birds and other wildlife.

The Sierra Nevada Region is a huge block-fault mountain range extending more than 430 miles northwest to southeast in the eastern one-third of California. In places it is almost 80 miles wide and is dissected by numerous rivers draining westward into the San Joaquin Valley. Dozens of its peaks rise above 14,000 feet and deep glaciated valleys enclose many picturesque lakes and rivers. Because of its elevation the Sierra Nevada contains a number of "life zones" and plant communities ranging from the "rain shadow" deserts to the east, across the glaciers and alpine fell-fields at the crest, to the hot interior foothills on the gentle western slopes. At elevations between 4,000 and 9,000 feet are to be found dense forests of pine and fir.

In the southern one-fifth of the state lie two large mountain masses and all of the large islands. The Transverse Ranges Region extends southeastward from Santa Barbara County to San Bernardino County and consists of the westernmost Santa Ynez and other low mountain groups and intervening valleys. Farther east are the San Gabriel Mountains which extend to Cajon Pass. East of this pass rise the San Bernardino Mountains with San Gorgonio Peak, 11,485 feet, as its supreme summit. These ranges are the only major east-west trending mountain ranges in the state. The lower slopes of these Transverse Ranges (especially the south-facing exposures) are clothed with chaparral scrub, and extensive coniferous forests cover the higher slopes until a timberline is reached at about 10,000 feet. The westernmost member of the Transverse Ranges, the Santa Monica Mountains, terminates at the seacoast. The northern group of the Channel Islands (Anacapa, Santa Cruz, Santa Rosa, and San Miguel) were once part of these mountains but are now separated by about 30 miles of ocean. To the southeast of them are the other Channel Islands—Catalina, San Clemente, San Nicolas, and the Santa Barbara Islands, none of which are geologically part of the northern group. Other islands of consequence to bird life off the California coast include the seven islets of the Farallon Islands located some 30 miles offshore from the Golden Gate, and Los Coronados

Islands (belonging to Mexico) which are situated just 8 miles from shore south of
San Diego.

The southwestern corner of California is occupied by mountainous land called
the Peninsular Ranges Region which extends from near the cities of Los Angeles
and Riverside south into Baja California. The average width of the Peninsular system is about 50 miles. With few exceptions the highest elevations in the Peninsular
Ranges are located close to the great fault scarp on the eastern side of the Ranges
with the highest peak being Mt. San Jacinto (10,508 feet). Santa Rosa Mountain
farther to the southeast rises 8,046 feet above sea level. In San Diego County the
highest peaks are Palomar Mountain (6,126 feet) and Cuyamaca Peak (6,515 feet).
The lower slopes of those mountains of the Peninsular Ranges adjacent to the Colorado Desert are sparsely vegetated. Dense stands of chaparral composed largely of
chamise and ribbonwood are to be found higher up and to the west. At 5,000 feet
to 6,000 feet this dense scrub gives way to coniferous forests of pine and fir. Live
oak woodlands are to be found at the middle elevations of those mountains closer
to the coast, as on Palomar Mountain.

The vast Mojave Desert and the much smaller Colorado Desert occupy one-
sixth of the state in its southeastern corner. To the east of the Peninsular Ranges
lies the Colorado Desert Region situated in a trough that continues southward as
the Gulf of California. It occupies about 2,000 square miles, includes more than 100
palm oases, and contains the recently created 60-mile-long Salton Sea. To the west
of the Peninsular Ranges lies the Pacific Ocean. Because of the diversity of habitats
to be found within a relatively short distance between the Colorado Desert and the
Pacific Ocean across the Peninsular Ranges, a California birding party in the spring
of 1972 established an all-time record of 227 bird species observed in a single day by
a single small party. This fact alone points up the remarkable variety of California
bird life. The great Mojave Desert Region to the north of the Colorado Desert covers about 25,000 square miles between the Sierra Nevada and the Nevada border
and the Colorado River. To the north it merges with the shadscale and sagebrush
scrubs of the Great Basin.

In addition to these natural regions, Californians have created extensive artificial habitats which have had differing effects upon bird life. Large urban and especially suburban complexes at San Francisco, Los Angeles, and San Diego are in a
sense special bird habitats as are the man-made agricultural lands, parks, golf
courses, cemeteries, parkways, reservoirs, garbage dumps, and the like. Rather than
being devoid of birds, some of these areas attract large numbers of birds and frequently of rather few types. People living in cities are often unaware of the numbers and variety of birds which share their environment with them.

The climate of most of California is characterized by only two well-marked seasons—rainy and non-rainy. The first normally starts in the north about late September or October and may last until April or May. It is a consequence of the
cyclonic storms generated in the Gulf of Alaska. Heavy rains, which often cause
serious floods, have totaled as much as 26 inches in a single day. Rainfall gradually

decreases from north to south and west to east except where mountains intervene, with the northwest coastal areas averaging more than 100 inches per year. At San Francisco the annual average is about 22 inches; at Los Angeles, 15 inches; and at San Diego, 10 inches. Bagdad, in Death Valley, experienced 760 rainless days early in the twentieth century, and no other place in the United States has ever experienced a longer rainless period. The northern portion of the state receives more rain than the southern part for essentially two reasons. The centers of the winter cyclonic storms are closer to northern California and in general, areas closer to the center of a low-pressure system receive more precipitation than areas far removed from the center. Additionally, northern California is affected by more cyclonic storms than the southern part of the state. In the northern hemisphere the flow of air around cyclonic storms is counterclockwise. Because of this fact, the moisture-bearing winds in front of an approaching California storm are from a southerly direction. These winds swing to the west as the storm reaches and passes over California. This also results in heavier precipitation on the south and west slopes of the mountains than on the north and east slopes. Summer rain in the form of tropical thunderstorms sometimes douses the eastern Transverse Ranges, the southern deserts, and the Peninsular Ranges. These irregular storms may begin as tropical cyclonic disturbances originating far to the south off the Pacific shores of Mexico. A more usual cause of the summer thunderstorms which account for a considerable portion of the total annual precipitation in the eastern and southeastern deserts are the so-called Sonora storms. These storms are caused by tongues of warm moist air that originate over tropical waters and enter the state from the southeast. These storms may reach as far north as the Klamath Mountains area and thunderstorms can occur throughout the mountainous regions, particularly in the Sierra Nevada, Cascades, and the Transverse and Peninsular Ranges, causing widespread forest fires.

Because of its extreme altitude, the Sierra Nevada is the coldest part of the state and one of the snowiest regions in the world. Some snow is to be found on the higher Sierran peaks throughout the year and there are still a few small glaciers extant there. Winters are long and severe with much snow and howling gales. Freezing temperatures occur there even in summer. California's lowest recorded temperature, –45°F., occurred in January, 1937, at Boca, Nevada County. Temperatures over 100°F. are usual in the deserts and some of the interior valleys during the summer. The highest temperature ever recorded in California and the United States was 134°F. at Death Valley on July 10, 1913.

It rarely snows in the valleys along the central and southern coast, but much snow falls in the higher reaches of the several mountain ranges of the state. In some parts of the Sierra Nevada the yearly snowfall averages more than 450 inches. The climate of the coastal areas is tempered by the prevailing moist westerly winds from the Pacific. These coastal areas usually have warm summers and cool frost-free winters. That stretch of coastline between Los Angeles and San Diego has one of the mildest climates to be found anywhere in the United States. Los Angeles temperatures average 55°F. in January and 73°F. in July. Small wonder then that the population center of the state is situated near there and that the greatest expansion of urban and suburban environments has occurred in the Los Angeles and Orange County areas. San Francisco is somewhat cooler as January temperatures average about 50°F. and July temperatures average about 60°F. Coastal low clouds and fog during summer and "tule" fogs in the Central Valley during the winter are important in limiting temperature variation between day and night in those areas.

A unique feature of California is its many belts of moisture and heat, some of which are only a few miles wide. The locations and directions of the mountains and interior valleys causes the climate to vary markedly from section to section. Also, up to a certain point, precipitation increases with increasing elevation. North-south mountain ranges may force prevailing westerly winds to rise and precipitate their moisture on the westerly slopes, resulting in cool dense forests, while the easterly slopes, located in the "rain shadow" of the mountains, receive but little moisture and desertlike conditions prevail.

Ocean currents are of considerable importance to the distribution of California's coastal and sea birds. The cool California Current from the north central Pacific Ocean is a sluggish flow of water about 400 miles wide. Between this current and the coast is a complex of eddies and countercurrents which are constantly changing with the seasons. One such is a deep (below 600 feet) countercurrent that flows to the northwest along the coast from Baja California to beyond Cape Mendocino. The waters of this current are warmer and more saline than are the surface waters. During the late fall, when the north winds are weak or absent, this current, now known as the Davidson Current, forms at the surface between the California Current and the mainland and it extends from the tip of Baja California to north of Point Conception. This countercurrent may be partially responsible for the concomitant appearance along the California coast of such tropical sea birds as Magnificent Frigatebirds, Red-billed Tropicbirds, Least Storm-Petrels, Craveri's Murrelets, and even Elegant Terns.

During the summer the strong northerly winds along the California coast maintain the well-developed current system, but as these winds diminish in the fall the California Current weakens, allowing the Davidson Current to form at the surface. An additional factor that contributes to the wealth of California's marine life (including birds) is the offshore displacement of surface waters by the strong and persistent northerly and northwesterly winds. Upwelling of deep cold water rich in dissolved nutrients replaces the wind-blown surface waters. These deep waters, rich in dissolved oxygen as well, result in a prodigious proliferation of phytoplankton that forms the base of virtually all marine food-chains. This upwelling is associated with winds from the north and northwest and consequently appears in southern and central California waters during May and June. Upwelling is strongest in northern California waters during July and August. The abundance of such pelagic birds as Sooty Shearwaters, jaegers, storm-petrels, albatrosses, and the like during this season is no doubt related to this phenomenon.

As a consequence of this diversity of climate, soils (of over 500 types), ocean currents, and physiography, coupled with complexity of its vegetation and habitats, California's bird list of more than 500 species is five-eighths of the total North American avifauna found north of Mexico. In addition, 276 species of birds of the 301 species which have bred in modern times regularly breed in California. This is second only to Texas (with more than 320 breeding species in modern times) and more bird species than breed in any of the countries of Europe west of the Soviet Union.

Distribution of California Birds

The birds of California are not a unique assemblage peculiar to this particular political unit. Rather, knowing no state or international borders, they freely move to and fro as part of a larger pulsating river of bird life which comprises the birds of North America—a more realistic zoogeographic unit. Unaware of the artificial borders drawn on a political map of North America, birds, unlike humans, are distributed across the continent by factors of food, nesting habitats, physical barriers, dispersal avenues, ancestral ranges, times and pathways of migration, population pressures, age groupings, and to some extent, human endeavors. To speak of the birds of California as an entity is for purposes of convenience only. Birds, being among the most mobile of all animals, constitute an extremely fluid population that changes from place to place, season to season, and year to year.

It is impossible to determine with any degree of accuracy the actual number of birds that inhabit California. Twenty billion birds has been suggested as a possible figure for all of North America north of Mexico in autumn. Bird populations within a specific area change constantly. For birds nesting in California, populations are highest during or near the end of the breeding season. In fact, their populations may double or treble between the onset of the nesting season and its end. But by the following year, at the beginning of the next breeding period, the rigors of migration, predation, disease, inclement weather, food shortages, and all the other natural hazards, have reduced the population from 50 to 60 per cent for most smaller land birds. For migratory species which do not nest within the state, there are peak periods when they may number in the millions. On a worldwide basis, some sea birds may be the most abundant of all bird species. In California (along the coast) during May, the population of Sooty Shearwaters may number in the tens of millions, but at other seasons it drops to tens of thousands or even lower.

What is the most abundant species of bird (of the more than 500 that have occurred) in California? This would also depend upon the season of the year, as obviously tens of millions of Sooty Shearwaters are within the state boundaries at *some* time of the year. During May there is probably no more abundant species. On a year-around basis perhaps it is the Mourning Dove, the Red-winged Blackbird, the House Sparrow, or the House Finch. The exploding population of Starlings makes them a strong and unwelcome contender for number one in the near future. It is significant to note that two of the possible leading species are introduced and undesirable immigrants.

As to California's rarest bird, the California Condor certainly comes to mind immediately. Many birds which do not breed in California and have been recorded here only once or twice in this century are certainly rare in California, but elsewhere may be very common. For nesting species, the Yellow Rail formerly nested within California in this century but must now be considered extirpated as a breeder and is certainly very rare at any time or place. Yet this rail, as well as the other members of its family, are difficult to see because of the denseness of their marsh habitat and the nature of their shy and skulking habits. Thus a bird such as the Black Rail, which is *rarely seen* but more frequently heard, is not really a rare bird as is the California Condor, which is relatively easy to see, but whose total world population of probably less than fifty makes it a rare bird in the absolute sense. Birds such as Piping Plovers, White-eyed Vireos, Golden-cheeked Warblers, and Wheatears, which have been recorded but once in California, are certainly rare *here*. The very small breeding population of Whip-poor-wills (probably no more than several pairs) in the Mt. San Jacinto region makes them a very rare breeder in the state, but elsewhere in North America they are abundant.

In habitats or communities that have not as yet reached their climax state—that is, they are still in the process of evolving by plant succession through a series of different stages—the bird populations change accordingly. In the classical succession of pond to climax coniferous forest, possibly six or seven distinct communities may follow each other within the space of one hundred years. The original pond community may have such birds as Pied-billed Grebes, several species of ducks, Belted Kingfishers, and other water-oriented species. The marsh community that follows may harbor Long-billed Marsh Wrens, American Coots, several species of rails, Red-winged Blackbirds, and so forth, but when a meadow and willow-alder-aspen community replaces the marsh, such birds as Western Meadowlarks, Lincoln's Sparrows, House Wrens, Red-breasted Sapsuckers, and Tree Swallows will move in. Eventually, when a montane or subalpine forest of coniferous trees invades the area as the climax community, a more stable population of Yellow-rumped Warblers, Red-breasted Nuthatches, Cassin's Finches, Hermit Thrushes, and Red Crossbills will become established. Thus, birds which were at one time common enough in a certain area, may in time become uncommon, rare, and finally disappear altogether.

Birds, then, are spatially and temporally distributed in California. No single species of bird occurs in *all* of California's natural habitats. Some birds with more generalized feeding requirements and habits are found in a number of habitats. The Common Raven, for example, is found in the deserts of California, in grasslands, on rocky cliffs, along the seacoast, in mountain forests, and above timberline in the alpine fell-fields. Being a predator and scavenger, it survives well almost anywhere. Birds with very restricted ranges and habitats because of food resources, nesting requirements, and vegetational cover requirements would include the Black Oystercatcher which is at home only on the rocky beaches of the offshore islands and mainland where it feeds and breeds. The Wrentit requires the very dense cover of the chaparral, northern coastal scrub, and the coastal sage scrub. Their cover requirements are so circumscribed that this species may not even cross roads and firebreaks which have been cut through their territories.

During the nesting season many birds, especially the males, become highly territorial, that is, they will vigorously defend a certain defined area from other members of the same species. This type of behavior then will restrict the distribution of birds to certain favorable places during the nesting season, but these territorial boundaries break down later and the entire population of a species becomes more fluid and some birds may even join together in large feeding aggregations. Where feeding grounds are some distance from the breeding area (as in sea birds), or are rich but restricted to a relatively small area (such as a marsh), foraging areas are frequently excluded from the defended territory but are part of the larger and undefended home range. For some birds, such as some alcids and storm-petrels, the nesting colonies may appear virtually deserted during the day because the majority of the colony is far away at sea and feeding while the rest of the birds are safe underground in their burrows. At night, however, the colony becomes a beehive of noise and activity as parent birds return from the sea to feed their hungry young. Birds, then, have certain preferred habitats for nesting and feeding. Those habitats and the birds which inhabit them will be more fully considered in Chapter Four.

The temporal distribution of the birds of California is essentially one of migration. Classically, migration is a north-south-oriented movement of birds between two home ranges. Bird migration, while not confined to the northern hemisphere, is best expressed there. However, in the mountainous western United States, an up-mountain and down-mountain movement of birds occurs that is called vertical migration. The migration of sea birds occurs primarily in the daytime and the birds feed en route, often lingering for some time in areas where food is plentiful. Some birds, such as hawks, swifts, and swallows, are also diurnal migrants which feed as they travel. Not much is known about the navigational techniques of sea birds such as albatrosses and shearwaters. Perhaps they are guided by the sun and stars, movements of water masses, ocean currents, shoreline configurations, and combinations of such factors. The diurnal land migrants probably follow conspicuous physiographic features such as coastlines, river valleys, and mountain ranges. In many instances, young birds migrating with adults learn the route as they go, while in other cases, the adults and young migrate at slightly different times. This means that the young must inherit the necessary navigational processes from their parents. Once under way, they must respond in the correct way to certain environmental cues. Such environmental cues may be celestial or terrestrial or both. Nocturnal migrants are primarily smaller land birds which must then spend much of the daylight hours feeding to restore the energy necessary for the next leg of the journey. Smaller birds are also safer from predators during their night flights. However, as they are guided primarily by the constellations, they often become disoriented on foggy or overcast nights and frequently collide with such brightly lighted objects as bridges, high-rise buildings, lighthouses, and radio and television transmitting towers. On such occasions the birds appear to be badly confused and disoriented and even fly directly down into the ground. Airport ceilometers, which measure the altitude of the cloud cover by shining a powerful searchlight vertically, often attract hundreds of birds which then may plunge to their deaths down the lethal light beam. Once safely aground after a night's flight, those birds which have alighted shortly after dawn, feed voraciously, drink, bathe, and rest themselves. They then may continue their northward journey in a more leisurely fashion, feeding as they go during the rest of the day. On the spring nights of rather heavy migrational flights it is possible to hear the chips, chirps, and chatters of the nocturnal migrants as they pass unseen overhead in their rush to the north. Although each of these migrants probably navigates by itself, the flocks remain in rather loose formation and possibly gain some reassurance from the voices of the other birds in the flock. These flocks may be of a single species or may be mixed assemblages of small land birds.

For some species, such as the Cliff Swallow, northward movements are more or less isochronal unless severe inclement weather interferes with the timetable. Other species are not quite so precise in the timing of their movements and are more subject to local weather conditions. The migration season is protracted in California. Among the earliest of northbound migrants are the diurnal Turkey Vultures, which begin to drift northward from Mexico in late January, although there are always small numbers of Turkey Vultures present in California. Allen's Hummingbirds (of the migratory race) normally begin to arrive in southern California during the second week of January and the first Rufous Hummingbirds appear about a week later. The spring migration for most species accelerates swiftly through March and early April and reaches a crescendo in late April and early May in the southern part of the state, and about a week later in northern California. Small migrants which may fly north for at least eight hours per night at 20 to 30 miles per hour can easily cover 200 to 300 miles in this time period and thus traverse the entire length of the state in just three or four nights. Compared with the fall migration, the spring migration appears to be a more vigorous and energetic affair. The birds are more conspicuous. They are in their finest and brightest plumage, they sing more, and they are literally here today and gone tomorrow. The fall migration seems more subdued and leisurely as if the birds were hesitant to leave the state. In the spring, with their juices flowing, it seems as if the birds can't wait to reach their breeding grounds.

The formation of migrational "waves" of birds does not occur with the same frequency or intensity as it does in the central and eastern portions of the continent. However, migrational bird "waves" do form in the far western migration stream when certain meteorological conditions prevail. During the spring migration season, the normal weather pattern is that of a persistent high-pressure system that predominates off the California coast during April and May. The resulting strong northwest winds (especially along the central and northern coastal areas where gusts occasionally reach 100 mph) slow down the northward surge of coastal migrants. When a low-pressure system replaces the high-pressure area, the northwest winds may abate or be replaced by light winds from the south or southeast, thus releasing a flood of dammed-up migrants into a typical migrational wave. In the Central Valley, the passage of a cold front is associated with the subsiding of the northwest winds on the coast. Thus, numbers of migrants become locally grounded as the cold front passes, with the resulting formation of a migrational wave. Passage of migrants out of the southeastern deserts is accomplished with the aid of shifting wind patterns also. Normally the high-pressure system off the California coast produces an intense onshore flow of marine air accompanied by coastal low clouds and fog which may extend inland for many miles, even to the fringes of the desert as at San Gorgonio Pass near Palm Springs. At these times gale-force winds rip eastward through the passes churning up clouds of sand and dust and pinning down the migrants. When these conditions abate, migrational waves then form as the migrants rush to resume their northward journey out of the desert. Even in the face of adverse winds, the migrants may continue to trickle northward following along the less windy routes. At these times, then, the desert oases and indeed the entire Coachella and Imperial Valleys with their green and irrigated fields and orchards become holding pockets for migrating birds.

The fall migration of small land birds is probably more protracted in time and place, while the spring migration routes are fairly well defined. Southbound shorebirds appear in July and the shorebird migration reaches a peak, or actually a plateau, during August and early September, after which it tapers off considerably, but not before leaving behind fairly large numbers of shorebirds that remain throughout the winter. Southbound land birds commence migration in August and most are gone by mid-October. Some migrants even depart or move through in July, and the Rufous Hummingbirds actually *ascend* to 6,000 feet and higher in the Sierra Nevada and other mountains to find the necessary flowers during their journey. The migratory status of California birds is fairly complex, but it does resolve itself into a rather definite pattern.

Examination of a map of North America reveals that migratory land birds entering California must have done so after crossing hundreds of miles of Mexican desert. However, the migrants can accomplish this in three days and enough oases and watercourses exist to provide them with essential food and water. Their passage through these sere lands happily coincides with the early flowering spring season and it affords them sufficient nectar and insects for survival. Migrant land birds, then, enter California from the south and the southeast and are greeted upon their arrival in the Golden State by more of the same—desert. Here too, however, the desert is in bloom, although the quality and intensity of this flowering season varies from year to year and is dependent to some extent upon the rains of the previous winter. Some of the migrants follow the inviting greenery of the Colorado River and ultimately cross the open deserts into the Great Basin. Some swing westward and follow the Owens River Valley to the north. Since most of the mountain ranges in the Great Basin are aligned in a north-south direction, the intervening valleys provide natural avenues for bird migration. The Imperial Valley in the Colorado Desert with its artificial oases and extensively irrigated agricultural fields provides welcome cover, food, and water. The California deserts are liberally sprinkled with natural oases and these become virtual bird traps in April and early May. Moreover, the numerous desert communities which increase and enlarge each year as more and more people retire to the desert, also provide the necessary cover, food, and water. Clearly, the majority of land bird migrants from the south (Mexico, Central and South America) enter California across the deserts of the state. Some spring migrants, following the Baja California peninsula, proceed along the California coast on their route, but the majority of migrants fan out from the deserts and follow the natural landforms which thus funnel them northward. Those following the eastern escarpment of the Sierra Nevada may reach higher elevations by following up the riparian watercourses in the canyons while others proceed northward at lower elevations. In late April and early May, when the surge of migration is at flood, the higher forests are still in the grip of winter and the migrants which eventually will populate those areas during the summer proceed upward slowly. Not only do the migrants move northward with the spring, but the spring season itself progresses northward and upward as well. Often, too-early migrants will be caught on their montane breeding grounds by late unseasonable snows that kill most available insect food. The newly arrived migrants cannot retreat downhill and therefore many starve and freeze to death.

Various low elevation passes enable the migrants to breast the mountains enclosing the Great Valley and proceed to the north by this wide and fruitful avenue. Others follow various valley systems through the Coast Range which are experiencing spring also. The climate of the lower reaches of the Coast Range is tempered to moderation by the adjacent Pacific Ocean and the birds encounter few climatic obstructions there. Nesting of some species is completed in the southern part of the state while May migrants are still passing through northern California en route to more boreal nesting areas. Those spring migrants that are considered rarities in California seem to occur with surprising regularity very late in the spring season. These birds are often warblers that appear late in May or in early June at scattered oases in the Mojave Desert and the Great Basin, and on the Farallon Islands.

During the fall migration the desert oases are not as productive as in the spring. The desert itself is uninviting, dry, flowerless, and exceedingly hot. The pattern of southbound migration in California is not entirely clear but it seems evident that there is a decided coastward shift of some southbound land birds. There is even some suspicion that in southern California at least, there is virtually no northward spring coastal movement of birds to speak of and the land birds seen along the coast at that season have traveled in a westerly and northwesterly direction to get there. From Crescent City to Point Arena, the California coastline extends in a more or less northwest-southeast direction. From Point Arena southward the coast swings abruptly southeastward. Indeed the coastline from San Diego to Point Arena is about 320° from true North (360°), or, stated another way, the coastline between San Diego and Point Arena, is inclined at a 40° angle to the meridians of longitude. The implications of this to the student of California migration are very great. If the "preferred direction" of flight of southbound migrants is south-oriented, then the coastal concentrations of migrants during the autumn months is easily explained. Such places as South Farallon Island, Point Reyes, and Point Bonita in Marin County, Pacific Grove and Carmel in Monterey County, Santa Barbara in Santa Barbara County, Los Angeles and Point Fermin in Los Angeles County, Dana Point in Orange County, and Solana Beach, Point Loma, and Imperial Beach in San Diego County are focal points for fall migration studies. In addition to the expected fall migrants, many of California's rare transients and casual land birds also occur in these coastal areas at this time. In fact, most of the extra-limital records of the rarer (in California) birds occur during the fall migration.

Heavy flights of southbound migrants, especially warblers, also pass through the Central Valley and the middle elevations of the Sierra Nevada. Especially favored feeding areas at dawn are around the perimeters of wet mountain meadows at the 6,000- to 7,000-foot level. Large numbers of small migrant land birds also follow southward along the eastern escarpment of the Sierra Nevada and these birds include among their numbers many from western Canada and Alaska. As the southbound migrants enter Mexico in August and September they encounter more or less favorable conditions in the western part of the country which will be undergoing a "rainy" season with concomitant production of plant and animal foods for the birds.

A small countercurrent of fall migration regularly develops among at least six species of California birds. Small flocks of Wood Storks from the mainland move northward from their Mexican breeding grounds during July, and substantial numbers assemble at the south end of the Salton Sea at least until early September. A few individuals are sprinkled along the coastal lagoons in southern California as well at this time. By mid-September, however, most have retreated southward again. Heermann's Gulls, which nest primarily on islands in the Gulf of California, also move northward at this time, although small numbers of Heermann's Gulls are present, at least in southern California, throughout the year. Although a small population of Elegant Terns nests near San Diego, a large influx of post-breeding birds from islands in the Gulf of California occurs in late July. Numbers increase through September but most birds have returned to the south by early October. Similarly, the little-known Craveri's Murrelet from islands in the Gulf of California appears in California coastal waters during August, September, and October.

With the rather sudden decline in the production of young California Brown Pelicans due to chlorinated hydrocarbons in the food of the adults that renders the female pelicans incapable of producing thick and durable egg shells, more attention has been paid to the origin of the flocks of Brown Pelicans seen along the California coast in late summer and fall. Intensive marking programs utilizing colored streamers affixed to the legs of nestling Brown Pelicans reared on islands in the Gulf of California has revealed that large numbers of these Mexican-born birds move northward with some adults into California coastal waters late in summer each year only to return south again in the late fall. It is not known whether these latter four sea birds from the Gulf of California cross the mainland from the northern Gulf to the southern California coast or whether they first make the long southward journey to the southern tip of the Baja California peninsula before turning northward into the Pacific Ocean. The very few records from the Salton Sea indicate a coastal route for most of these birds. The fairly regular appearance in late summer of Blue-footed and Brown Boobies and the Yellow-legged race of the Western Gull at the Salton Sea indicates that at least some of the Mexican sea birds choose the overland route. The only land bird that seems to display this type of predictable northward fall "migration" is the Tropical Kingbird. They regularly occur in small numbers, particularly along the coast, during September, October, and into November. Least Storm-Petrels and Red-billed Tropicbirds, also from Mexican waters, probably exhibit an irregular pattern of coastal northward migration, although in very small numbers. During 1970 some 3,000 Least Storm-Petrels occurred off San Diego, indicating the possible sporadic nature of these movements.

California birds can conveniently be categorized by their migratory or non-migratory status in the state. RESIDENTS are those species that do not enter or leave the state in migration. Generally, these birds do not move very far in the course of their lives. However, some residents may breed in one part of the state, migrate a short distance, and winter in another part. California Quail, Acorn Woodpeckers, and Wrentits are examples of relatively sedentary species whose movements are minimal. On the other hand, American Robins, Dark-eyed Juncos ("Oregon" type), and White-crowned Sparrows which nest in northern and/or mountainous parts of California spend the winter in the lowlands and/or southern parts of the state. It must be pointed out that because of the large size and diverse nature of California it is often impossible to easily categorize each of California's birds in this manner. For example, the Varied Thrush and the Lewis' Woodpecker are common enough residents in the northern and western parts of the state, but in southern California are irregular visitors in the fall and winter. Some species, such as Chestnut-backed Chickadees, are resident in coastal areas from Morro Bay, San Luis Obispo County, northward, but never reach southern or eastern California. Additionally, the migratory status of each species must be further qualified by such subjective designations as *common, uncommon,* and *rare* (not rarely seen, but rare in the absolute numerical sense). Also, these designations must obviously refer to *preferred habitat.* The Acorn Woodpecker is common enough in its "preferred" and required habitat of oak woodlands and would be extremely rare (or well nigh impossible) on the hot creosote bush flats of the Mojave Desert. Thus, in preferred habitat, the Acorn Woodpecker is a *common* resident; the Black-backed Three-toed Woodpecker is an *uncommon* resident; and the California Condor (although easily seen at times) is a *rare* resident. Some 164 or 31 per cent of California's birds may be considered essentially as *residents*.

The PURE TRANSIENTS are birds that migrate through California in spring and/ or fall and *do not nest* in the state. Some of the rarer pure transients are found primarily in the fall and have never been recorded in the spring. Pure transients are usually birds that nest to the north of California and spend the winter somewhere to the south of the state. Within a given species, for example the Whimbrel, some members of this highly migratory species spend the winter in the state but most continue flying to the south from their arctic breeding grounds. In the spring, however, almost all of them continue on north to Canada and Alaska and none spend the summer months in California. However, virtually the entire population of Rufous Hummingbirds in California is purely transient. In the case of the Baird's Sandpiper, which winters in South America, there are no winter or summer records for California. The Northern Phalarope exemplifies a common pure transient; the Baird's Sandpiper is an uncommon pure transient; and the Bobolink is a rare fall pure transient. Pure transients comprise about 4 per cent or 19 species of California's birds.

Another form of transient situation exists among California's birds. There are those transient species whose status in California is complex and is not as easily designated as pure transient. These birds fall roughly into three broad categories. First, there are those birds whose distribution is such that some members of the population breed in the state and other members (they may even be of different races) proceed through the state as transients to breed in Oregon, Washington, Canada, or Alaska. The Western Tanager is a case in point. Second, there are the transients from breeding grounds to the north of California. Some continue on south through the state to spend the winter to the south of California, perhaps in Mexico, as does the Pintail. However, tens of thousands of Pintails spend the winter in California as winter visitors and small numbers are even resident. Third, there is the case of a bird such as the Ruby-crowned Kinglet where some of the population that breeds in California remains in the state throughout the year as residents, while other members of this species depart for Mexico in the fall to return again to nest in California the following year. The situation is further complicated by such birds as the Spotted Sandpiper, part of whose population is *transient* from the north through the state, part of the population from the north of California *winters* in the state, and another group of Spotted Sandpipers is *resident* in the state throughout the year. Various combinations of these situations also occur to further complicate this type of categorization. The term COMPLEX TRANSIENT is used for such transients. Eighty of California's birds, or 16 per cent, fall within this category.

WINTER VISITORS are those birds whose breeding range is somewhere to the north of California. In the autumn they migrate south to California and spend the winter months. The following spring they return to the northern breeding areas once more. As previously mentioned, some birds of a given species may be both transients and winter visitors. For example, the transient Pintails that migrate early in the fall continue on to spend the winter in Mexico. Those that follow later spend the winter in California. The Heermann's Gull, which nests in Mexico, migrates north in the fall in great numbers and is a very common winter visitor along the coast although there are some non-breeding Heermann's Gulls present during the summer as well. It is interesting to note that the similar and closely related Gray Gull of South America exhibits the same migrational pattern, except in reverse. After the nesting season in Chile they migrate south during their "fall" season. Whistling Swans are common winter visitors in the northern half of the state, but in southern California they are rare. Rough-legged Hawks are winter visitors throughout the state, but they rank from almost rare in the southern portion to fairly common in the far northern parts. Rock Sandpipers are rare but regular winter visitors to certain favored coastal areas primarily in the northern half of California. Birds that are essentially winter visitors to California number 46 species or about 10 per cent of the state's species.

SUMMER VISITORS is the designation given to those birds whose winter range is somewhere to the south of California. They migrate north in the spring, nest somewhere in California, and return to their southerly winter homes again in the autumn. Occasionally a few members of this group spend the winter in the southern parts of the state. In this group are some species whose winter homes are far to the south in South America. Western Tanagers, which spend the winter months from Mexico to Costa Rica, are common summer visitors in the montane forests throughout the state. Fulvous Tree Ducks are uncommon summer visitors in the extreme southern part of California and Summer Tanagers are rare and very local summer visitors, again in the southern portion. However, along the Colorado River in California the Summer Tanagers are uncommon summer visitors. There are 32 birds in this group, representing about 6 per cent of California's bird species.

A small group of birds can be described as POST-BREEDING or FALL VISITORS. These are post-breeding birds from Mexico that come north in late summer, remain well into autumn, and return to their southern homes before winter. Such species as Least Storm-Petrels, Black Storm-Petrels (present during *our* summer and early fall, but *their* fall), many of the Brown Pelicans, Laughing Gulls, Western Gulls of the Yellow-legged race, Craveri's Murrelets, Elegant Terns, and Tropical Kingbirds are included in this group. Fall visitors constitute less than 1 per cent of California's bird species. The Elegant Tern is a common post-breeding or fall visitor; the Tropical Kingbird is uncommon, and the Craveri's Murrelet is rare.

PERENNIAL VISITORS, amounting to less than 1 per cent of California's birds, are those few species that are present somewhere in California throughout the year, but do not nest in the state. They are sea birds such as Black-footed Albatrosses and Sooty Shearwaters, whose populations in California are constantly in a state of flux. At certain seasons they are more numerous than at others, but there are always some along the California coast. Those of the species that occur during their nesting season are juveniles and non-breeding adults.

Some of the less common birds whose numbers are sporadic from year to year or which occur in some years and are absent in others can be termed IRREGULAR VISITORS and comprise less than 1 per cent of California's bird species. Different species may be expected at different seasons. In some cases, such as the Bohemian Waxwings, their numbers may be substantial when they arrive in late fall and winter. Others, like the Flesh-footed Shearwaters are scarce but fairly regular each year and may occur anywhere offshore at any time.

CASUAL VISITORS and ACCIDENTALS occur unexpectedly, are unpredictable and very rare in California, and some may occur by chance anywhere and at any time. The Cape Petrel that occurred off Monterey on September 9, 1962, is one of the extremely few known appearances of this accidental Antarctic species north of the equator. A rare bird may occur more than ten times and be considered as casual. There are perhaps a dozen or so records of the Laysan Albatross off the California coast, but it still must be regarded as casual until more pelagic fieldwork reveals a definite and predictable pattern. Other *casual visitors* include Little Blue Herons, Emperor Geese, Long-tailed Jaegers, and Eastern Phoebes. White-tailed Tropicbirds, Wandering Albatrosses, Kittlitz's Murrelets, Black-billed Cuckoos, Red-headed Woodpeckers, Blue Jays, and Red-faced Warblers are among the group of *accidentals* or birds that have occurred in California about ten times or less since 1900. Astonishingly, there are 128 birds of these types and they constitute 26 per cent of the state list.

Most California birds fit fairly well into one of the above status categories but there are always the exceptions to the general rules. Numerous non-breeding adults and immatures of several species of shorebirds and some species of gulls spend the summer months (June–September) along the California coast. The shorebirds represent small groups whose larger populations are transient in the spring. The different summering coastal gulls are from species which normally winter along the California coast. Many immature Western Gulls are to be found along the coast in summer as well. The adults nest on some of the offshore islands. Among the various species of shorebirds that migrate south through California in the fall there are those species such as the Lesser Yellowlegs, Baird's Sandpipers, and Wilson's Phalaropes that normally do not winter in California at all. Among other fall transients, such as Sanderlings, Greater Yellowlegs, and Western Sandpipers, substantial segments of those populations winter in California.

Some 32 or about 6 per cent of California's birds defy pigeonholing and are actually various combinations of the above general groupings. Also, two species, the Pintail and the Brant are both winter visitors and transients. However, perhaps 20 per cent of the Pintail population is transient and 85 per cent of the Brant population is as well.

CHAPTER 2

Birds and Bird Study

MORE PEOPLE SEEK and study birds than study any other group of animals, with the possible exception of insects. Certainly among the vertebrates, birds are the most interesting to the layman. It has been estimated that there are more than two million birdwatchers in the United States. They range in intensity of interest from the backyard birdwatcher who does no more than observe the local birds attracted by home bird-feeders to the inveterate birder with an insatiable appetite for seeing new birds who stalks them from the rain forests of the Congo, through the deserts of the Middle East, to the high altiplanos of the Andes. Most birdwatchers fall somewhere between these two extremes, but the term "birder" is preferred by this group to such titles as birdwatcher, bird fancier, and bird lover. The Australians have a good word for themselves—"birdos." This author is a birder with an insatiable appetite for new "life" birds who has chased and stalked them on all continents except Antarctica since 1942, when, at the age of twelve, he had to satisfy a nature requirement by identifying a dozen wild birds in order to become a First Class Boy Scout. Since then, more than 3,800 species have been added to that original dozen.

Most professional ornithologists acquired their interest in birds when young teenagers and some of the great men of both professional and amateur ornithology began before they were twelve years of age. However, today, with more people retiring at a younger age, with increasing numbers of people living longer to enjoy their retirement years, with more people traveling, trailering, and camping than ever before, more people are interesting themselves in birds at an older age. The growing feeling and concern among Americans for their environment and their natural world has also contributed to the growth of birding as a hobby and sport. The American Birding Association, conceived by James Tucker of Austin, Texas, in 1968 and established in 1969 by him and some of America's most ardent birders, quickly captured the imagination of birders here and abroad and soon became synonymous with American birding.

Birding can be enjoyed almost anytime and anywhere, even in the cities. People watch birds from their office windows, on their way to and from work, in city parks, on golf courses, at home, on special weekend trips, and on extended vacations. Birding requires very little formal equipment and no previous training. The basic "birding kit" consists of a good pair of prism binoculars and a guide to bird identification. It is wise to obtain the very best binoculars one can afford and good ones can last a lifetime. Those with "central focus" are best, and they can frequently be adjusted to focus to within 15 feet. Most active birders use binoculars with an optical combination of 8x40, 9x35, or 10x50. The first number refers to the magnification and the second and larger number to the light-gathering aperture expressed in millimeters. Other factors being equal, binoculars with a quotient of at least 5 (obtained by dividing the aperture by the magnification) results in the most brilliant image especially in dim light or at dusk. Wide-angle features are of additional value. Birding binoculars are often subjected to pretty rough treatment in the course of strenuous birding. They may be dropped, bounced against rocks, tumbled about in jeeps, rained upon, and even immersed in water. The best and most expensive binoculars are fairly waterproof and shock-resistant. In the humid tropics there is an additional hazard—air conditioning. Binoculars or a telescope (and cameras and lenses as well) after having been used in the hot and humid field and brought into a chilled automobile or hotel, contain air of high humidity. When quickly chilled the moisture condenses within the instrument—on the prisms and behind the lenses. In time it may or may not evaporate. If it does, a dirty film may be deposited anyway. When emerging from an air-conditioned auto or building into the hot, humid, tropical air the same problem exists because if the binoculars have been chilled, the hot wet outside air will condense on the metal and glass. It can be easily wiped from the outside surfaces, but it is almost impossible to clean from within. Since air-conditioned air may be somewhat dehumidified it is best to wrap the optical instruments in plastic bags before leaving the air conditioning and allow the instrument to warm up slowly outside before unwrapping it. When entering air conditioning it is best not to allow the binoculars to get chilled. Storage under insulation far from the air register is usually all that is required. The author's first day of birding in Panama was a frustrating experience because of this problem. Here were forests filled with legendary and gorgeous tropical birds, most of which were life birds, but they could only be dimly seen as if through a dense fog. On extended trips such as this it is wise to carry a spare pair of small binoculars. What could be more exasperating to a birder than to travel half way around the world at great expense only to be able to see nothing once there? And it is not always possible to purchase a new binocular when you are a hundred miles upriver from Kuala Lumpur in the Taman Nagara of Malaysia.

A prism telescope, usually mounted on a tripod, but sometimes used on a gunstock, is a valuable adjunct to binoculars. It is small, lightweight, and compact compared with the cumbersome reflecting telescope used in astronomy. For water-fowl and shorebirds it is almost indispensable. These water birds are invariably found in the open and sometimes at long distance or across an impassable stretch of mud or marsh. Also, viewing at long range is less likely to frighten the birds away. 'Scoping a flock of birds with a telescope mounted on a tripod is the best way to search for unusual species and to make an accurate count of the flock and deter-mine its composition. A prism telescope with a single eyepiece of 25x is satisfactory. Turrets which hold up to four oculars are available to be mounted on the telescope and the usual combination of eyepieces is 20x, 30x, 40x, and 60x, although the lat-ter is difficult to use on terrestrial objects because of atmospheric interference. Tele-scopes with "zoom" optics are more compact and achieve the same results. One of the newer pieces of birding instrumentation is the compact casette tape-recorder. Some birders carry a complete set of bird songs for all North American birds with them when birding. Birds, even non-territorial birds, frequently respond to record-ings of their species and can be lured into the open for viewing by playing the ap-propriate song or call. Another technique, often employed specifically for rails, owls, or other special birds, is to record a number of sequences of the same song from a record or other source. Territorial birds are especially responsive, and diffi-cult-to-see species can be lured into the open in this manner. A similar use of the tape-recorder is to record the voice of an unseen bird and play it back to entice the singer into the open. This is an especially effective technique as the singer is prob-ably territorial to begin with and a "fresh" field recording is often better than a "stale" one taken from what may have been a poor record. A further use of the tape-recorder is as a field stenographer for the recording of field notes and descrip-tions. It is particularly useful this way when employed in a place where the birds are unfamiliar to the observer. Field descriptions can be spoken into the recorder while actually observing the bird in question. Later, the notes or lists may be transcribed into a journal. Some of the more advanced and sophisticated birders of today even go equipped with cameras and powerful telephoto lenses so as to be able to docu-ment the sightings of rare and unusual birds.

For the birds of North America, excellent field guides to identification are avail-able. This is true for other parts of the world as well. For some regions, unfortu-nately, there is little or nothing available in modern books. Good to excellent bird books exist for North America, Mexico, Europe, Japan, Africa, Australia, New Zea-land, India, Burma, and parts of southeast Asia. South America, with more birds than any other continent lacks bird books for many important areas and there is virtually nothing for China at all. In time, however, these gaps will be filled in. Not all of the foreign bird books are field guides, however. Field guides are small enough to fit into a jacket pocket or into a small shoulder bag. They contain a great deal of condensed information and colored illustrations of all the birds of a particular region. In the United States and elsewhere, small field checklists are fre-quently available from local bird clubs or museums. Many states have state bird books that summarize the status and distribution of their birds. Most good field ornithologists (amateur and professional alike) never go birding without pad and pencil. Sooner or later even the experts come upon a bird that defies precise identification. It is essential under those circumstances to make detailed and accurate notes *in the field* of the bird in question. All information about the appearance, voice, and behavior of the bird should be noted down *at the time* plus other information concerning location, time, weather, optical instruments used, visibility, and other observers present. These notes should be submitted (in California) to the Rare Bird Committee, Point Reyes Bird Observatory, Mesa Road, Bolinas, California 94924. This documentation is essential if an accurate account of California birds is to be maintained.

Birds are to be found almost all over California at any time of the year. However, because of the spatial and temporal distribution of California birds, different areas and habitats are best visited at certain times of the year which coincide with the preferences and activities of the birds themselves. Sea birding, or pelagic birding as it is called, is good any time of the year but better for special species at certain times. There is no season when some species of true pelagic birds may not be seen off the coast of California. In fact, pelagic birding is no better anywhere in the United States than in California. Sea trips taken during the winter months will always produce Black-legged Kittiwakes, Northern Fulmars, possibly Manx and Short-tailed Shearwaters, small numbers of jaegers, and a number of alcids. Midsummer pelagic trips should produce some storm-petrels, especially Black Storm-Petrels off southern California, Black-footed Albatrosses, a few jaegers, often thousands of Sooty Shearwaters, Pink-footed Shearwaters, and a few alcids. Spring and fall are by far the best seasons offshore. In spring tens of thousands (and more) of Sooty Shearwaters can be seen in a few hours. Sprinkled among them will be smaller numbers of Pink-footed Shearwaters. Jaegers will be numerous as will Northern and Red Phalaropes. Arctic Terns and the stunning Sabine's Gulls will be in high spring plumage as they migrate to their far arctic nesting grounds. Loons by the thousands move northward closer to the coast. Small numbers of storm-petrels and alcids also occur. Close to some of the offshore islands populations of Western Gulls, Brandt's and Pelagic Cormorants, several species of alcids, and, formerly at least, Brown Pelicans are abundant. Wandering Tattlers and Black Oystercatchers occur on the rocky shores. But it is the late summer and fall seasons at sea that capture the imagination of California birders, for it is at this time of the year that the casual and irregular sea birds might appear. Hopes are always high for Laysan Albatrosses, Flesh-footed Shearwaters, New Zealand Shearwaters, Wilson's Storm-Petrels, Least Storm-Petrels, Craveri's Murrelets, Long-tailed Jaegers, Red-billed Tropicbirds or such accidentals as Cape Petrels, Galapagos Storm-Petrels or even some bird new to the state such as a Harcourt's Storm-Petrel or a Wedge-tailed Shearwater.

Shore birding is best done during spring, fall, and winter at which time the beaches, estuaries, mud flats, and salt-water marshes are teeming with shorebirds, gulls, terns, and waterfowl. Coastal thickets, especially on headlands, islands, and promontories are best searched for small land birds during September and October at which time the rare transients and casuals are most likely to occur. The most rewarding time to visit the desert is spring. The climate is at its best, although it is often windy. Desert plants are in bloom and there is copious plant and insect food for the birds. Resident desert birds are in full song and nesting. The many desert oases are swarming with migrants and the turnover is rapid as new species replace old day by day. The foothills are at their best in late spring and early summer. Chaparral, savannah, and oak woodlands harbor many species of residents and migrants during the spring also. The mountains are best during the summer after spring has made the long climb upward from the valleys and deserts below. Resident songbirds have arrived and are in full song and there is much bird activity in general. For the hardy birder, winter is the season to head north for the snowbound counties of northern and northeastern California. The waterfowl will have moved south into the Great Valley and Tule, Lower Klamath, Eagle, Honey, and Goose Lakes will be frozen, but this is the time of year for such great California rarities as Great Gray and Snowy Owls, Gyrfalcons, Common Redpolls, and Snow Buntings. Bald Eagles, Rough-legged Hawks, Black-backed Three-toed Woodpeckers, Bohemian Waxwings, Rosy Finches, Tree Sparrows, and three species of longspurs make for exciting birding in the north of California. Along the rainy northwest coast may be found such rare California species as Emperor Geese, Harlequin Ducks, "Eurasian" Green-winged Teal, Rock Sandpipers, Ruffed Grouse, Gray Jays, and Black-capped Chickadees. Birding on the many federal and state waterfowl refuges in the Great Valley and the Imperial Valley is exciting as hundreds of thousands of ducks and geese regularly spend the winters there. The Salton Sea is excellent in fall, winter, and spring but temperatures of 120° during July and August repel all but the most dedicated and persistent of birders. It is during these hot summer months that some of the best birds appear at the south and north ends of the Salton Sea. Magnificent Frigatebirds, Wood Storks, Roseate Spoonbills, Laughing Gulls, Gull-billed Terns, and Black Skimmers are some of the specialties that may be found there from July to September. The lower Colorado River Valley from Yuma to Needles contains certain birds such as Inca Doves, Cardinals, Harris' Hawks, Summer Tanagers, Lucy's Warblers, Yellow-billed Cuckoos, Black Rails, Great-tailed Grackles, and Bronzed Cowbirds, birds not easily found elsewhere in California. In addition, there is a good flow of migrants through this valley in spring. Desert oases such as those at Deep Springs Valley Oasis, Scotty's Castle, Furnace Creek Ranch, the Amargosa River, and Saratoga Springs, in addition to attracting large numbers of migrants in spring, are the source of a number of rare transients and casuals in very late spring (late May and early June) and from September to November.

It has been said that the only cure for the affliction of birding is to arise at dawn and sit in a bog. While it is true that birds are early risers, birders must surpass them in this for best results. For land birds and some other groups as well, dawn is the most important time of the day. Birds have such a high rate of metabolism compared to other vertebrates that their most constant activity is a search for food. After a long night of fasting, birds begin their day with their most important function—feeding. It is primarily for this reason that birds are most active in the early morning and then again in the late afternoon. In the northern latitudes and in the higher altitude habitats, bird action is likely to continue throughout the day with some slowdown in the middle of the day. Nesting birds are more likely to remain active longer in search of food for the nestlings. In the northern and higher altitude habitats, the days are cooler and the birds do not need to retreat to the shade to reduce physical exertion and cool themselves. In the deserts and tropics however, the cessation of bird song and movement by midmorning is dramatic except on cool, overcast, or drizzly days. For shorebirds, dawn is not as critical as is the change in the tidal flow. They spend the hours of the high tides sleeping and loafing in the salt-water marshes and on sandbars. When the tide turns, they become highly animated and commence their activity by flying to the appropriate areas of mud being exposed by the ebbing tide where they begin to feed immediately.

Besides the milkmen, probably no other group of people has witnessed so many sunrises as have birders. A well-planned birding trip often involves arrival at a marsh before dawn to catch the dawn chorus of the unseen marsh birds. This may be followed by a trip to a nearby woodland for early morning land birding and then a midday drive to a shore or aquatic habitat for water birds. Afternoon hours are good for shorebirds, and late afternoon is again good for land birds. Birding often continues after dark in search of night birds such as goatsuckers and owls.

While birding "dress" is as individualistic as the birds themselves, there are a few sensible rules to follow. Birds are startled and frightened by sudden movements of conspicuous objects. Birding clothes should be of inconspicuous colors such as browns and greens or earth colors. Birds are color and motion conscious, having excellent vision for both. They are not nearly so frightened by noises, although sudden sharp sounds will often startle them into flight. When birding, it is best to dress in subdued hues, move slowly and quietly, and speak softly. A whistle is frequently more effective in calling a comrade than a shout which is likely to startle the birds. White clothing is probably the very worst for fieldwork. A wide-brimmed hat is an essential item of clothing to shade the eyes for better visibility. It is tempting to wear shorts for desert birding, but tough long trousers are better for repelling spines, thorns, and rocks. Hiking shoes are superior to tennis shoes for the same reason although tennis shoes are worn by many birders for general land birding and marsh birding. They have the advantages of being light in weight, suffer no permanent damage when soaked, and dry out quickly. Pelagic birding offers its special challenges to the landlubber. The best vantage point for viewing fast-flying sea birds that appear and disappear between wave crests is high up and in the forward part of the boat. Waterproof slickers are essential for those who would endure the waves breaking over the bow. Seasickness is no respecter of birders. There are many antimotion-sickness pills available but they frequently result in drowsiness and the sufferer could be sound asleep when the best bird of the day is seen. Sea-sick-prone birders have found that a good supply of bland dry crackers is an effective preventative.

To the uninitiated, the identification of wild birds in the field seems to be nothing short of wizardry. A speck on the horizon, a dot in the sky, a formless shape huddled in a tree, a distant blob on a lake, a hummingbird zooming past at 50 miles per hour, a chip, a lisp of a song, a chirp, a hoot in the night, a silhouette against the sunset—all of these and more, if they are birds, can be identified with uncanny precision by expert birders. These people do not possess occult powers nor are they clairvoyant. Years of familiarity with the bird's form, behavior, nuances of flight and action, voice, and other "field marks" are instantaneously run through the mental computer. At first the bird is mentally assigned to its correct taxonomic family and then quickly run down to species. Processes of elimination are also employed in this rapid process. Surprisingly, all of the field marks of a bird need not necessarily be perceived for correct identification. Often, after the correct family is mentally noted, a single significant field mark (from a number of possible ones) is sufficient to clinch the identification. For example, if a distant mote of a small pelagic bird is determined to be a storm-petrel and its lazy languid flight reminds the observer of a Black Tern, then there can be little doubt that the speck on the horizon was a Black Storm-Petrel. Other birds such as winter-plumaged longspurs and wood warblers in fall plumage may not be so simple, but in the case of the longspurs, their call notes would be quite sufficient for identification. This kind of skill is developed after study of books, pictures, sound recordings, and frequent contact with the birds in the field. Advice and tips from other birders is invaluable.

Birding is similar to other "collecting" hobbies in one respect. In the case of birding, the collected item is most frequently the *name* of a bird added to some sort of list after it has been seen or heard for the first time. Very few birders attempt to collect photographs they have themselves obtained of wild birds they have seen. An important virtue of this type of "collection" is that the "trophy" lives on to be enjoyed by others after it has been "collected" for a list. This is very close to "having one's cake and eating it too." In the early days of bird study, the collection of sets of birds' eggs was an important phase of ornithology. Today it is done rarely; usually only in the case of the first discovery of the nest. Early ornithologists shot a great many birds for collections and these were indispensable for certain studies, but they also argued that birds could not be identified in any other fashion. Today, expert field ornithologists can correctly identify (at least to species) virtually every bird they see or hear and at almost any distance.

List-keeping is but one of several types of activities amateur ornithologists engage in. It is by far the most popular phase of the hobby and forms the common denominator by which birders may compare their results. Careful lists of birds and field journals often form the basis for later distributional and behavioral studies of great importance. The basic and most sacrosanct list is the "life list." It does not pretend any scientific merit and is kept for purely personal reasons. Basically, the life list contains the names of all of the different species of birds seen or heard during the life of the birder. Since this list is such a personal thing, complete unanimity does not exist among birders as to what this list should contain. A very few birders even include birds that they have found dead (and never have seen in life) on their "life" lists! However, most life lists are basically the same—lists of birds seen or heard alive, although considerable disagreement exists among birders regarding the inclusion of birds that have been *heard* but never *seen*. Rails, owls, and goatsuckers are particularly bothersome in this regard because of their retiring and/or nocturnal habits. To birders, the most important types of life lists are the world list, the North American (north of Mexico) list, and their own state list. Several plateaus or hurdles have been agreed upon which represent milestones to list-keeping. A world list of at least 3,000 birds is a minor triumph; 600 birds is the major goal for a North American list; and 400 of the 500 or so California species is considered to be some sort of accomplishment. This type of listing is strictly for fun, but is taken very seriously by the listers. The different types of lists kept by listers is almost limitless. Other popular lists include garden lists, county lists, year lists (of birds seen in a year either in North America, the world, or within a state), lists of birds seen or heard during special counts or censuses, lists of orders and families, country lists, continent lists, lists of birds seen *in* one place or even *from* one place, lists of birds seen on certain dates, lists of birds that have been heard, lists of birds whose nests have been found, lists of birds successfully photographed, tape-recorded, or mist-netted and banded, and so forth. At least one birder keeps a list of his lists! It can surely be said that no avid and energetic birder is list-less.

However, listing *per se* is really but one phase of bird study for the amateur. Special counts and censuses form another activity in which many birders become involved. Some of these counts are really just games while others yield valuable census data, which over the years, becomes a priceless source of population information on different species whose status seems to be changing. Probably the most demanding list game played by active and enthusiastic birders is the "big day," "lethal tour," or "grim grind." When first instituted on the east coast it was called a "century run," the object being for a single party of birders (three or four, or as many as would fit in a car comfortably) to see at least 100 species of birds within one day in spring. It soon became evident that many more than 100 were possible. In fact, one of the earliest attempts, in New Jersey, bettered 150. The first single party big day list of more than 200 was accomplished in southern California in the spring of 1959. Since then more than 200 species recorded between midnight and midnight has been accomplished several times by single parties. Other types of listing games include "round-ups," big day multiple parties, five-day marathons, and so forth. These "games" are not without real merit, however, for if continued over a period of years, they reveal information about migration chronology, migration routes, weather factors, bird distribution during migration, and the composition of migratory flocks.

The annual Christmas Censuses sponsored by the National Audubon Society since 1900 are an unparalleled source of winter bird population data stretching unbroken for some census areas for more than 70 years. At a time when we are becoming increasingly more concerned about the actual or fancied decline in bird life, these counts represent a vital source of data. Annual breeding bird censuses also sponsored by the National Audubon Society are excellent sources of hard information about summer bird populations in the United States. These censuses and the annual winter bird population studies are conducted by thousands of interested and serious birders throughout the country. In 1971, 963 Christmas Censuses were taken by 18,798 participants who tallied 583 species in the United States and Canada. A newer type of annual bird census was instigated by the Migratory Bird Population Survey of the U.S. Fish and Wildlife Service, Laurel, Maryland. In this "strip" census, fifty stations spaced at 0.5 mile intervals are censused from a car along a prescribed route. The census commences 30 minutes before sunrise and must be completed at the fiftieth station within 4½ hours. At each stop, which lasts for 3 minutes, all birds heard and all those seen within ¼ mile of the car are counted. In 1972 more than 130 such strip censuses were completed in California alone. They included a variety of habitats from deserts, through foothills and forests, to mountaintops. Many types of habitats chosen at random all over the country are censused this way during the nesting season and in time a picture of changing bird populations and habitats should emerge.

Bird banding, another phase of amateur (and professional) bird study, is a specialized endeavor to which a minority of birders finally turn. The bands, streamers, or other marking devices enable the tagged bird to be traced in the event of recovery. Affixing colored streamers or marking birds with colored dyes is useful in special projects involving larger birds such as pelicans, gulls, cranes, and waterfowl. If the birds are sighted after release at some distance from the point of original capture, then timing, routes, and other factors of dispersion may be determined. It was by this method that the northward movement of Mexican-born Brown Pelicans into California coastal waters was ascertained. By far the most widespread method of tagging birds is by the use of lightweight aluminum leg bands. Birds are captured in traps or mist nets, weighed, aged, measured, sexed, banded, and released. The recovery probability for small land birds is very low, but essential information about body weights, ectoparasites such as bird lice, blood samples, molting, migratory flock compositions, longevity, sex and age ratios, survivorship, skeletal ossification, and many other factors have emerged from this most valuable technique. In addition, some of California's most casual and irregular birds have been netted by the bird banders on South Farallon Island and other prominent banding stations in the state.

Bird photography is a difficult and demanding phase of bird study. For more than mediocre results, costly equipment of high precision and quality is required. To achieve a recognizable image on film is a far different problem than obtaining a quality portrait of such shy, mobile, and elusive creatures as birds. Few other photographic subjects are as difficult to capture successfully on film. A small number of birders gravitate to bird photography after they have pretty well filled out their life lists of North American birds. Stalking wild birds with camera in hand is the simplest and most direct technique and it is sometimes successful for larger birds. In most instances, however, the photographer must lure the birds to him with water and/or food, or station himself at a place to which birds regularly come. Feeding or resting areas, roosts, favorite perches, display and strutting grounds, and nest sites are such places and usually the photographer must conceal himself nearby in a bird blind or in some other way. Besides the necessary photographic equipment and the skill to use it, the most important requisites for the successful bird photographer are a thorough knowledge of his subjects and their habits, coupled with almost infinite patience. It is not surprising then that so few birders eventually turn to this phase of the birding sport.

With the advent of small, high-quality tape recorders and sensitive microphones suitable for field use, some birders have become skillful at recording bird sounds and have developed extensive tape libraries. This is also a challenging phase of bird study, which like bird photography, demands complete attention to the immediate subject to the exclusion of all else at the time. Real contributions to ornithology can be made by amateur recorders. Although the sounds of North American birds have been fairly well recorded, much work still remains to be done, especially in the tropics. The Moore Laboratory of Ornithology at Occidental College, Los Angeles, has a fine collection of neotropical bird recordings and welcomes acquisitions of new recordings for their tape library.

An even smaller number of birders becomes involved with bird illustration and painting. Since this does require special skill, talent, and training, relatively few people can achieve professional results. Virtually all the renowned bird artists are birders whose talents are so essential to the production of quality bird books.

For those whose ability to travel far from home is limited, birds can be lured to the home garden with food and water. Birds are very fond of bathing, and drinking is, of course, essential. Even more effective than pools of water as a bird attractant is *dripping* water. Water slowly dripping into a pool situated close to protective and secure cover is almost irresistible to small birds. A wide variety of bird foods can also be used, and some of the most popular are bird seed, chick scratch, bread crumbs, suet, peanut butter, oranges (sliced open), raisins, peanuts, many types of pulpy fruits, and sunflower seeds. Hummingbirds are quickly attracted to special hummingbird feeders filled with sweet syrup colored red. Some California "garden lists" exceed 100 species.

Those just starting out as birdwatchers quickly learn that it is a most popular and congenial hobby and sport. Birders naturally gravitate to the selected places where birds are most apt to be found and it is not long before the beginner meets others with the same interest. Bird clubs, Audubon Societies, and ornithological groups are scattered throughout California and offer informative and entertaining meetings, programs, field trips, seminars, courses, and even travel tours for birdwatching. Once an individual becomes a birder, he will find that he has entered a grand international fraternity and has access to birding contacts and new friends throughout the world. It was this author's privilege to travel throughout the Pacific area a few years ago, and in every city from Auckland, New Zealand, throughout Australia and New Guinea, through Kuala Lumpur, Malaysia, and Bangkok, Thailand, to Tokyo, Japan, he met new birders who were willing to befriend a stranger and guide him to local birding areas. It is difficult to conceive of another interest which has such universal appeal and in which total strangers can so quickly become lifelong friends. There is a spirit of competition among birders, but it is a healthy spirit, and it really is one of cooperation because other than seeing a new life bird for one's self, there is nothing more gratifying in the hobby and sport of birding than to show a life bird to someone else.

CHAPTER 3

Annotated List of
the Birds of California

THE FOLLOWING 518* species of birds are positively known to have occurred in
California and are substantiated by specimens, photographs, or well-documented
field descriptions that have been accepted by the Rare Bird Committee of the Cali-
fornia Field Ornithologists, Point Reyes Bird Observatory. Of these, 509 are native
or self-introduced birds and nine are well-established introduced species either from
North America (Turkey) or from elsewhere (Ring-necked Pheasant, Chukar, Gray
Partridge, Rock Dove, Spotted Dove, Ringed Turtle Dove, Starling, and House
Sparrow). A total of 302 species breed or have bred in California of which 277 are
regular nesters, 23 are former nesters, irregular nesters, unknown nesters (Marbled
Murrelet), rare nesters, or new nesters, and at least two species (Brant and Snow
Goose) were probably cripples that remained to breed in the state. The California
State Department of Fish and Game has, from time to time, attempted to introduce new species of game birds into the state. Such birds as Bobwhite, European
Partridge, and Woodcock may occasionally be encountered. Other semi-successful
exotics that have escaped or have been released into the wild, especially in the
warmer southern one-third of the state, include Yellow-headed and other *Amazona*
sp. parrots, "red-headed" parrots, Blue-rumped Parrotlets, Canary-winged and other
species of Parakeets, Budgerigars, Peafowl, Red-whiskered Bulbuls, Brazilian Cardinals, Blue-gray Tanagers, and flamingoes of several species. Some of these birds have
succeeded in nesting successfully in the wild state. Small exotic land birds such as
African Bishops, European Goldfinches, and Java Finches are frequently reported
but they can always be dismissed for what they are. Exotic waterfowl are more trou-
blesome. Ducks and geese are powerful fliers and a number of Asiatic types have
reached Alaska and the Aleutians. Waterfowl are frequently kept in captivity by
zoos, game parks, and private collectors and they often escape, join the flocks of

* Note—In 1974, seven new species were added to the state list, bringing the state total to 525. These
birds do not appear in their proper places below but are listed on p. xxii.

wild waterfowl, and revert to the "wild" state. It then becomes almost impossible to know for certain whether a "possible" alien waterfowl is an escapee or not and each occurrence must be judged on its own merit based upon the probability of that species arriving in California by itself. The Red-breasted Geese that traveled with the wild Snow Geese in the Imperial Valley in 1969 gave every appearance of being wild birds but the likelihood is very small when their breeding range (central Asia), their wintering grounds (to the Caspian Sea), and their probable routes of migration are considered. Later it was positively established that a number of birds of this species had indeed escaped from an obscure "game park" in southern Oregon. Also, the Red-breasted Goose, a very beautiful bird, is much desired and frequently found in private waterfowl collections. Such facts must be considered when evaluating the status of such other "California" exotics as Falcated and Baikal Teal and Ruddy Sheld-ducks. Enough Tufted Ducks have appeared in Alaska and the mid-Pacific to demonstrate their propensity for travel. Considering that they are an abundant species within their range, are far-flying travelers, and that they normally occur in eastern Asia, they have been placed on the California list.

Exotic hawks and other birds of prey are another problem because of their importation for falconry. Roadside Hawks, Harris' Hawks, and Caracaras from Mexico and others from even further afield have been loosed into California's skies. Most of these birds can easily be recognized for what they are by the jesses they usually wear.

The birds listed here have occurred within the previously defined ornithological borders of the state, that is, they have appeared within 100 statute miles of the seacoast or an offshore island measured at right angles to the nearest part of that coast. They must also have been located north of the Mexican border and south of the Oregon border if those lines were extended 100 statute miles out to sea at the same latitudes. Also, the birds must have occurred on the California side of the Colorado River or less than one-half the distance to the Arizona shore.

The nomenclature used generally follows the A.O.U. *Checklist of North American Birds,* Fifth Edition, 1957 and its Thirty-second Supplement (1973), but there have been some changes included. The taxonomic status of a number of species is still unsettled and such are so indicated. A number of birds are listed in *italics* and indented under the name of the species. Such birds were listed as separate species in the 1957 *Checklist* but they are treated here as well-marked subspecies. Other well-marked subspecies are *not* so indicated. Other species treated as subspecies in the 1957 *Checklist* are considered here as full species and are so indicated. The author realizes that full agreement does not and will not exist regarding certain taxonomic revisions.

The Annotated List includes the *seasonal status* of *most* of the population of each species and takes no notice of extremes in date or range within California. In certain cases, this seasonal status varies with the region of the state and it is so indicated.

The following terms are used to indicate the *seasonal status* of each bird and often they are combined to better delineate a more complex situation:

RESIDENTS—do not enter or leave the state in migration; 164 species or 31 per cent

PURE TRANSIENTS—migrate through the state; do not breed in California; 19 species or 4 per cent

COMPLEX TRANSIENTS—migrate through the state; some winter or breed in California; 80 species or 16 per cent

WINTER VISITORS—breed to the north of the state; spend the winter in California; 46 species or 10 per cent

SUMMER VISITORS—breed in the state; spend the winter to the south of California; 31 species or 6 per cent

FALL or POST-BREEDING VISITORS—breed to the south of the state; come north to California after their breeding season and return to the south before the winter or following spring; less than 1 per cent

PERENNIAL VISITORS—do not breed in the state; some are present throughout the year in California; they are all sea birds; less than 1 per cent

IRREGULAR VISITORS—numbers and visitations vary from year to year; do not breed in California; less than 1 per cent

CASUAL VISITORS and ACCIDENTALS—unexpected and unpredictable; 128 or 26 per cent, of which 81 species are accidentals that have occurred about 10 or fewer times since 1900. Of the 81 accidentals, 42 have occurred but once or twice since 1900.

About 6 per cent of California's birds cannot easily be classified by the above status categories.

Birds are also designated as COMMON, UNCOMMON, or RARE in preferred habitat. These are subjective designations and refer to absolute population numbers rather than to ease of observation.

The Annotated List indicates the preferred habitat of the bird for breeding, feeding, and migration.

The *general* geographic range for each species within California is also described.

Where a specimen or satisfactory recognizable photograph of a species in question has been secured, it has been so indicated.

Loons

COMMON LOON *(Gavia immer)*

Seasonal status—winter visitor, October through April; *habitat*—seacoast, bays, occasionally large lakes; *breeds* or bred on large lakes of Modoc Plateau; *range in California*—length of state.

Yellow-billed Loon—winter plumage

YELLOW-BILLED LOON *(Gavia adamsii)*
　　Seasonal status—casual visitor in winter; *habitat*—seacoast, large bays; *range in California*—most of records from Bodega Bay, Sonoma County, to Monterey Bay, Monterey County; *note*—likely to have been overlooked prior to 1967 and probably a rare but regular winter visitor.

PACIFIC LOON (formerly Arctic Loon) *(Gavia pacifica)*
　　Seasonal status—common winter visitor, September to May; *habitat*—seacoast, large bays; *range in California*—length of state; *note*—most pelagic of loons; may be distinct species from Arctic Loon *(Gavia arctica)* of Eurasia.

RED-THROATED LOON *(Gavia stellata)*
　　Seasonal status—common winter visitor, September to May; *habitat*—seacoast, large bays; *range in California*—length of state.

Grebes

RED-NECKED GREBE *(Podiceps grisegena)*
　　Seasonal status—uncommon winter visitor, October to April, south to Monterey County; rare south of there; *habitat*—seacoast, large bays, estuaries; *range in California*—length of state, but very rare in southern one-third.

HORNED GREBE *(Podiceps auritus)*
　　Seasonal status—winter visitor, October to April; *habitat*—seacoast, bays, estuaries; *range in California*—length of state; *note*—confined exclusively to salt water.

EARED GREBE *(Podiceps nigricollis)*
Seasonal status—common resident; *habitat*—for *breeding*, mostly on interior lakes east of the Sierra Nevada; in fall, population shifts coastward and generally inhabits bays, estuaries, lakes near seacoast, lagoons, and harbors; *range in California*—length of state; *note*—has bred as far south as San Diego County.

LEAST GREBE *(Podiceps dominicus)*
Seasonal status—accidental; *habitat*—fresh-water lakes bordered by cattails and tules; *range in California*—only recorded from lower Colorado River Valley near Imperial Dam (at West Pond), Imperial County, where it is known to have *bred* in 1946; *note*—present status uncertain because of possible errors in field identification. Specimen.

Western Grebe

WESTERN GREBE *(Aechmophorus occidentalis)*
Seasonal status—common resident; *habitat*—for *breeding*, large northern lakes; in fall, population shifts to seacoast, large bays, and coastal lagoons, from September to April; *range in California*—length of state; *note*—has bred as far south as the Salton Sea.

PIED-BILLED GREBE *(Podilymbus podiceps)*
Seasonal status—common resident; *habitat*—for *breeding*, small fresh-water lakes and ponds with marsh vegetation; in winter, some occur on ocean, bays, coastal lagoons, estuaries; *range in California*—length of state.

Albatrosses

WANDERING ALBATROSS *(Diomedea exulans)*
Seasonal status—accidental; *habitat*—seacoast, open sea; *note*—one record, The Sea Ranch, Sonoma County, July 11–12, 1967. Photograph.

SHORT-TAILED ALBATROSS *(Diomedea albatrus)*
Seasonal status—accidental; *habitat*—open sea; *note*—formerly fairly common; one record since 1900—a single bird 70 miles west of San Francisco, San Francisco County, Feb. 17, 1946.

Black-footed Albatross

BLACK-FOOTED ALBATROSS *(Diomedea nigripes)*
Seasonal status—perennial visitor in small numbers; *habitat*—open sea; *range in California*—length of state although more numerous from Monterey County northward; *note*—most common during summer months.

LAYSAN ALBATROSS *(Diomedea immutabilis)*
Seasonal status—casual visitor, October through March; *habitat*—open sea, well away from coast; *range in California*—length of state; *note*—has been noted more frequently from Monterey northward; commercial fishermen in northern California report regular sightings of "white" albatrosses far at sea off the California coast and this species probably occurs with some regularity throughout the year within 100 miles off the coast at least off Mendocino, Humboldt, and Del Norte counties.

Fulmars and Shearwaters ·

CAPE PETREL *(Daption capense)*
Seasonal status—accidental; *habitat*—open sea; *note*—one record; one bird at Monterey Bay, Monterey County, Sept. 9, 1962. Sight record.

NORTHERN FULMAR *(Fulmarus glacialis)*
Seasonal status—winter visitor, occasionally common; *habitat*—open sea, seacoast, harbors; *range in California*—length of state.

Northern Fulmar
—light phase

PINK-FOOTED SHEARWATER *(Puffinus creatopus)*
Seasonal status—perennial visitor but numbers greater during the summer; *habitat*—open sea; *range in California*—length of state.

FLESH-FOOTED SHEARWATER *(Puffinus carneipes)*
Seasonal status—rare irregular visitor; *habitat*—open sea; *range in California*—length of state.

Pink-footed Shearwater

NEW ZEALAND SHEARWATER *(Puffinus bulleri)*
Seasonal status—fall visitor or fall transient; *habitat*—open sea; *range in California*—length of state although most birds occur in vicinity of Monterey Bay; *note*—peak numbers occur during September and October but numbers in Monterey Bay fluctuate from year to year; at times hundreds are present.

SOOTY SHEARWATER *(Puffinus griseus)*
Seasonal status—perennial visitor, at times abundant; most numerous from April through November; *habitat*—open sea but frequently observed from favorable shore points; *range in California*—length of state.

SHORT-TAILED SHEARWATER *(Puffinus tenuirostris)*
Seasonal status—irregular visitor or fall and early winter transient in very small numbers; *habitat*—open sea; *range in California*—length of state; *note*—status is unclear; formerly common a few times but now rarely observed.

MANX SHEARWATER *(Puffinus puffinus)*
Seasonal status—irregular fall and winter visitor, sometimes common; *habitat*—open sea; *range in California*—length of state; *note*—small numbers undoubtedly occur each year.

Storm-Petrels

FORK-TAILED STORM-PETREL *(Oceanodroma furcata)*
Seasonal status—uncommon resident; *habitat*—for breeding, small offshore islands; in non-breeding season, open sea; *range in California*—for *breeding,* small islets off coast of Del Norte and Humboldt counties; length of state during non-breeding season; *note*—population seems to have declined in recent years; strong onshore winds sometimes force this pelagic storm-petrel close to shore and into bays and harbors.

LEACH'S STORM-PETREL *(Oceanodroma leucorhoa)*
Seasonal status—occurs in two roles; "white-rumped" race is summer visitor to northern California and is spring and fall transient to and from nesting islands; "dark-rumped" races come north from Mexican nesting islands as post-breeding or fall visitors and are quite rare; *habitat*—open sea in non-breeding season; "white-rumped" (or Beal's race) *breeds* on Farallon Islands and islets off Del Norte and Humboldt counties.

ASHY STORM-PETREL *(Oceanodroma homochroa)*
Seasonal status—may be resident but there are almost no early spring records; *habitat*—for breeding; offshore islands; otherwise open sea; *range in California*—most of population *breeds* on Farallon Islands but small numbers nest on San Miguel and Santa Cruz Islands and on Los Coronados Islands just south of the Mexican border; *note*—occurs north to the Oregon border.

GALAPAGOS STORM-PETREL *(Oceanodroma tethys)*
Seasonal status—accidental; *habitat*—open sea; *note*—one record: one bird at Carmel, Monterey County, Jan. 21, 1969. Specimen.

HARCOURT'S STORM-PETREL *(Oceanodroma castro)*
Seasonal status—accidental; *habitat*—open sea; *note*—one record: one bird 25 miles west of Mission Bay, San Diego County, Sept. 12, 1970. Sight record.

BLACK STORM-PETREL *(Oceanodroma melania)*

Seasonal status—primarily a post-breeding summer visitor from May through October; very few recorded in winter; *habitat*—open sea; *note*—not recorded north of Marin County but breeds on Los Coronados Islands just south of Mexican border.

LEAST STORM-PETREL *(Halocyptena microsoma)*

Seasonal status—irregular post-breeding visitor during August and September; *habitat*—open sea; *range in California*—extreme southern waters between San Diego and San Clemente Island; *note*—absent some years, abundant in others; more than 3,000 observed Sept. 17, 1970.

WILSON'S STORM-PETREL *(Oceanites oceanicus)*

Seasonal status—accidental or possibly casual visitor from late August to November; *habitat*—open sea; *range in California*—length of state.

Wilson's Storm-Petrel

Tropicbirds

RED-BILLED TROPICBIRD *(Phaethon aethereus)*

Seasonal status—rare irregular post-breeding visitor from June to October; *habitat*—open sea; *range in California*—north to at least Morro Bay, San Luis Obispo County; *note*—most observations are from near San Clemente Island during August and September; two birds wintered at Santa Barbara 1954-1955.

WHITE-TAILED TROPICBIRD *(Phaethon lepturus)*

Seasonal status—accidental; *habitat*—open sea; *note*—one record: one bird at Newport, Orange County, May 24 to June 23, 1964. Photograph.

Red-billed Tropicbird

Pelicans

WHITE PELICAN *(Pelecanus erythrorhynchos)*
Seasonal status—winter visitor and transient; *habitat*—in transit may be seen almost anywhere; winters on larger coastal bays and larger lakes in southwestern and southern portion; *range in California*—length of state; *note*—no longer known to breed in California; formerly *nested* from Tule Lake, Siskiyou County, and lakes to Modoc County south to the Salton Sea. Transient flocks are most frequently seen in March, April, and October.

White Pelican

BROWN PELICAN *(Pelecanus occidentalis)*

Seasonal status—formerly a common resident, now decreasing in numbers; also occurs as post-breeding or fall visitor from Mexico; *habitat*—open sea, seacoast, larger bays, harbors, breakwaters; *range in California*—viable *breeding* colonies existed on Anacapa Island, Santa Barbara Island, Santa Cruz Island, and San Miguel Island; a small colony at Bird Island, Point Lobos Reserve, Monterey County, is northernmost breeding station; non-breeding birds ranged length of the state; *note*—viability of present colonies due to chlorinated hydrocarbon residues is in doubt; there is a large influx of immature birds from Mexican colonies (as determined by tagging operations on the Mexican breeding islands) each summer, the birds remaining until October and then returning to the south.

Boobies

BLUE-FOOTED BOOBY *(Sula nebouxii)*

Seasonal status—irregular (?) casual post-breeding visitor during late summer and early fall; *habitat*—mostly the Salton Sea but birds have been picked up on roads and have been seen on several fresh-water lakes in southern California and on the seacoast; *range in California*—coastwise as far north as Monterey; *note*—also recorded on the Colorado River; highest count at Salton Sea was 48, Sept. 6, 1971.

Blue-footed Boobies

BROWN BOOBY *(Sula leucogaster)*

Seasonal status—rare irregular post-breeding visitor; *habitat*—seacoast, Salton Sea, Colorado River; *range in California*—coastwise as far north as Prince Islet off San

Miguel Island; has occurred at Imperial Dam on Colorado River; *note*—on Salton Sea outnumbered by Blue-footed Boobies 20:1 in late summer.

Cormorants

DOUBLE-CRESTED CORMORANT *(Phalacrocorax auritus)*
Seasonal status—resident; *habitat*—seacoast, bays, estuaries, harbors, larger freshwater lakes, rivers, and marshes; *range in California*—along the seacoast; *breeds* north to Farallon Islands, primarily on offshore islands; also breeds along Colorado River and larger lakes inland from Clear Lake, Modoc County, south to Salton Sea, Imperial County; *note*—no longer breeds in some of former nesting sites in Sacramento and San Joaquin valleys.

*Double-crested
Cormorant*

OLIVACEOUS CORMORANT *(Phalacrocorax olivaceus)*
Seasonal status—accidental; *note*—two records at Imperial Dam, Imperial County, Apr. 13, 1971 and Apr. 22-23, 1972. Photograph.

BRANDT'S CORMORANT *(Phalacrocorax penicillatus)*
Seasonal status—common resident; *habitat*—seacoast, offshore islands, and sea cliffs; *range in California*—*breeds* or has bred along the entire coast on the mainland and on islands and islets; *note*—limited exclusively to salt water.

PELAGIC CORMORANT *(Phalacrocorax pelagicus)*
Seasonal status—resident; *habitat*—seacoast, offshore islands, sea cliffs; *range in California*—*breeds* or has bred along coast from Santa Barbara Island north to Del Norte County; *note*—limited exclusively to salt water; small numbers still breed at Point Loma, San Diego County.

Frigatebirds

MAGNIFICENT FRIGATEBIRD *(Fregata magnificens)*
Seasonal status—rare post-breeding or fall visitor; *habitat*—Salton Sea and seacoast; *range in California*—since 1900 none recorded further north than Marin County; recorded irregularly from the Salton Sea.

Magnificent Frigatebird—female

Herons and Bitterns

GREAT BLUE HERON *(Ardea herodias)*
Seasonal status—common resident; *habitat*—salt-water marshes, estuaries, and mud flats; fresh-water lakes, rivers, and marshes; *range in California*—length of state; does not *breed* in eastern portion of state except at Salton Sea and Colorado River.

GREEN HERON *(Butorides virescens)*
Seasonal status—resident but part of the population leaves the state for the winter; *habitat*—fresh-water lakes, marshes, streams; rarely found in salt-water marshes; *range in California*—length of state; *breeds* in lowlands of western and southern portions.

LITTLE BLUE HERON *(Florida caerulea)*
Seasonal status—casual visitor with most records in fall; *habitat*—coastal lagoons, salt-water marshes, bays, estuaries; *range in California*—north to Marin County; *note*—formerly accidental; increase in recent sightings may reflect better fieldwork.

Great Blue Heron

CATTLE EGRET *(Bubulcus ibis)*

Seasonal status—resident in Imperial Valley; *habitat*—primarily cattle pastures with cattle; *range in California*—first found *breeding* at south end of Salton Sea in 1970 after having first been seen in California in 1964; has occurred almost length of state but most of population confined to the Imperial Valley.

REDDISH EGRET *(Dichromanassa rufescens)*

Seasonal status—casual visitor with most records from summer and fall; *habitat*—coastal lagoons, salt-water marshes, and mud flats; *range in California*—has occurred at Salton Sea and Colorado River but most records are from coastal southern California.

GREAT EGRET *(Casmerodius albus)*

Seasonal status—resident; *habitat*—coastal lagoons, salt-water marshes and mud flats, margins of larger rivers and lakes; *range in California*—*breeds* or has bred length of the state; withdraws from northeastern portions in winter.

SNOWY EGRET *(Egretta thula)*

Seasonal status—resident; *habitat*—coastal lagoons, salt-water marshes, bays, estuaries, fresh-water marshes, rivers, lakes, and streams; *range in California*—most of state; not normally found in northern one-fourth; *breeds* or has bred very locally at Salton Sea and in San Joaquin Valley.

LOUISIANA HERON *(Hydranassa tricolor)*

Seasonal status—casual visitor; *habitat*—coastal lagoons, mud flats, estuaries; *range in California*—primarily coastal southern California; has reached Honey Lake, Lassen County.

BLACK-CROWNED NIGHT HERON *(Nycticorax nycticorax)*

Seasonal status—resident; *habitat*—salt-water marshes, fresh-water marshes; roosts in dense groves of trees usually, but not necessarily, near water; *range in California*—length of state as *breeder.*

YELLOW-CROWNED NIGHT HERON *(Nyctanassa violacea)*

Seasonal status—accidental; *habitat*—salt-water and fresh-water marshes; *note*—at least nine records of probably six individuals, as follows: one near Venice, Los Angeles County, June 1951; one at Imperial Beach, San Diego County, Nov. 3, 1962; one at Claremont, Los Angeles County, Mar. 27–Apr. 6, 1963; one at Harbor Park, Los Angeles County, May 1963; one at Imperial Beach, San Diego County, Oct. 22–25, 1963; and what was probably the same individual occurred near San Rafael, Marin County, July 12–Aug. 25, 1968, May 3–Sept. 3, 1969, May 10–July 27, 1970, and spring and summer of 1972.

LEAST BITTERN *(Ixobrychus exilis)*

Seasonal status—uncommon resident but part of population migrates south in fall; *habitat*—fresh-water marshes; *range in California*—primarily San Joaquin Valley south to Salton Sea and Colorado River as *breeder.*

AMERICAN BITTERN *(Botaurus lentiginosus)*

Seasonal status—resident; *habitat*—fresh-water and occasionally salt-water marshes; *range in California*—*breeds* throughout length of state west of Sierra Nevada and in suitable marshes in the southern portion.

Storks

WOOD STORK *(Mycteria americana)*

Seasonal status—uncommon and very local post-breeding visitor; *habitat*—fresh-water or salt-water sloughs, mud flats, and marshes; *range in California*—primarily south end of Salton Sea, lower Colorado River Valley, and coastal lagoons of San Diego County; *note*—normally arrives in early July and remains until late September; formerly more widespread in state, even to Modoc County, but most of the birds visiting state today are the 100–200 in the Salton Sea area each year.

Wood Stork

Ibises and Spoonbills

WHITE-FACED IBIS *(Plegadis chihi)*
Seasonal status–resident; *habitat*–fresh-water marshes, cultivated and irrigated fields; *range in California*–has *bred* as far north as Honey Lake, Lassen County, and Tule and Lower Klamath Lakes, Siskiyou County; now confined as a breeder to a few areas in the San Joaquin Valley and the south end of the Salton Sea; vagrants occur the length of state; *note*–irregularly occurs on the coast, even north to Humboldt Bay.

White Ibis

WHITE IBIS *(Eudocimus albus)*
Seasonal status–accidental; *note*–one definite record of one bird at Point Loma, San Diego County, Nov. 20, 1935 (specimen); other records are one at Palo Verde, Imperial County, March 1914, and one at Bolinas, Marin County, May 14–Sept. 9, 1971 both of which may have been escapes.

ROSEATE SPOONBILL *(Ajaia ajaja)*
Seasonal status–accidental/casual visitor; *habitat*–shores of marshes and rivers; *range in California*–most of the records are from the Salton Sea; also one record from lower Colorado River and another from Mendota, Fresno County; *note*–all records fall between May and October and the species is probably a post-breeding visitor from Mexico.

Swans, Geese, and Ducks

WHISTLING SWAN *(Olor columbianus)*
  Seasonal status—winter visitor; *habitat*—usually large fresh-water lakes and ponds; also occurs on larger sheltered bays; *range in California*—primarily northern half of state; uncommon in southern portion.

Whistling Swan

TRUMPETER SWAN *(Olor buccinator)*
  Seasonal status—casual winter visitor; *habitat*—large fresh-water lakes and ponds; also occurs occasionally on large protected saltwater bays; *range in California*—primarily northern one-third of state; *note*—may be looked for among large flocks of Whistling Swans.

CANADA GOOSE *(Branta canadensis)*
  Seasonal status—common winter visitor; *habitat*—fresh-water lakes and marshes; coastal bays and lagoons; cultivated lands; *range in California*—length of state; *note*—four fairly well-marked subspecies of the Canada Goose occur—Western, Lesser, White-cheeked, and Cackling; the White-cheeked race *(B. c. canadensis)* *breeds* on the Modoc Plateau.

BRANT *(Branta bernicla)*
  "American" Brant: *Seasonal status*—casual visitor in winter; *habitat*—larger shallow coastal bays where eelgrass is plentiful; *range in California*—length of state.
  "Black" Brant: *Seasonal status*—winter visitor, transient; *habitat*—same as for

"American" Brant; *range in California*—length of state with largest concentrations on Humboldt Bay, Tomales Bay, Morro Bay, and south San Diego Bay; *note*—many birds winter on the coastal lagoons of Baja California, occurring in California as spring and fall transients.

EMPEROR GOOSE *(Philacte canagica)*

Seasonal status—casual winter visitor; *habitat*—with other geese in fresh-water marshes and in open agricultural fields; occasionally found along seacoast on reefs, bays, and estuaries; *range in California*—primarily northern California; very few records for southern half of state.

White-fronted Goose

WHITE-FRONTED GOOSE *(Anser albifrons)*

Seasonal status—winter visitor, September through April; *habitat*—fresh-water lakes and marshes, open agricultural land with other geese; *range in California*—length of state but much more numerous in northern half of state.

SNOW GOOSE *Chen caerulescens)*—a polymorphic species

Lesser Snow Goose (the white morph; formerly *Chen hyperborea*):

Seasonal status—common winter visitor, September through April; *habitat*—fresh-water marshes and lakes, open grain fields, and agricultural lands; rare on salt-water bays; *range in California*—length of state; *note*—largest concentrations in California occur on waterfowl refuges in the Central Valley; in southern California occurs primarily at south end of Salton Sea and lower Colorado River Valley.

"BLUE" GOOSE (the dark morph)

Seasonal status—rare winter visitor; *habitat*—same as for the white morph with which it associates; *range in California*—length of state; most southern California records are from the very few that winter each year in the Imperial Valley.

ROSS' GOOSE *(Chen rossii)*
Seasonal status–winter visitor from late September to mid-April; *habitat*–same as for Snow Goose and very rare on salt water; *range in California*–primarily the refuges and wildlife areas of the Sacramento and San Joaquin valleys where virtually the entire world population of perhaps 15,000 birds occurs; a very small number winter each year at the south end of the Salton Sea with the Snow Geese.

BLACK-BELLIED TREE DUCK *(Dendrocygna autumnalis)*
Seasonal status–accidental; *note*–three records: one in Imperial Valley, Imperial County, "fall of 1912"; one near Calipatria, Imperial County, June 12, 1951; and 1-4 at south end of Salton Sea, Imperial County, June 2–Aug. 5, 1972. Specimen.

FULVOUS TREE DUCK *(Dendrocygna bicolor)*
Seasonal status–uncommon summer visitor, April through October; *habitat*–fresh-water marshes; *range in California*–declining because of diminishing habitat for nesting; *breeds* as far north as Merced County but spottily; most consistent breeding areas are near south end of Salton Sea; *note*–some disperse to north after breeding season; there are a few winter records.

MALLARD *(Anas platyrhynchos)*
Seasonal status–common resident and winter visitor; *habitat*–fresh-water lakes, ponds, rivers, and marshes; *range in California*–length of state but much more numerous as wild birds in the northern half; many local birds, especially in parks are not truly wild birds; *breeds* throughout state; *note*–second only to Pintail in wintering population in the Central Valley with numbers exceeding 1,000,000.

BLACK DUCK *(Anas rubripes)*
Seasonal status–accidental; *note*–three records: one in Lower Klamath basin, Klamath County, "Nov. 1962"; another there "Sept. 1963"; and one at Biggs, Butte County, Dec. 17, 1970. Specimen.

GADWALL *(Anas strepera)*
Seasonal status–resident, transient, and winter visitor; *habitat*–fresh-water lakes, ponds, and marshes; *range in California*–length of state; *breeds* in Sacramento and San Joaquin valleys.

PINTAIL *(Anas acuta)*
Seasonal status–complex transient and winter visitor; some are resident; *habitat*–fresh-water lakes, ponds, and marshes; salt-water bays, lagoons, and estuaries; *range in California*–length of state; *note*–possibly most abundant waterfowl in California during winter; most certainly so in northern portion where wintering population in Sacramento Valley yearly reaches 3,000,000 birds; *breeds* or has bred locally from Modoc County to San Diego County.

GREEN-WINGED TEAL *(Anas crecca)*
"American" Green-winged Teal (formerly *Anas carolinensis*)
Seasonal status–primarily a winter visitor, September through April but some of population is transient through state; *habitat*–fresh-water lakes, ponds, and marshes; salt-water bays and estuaries; *range in California*–length of state; small numbers *breed* in California.

Pintail

"*Eurasian*" *Green-winged Teal*

Seasonal status—casual winter visitor; *habitat*—same as for "American" Green-winged Teal; *range in California*—length of state.

BLUE-WINGED TEAL *(Anas discors)*

Seasonal status—primarily an uncommon winter visitor; *habitat*—fresh-water lakes, ponds, streams; occasionally occurs on estuaries; *range in California*—length of state but *breeds* in northeast region; more abundant in northern half of state.

CINNAMON TEAL *(Anas cyanoptera)*

Seasonal status—resident in southern half of state; uncommon during winter in northern half; many birds from entire state withdraw to south in winter; *habitat*—fresh-water lakes, rivers, ponds, and streams; rare on salt water; *range in California*—length of state as *breeding;* almost completely absent from humid northwest coastal region.

EUROPEAN WIGEON *(Anas penelope)*

Seasonal status—rare winter visitor; *habitat*—usually in company of American Wigeon; *range in California*—length of state.

AMERICAN WIGEON *(Anas americana)*

Seasonal status—primarily winter visitor August through April; *habitat*—fresh-water marshes, ponds, and lakes; salt-water bays and estuaries; *range in California*—length of state; in northern half it ranks number three in abundance behind Pintail and Mallard; in southern California numbers equal or exceed Pintails; *note*—many are spring and fall transients to and from Mexico; has *bred* in California but these may have been cripples.

NORTHERN SHOVELER *(Anas clypeata)*

Seasonal status—primarily a common winter visitor from late August to late

April; very few are resident; *habitat*—fresh-water lakes, ponds, marshes; salt-water bays and estuaries; *range in California*—length of state; *breeds* in small numbers in Central Valley and northeast portion.

WOOD DUCK *(Aix sponsa)*

Seasonal status—uncommon resident; *habitat*—fresh-water ponds, sloughs, and rivers which are bordered by trees; *range in California*—length of state but quite rare in southern one-third; *breeds* locally in Sacramento and San Joaquin valleys and few areas to the west in valleys of Coast Range; *note*—most southern California breeding birds are those that have been captured and released for show on various park lakes.

REDHEAD *(Aythya americana)*

Seasonal status—primarily a winter visitor, but some birds are resident; winter birds occur from September to April; *habitat*—prefers fresh-water marshes and lakes; a few occur on salt-water bays and estuaries; *range in California*—length of state; still *breeds* locally on northernmost refuges and in Central Valley.

RING-NECKED DUCK *(Aythya collaris)*

Seasonal status—primarily a winter visitor September to May; *habitat*—prefers fresh-water lakes and ponds; *range in California*—length of state; small numbers *breed* locally in northern Sierra Nevada.

Canvasback

CANVASBACK *(Aythya valisneria)*

Seasonal status—winter visitor, September to May; *habitat*—primarily salt-water bays and estuaries; also fresh-water lakes and large rivers; *range in California*—length of state.

GREATER SCAUP *(Aythya marila)*

Seasonal status—winter visitor, uncommon in southern California and more common in northern half of state; *habitat*—salt-water bays, lagoons, estuaries; *range in California*—length of state in coastal areas.

LESSER SCAUP *(Aythya affinis)*

Seasonal status—common winter visitor September to May; *habitat*—salt-water bays, lagoons, and estuaries; larger fresh-water lakes, ponds, and rivers; *range in California*—length of state; a few, probably cripples, have *bred* in northeast portion.

TUFTED DUCK *(Aythya fuligula)*

Seasonal status—accidental; *note*—five records: one in Livermore Valley, Alameda County, "between Dec. 23, 1948 and Jan. 8, 1949"; one at Arcata, Humboldt County, April 10–Nov. 4, 1968; one at Felt Lake, San Mateo County, Feb. 4–March 7, 1971; one at Stow Lake, San Francisco County, Feb. 15–March 3, 1972; and one at Lake Sherwood, Ventura County, Jan. 25–Feb. 10, 1973. Specimen.

COMMON GOLDENEYE *(Bucephala clangula)*

Seasonal status—winter visitor, October to April; *habitat*—salt-water bays, lagoons, estuaries; occasional on fresh-water lakes; *range in California*—length of state but commoner in northern portion.

BARROW'S GOLDENEYE *(Bucephala islandica)*

Seasonal status—primarily an uncommon winter visitor and possible resident; *habitat*—in winter, salt-water bays, lagoons, estuaries; occasionally on fresh-water lakes (especially Lake Merritt in Oakland); formerly *bred* on small timber-bordered lakes in Sierra Nevada and Cascades but may no longer do so; *range in California*—primarily northern half of state coastwise; very rare in southern California.

BUFFLEHEAD *(Bucephala albeola)*

Seasonal status—winter visitor, October to April; *habitat*—salt-water bays, lagoons, estuaries; *range in California*—length of state; *breeds* or has bred in small numbers on lakes of northeastern portion and northern Sierra Nevada.

OLDSQUAW *(Clangula hyemalis)*

Seasonal status—uncommon to rare winter visitor, October to May; *habitat*—seacoast, larger bays, and estuaries; *range in California*—length of state; *note*—becomes rarer from north to south in state.

HARLEQUIN DUCK *(Histrionicus histrionicus)*

Seasonal status—rare winter visitor; *habitat*—seacoast; *range in California*—length of state although very rare in southern one-third; has *bred* on tumbling mountain streams of Sierra Nevada but no recent evidence of this.

KING EIDER *(Somateria spectabilis)*

Seasonal status—accidental with most occurrences during winter season; *note*—nine records: one at Suisun Marshes, Solano County, "winter 1902-1903"; three at Tomales Bay, Marin County, Dec. 16, 1933; one at Monterey, Monterey County, Feb. 3–March 16, 1958; one at Pacific Grove, Monterey County, March 21-26,

1959; one at Monterey, Monterey County, June 24–25, 1959; one at Moss Landing, Monterey County, March 25–Aug. 26, 1961; one at Bodega Bay, Sonoma County, Sept. 17, 1961; one at Monterey, Monterey County, Dec. 24, 1969–March 28, 1971 and "January"–March 11, 1972. Specimen.

WHITE-WINGED SCOTER *(Melanitta deglandi)*
Seasonal status–winter visitor, September through April; *habitat*–seacoast, larger salt-water bays; *range in California*–length of state; *note*–may be conspecific with Palearctic Velvet Scoter *(Melanitta fusca)*. Frequently found with Surf Scoters in harbors.

SURF SCOTER *(Melanitta perspicillata)*
Seasonal status–common winter visitor, October to May; a few remain through the summer as non-breeders; *habitat*–seacoast, harbors, salt-water bays and estuaries; *range in California*–length of state.

BLACK SCOTER *(Melanitta nigra)*
Seasonal status–uncommon to rare winter visitor, October to May; *habitat*–seacoast, salt-water bays and estuaries; *range in California*–length of state although increasingly rarer to south.

RUDDY DUCK *(Oxyura jamaicensis)*
Seasonal status–common resident; *habitat*–in breeding season, fresh-water lakes and ponds; in non-breeding season, lakes, ponds, salt-water bays, lagoons, estuaries, and harbors; *range in California*–length of state; decided fall movement from interior *breeding* lakes to coastal waters.

HOODED MERGANSER *(Lophodytes cucullatus)*
Seasonal status–uncommon winter visitor, October to April; *habitat*–fresh-water ponds, lakes, and rivers; salt-water lagoons, sloughs; *range in California*–length of state, but rare in southern half; *breeding* recorded from Mountain Meadow, Lassen County.

*Red-breasted Merganser
    –female*

COMMON MERGANSER *(Mergus merganser)*

Seasonal status—part of population is resident in state; others are winter visitors from north; *habitat*—for *breeding,* fresh-water lakes and fast-running rivers and streams; *range in California*—for breeding, north coastal and north central regions and northern Sierra Nevada; in winter, length of state but commoner in northern half; *note*—in non-breeding season many Common Mergansers are found in coastal areas as on lagoons, estuaries, and protected bays; not found on ocean; also occurs on larger lakes and rivers.

RED-BREASTED MERGANSER *(Mergus serrator)*

Seasonal status—common winter visitor, October to May; *habitat*—seacoast, bays, estuaries, lagoons; uncommon on fresh-water lakes near seacoast; *range in California*—length of state.

American Vultures

TURKEY VULTURE *(Cathartes aura)*

Seasonal status—part of population is resident, part is migratory; *habitat*—forages over open country of mountains, grasslands, deserts, savannahs, and agricultural lands; *range in California*—length of state; *breeds* throughout state in suitable well-hidden cavities in cliff-faces, brush, logs, etc.; *note*—migratory birds enter or transit through state in February and March and leave about October.

Turkey Vulture

*California Condor
—subadult*

CALIFORNIA CONDOR *(Gymnogyps californianus)*
Seasonal status—rare resident; *habitat*—for *breeding,* cavities or caves in cliff-faces; forages over mountains, grasslands, and savannahs (especially large ranches) for carrion; *range in California*—most birds nest and roost in Sespe Wildlife Area of Los Padres National Forest, Ventura County, and forage northwards into southern foothills of Sierra Nevada in Kern and Tulare counties; smaller group roosts and moves northwards from Santa Barbara County sometimes as far north as Santa Clara County; some birds from Sespe Wildlife Area also move towards Santa Barbara, San Luis Obispo, and Monterey counties; *note*—present population between 40 and 60 birds.

Kites, Hawks, and Harriers

WHITE-TAILED KITE *(Elanus leucurus)*
Seasonal status—resident; *habitat*—open cultivated bottomland with scattered trees, savannahs, and grassy foothill slopes with scattered oaks; *range in California*—length of state in suitable habitat west of the Sierra Nevada and deserts; *note*—encouraging upsurge in populations may be due to expansion of irrigation and agricultural areas which are inhabited by meadow mice, its preferred food; accepts orchards (even low citrus) and windbreaks of exotic trees for *nesting* near suitable open areas for hunting.

MISSISSIPPI KITE *(Ictinia mississippiensis)*
Seasonal status—accidental; *note*—four records: one at Goleta, Santa Barbara County, June 18, 1933; one at Furnace Creek Ranch, Inyo County, June 2–5, 1968; one at Santa Barbara, Santa Barbara County, June 3, 1970; and two at Furnace Creek Ranch, Inyo County, May 20–21, 1973. Specimen.

White-tailed Kite

GOSHAWK *(Accipiter gentilis)*

Seasonal status—uncommon resident; uncommon winter visitor; *habitat*—in summer on breeding grounds, forests of Canadian Life Zone; during winter, those that are in lowlands frequent riparian woodlands and broken woodlands; *range in California*—has been recorded from length of state but *breeds* primarily at higher elevations in northern one-third of state and south in Sierra Nevada to at least Greenhorn Mountain in Kern County; also recorded in summer from Mt. Pinos, Ventura County, and Mt. San Jacinto, Riverside County.

SHARP-SHINNED HAWK *(Accipiter striatus)*

Seasonal status—winter visitor and resident; *habitat*—in breeding season, open woodland; during winter, almost all habitats except desert, grasslands, and aquatic and marsh habitats; *range in California*—for *breeding,* northern half of state; otherwise, length of state from September to April.

COOPER'S HAWK *(Accipiter cooperii)*

Seasonal status—primarily resident but small numbers from north are winter visitors; *habitat*—*breeds* in open woodland, riparian woodland, and broken woodland; *range in California*—length of state, but least common in northwest and southeast portions.

RED-TAILED HAWK *(Buteo jamaicensis)*

Western Red-tailed Hawk

Seasonal status—common resident; small numbers are transient; *habitat*—grasslands and savannah, open woodlands, desert, chaparral; *range in California*—length of state; *breeds* in almost any suitable habitat with cliffs or tall trees for nesting or roosting.

Harlan's Hawk (formerly *Buteo harlani*)

Seasonal status—casual winter visitor; *habitat*—open country; *range in California*—

Red-tailed Hawks

most records from Honey Lake basin, Lassen County, but also recorded from Central Valley south to southern California.

RED-SHOULDERED HAWK *(Buteo lineatus)*

Seasonal status—resident; *habitat*—very partial to riparian and dense oak woodlands; *range in California*—*breeds* in appropriate habitat in Central Valley and coastal lowlands of southern California; less common in northern coastal woodlands.

BROAD-WINGED HAWK *(Buteo platypterus)*

Seasonal status—casual visitor with almost all records between October and March; *habitat*—lowlands with woodland, riparian, or other open vegetation; *range in California*—has been recorded from Marin County south to San Diego County with most records near coast; one record, Nov. 1972, from Furnace Creek Ranch, Death Valley, Inyo County; *note*—may be a rare but regular fall transient coastwise.

SWAINSON'S HAWK *(Buteo swainsoni)*

Seasonal status—summer visitor and transient; *habitat*—grasslands, oak woodlands, savannah; *range in California*—as transient, length of state; *breeds* in Great Basin, sparingly in Sacramento and San Joaquin valleys, and south in coastal woodlands to San Luis Obispo County; *note*—majority of spring flocks are noted in March and early April although migratory flocks have been observed in late February; fall migration occurs during September and October but fall flocks are unknown; no authentic winter records.

ZONE-TAILED HAWK *(Buteo albonotatus)*

Seasonal status—accidental; *note*—11 records since 1900, as follows—six from San Diego County, two from Inyo County, and one each from Riverside, San Bernardino, and Imperial counties. Specimen.

ROUGH-LEGGED HAWK *(Buteo lagopus)*

Seasonal status—winter visitor, October to April; *habitat*—open country including grasslands, sagebrush flats, agricultural land, plains; *range in California*—length of state but commonness decreases from north to south; *note*—occurs each year but numbers fluctuate from year to year; most abundant in northern Central Valley and northeastern portion.

FERRUGINOUS HAWK *(Buteo regalis)*

Seasonal status—winter visitor, September to April; *habitat*—open grasslands, plains, and foothills; *range in California*—length of state.

HARRIS' HAWK *(Parabuteo unicinctus)*

Seasonal status—casual visitor or rare resident; *habitat*—riparian woodlands; *range in California*—formerly occurred as *breeding* in the Imperial Valley, now accidental there; rare resident along lower Colorado River between Topock, Arizona and Yuma, Arizona.

GOLDEN EAGLE *(Aquila chrysaëtos)*

Seasonal status—resident; *habitat*—open rolling country of light woodlands and savannahs, grasslands, desert edge, and farms and ranches; *range in California*—length of state where it *breeds* in suitable trees or cliff sites; scarce in southeastern desert portion.

BALD EAGLE *(Haliaeetus leucocephalus)*

Seasonal status—uncommon winter visitor October to April; small number are resident; *habitat*—seacoast, islands, sea cliffs, large lakes, and large rivers, coastal lagoons; *range in California*—formerly length of state *breeding* from northern portions south to San Clemente Island; now breeds only in a few localities in northern portion of state; ranges the length of state but commoner in northern parts; *note*—no longer nests on any of the coastal islands in southern California; small numbers winter on the larger lakes and reservoirs in southern California.

Marsh Hawk—female

MARSH HAWK *(Circus cyaneus)*
Seasonal status—resident and lesser number of winter visitors, September to April; *habitat*—fresh-water and salt-water marshes, grasslands, desert sinks, and mountain meadows; *range in California*—length of state for *breeders* and in migration.

Osprey

Ospreys

OSPREY *(Pandion haliaetus)*
Seasonal status—primarily a spring and fall transient; a small number winter in the state and some are residents; *habitat*—seacoast, coastal lagoons, large bays, estuaries, rivers, and large lakes; *range in California*—length of state, normally west of the deserts; formerly nested on the larger offshore islands but no longer; *breeds* mostly in northern half of state on larger lakes and rivers.

Falcons

GYRFALCON *(Falco rusticolus)*
Seasonal status—accidental; *note*—one record; one bird at Tule Lake, Siskiyou County, Oct. 23, 1948. Specimen.

PRAIRIE FALCON *(Falco mexicanus)*
Seasonal status—resident; *habitat*—open country of interior grasslands, deserts, and agricultural lands; *range in California*—length of state except humid northwest coastal belt; *breeds* near suitable habitat, but on cliff-faces, earthen mounds, and rocks; *note*—nest-robbing by people wanting young falcons has caused alarming decline in population.

Prairie Falcons

PEREGRINE FALCON *(Falco peregrinus)*
Seasonal status—very rare resident; uncommon transient and winter visitor; *habitat*—seacoast, islands, sea cliffs, and almost any interior habitat for foraging except dense forest; *range in California*—length of state; formerly *bred* along seacoast and on offshore islands; known viable eyries fewer than five in entire state today; *note*—abrupt decline in population probably due to ingestion of chlorinated hydrocarbons and nest-robbing by people wanting young falcons.

MERLIN *(Falco columbarius)*
Seasonal status—uncommon transient and winter visitor, late September to May; *habitat*—seacoast, open woodlands, savannahs, and grasslands; *range in California*—length of state.

AMERICAN KESTREL *(Falco sparverius)*
Seasonal status—common resident with additional birds wintering in California from the north; *habitat*—open country such as deserts, grasslands, savannahs, open woodlands, agricultural lands, and ranches; *range in California*—length of state; *breeds* throughout state except above timberline.

Grouse

BLUE GROUSE *(Dendragapus obscurus)*
Seasonal status—resident, but numbers seem to be declining; *habitat*—montane forest of the upper Transition and Canadian Life Zones; *range in California*—dense forests of the northwestern and north central portions, Warner Mountains, entire Sierra Nevada south through higher mountains of the Tehachapis; also reported from Panamint Mountains, White Mountains, and Mt. San Jacinto

in Peninsular Ranges; *note*—in late summer some grouse move to higher elevations of the Hudsonian Zone before returning to somewhat lower elevations for
the winter; the race on Mt. Pinos, Kern County, has not been observed in recent
years.

RUFFED GROUSE *(Bonasa umbellus)*
Seasonal status—rare and local resident; *habitat*—dense growth along streams in
steep canyons; *range in California*—locally in Humboldt and Del Norte counties
in humid northwest coastal region; also very locally in Trinity and Siskiyou
counties. Most probably *breeds* in state.

SHARP-TAILED GROUSE *(Pedioecetes phasianellus)*
Note—extirpated from California since 1915; formerly resident in rolling grasslands of northeastern plateau region.

SAGE GROUSE *(Centrocercus urophasianus)*
Seasonal status—resident; *habitat*—flatlands containing extensive stands of Great
Basin sagebrush; *range in California*—*breeds* in northeastern portion and Great Basin south to about Lake Crowley, Mono County; *note*—has disappeared from
much of its former range; very local now.

Sage Grouse—male

Quails and Pheasants

CALIFORNIA QUAIL *(Lophortyx californicus)*
Seasonal status—common resident; *habitat*—chaparral, brushlands, riparian
growth, and edges of agricultural lands; *range in California*—*breeds* length of state
except higher portions of Sierra Nevada above Upper Sonoran Zone and the
southeastern deserts; *note*—a distinct race exists on Catalina Island.

California Quail
—male

GAMBEL'S QUAIL *(Lophortyx gambelii)*
Seasonal status—common resident; *habitat*—more densely vegetated portions of desert as along ravines, arroyos, washes, and hillsides; requires drinking water nearby; *range in California*—Mojave and Colorado Deserts. *Breeds.*

MOUNTAIN QUAIL *(Oreortyx pictus)*
Seasonal status—resident; *habitat*—primarily mountain chaparral, brushlands, edges of woodlands and coniferous forests; *range in California—breeds* length of state in suitable habitat; north central, north coastal, and northeastern portions, Sierra Nevada, mountains of Great Basin, Transverse Ranges, and Peninsular Ranges south to Mexican border; *note*—vertical down-mountain walking migration to escape winter snows occurs in fall.

RING-NECKED PHEASANT *(Phasianus colchicus)*—INTRODUCED into California
Seasonal status—resident; *habitat*—brushy fields, agricultural land, stubble fields; *range in California*—widely planted throughout state in suitable habitat. *Breeds.*

CHUKAR *(Alectoris chukar)*—INTRODUCED into California
Seasonal status—resident; *habitat*—arid foothills with rocky areas, along the desert and valley edges; *range in California*—widely planted throughout state in suitable habitat with "guzzlers" provided to supply necessary drinking water. *Breeds.*

GRAY PARTRIDGE *(Perdix perdix)*—INTRODUCED into California
Seasonal status—resident; *habitat*—brush-bordered agricultural lands; *range in California*—introduced in extreme eastern Modoc and Lassen counties; *note*—successful establishment of this bird is uncertain.

Turkeys

TURKEY *(Meleagris gallopavo)*—INTRODUCED into California
Seasonal status—resident; *habitat*—oak woodlands, riparian woodlands, pine forests of Transition Zone; *range in California*—known to be established in Mendocino, Santa Clara, Monterey, San Luis Obispo, Santa Barbara, and Riverside counties. *Breeds.*

Turkeys

Cranes

SANDHILL CRANE *(Grus canadensis)*
Seasonal status—most of the California birds are "Lesser" Sandhill Cranes that are winter visitors from October to April; a small number are the resident "Greater" Sandhill Cranes; *habitat*—for wintering birds, agricultural lands, grain fields, stubble fields, and open areas at edge of large fresh-water lakes and rivers; for *breeding,* open country near lakes and fresh-water marshes in northeastern portion of state; *range in California*—for transients, length of state; for residents and winter visitors, most winter south to central San Joaquin Valley and the Carrizo Plain in eastern San Luis Obispo County; formerly, good numbers reached the Imperial Valley but now only small numbers of transients and winter visitors.

Sandhill Cranes

Rails, Gallinules, and Coots

CLAPPER RAIL *(Rallus longirostris)*
Seasonal status—resident; *habitat*—for the two coastal races, salt-water tidal marshes; for the single inland race, fresh-water and brackish-water marshes; *range in California*—isolated coastal salt-water marshes from Marin County south to San Diego County; for the "Yuma" Clapper Rail, marshes at south end of Salton Sea and in lower Colorado River Valley; *note*—the three races of this species in California are endangered species. *Breeds.*

VIRGINIA RAIL *(Rallus limicola)*
Seasonal status—resident; *habitat*—primarily fresh-water marshes, but also edges of salt-water or brackish-water marshes; *range in California*—length of state but there is some movement to the south and to lower elevations of the birds from the northern and mountainous regions. *Breeds.*

SORA *(Porzana carolina)*
Seasonal status—most are resident; some withdrawal of northern birds and birds of mountainous regions to the south during the winter; *habitat*—fresh-water marshes, but in winter there is a large influx of birds into salt-water marshes; *range in California*—length of state. *Breeds.*

YELLOW RAIL *(Coturnicops noveboracensis)*
Seasonal status—recent observations are so few that it must be regarded as accidental now with most records during winter; *habitat*—for *breeding*, fresh-water

Sora

marshes and marshy meadows; in winter, has been observed in salt-water marshes; *range in California*—formerly *nested* east of Sierra Nevada in Mono County; during winter it has been recorded from Humboldt County south to at least Orange County and at a few inland locations.

BLACK RAIL *(Laterallus jamaicensis)*

Seasonal status—status still uncertain; some are resident and some are migratory; rarely observed; *habitat*—salt-water marshes; also brackish-water and fresh-water marshes and meadows; *range in California*—coastwise from Marin County to San Diego County; known to have *bred* at Morro Bay, San Luis Obispo County, and in San Diego County; some non-breeding inland occurrences, but most consistently seen and heard from April to June in lower Colorado River Valley at West Pond, Imperial County.

PURPLE GALLINULE *(Porphyrula martinica)*

Seasonal status—one record: one bird at Point Loma, San Diego County, Oct. 1, 1961. Specimen.

Common Gallinule

COMMON GALLINULE *(Gallinula chloropus)*

Seasonal status—most are resident, but part of population withdraws south in winter; *habitat*—fresh-water marshes and marsh-bordered lakes and streams; *range in California*—mid-Sacramento Valley south to Mexican border and coastwise south as well; very rare in salt-water marshes; also occurs in suitable habitat in southeastern portion of state. *Breeds.*

American Coot

AMERICAN COOT *(Fulica americana)*

Seasonal status—common resident; *habitat*—*breeds* only in freshwater marshes and marsh-bordered lakes and streams; in winter, large numbers move coastward to salt-water marshes and tidal estuaries; occasionally observed at sea; *range in California*—length of state.

Oystercatchers

AMERICAN OYSTERCATCHER *(Haematopus palliatus)*

Seasonal status—accidental; *note*—at least three records since 1900—one at White's Landing, Santa Catalina Island, Feb. 12, 1910; one on Anacapa Island from 1964 to 1973 was probably same individual; and one at Avila Beach, San Luis Obispo County, Oct. 25, 1964–Feb. 20, 1965; also recorded from Los Coronados Islands, Baja California del Norte. Specimen.

*American
Oystercatcher*

BLACK OYSTERCATCHER *(Haematopus bachmani)*
   Seasonal status—resident; *habitat*—rocky shores and reefs of offshore islands and
   mainland; *range in California*—regularly *breeds* as far south on mainland as about
   Morro Bay but on islands, as far south as at least to Los Coronados; occasionally
   occurs on mainland south of Morro Bay, San Luis Obispo County as far south as
   San Diego County.

Plovers

SEMIPALMATED PLOVER *(Charadrius semipalmatus)*
   Seasonal status—winter visitor, August to end of May; also transient spring and
   fall; *habitat*—tidal mud flats and estuaries; *range in California*—coastwise, length
   of state; few inland records.
PIPING PLOVER *(Charadrius melodus)*
   Seasonal status—accidental; one record: one bird at Goleta, Santa Barbara County,
   Apr. 14–18, 1971, Dec. 16, 1971–Apr. 22, 1972, and winter 1972–1973. Photograph.
SNOWY PLOVER *(Charadrius alexandrinus)*
   Seasonal status—resident; *habitat*—typically sea beaches, but also shores of some in-
   land brackish lakes; *range in California*—length of state. *Breeds*.
WILSON'S PLOVER *(Charadrius wilsonia)*
   Seasonal status—accidental; *note*—one record since 1900: a single bird at Imperial
   Beach, San Diego County, May 11, 1918. Specimen.

KILLDEER *(Charadrius vociferus)*

Seasonal status—common resident; *habitat*—tidal flats and estuaries; shores of lakes, rivers, and ponds; greenswards, irrigated fields, and meadows; *range in California*—length of state. *Breeds.*

Killdeer

MOUNTAIN PLOVER *(Charadrius montanus)*

Seasonal status—winter visitor September to March; *habitat*—freshly-plowed fields, short grass plains; *range in California*—principally the San Joaquin Valley in suitable habitat on the west and central portions; favored areas are near Blackwell's Corner, Kern County, Carrizo Plain, San Luis Obispo County, and Imperial Valley, Imperial County; also known from coastal plains of Ventura and Orange counties.

AMERICAN GOLDEN PLOVER *(Pluvialis dominica)*

Seasonal status—uncommon or rare fall transient or winter visitor; *habitat*—tidal flats, irrigated fields, meadows of short grass; *range in California*—length of state in coastal areas.

BLACK-BELLIED PLOVER *(Pluvialis squatarola)*

Seasonal status—common winter visitor and transient, August to May; *habitat*—tidal mud flats and occasionally on sea beaches and exposed reefs; *range in California*—length of state.

Sandpipers

SURFBIRD *(Aphriza virgata)*

Seasonal status—winter visitor and spring and fall transient, August to May; *habitat*—reefs, rocky shores, and breakwaters of mainland and offshore islands; *range in California*—length of state.

RUDDY TURNSTONE *(Arenaria interpres)*

Seasonal status—winter visitor and spring and fall transient, August to May; *habitat*—tidal flats, estuaries, mud flats, sea beaches, rocky shores; *range in California*—length of state.

BLACK TURNSTONE *(Arenaria melanocephala)*

Seasonal status—winter visitor and spring and fall transient, July to May; *habitat*—rocky beaches, reefs, breakwaters, and occasionally sea beaches; *range in California*—length of state.

COMMON SNIPE *(Capella gallinago)*

Seasonal status—resident but southward and coastward shift of population occurs in fall as birds leave their breeding areas in northern and northeastern portions of the state for the winter; *habitat*—wet meadows, fresh-water marshes, and grassy margins of rivers, lakes, and streams; *range in California*—length of state, but *breeds* in northern and northeastern portions.

EUROPEAN JACKSNIPE *(Lymnocryptes minimus)*

Seasonal status—accidental; *note*—one record; one bird near Marysville Buttes, Butte County, Nov. 20, 1938. Specimen.

LONG-BILLED CURLEW *(Numenius americanus)*

Seasonal status—Transient, winter visitor, and resident; *habitat*—in areas where it occurs as winter visitor or transient, prefers tidal mud flats, estuaries, salt-water marshes, and grasslands; for breeding it requires grasslands with lakes or marshes nearby; *range in California*—for *breeding,* northeast region; otherwise, length of state.

Whimbrel

WHIMBREL *(Numenius phaeopus)*

Seasonal status—winter visitor and spring and fall transient, July to May; *habitat*—estuaries, tidal mud flats, sea beaches, short grass fields near water; *range in California*—length of state.

UPLAND SANDPIPER *(Bartramia longicauda)*
Seasonal status—accidental; *note*—four records since 1900: one at Needles Landing
on Lake Havasu, San Bernardino County, Sept. 11, 1952; one at Furnace Creek
Ranch, Inyo County, May 13, 1959; one on the Farallon Islands Aug. 22–24,
1968 and another there May 23, 1969. Specimen.

SPOTTED SANDPIPER *(Actitis macularia)*
Seasonal status—resident, spring and fall transient; *habitat*—shores of islands, estuaries, lakes, rivers, ponds, and streams, preferably where there are rocks, gravel,
or pebbles; *range in California*—length of state for transient birds; *breeds* in mountainous areas of northern half of state at which time they are absent from southern California where they winter.

WANDERING TATTLER *(Heteroscelus incanus)*
Seasonal status—transient, winter visitor, and perennial visitor; *habitat*—offshore islands, reefs, breakwaters, rocky beaches; *range in California*—length of state; *note*—
wintering birds are generally found south of Monterey Bay.

WILLET *(Catoptrophorus semipalmatus)*
Seasonal status—perennial visitor, spring and fall transient, winter visitor; *habitat*—
for non-breeding, sea beaches, mud flats, estuaries, salt-water marshes; for breeding, wet grassy meadows close to lakes; *range in California*—in non-breeding season, length of state; for *breeding,* northeast portion including localities in Modoc,
Lassen, and Plumas counties.

SOLITARY SANDPIPER *(Tringa solitaria)*
Seasonal status—uncommon pure transient, spring and fall; *habitat*—confined to
fresh-water habitats such as small ponds, streams, small rivers, rain pools, and
small canals where it forages alone along the water's edge; *range in California*—
generally, length of state.

GREATER YELLOWLEGS *(Tringa melanoleuca)*
Seasonal status—spring and fall transient and winter visitor, July to May; *habitat*—
estuaries, mud flats, salt-water marshes, shores of small lakes and ponds; *range in
California*—length of state.

LESSER YELLOWLEGS *(Tringa flavipes)*
Seasonal status—primarily a pure transient although there are some winter records; most of the spring migrants move through in April and fall migration occurs from July to October; *habitat*—salt-water marshes, estuaries, mud flats, and
occasionally along margins of fresh-water ponds; *range in California*—length of
state.

RED KNOT *(Calidris canutus)*
Seasonal status—primarily a pure transient, spring and fall, although small numbers winter, especially in southern California; most of spring migrants move
through in April and early May and fall migration occurs during August and
September; *habitat*—estuaries, mud flats, and salt-water marshes; *range in California*—coastwise primarily, length of state.

ROCK SANDPIPER *(Calidris ptilocnemis)*
Seasonal status—rare winter visitor, November to April; *habitat*—rocky shores, reefs, breakwaters; *range in California*—coastwise from Del Norte County south to Los Angeles County (at Los Angeles harbor).

SHARP-TAILED SANDPIPER *(Calidris acuminata)*
Seasonal status—accidental; *note*—at least seven records since 1900: one at San Diego, San Diego County, Sept. 16, 1921; one near Oakland, Alameda County, Oct. 10–26, 1959; one at Abbott's Lagoon, Marin County, Sept. 3, 1968; one at Goleta, Santa Barbara County, Sept. 13–21, 1969; one at Bodega Bay, Marin County, Oct. 13–Nov. 4, 1969 (and an additional four there Nov. 4, 1969); four to six on Humboldt Bay, Humboldt County, Oct. 16–30, 1969; and two at Olema, Marin County, Nov. 4, 1969. All of the records falling between Sept. 3 and Nov. 4 may indicate that this species is a regular but very rare pure fall transient through this region. Specimen.

PECTORAL SANDPIPER *(Calidris melanotos)*
Seasonal status—pure transient, uncommon in fall and very rare in spring; *habitat*—prefers drier portions of mud flats and grassy borders of estuaries and bays; *range in California*—length of state.

WHITE-RUMPED SANDPIPER *(Calidris fuscicollis)*
Seasonal status—accidental; *note*—one record: one bird at the north end of the Salton Sea, Riverside County, June 7, 1969. Specimen.

BAIRD'S SANDPIPER *(Calidris bairdii)*
Seasonal status—pure transient, uncommon to rare in fall (late June to late September) and very rare in spring (late April to early May); *habitat*—prefers drier areas of lakes, estuaries, mud flats with low grasses; *range in California*—length of state.

LEAST SANDPIPER *(Calidris minutilla)*
Seasonal status—primarily a winter visitor and spring and fall transient although some of population might be considered perennial visitors as there are small numbers present each summer; *habitat*—estuaries, mud flats, salt-water marshes, margins of rivers, lakes, and ponds; *range in California*—length of state.

CURLEW SANDPIPER *(Calidris ferruginea)*
Seasonal status—accidental; *note*—two records: one at Rodeo Lagoon, Marin County, Sept. 7, 1966 and one at Pescadero, San Mateo County, Sept. 17, 1972. Photograph.

DUNLIN *(Calidris alpina)*
Seasonal status—spring and fall migrant and winter visitor, October to May; *habitat*—estuaries, mud flats, salt-water marshes; *range in California*—length of state; *note*—fall transient and winter visitors arrive later than other sandpipers and reach very large populations in late fall and winter.

SEMIPALMATED SANDPIPER *(Calidris pusillus)*
Seasonal status—accidental or possibly casual visitor or spring (early May) and fall transient; *habitat*—mud flats, estuaries, sandbars; *range in California*—eight of

eleven California records are for the Salton Sea in spring; two of the records are coastal and occurred in fall; the additional record is for inland in spring; *note—* may be a regular but very rare transient easily overlooked because of similarity to Western Sandpiper.

WESTERN SANDPIPER *(Calidris mauri)*
*Seasonal status—*common spring and fall transient and winter visitor, July to May; *habitat—*estuaries, mud flats, salt-water marshes, shores of lakes, ponds, and rivers; *range in California—*length of state.

Western Sandpiper

SANDERLING *(Calidris alba)*
*Seasonal status—*common spring and fall transient and winter visitor, August to May; most abundant during migration and small numbers are frequently noted in summer; *habitat—*primarily sea beaches but also occasionally found on reefs, breakwaters, and tidal mud flats; *range in California—*length of state.

SHORT-BILLED DOWITCHER *(Limnodromus griseus)*
*Seasonal status—*primarily a spring and fall transient and winter visitor, July to May; small numbers occasionally linger through the summer in southern California; *habitat—*estuaries, mud flats, salt-water marshes and less frequently in fresh-water habitats; *range in California—*length of state; *note—*probably occurs with greater regularity in salt-water habitats than fresh as opposed to the very similar Long-billed Dowitcher.

LONG-BILLED DOWITCHER *(Limnodromus scolopaceus)*
*Seasonal status—*primarily a spring and fall transient and winter visitor, July to May; small numbers occasionally linger through the summer in southern California; *range in California—*length of state; *note—*this species prefers fresh-water habitats and is therefore the more common inland dowitcher in the Imperial and Central valleys during spring migration.

STILT SANDPIPER *(Micropalma himantopus)*

Seasonal status—rare transient everywhere in state except at south end of Salton Sea where they are regular but uncommon spring and fall transients and winter visitors, August to late April; *habitat*—mud flats, borders of lakes, sloughs, and ponds; *range in California*—primarily the Salton Sea, at the south end; very rare on the coast.

BUFF-BREASTED SANDPIPER *(Tryngites subruficollis)*

Seasonal status—accidental; *note*—five records: one at Morro Bay, San Luis Obispo County, Sept. 14, 1923; one at Furnace Creek Ranch, Inyo County, July 1-5, 1935; two at Goleta, Santa Barbara County, Sept. 10-26, 1964; one at Carlsbad, San Diego County, Sept. 16, 1967; and one on the Palos Verdes Peninsula, Los Angeles County, Sept. 5-17, 1971. Specimen.

MARBLED GODWIT *(Limosa fedoa)*

Seasonal status—common spring and fall transient and winter visitor, July to May; *habitat*—estuaries, mud flats, salt-water marshes, sea beaches, and wet meadows; *range in California*—length of state; *note*—occasionally seen in summer; suspected of breeding in northeastern portion.

Marbled Godwits

HUDSONIAN GODWIT *(Limosa haemastica)*

Seasonal status—accidental; *habitat*—as for other godwits; *note*—one record: one bird at Arcata, Humboldt County, Aug. 9-10, 1973. Photograph.

BAR-TAILED GODWIT *(Limosa lapponica)*

Seasonal status—accidental; *note*—one record: one bird at Arcata, Humboldt County, July 11-17, 1968. Specimen.

RUFF *(Philomachus pugnax)*
Seasonal status—very casual visitor, September to April; at least 16 records from
1961 to 1972; *habitat*—mud flats, margins of sloughs and ponds; *range in California*—recorded from Siskiyou County to San Diego County and most records are
from coastal areas during the fall. Specimen.

Avocets and Stilts

AMERICAN AVOCET *(Recurvirostra americana)*
Seasonal status—summer visitor in northern and northeastern portions; resident
in southern half of state but population from northern areas moves southward
in fall and some birds leave the state for the winter; do not normally winter
north of San Francisco area in any numbers and large numbers winter in southern California; *habitat*—estuaries, mud flats, and shallow pools for feeding; interior alkaline lakes and fresh-water ponds and sloughs for nesting; *range in California*—for *breeding,* length of state.

BLACK-NECKED STILT *(Himantopus mexicanus)*
Seasonal status—primarily a summer visitor from April to October; birds in the
extreme southern portion (as at the Salton Sea) are resident or at least occur
there throughout the year—it is uncertain whether they are the same individuals
or not; small numbers winter on coast of southern California; *habitat*—margins
of shallow pools, salt, fresh, or brackish; along borders of sloughs and ponds;
range in California—length of state, but not as *breeder* north of about San Francisco.

Black-necked Stilt

American Avocet—winter plumage

Phalaropes

RED PHALAROPE *(Phalaropus fulicarius)*

Seasonal status—primarily a pure transient, spring and fall; majority of spring birds pass north in late April and May and southbound birds occur mostly from late September to early December; *habitat*—primarily open sea well out from shore but flocks are sometimes noted close to land and occasionally even in bays and coastal lagoons; a few sometimes can be found among the large flocks of Northern Phalaropes on bays and ponds; *range in California*—length of state.

*Wilson's Phalarope
—female*

WILSON'S PHALAROPE *(Steganopus tricolor)*

Seasonal status—in non-breeding areas it is a spring and fall transient; during spring migration (late April through May) it is less common than during fall migration (July to October); summer resident in breeding areas; *habitat*—during non-breeding season, coastal lagoons, salt-water ponds, and estuaries; for *breeding*—fresh-water marshes and ponds; *range in California*—during migration, from about Sonoma County south; for *breeding,* northeastern Great Basin region south to Inyo County, north-central portion in Siskiyou County, and portions of San Joaquin Valley.

NORTHERN PHALAROPE *(Lobipes lobatus)*

Seasonal status—common pure transient, spring and fall; spring migration occurs chiefly during April and May and fall migration July to November; *habitat*—coastal waters and less often, far at sea; bays, lagoons, estuaries, salt-water ponds; *range in California*—coastwise, length of state.

Jaegers and Skuas

POMARINE JAEGER *(Stercorarius pomarinus)*
Seasonal status–primarily a transient, spring (March and April) and fall (August to November) but small numbers remain in California waters during the winter; *habitat*–open sea; *range in California*–coastwise, length of state; *note*–greater numbers appear during fall migration and this is the commonest jaeger seen on the open sea.

Pomarine Jaeger

PARASITIC JAEGER *(Stercorarius parasiticus)*
Seasonal status–primarily a transient, spring (March to May) and fall (July to November), but frequently seen off southern California during winter; *habitat*–seacoast, sometimes flying in over the dunes to forage in the coastal lagoons among the assembled gulls and terns; *range in California*–length of state coastwise; *note*–this is the commonest jaeger normally seen close to the coast and from the shore; numbers are greater in fall than spring.

LONG-TAILED JAEGER *(Stercorarius longicaudus)*
Seasonal status–casual pure transient in fall; *habitat*–open sea; *range in California*–coastwise, length of state; *note*–most records fall between July and October and are from observations made well out to sea.

SKUA *(Catharacta skua)*
Seasonal status–very rare transient, spring and fall; spring records are from February to May and are very few; most fall records occur in September and October; *habitat*–open sea; *range in California*–coastwise, length of state with most records from Monterey Bay.

Gulls and Terns

GLAUCOUS GULL *(Larus hyperboreus)*
Seasonal status—rare winter visitor, November to April; *habitat*—seacoast, bays, estuaries, garbage dumps; *range in California*—length of state although occurs more frequently in northern portion.

GLAUCOUS-WINGED GULL *(Larus glaucescens)*
Seasonal status—common winter visitor, October to late April; *habitat*—seacoast, bays, sea beaches, garbage dumps; *range in California*—coastwise, length of state although increasingly more common to the north.

WESTERN GULL *(Larus occidentalis)*
Seasonal status—common resident; *habitat*—offshore islands, seacoast, sea beaches, bays, lagoons, estuaries; *range in California*—coastwise, length of state; *breeds* on offshore islands; also on mainland sea cliffs as far south as Morro Bay, San Luis Obispo County; *note*—"Yellow-legged" race from Gulf of California is an uncommon but probably regular post-breeding visitor to the Salton Sea during summer in small numbers.

Western Gull

HERRING GULL *(Larus argentatus)*
Seasonal status—winter visitor, September to May; *habitat*—seacoast, sea beaches, estuaries, bays, lakes, garbage dumps; *range in California*—length of state but commoner in northern half.

THAYER'S GULL *(Larus thayeri)*
Seasonal status—rare to uncommon winter visitor; *habitat*—seacoast, sea beaches, estuaries, bays and harbors, sewage outfalls, lagoons, and lakes near seacoast; *range in California*—has been recorded coastwise length of state but because of difficulty of identification, actual range is uncertain; *note*—this gull has recently been elevated to full species status from a subspecies of Herring Gull.

CALIFORNIA GULL *(Larus californicus)*

Seasonal status—common spring and fall transient and winter visitor, July to May; summer visitor to Modoc Plateau where they breed in compact colonies on some of the large lakes; *habitat*—most diverse for any of the California gulls: open sea, seacoast, sea beaches, estuaries, salt-water marshes, bays and harbors, garbage dumps, lakes, rivers, fresh-water marshes, flooded agricultural lands, greenswards; *range in California*—as *breeder* in northeastern plateau region; at other times, length of state; *note*—for an inland-nesting gull, this species ventures further out to sea than any of the others except such pelagic gulls as Sabine's and Black-legged Kittiwake; in a sense this species is resident since there are always large numbers in the state in any season.

RING-BILLED GULL *(Larus delawarensis)*

Seasonal status—common winter visitor or even perennial visitor; numbers diminish during June and July as some birds move northeastward and out of the state; *habitat*—seacoast, estuaries, sea beaches, bays and harbors, fresh-water rivers, lakes, ponds, and marshes, irrigated fields and freshly-plowed land; *range in California*—length of state, but *breeds* at a few lakes in northeastern portion of state.

BLACK-TAILED GULL *(Larus crassirostris)*

Seasonal status—accidental; *note*—one record: an adult female was collected at San Diego Bay, San Diego County, Nov. 26, 1954. It should be noted that some doubt exists as to the true status of this Japanese gull in California since there is a strong possibility that it arrived in San Diego Bay in conjunction with a U.S. naval vessel from Japanese waters. Specimen.

MEW GULL *(Larus canus)*

Seasonal status—winter visitor, October to April; *habitat*—seacoast, sea beaches, bays and harbors, mud flats near seacoast; *range in California*—coastwise, length of state; *note*—these gulls arrive in northern California in October and they slowly drift southward not arriving in southern California until November or early December.

BLACK-HEADED GULL *(Larus ridibundus)*

Seasonal status—accidental; *note*—two records: one near Richmond, Alameda County, Jan. 23-24, 1954 and one at Arcata, Humboldt County, July 16-17, 1972. Photograph.

LAUGHING GULL *(Larus atricilla)*

Seasonal status—possibly now a post-breeding visitor to the Salton Sea during July and August; elsewhere, accidental; *range in California*—primarily the south end of the Salton Sea; there are a few southern coastal records; this species formerly *bred* in small numbers on islands at the south end of the Salton Sea.

FRANKLIN'S GULL *(Larus pipixcan)*

Seasonal status—casual visitor with most records during spring and fall; *habitat*—estuaries, bays, mud flats, lagoons, fresh-water lakes; *range in California*—chiefly the southern portion and southwest coast; many records from the Salton Sea; a number of winter records from as far north as San Francisco.

BONAPARTE'S GULL *(Larus philadelphia)*
Seasonal status—spring and fall transient and winter visitor, September to June; *habitat*—open sea, seacoast, bays and harbors, estuaries, mud flats, larger lakes and rivers; *range in California*—length of state; *note*—winters in large numbers off southern California coast; especially attracted to sewage outfalls.

LITTLE GULL *(Larus minutus)*
Seasonal status—accidental; *note*—two records: one near Mecca, Riverside County, Nov. 16–21, 1968 and one at Redondo Beach, Los Angeles County, Dec. 22–25, 1969. Photograph.

HEERMANN'S GULL *(Larus heermanni)*
Seasonal status—post-breeding summer and fall visitor; perennial visitor in that some birds are present in coastal southern California throughout the year; numbers diminish between January and March as most of the population returns south to the Mexican nesting islands; *habitat*—seacoast, sea beaches, estuaries, lagoons, bays and harbors; *range in California*—length of state along the seacoast including the offshore islands.

BLACK-LEGGED KITTIWAKE *(Rissa tridactyla)*
Seasonal status—irregular visitor during winter, September to May; *habitat*—open sea, seacoast, and occasionally bays and harbors; *range in California*—coastwise, length of state; *note*—occurs every winter but abundant during some years; a few birds have been noted throughout the summer on the southern California coast.

SABINE'S GULL *(Xema sabinii)*
Seasonal status—pure transient spring (mid-April to late May) and fall (mid-August to late October); *habitat*—open sea; extraordinary elsewhere; *range in California*—well offshore, length of state.

GULL-BILLED TERN *(Gelochelidon nilotica)*
Seasonal status—uncommon summer visitor; *habitat*—feeds along shores of Salton Sea and hunts for grasshoppers and crickets over freshly plowed fields; *range in California*—south end of Salton Sea where small breeding colony exists at mouth of New River; *note*—present from late March to September; one winter record.

FORSTER'S TERN *(Sterna forsteri)*
Seasonal status—resident although there is some withdrawal to south for the winter; *habitat*—seacoast, estuaries, bays and harbors, larger rivers, and freshwater and alkaline lakes; *range in California*—breeds on some lakes in northeastern plateau region, near San Diego, and in a few fresh-water marshes of Central Valley; otherwise length of state but not found north of Marin County in winter.

COMMON TERN *(Sterna hirundo)*
Seasonal status—primarily a pure transient, spring (mid-April to early June) and fall (late July to mid-November) although a few winter in southern California each year; *habitat*—seacoast, estuaries, bays and harbors, lagoons; *range in California*—coastwise, length of state; *note*—more abundant in fall.

ARCTIC TERN *(Sterna paradisaea)*
Seasonal status—uncommon pure transient, spring (mid and late May) and fall

(late August to mid-October); *habitat*—open sea; extraordinary elsewhere; *range in California*—coastwise well offshore, length of state. *Note*—commoner in fall.

LEAST TERN *(Sterna albifrons)*

Seasonal status—summer visitor, mid-April to mid-October; *habitat*—seacoast, estuaries, bays and harbors; *range in California*—formerly *bred* as far north as Monterey County but now only as far north as Ventura County; wanders north to San Francisco.

ROYAL TERN *(Thalasseus maximus)*

Seasonal status—primarily a post-breeding late summer, fall, and early winter visitor from Mexico; most birds depart for south by end of January although they have been recorded every month of the year; *habitat*—seacoast, offshore islands, bays, and estuaries; *range in California*—coastwise north to about Marin County; first recorded *breeding* in California, near San Diego during May–June 1959 and again in 1960; no breeding records since then.

ELEGANT TERN *(Thalasseus elegans)*

Seasonal status—most birds are post-breeding summer and fall visitors from Mexico; *habitat*—seacoast, offshore islands, estuaries, large bays and harbors, mud flats; *range in California*—recorded as far north as at least to Sonoma County; first recorded *breeding* in United States was near San Diego April–May, 1959; has bred there intermittently ever since; *note*—prior to 1950 this species was considered quite rare in California and there is little doubt in view of breeding range expansion that this species has truly exhibited a range and population expansion within recent years; thousands sometimes reach Monterey County.

Caspian Tern

CASPIAN TERN *(Hydroprogne caspia)*

Seasonal status—perennial visitor although numbers much reduced in winter; *habitat*—estuaries, bays, harbors, large rivers and lakes, lagoons; *range in California*—length of state; has *bred* from Siskiyou to Imperial counties but now much reduced as breeder because of disappearance of suitable fresh-water marsh habitat; *note*—very rare in northern California in winter.

BLACK TERN *(Chlidonias niger)*

Seasonal status—primarily a spring and fall transient and summer visitor, mid-April to early October; *habitat*—primarily fresh-water lakes, marshes, and ponds although sometimes noted at coastal lagoons and along the seacoast; *range in California*—recorded as *breeding* (at least formerly) from northern and north-eastern California south through Central Valley; *note*—these terns occur from April through summer near the south end of the Salton Sea but no evidence of their nesting there has been obtained; thousands spend the summer near the north end of the Sea as well.

Skimmers

BLACK SKIMMER *(Rynchops niger)*

Seasonal status—very rare post-breeding summer and fall visitor from Mexico; *habitat*—seacoast, shallow bays and estuaries; *range in California*—north to Bodega Bay, Sonoma County; *note*—first recorded in state at mouth of Santa Ana River, Orange County, Sept. 8, 1962; first recorded at Salton Sea near mouth of Whitewater River, Riverside County, July 3, 1968; numerous records since then and first *breeding* at the mouth of the New River at the south end of the Salton Sea, July 1972, indicates a positive range expansion in recent years.

Black Skimmers

Auks, Murres, and Puffins

COMMON MURRE *(Uria aalge)*

Seasonal status—resident; *habitat*—seacoast, offshore islands; *range in California*—length of state but uncommon south of about Monterey County; *breeds* from about Humboldt County south to Marin County and formerly as far south as Prince Islet off San Miguel Island, Santa Barbara County; *note*—breeding metropolis is probably Farallon Islands and other breeding islets are widely scattered and few.

THICK-BILLED MURRE *(Uria lomvia)*
 Seasonal status—accidental; *note*—six records all from or very near to Monterey Bay: 1964, 1965, 1966, 1968, 1969, and 1972 (4 records in fall, others from February and April). Specimen.

Thick-billed Murre

PIGEON GUILLEMOT *(Cepphus columba)*
 Seasonal status—resident; *habitat*—during breeding season, vicinity of coastal sea cliffs and offshore islands; rest of year, far at sea or scattered along seacoast; *range in California*—length of state, but very rare along southern California seacoast; *breeds* from Del Norte County south to about Avila, San Luis Obispo County, on the mainland coast and south to the Santa Barbara Islands offshore.

MARBLED MURRELET *(Brachyramphus marmoratus)*
 Seasonal status—probably resident, although numbers increase during winter; nowhere common; *habitat*—open sea, seacoast; *range in California*—probably *breeds* inland from immediate coast in Humboldt and Del Norte counties but nest not yet found in North America.

KITTLITZ'S MURRELET *(Brachyramphus brevirostris)*
 Seasonal status—accidental; *note*—one record: one at La Jolla, San Diego County, Aug. 16, 1969. Specimen.

XANTUS' MURRELET *(Endomychura hypoleuca)*
 Seasonal status—resident; *habitat*—offshore islands, seacoast; *range in California*—*breeds* north to at least Anacapa Island on offshore islands; in late summer and fall ranges as far north as Monterey Bay, north of which it is very rare; numbers decline in winter as birds move south and out to sea.

CRAVERI'S MURRELET *(Endomychura craveri)*
Seasonal status—uncommon to rare (possibly irregular in numbers) post-breeding summer and fall visitor from Mexico; *habitat*—open sea; *range in California*—north to Monterey Bay; *note*—probably occurs each year in varying numbers but difficulty of identification makes status uncertain.

ANCIENT MURRELET *(Synthliboramphus antiquus)*
Seasonal status—uncommon and irregular (as to numbers) winter visitor, October to April; *habitat*—open sea, seacoast; *range in California*—length of state.

CASSIN'S AUKLET *(Ptychoramphus aleuticus)*
Seasonal status—resident; *habitat*—open sea; *range in California*—length of state; *breeds* on offshore islands and islets from Humboldt County south to Santa Barbara Islands, Santa Barbara County; metropolis for breeding is Farallon Islands.

PARAKEET AUKLET *(Cyclorrhynchus psittacula)*
Seasonal status—very rare winter visitor or casual visitor; *habitat*—open sea, seacoast; *range in California*—length of state.

RHINOCEROS AUKLET *(Cerorhinca monocerata)*
Seasonal status—most are winter visitors, October to April; *habitat*—open sea; *range in California*—length of state; *note*—at times abundant; a small population *breeds* on Castle Island, Del Norte County.

HORNED PUFFIN *(Fratercula corniculata)*
Seasonal status—very rare winter or casual visitor; *habitat*—open sea; *range in California*—length of state, but most records are north of Monterey including some summer records and are of dead remains; live birds sighted in 1971, 1972, and 1973.

TUFTED PUFFIN *(Lunda cirrhata)*
Seasonal status—resident, although population disperses away from breeding islands during non-breeding season; *habitat*—offshore islands, open sea; *range in California*—*breeds* or has bred on offshore islands and islets south to Anacapa Island, Ventura County; has occurred length of state; *note*—very rare away from breeding islands during breeding season; at other times, birds move far out to sea.

Pigeons and Doves

BAND-TAILED PIGEON *(Columba fasciata)*
Seasonal status—resident; *habitat*—Transition Zone pine and oak forests, oak woodlands, and oak-lined canyons; *range in California*—length of state, west of Sierra-Cascade axis. *Breeds.*

ROCK DOVE *(Columba livia)*—INTRODUCED into California
Seasonal status—resident; *habitat*—cities, towns, suburbs, farms; *range in California*—length of state; *breeds* wherever it occurs but some wilder pigeons may occasionally be found nesting on remote sea cliffs.

WHITE-WINGED DOVE *(Zenaida asiatica)*

Seasonal status—primarily a summer visitor, early April to October; *habitat*—Sonoran and Colorado Deserts; *range in California*—southeastern desert areas, but stragglers reach the coast in fall and winter; recorded north to Humboldt County. *Breeds* only in desert habitat.

MOURNING DOVE *(Zenaida macroura)*

Seasonal status—resident, but many birds move south in fall and return in spring; *habitat*—*breeds* in oak woodland, savannah, farms, ranches, cities, suburbs, desert; *range in California*—length of state.

Mourning Dove

SPOTTED DOVE *(Streptopelia chinensis)*—INTRODUCED into California

Seasonal status—resident; *habitat*—cities, towns, and suburbs; *range in California*—metropolis of population is Los Angeles but widespread in Ventura, Orange, San Diego, and western Riverside counties. *Breeds.*

RINGED TURTLE DOVE *(Streptopelia risoria)*—INTRODUCED into California

Seasonal status—resident; *habitat*—city parks; *range in California*—confined chiefly to city parks in Los Angeles as at Pershing Square, MacArthur Park, L.A. City Hall and Public Library grounds, and north Olvera Street; occasionally found in suburban areas. *Breeds.*

GROUND DOVE *(Columbina passerina)*

Seasonal status—resident; *habitat*—riparian woodlands, desert thickets, orchards, edges of agricultural land where brush is thick; *range in California*—primarily lower Colorado River Valley, Imperial Valley, but has spread northwestward in Coachella Valley, Orange County, and sparingly into western Riverside County. *Breeds.*

INCA DOVE *(Scardafella inca)*

Seasonal status—probably resident but very local and uncommon; *range in California*—*breeds* at settlement on California side of Colorado River at Parker Dam, San Bernardino County; *note*—a few records for southern California.

Cuckoos and Roadrunners

YELLOW-BILLED CUCKOO *(Coccyzus americanus)*
Seasonal status—rare summer visitor; *habitat*—riparian woodlands with dense tangles of vines; *range in California*—as migrant, almost unknown away from lower Colorado River Valley today; status uncertain as numbers have diminished in recent years despite intensification of field birding; probably still *breeds* in a few localities in San Joaquin and Sacramento valleys; *note*—most frequently observed as spring transient in lower Colorado River Valley during late May and early June.

Black-billed Cuckoo

BLACK-BILLED CUCKOO *(Coccyzus erythrophthalmus)*
Seasonal status—accidental; *note*—one certain record: one bird at Point Reyes, Marin County, Sept. 22, 1965. Photograph.

ROADRUNNER *(Geococcyx californianus)*
Seasonal status—resident; *habitat*—desert where brush is thicker, edges of chaparral, edges of agricultural land; *range in California*—today, primarily southern half of state at lower elevations; east of Sierras to northern Inyo County, west of Sierras north to north end of Sacramento Valley, and in coastal regions occasionally north to Humboldt County; *note*—becoming increasingly scarcer in northern portions of its range. *Breeds.*

Barn Owls

BARN OWL *(Tyto alba)*
Seasonal status—resident; *habitat*—must have open fields, meadows, lawns, desert, and even short-grass marshy meadows and beaches for hunting in addition to suitable trees, caves, tunnels, mines, buildings, bridges, and vertical holes for roosting and *nesting; range in California*—length of state at low elevations.

Barn Owl

Typical Owls

SCREECH OWL *(Otus asio)*

Seasonal status—resident; *habitat*—broken woodland of oaks, conifers, or mixed hardwoods and conifers, savannah, riparian woodland, piñon pines and junipers, suburbs, small towns, farms, and ranches; *range in California*—length of state at lower elevations, except in north central portion and most of eastern and southeastern portion; a race occurs in the Inyo region of Owens Valley and mountains eastward to edge of Death Valley. *Breeds.*

FLAMMULATED OWL *(Otus flammeolus)*

Seasonal status—primarily a summer resident; *habitat*—requires Ponderosa Pine forests or other mixed coniferous forests of Transition Life Zone; *range in California*—incompletely known because of retiring nature of this owl; has been found in northern inner Coast Range, Sierra Nevada, Transverse Ranges, and Peninsular Ranges south to Palomar Mountain, San Diego County; also occurs in some higher desert ranges as at Clark Mountain, San Bernardino County. *Breeds.*

GREAT HORNED OWL *(Bubo virginianus)*

Seasonal status—resident; *habitat*—broken woodland of oaks or coniferous-deciduous forest, thickly-wooded canyons, desert, riparian woodland; *range in California*—length of state. *Breeds.*

SNOWY OWL *(Nyctea scandiaca)*

Seasonal status—accidental, winter; *note*—known to have reached California during the winters of 1896–97, 1908–09, 1916–17, and 1966–67 (near Arcata, Humboldt County). Specimen.

PYGMY OWL *(Glaucidium gnoma)*

Seasonal status—resident; *habitat*—woodland, mixed coniferous and deciduous woods, edges of coniferous forest; most common in the Transition Life Zone; *range in California*—length of state but absent from northeast plateau region, Central Valley, southeastern deserts, and south coast region. *Breeds.*

ELF OWL *(Micrathene whitneyi)*

Seasonal status—very rare summer visitor; *habitat*—riparian woodland, oases, Saguaro Cacti; *range in California*—formerly lower Colorado River Valley; now only known from a few oases in northern Colorado Desert. *Breeds.*

BURROWING OWL *(Speotyto cunicularia)*

Seasonal status—resident; *habitat*—dry, open, rolling hills, grassland, desert floor, agricultural land, open bare ground; *range in California*—length of state except mountains and northwest humid coastal forest; occurs on larger offshore islands. *Breeds.*

SPOTTED OWL *(Strix occidentalis)*

Seasonal status—resident; *habitat*—densely forested shady canyons, dense coniferous forest; *range in California*—three large disjunct populations located in the northwest portion of the state, the main Sierra Nevada, and the Transverse and Peninsular Ranges south to Palomar Mountain, San Diego County; a small isolated population exists in Muir Woods, Marin County. *Breeds.*

GREAT GRAY OWL *(Strix nebulosa)*

Seasonal status—rare resident; *habitat*—dense fir forests of the upper Transition and Canadian Life Zones preferably interspersed with meadows for hunting; *range in California*—central and northern Sierra Nevada and a few old records for north central California in the Central Valley; occasionally occurs in Lower Klamath Basin, Siskiyou County, in winter; *note*—most frequently seen in the Canadian Zone forests along the borders of the meadows in Yosemite National Park. *Breeds.*

LONG-EARED OWL *(Asio otus)*

Seasonal status—resident but populations shift about in unknown pattern; *habitat*—riparian woodlands and stands of live oaks along watercourses; *range in California*—length of state. *Breeds.*

Long-eared Owl

SHORT-EARED OWL *(Asio flammeus)*

Seasonal status—resident, winter visitor, and transient; *habitat*—salt-water marshes, tall grass meadows, fresh-water marshes, agricultural lands; *range in California*—for *breeding,* formerly at least, length of state; now known primarily as a non-breeder.

SAW-WHET OWL *(Aegolius acadicus)*

Seasonal status—uncommon resident; *habitat*—dense coniferous forest, broken woodland or broken forest; *range in California*—poorly understood; known from Cascades, Sierra Nevada, and Transverse and Peninsular Ranges in southern California; has appeared in lowland brush and desert areas and coastal locations. *Breeds.*

Goatsuckers

WHIP-POOR-WILL *(Caprimulgus vociferus)*

Seasonal status—very rare and local summer visitor; *habitat*—open pine and oak woodland near streamsides; *range in California*—birds of the Arizona or "Stephen's" race of the Whip-poor-will were first discovered near Lake Fulmor near Mt. San Jacinto, Riverside County, May 2, 1968, and were seen and heard again in 1969, 1970, 1971, 1972, and 1973. It is presumed that they *bred* in 1972. An "Eastern" Whip-poor-will was netted on Pt. Loma, San Diego County, Nov. 14, 1970. Photograph.

POOR-WILL *(Phalaenoptilus nuttallii)*

Seasonal status—primarily a summer visitor, April to November in the northern half of the state; some may over-winter by hibernating; one race is resident in the southeastern part of the state; *habitat*—chaparral, piñon-juniper woodland, brushy slopes, desert washes and desert floor with scattered bushes; *range in California*—length of state except humid northwestern portion and Central Valley. *Breeds.*

Common Nighthawk—female

COMMON NIGHTHAWK *(Chordeiles minor)*
Seasonal status—summer visitor and transient, April to end of October; *habitat*—coniferous forest of Transition and lower Canadian Life Zones; forages over lakes, valleys, meadows, and rivers; *range in California*—for *breeding,* Cascades, Sierra Nevada, and in the Transverse Ranges, the San Bernardino Mountains.

LESSER NIGHTHAWK *(Chordeiles acutipennis)*
Seasonal status—summer visitor, February to October; *habitat*—drier portions of southern half of state preferring floors of deserts and drier valleys with sparse vegetation; *range in California*—southern portion of state including Colorado and Mojave Deserts, San Joaquin Valley, and southwest coastal region. *Breeds.*

Swifts

BLACK SWIFT *(Cypseloides niger)*
Seasonal status—summer visitor and transient, April to October; *habitat*—for nesting, sea cliffs and steep-walled canyons with nearby waterfalls; *range in California*—known *breeding* areas include San Jacinto and San Bernardino Mountains in southern California, sea cliffs in San Mateo, Monterey, and Santa Cruz counties, Berry Creek Falls, Santa Cruz County, and behind waterfalls in MacArthur-Burney Falls State Park, and Yosemite, King's Canyon, and Sequoia National Parks.

CHIMNEY SWIFT *(Chaetura pelagica)*
Seasonal status—casual or very rare spring pure transient; *range in California*—most of the records are from southern California; *note*—of 11 records (1930, 1968, 1969, 1970, 1971, 1972, 1973), ten occurred in late May and early June and one occurred May 6 (1930).

VAUX'S SWIFT *(Chaetura vauxi)*
Seasonal status—summer visitor and and transient, late April to October; over most of the state these swifts are transients; *habitat*—for *breeding,* forests of Douglas Fir and Coast Redwood; in migration they follow desert and interior valleys, mountain ridges, and the coastline; *range in California*—length of state in migration; *breeds* in narrow coastal belt from Del Norte County south to Santa Cruz County.

White-throated Swift

WHITE-THROATED SWIFT *(Aeronautes saxatalis)*
Seasonal status—resident and summer visitor; larger part of population leaves state for winter (October to March); *habitat*—forages over deserts, foothills, mountains, seacoast; roosts in deep crevices in cliffs, canyons, bluffs, and rocks; *range in California*—more arid regions of the state east and south of the northwest humid coastal belt. *Breeds.*

Hummingbirds

BLACK-CHINNED HUMMINGBIRD *(Archilochus alexandri)*
Seasonal status—summer visitor, April to September; *habitat*—riparian woodlands, brush-bordered oak canyons, orchards, edges of agricultural land where bordered by trees; *range in California*—southern California, west of the deserts, San Joaquin and Sacramento valleys, Coast Range north to about San Francisco. *Breeds.*

Black-chinned Hummingbird—female

COSTA'S HUMMINGBIRD *(Calypte costae)*
Seasonal status—primarily a summer resident, late February to September; some winter in the Colorado and Sonoran Deserts of the southeastern region; *habitat*—primarily Colorado, Mojave, and Sonoran Deserts but also occurs in drier foothills of brush and chaparral in the interior valleys; *range in California*—*breeds* in southern portion of state including southeastern deserts, coastal region north to Santa Barbara County, and drier western edge of San Joaquin Valley north to Stanislaus County; recorded breeding at Palos Verdes Peninsula, Los Angeles County, as early (?) as Dec. 1.

ANNA'S HUMMINGBIRD *(Calypte anna)*
Seasonal status—common resident; *habitat*—chaparral, broken woodland, or mixed woodland and chaparral; *range in California*—southwestern region west of the deserts north to about San Francisco; length of Central Valley; *note*—a northward and up-mountain population movement occurs in midsummer. *Breeds.*

BROAD-TAILED HUMMINGBIRD *(Selasphorus platycercus)*

Seasonal status—uncommon summer resident; *habitat*—piñon-juniper woodland; *range in California*—this Rocky Mountain and Great Basin hummingbird is normally found only in the White, Panamint, Clark, and New York Mountains along the eastern border of the state; a male was at Big Pine in the Owens Valley, Inyo County, May 28, 1972, and another male at Arrastre Creek in the San Bernardino Mountains May 13, 1972, which may indicate *breeding* elsewhere in the state.

RUFOUS HUMMINGBIRD *(Selasphorus rufus)*

Seasonal status—primarily a spring and fall transient, but summer visitor to humid coastal coniferous forest; spring flight passes through southern California from late January to about mid-April; fall flight occurs primarily during July and August; *habitat*—for *breeding,* broken Coast Redwood and Douglas Fir forests; *range in California*—length of state west of the deserts, Sierra Nevada, and Cascades; *note*—southbound migrants move up-mountain (even to 13,200 feet) in the Sierra Nevada and southward through the mountain meadows of the upper Transition and Canadian Life Zones.

ALLEN'S HUMMINGBIRD *(Selasphorus sasin)*

Seasonal status—one race is migratory during spring (mid-January to mid-March), is a summer resident until southbound migration occurs during July and August, and normally does not winter; one race is non-migratory; *habitat*—coastal chaparral where there are ravines and canyons for breeding; some southbound migrants also utilize mountain meadows of the Sierra Nevada and other ranges; *range in California*—coastwise, nearly length of state; *breeds* from Santa Barbara County north to Del Norte County; non-migratory race inhabits San Clemente, Santa Catalina, Santa Cruz, and Santa Rosa Islands as well as Palos Verdes Peninsula, Los Angeles County.

CALLIOPE HUMMINGBIRD *(Stellula calliope)*

Seasonal status—as lowland transient during April and May; as summer visitor to montane forests during May to early September; *habitat*—during spring migration, lowlands and chaparral west of the deserts; fall migrants utilize mountain meadows as they move south; breeds in the montane forests of Transition and Canadian Life Zones as well as lower levels of subalpine forest; *range in California*—length of state exclusive of southeastern deserts and northwestern humid coniferous forests; *breeds* in Cascades, Warner Mountains, Sierra Nevada, White Mountains, Panamint Mountains, and the Transverse and part of the Peninsular Ranges in southern California, *note*—most of the males leave their breeding areas by the end of June.

BROAD-BILLED HUMMINGBIRD *(Cynanthus latirostris)*

Seasonal status—accidental; *note*—five records: one at San Diego, San Diego County, "mid-November 1961 to mid-March 1962"; one near Imperial Beach, San Diego County, Oct. 14, 1962; two near Imperial Beach, San Diego County, Nov. 9, 1963; one at Redlands, San Bernardino County, January 2–mid-February 1964; and one at Pacific Grove, Monterey County, April 21, 1969. Photograph.

Kingfishers

BELTED KINGFISHER *(Megaceryle alcyon)*
Seasonal status—resident but there is a north-south spring and fall shift in population as well as an up- and down-mountain movement; *habitat*—seacoast, estuaries, bays, harbors, offshore islands, fresh-water lakes, rivers, streams, and ponds; *range in California*—length of state west of the southeastern deserts; *breeds.*

Belted Kingfisher—male

Woodpeckers

COMMON FLICKER *(Colaptes auratus):* three types of flickers formerly classified as three distinct species have been combined into one species; hybrids between "Yellow-shafted" and "Red-shafted" are not rare.

"Yellow-shafted" Flicker
Seasonal status—rare winter visitor, October to April; *habitat*—open woodland, savannah; *range in California*—length of state.

"Red-shafted" Flicker (formerly *Colaptes cafer*)
Seasonal status—common resident plus some winter visitors from north; *habitat*—open woodland, savannah; *range in California*—length of state except Mojave and Colorado Deserts and southern portion of Great Basin Desert. *Breeds.*

"Gilded" Flicker (formerly *Colaptes chrysoides*)
Seasonal status—uncommon to rare resident; *habitat*—Sonoran Desert and lower Colorado River Valley; *range in California*—extreme eastern Riverside and Imperial counties; *breeds; note*—for some inexplicable reason, this form has all but disappeared from California in recent years except near Cima, San Bernardino County.

PILEATED WOODPECKER *(Dryocopus pileatus)*
Seasonal status—resident, not common; *habitat*—coniferous forest; *range in Califor-*

nia–northern portion of state in Coast Range (south to Sonoma and Napa counties), Cascades, and Sierra Nevada south to Greenhorn Mountain, Kern County. *Breeds.*

GILA WOODPECKER *(Centurus uropygialis)*

Seasonal status–uncommon to rare resident; *habitat*–riparian woodland, Saguaro Cacti; *range in California*–along Colorado River in eastern Riverside and Imperial counties and Imperial Valley; *note*–now very rare in Imperial Valley and very local in lower Colorado River Valley. *Breeds.*

RED-HEADED WOODPECKER *(Melanerpes erythrocephalus)*

Seasonal status–accidental; *note*–two records: dead remains found at La Puente, Los Angeles County, May 20, 1962 and one bird near Niland, Imperial County, July 17–Aug. 22, 1971. Specimen and photograph.

ACORN WOODPECKER *(Melanerpes formicivorus)*

Seasonal status–common resident; *habitat*–oak woodland or mixed oak and coniferous woodland; *range in California*–*breeds* throughout most of state west of deserts and Sierra Nevada; in Coast Range breeds as far north as Marin County although birds have reached Humboldt County; small numbers occur in Lassen County between Janesville and Susanville; occurs south to Mexican border along western slope of Sierra Nevada and in Coast Range.

LEWIS' WOODPECKER *(Asyndesmus lewis)*

Seasonal status–resident within state but irregular shifts in population occur; *habitat*–oak woodland and savannah, broken forests of deciduous and coniferous trees (primarily pines and oaks); *range in California*–*breeds* from northernmost counties south through Coast Range to San Luis Obispo County and south through Sierra Nevada to Kern County; absent from northwest humid coniferous forest belt of the coastal fog zone; occasionally "invades" southern California in large flights during winter.

YELLOW-BELLIED SAPSUCKER *(Sphyrapicus varius)*

Seasonal status–accidental; *note*–three records: one near Bard, Imperial County, Dec. 18, 1938; one at Imperial Beach, San Diego County, Dec. 20, 1969; one at Scotty's Castle, Inyo County, Oct. 24, 1971. Specimen. *Note*–this species and the two following sapsuckers are considered by some authorities to be of a single species and the three races, collectively called "Yellow-bellied Sapsucker."

RED-NAPED SAPSUCKER *(Sphyrapicus nuchalis)*

Seasonal status–resident and winter visitor; *habitat*–for *breeding,* riparian woodlands of aspens, cottonwoods, and willows; in winter, orchards, riparian woodlands, and mesquite thickets in desert; *range in California*–*breeds* on Modoc Plateau; winters in lower Colorado River Valley and occasionally westward to the coast; *note*–northern summer residents move southward and they are augmented by incoming wintering birds from the north and northeast.

RED-BREASTED SAPSUCKER *(Sphyrapicus ruber)*

Seasonal status–resident within state but winters (October to March) in lowlands; *habitat*–for *breeding,* broken coniferous (montane) forest of Transition Life Zone; *range in California*–for *breeding,* south in Coast Range to Mendocino

County, Cascades east to Warner Mountains, length of Sierra Nevada, Mt. Pinos in Ventura County, and at scattered locations in the Transverse and Peninsular Ranges; winters in lowlands west of the deserts.

Red-naped Sapsucker

WILLIAMSON'S SAPSUCKER *(Sphyrapicus thyroideus)*
~~Seasonal~~ *status*—resident, but some down-mountain drifting in winter, sometimes to seacoast; *habitat*—higher portions of montane forest but especially subalpine forests of Canadian and Hudsonian Life Zones; *range in California*—Siskiyou and Trinity Mountains east to Warner Mountains and south along Sierra Nevada, Mt. Pinos in Ventura County, and Transverse and Peninsular Ranges spottily as far south as Palomar Mountain, San Diego County. *Breeds.*

HAIRY WOODPECKER *(Dendrocopos villosus)*
Seasonal status—resident; *habitat*—montane forest of Transition Life Zone; also broken and mixed coniferous and deciduous forest; *range in California*—length of state except Central Valley and deserts of the eastern and southeastern portions. *Breeds; note*—some down-mountain fall and winter movement to lowlands.

DOWNY WOODPECKER *(Dendrocopos pubescens)*
Seasonal status—resident; *habitat*—riparian woodlands; *range in California*—length of state except eastern slope of Sierras from Lake Tahoe south and entire eastern and southeastern desert areas. *Breeds.*

LADDER-BACKED WOODPECKER *(Dendrocopos scalaris)*
Seasonal status—resident; *habitat*—low and high deserts, piñon-juniper woodlands; *range in California*—Colorado and Mojave Deserts; *note*—*breeding* ranges of this species and Nuttall's Woodpecker overlap at Morongo Valley, San Bernardino County.

NUTTALL'S WOODPECKER *(Dendrocopos nuttallii)*
Seasonal status—common resident; *habitat*—oak woodlands; *range in California*—Coast range north to Mendocino County, interior southern California west of

deserts north to head of Central Valley and along the western foothills of the Sierra Nevada. *Breeds.*

WHITE-HEADED WOODPECKER *(Dendrocopos albolarvatus)*
Seasonal status—resident; *habitat*—montane forests of pine and fir; *range in California*—mountain areas north and west of the Sacramento Valley (on the west side, south to Colusa County) but not including the humid coastal coniferous forest; Warner Mountains south through Cascades and Sierra Nevada to Mt. Pinos in Ventura County; Transverse and Peninsular Ranges south to Palomar Mountain, San Diego County. *Breeds.*

BLACK-BACKED THREE-TOED WOODPECKER *(Picoides arcticus)*
Seasonal status—uncommon to rare resident; *habitat*—Lodgepole Pine forests of subalpine region; primarily the Hudsonian Life Zone; *range in California*—Cascade Mountains and northern and central Sierra Nevada; *note*—occurs less commonly in the Red Fir forests of the Canadian Life Zone. *Breeds.*

Tyrant Flycatchers

EASTERN KINGBIRD *(Tyrannus tyrannus)*
Seasonal status—casual or very rare transient and summer visitor; *habitat*—open country with "edges" of woodland or scattered trees; *range in California*—numerous records scattered throughout the state; possibly *breeding* in northeast portion—Modoc County south to Inyo County; definitely *bred* at Honey Lake, Lassen County, in 1971.

THICK-BILLED KINGBIRD *(Tyrannus crassirostris)*
Seasonal status—accidental; *note*—four records: one near Imperial Beach, San Diego County, Oct. 19, 1965; one at Bonita, San Diego County, Dec. 26–27, 1966; one at Point Loma, San Diego County, Dec. 3, 1966; and another there, Oct. 18–23, 1967. Photograph.

TROPICAL KINGBIRD *(Tyrannus melancholicus)*
Seasonal status—uncommon to rare but regular post-breeding fall visitor; *habitat*—savannah, agricultural areas, open woodlands; *range in California*—primarily near the coast, length of state; *note*—these birds appear late in September, remain through November and presumably depart for the south in early December although there are a number of winter records.

WESTERN KINGBIRD *(Tyrannus verticalis)*
Seasonal status—common transient and summer visitor, late March to September; *habitat*—open country such as savannah, agricultural lands bordered by trees, plains; *range in California*—length of state but absent from northwest coastal forests and southeastern deserts. *Breeds. Note*—no satisfactory winter records.

CASSIN'S KINGBIRD *(Tyrannus vociferans)*
Seasonal status—resident, but of irregular occurrence; *habitat*—dry open savannah country as found in interior valleys west of the deserts; *range in California*—pri-

marily confined to the southwestern coastal region north to about Santa Cruz County on the coast and Alameda County interiorly; also as summer visitor to Providence Mountains in eastern San Bernardino County. *Breeds.*

SCISSOR-TAILED FLYCATCHER *(Muscivora forficata)*
Seasonal status—casual visitor; *habitat*—more or less open country; *range in California*—length of state north to Humboldt County; *note*—rare and irregular.

Scissor-tailed Flycatcher

GREAT CRESTED FLYCATCHER *(Myiarchus crinitus)*
Seasonal status—accidental; *note*—four records: two at Farallon Islands, Sept. 25, 1967; two at Farallon Islands, Oct. 13, 1970; one at Point Fermin, Los Angeles County, Sept. 26, 1970; one at Farallon Islands, Sept. 18, 1971. Specimen.

WIED'S CRESTED FLYCATCHER *(Myiarchus tyrannulus)*
Seasonal status—rare summer visitor, late April to September; *habitat*—oases and riparian woodlands; *range in California*—lower Colorado River Valley and Morongo Valley in San Bernardino County. *Breeds.*

ASH-THROATED FLYCATCHER *(Myiarchus cinerascens)*
Seasonal status—summer resident, early April to mid-September; *habitat*—high desert, piñon-juniper woodlands, desert edge, chaparral, riparian woodland, open oak woodland; *range in California*—north to Mendocino, Trinity, Siskiyou, and Modoc counties; *breeds; note*—small numbers may winter in southern California.

OLIVACEOUS FLYCATCHER *(Myiarchus tuberculifer)*
Seasonal status—accidental; *note*—one record: one at Furnace Creek Ranch, Inyo County, Nov. 23, 1968. Specimen.

EASTERN PHOEBE *(Sayornis phoebe)*
Seasonal status—casual visitor; *habitat*—open woodlands, riparian woodland; often found near water; *range in California*—recorded north to at least Marin County; *note*—most records fall between September and April.

BLACK PHOEBE *(Sayornis nigricans)*
Seasonal status—common resident; *habitat*—almost always found close to fresh water—lakes, streams, rivers, ponds, irrigation canals; *range in California*—at lower

elevations length of state west of Sierra Nevada north to head of Sacramento Valley and to Del Norte County; *breeds* near water and often places nest on some artificial object such as culvert, bridge, building, etc.

SAY'S PHOEBE *(Sayornis saya)*
Seasonal status – resident in state but during fall there is a movement of birds from the eastern and southern desert areas westward and northwards towards the coast; some birds remain in the desert areas throughout the year and others move westward in late September and remain in coastal areas until April; *habitat* – arid scrub and desert during the breeding season; more open country during the western excursion; *range in California* – for *breeding,* more arid regions east of Sierra Nevada but also drier interior valleys of Coast Range and San Joaquin Valley north to Contra Costa County; in non-breeding season occurs north to at least Sonoma County on the coast and to the north end of the Sacramento Valley; also occurs on all large southern islands.

WILLOW FLYCATCHER *(Empidonax traillii)*
Seasonal status – summer resident, late April to September; *habitat* – typically a riparian bird, especially for *breeding;* favors willows surrounded by meadows and near water; *range in California* – length of state in suitable habitat but not at high elevations, nor in humid northwest coniferous forests, nor southeastern deserts during breeding season; crosses deserts as transient; *note* – this flycatcher has been elevated to species status but may still be referred to as the "Traill's" Flycatcher.

LEAST FLYCATCHER *(Empidonax minimus)*
Seasonal status – accidental; *note* – ten records since 1900, nine of which were obtained on the Farallon Islands during June and between September and November, 1969–1971; one additional record – Point Reyes, Marin County, Sept. 9, 1969. Specimen.

HAMMOND'S FLYCATCHER *(Empidonax hammondii)*
Seasonal status – transient and summer visitor, April to October; *habitat* – for *breeding,* subalpine forests of Red Fir in the Canadian Life Zone and Lodgepole Pine in the Hudsonian Life Zone; transient through deserts; *range in California* – for *breeding;* northern California mountains (exclusive of the Coast Range) south through Sierra Nevada to Tulare County; *note* – positive field identification can be made by voice on the breeding grounds; commonly mist-netted at desert stations during spring migration.

DUSKY FLYCATCHER *(Empidonax oberholseri)*
Seasonal status – transient and summer visitor, April to October; *habitat* – for *breeding,* open areas of mountain chaparral with scattered coniferous trees; in migration, transient through the southeastern deserts; *range in California* – for *breeding,* length of state in most major mountain masses.

GRAY FLYCATCHER *(Empidonax wrightii)*
Seasonal status – transient and summer resident, April to October; *habitat* – for *breeding,* piñon-juniper woodland, mixed Great Basin Sagebrush and pines, arid forest; in winter, riparian woodlands; *range in California* – *breeds* in northeastern

Basin and Ranges Region from Modoc County south to Inyo County; some of population winters in southern California.

WESTERN FLYCATCHER *(Empidonax difficilis)*

Seasonal status—transient and summer visitor, March to October; *habitat*—for *breeding,* humid coniferous forest, well-shaded woodlands or forests with running water close at hand, deep, shaded canyons; *range in California*—length of state west of Sierra Nevada except for Warner Mountains; transient through southeastern deserts.

COUES' FLYCATCHER *(Contopus pertinax)*

Seasonal status—accidental; *note*—at least five records: one at Salton Sea, Imperial County, Oct. 4, 1952; one near Holtville, Imperial County, Sept. 29, 1965; one at Griffith Park, Los Angeles County, Dec. 31, 1967–March 24, 1968; one at Monterey, Monterey County, Dec. 27–29, 1968; one at Brock Ranch, Imperial County, Oct. 22, 1972 to "spring" 1973. Specimen.

WESTERN WOOD PEWEE *(Contopus sordidulus)*

Seasonal status—transient and summer visitor, April to September; *habitat*—for *breeding,* broken woodland or mixture of deciduous and coniferous forest; common transient through lowlands of southern and central California; *range in California*—*breeds* in appropriate habitat, length of state and across entire northern portion.

OLIVE-SIDED FLYCATCHER *(Nuttallornis borealis)*

Seasonal status—transient and summer visitor, April to September; *habitat*—for *breeding,* montane and subalpine forests of coniferous trees including Transition and Canadian Life Zones; *range in California*—in appropriate habitat, length of state. *Note*—partial to tall trees including eucalyptus in northern lowlands.

VERMILION FLYCATCHER *(Pyrocephalus rubinus)*

Seasonal status—rare resident on breeding grounds; irregular winter visitor elsewhere; *habitat*—desert riparian woodlands and oases with open water available; also desert thickets if water is nearby; *range in California*—Colorado and Sonoran Deserts; stragglers often reach coastal areas after breeding season; has ranged as far north as San Joaquin County; *note*—most persistent population is at Covington Park, San Bernardino County, where it regularly *breeds.*

Larks

HORNED LARK *(Eremophila alpestris)*

Seasonal status—common resident and winter visitor; *habitat*—grasslands, shortgrass plains, plowed agricultural land; *range in California*—length of state except Sierra Nevada and humid coniferous and montane length of northwest portion. *Breeds.*

Horned Lark—male

Swallows

VIOLET-GREEN SWALLOW *(Tachycinetta thalassina)*
Seasonal status—transient and summer visitor, February to October; some winter in lowland coastal regions also; *habitat*—open forest or woodland of deciduous, coniferous, or mixed trees when on breeding grounds; elsewhere, open country for foraging; *range in California*—for *breeding,* length of state west of southeastern deserts.

TREE SWALLOW *(Iridoprocne bicolor)*
Seasonal status—summer visitor and resident; *habitat*—for *breeding,* any suitable area of trees with woodpecker holes from sea level to subalpine forest; otherwise, open areas especially near lakes, rivers, sloughs, lagoons, and even salt-water marshes; *range in California*—length of state and west of the southeastern deserts.

BANK SWALLOW *(Riparia riparia)*
Seasonal status—transient and summer visitor, April to late September; *habitat*—for breeding, lowland country with appropriate soft banks or bluffs into which the birds must dig burrows for nesting; elsewhere, in migration, they may be found mixed with other migrating and foraging swallows over open country and open water; *range in California*—for *breeding,* scattered suitable localities, few in number, throughout state west of southeastern deserts.

ROUGH-WINGED SWALLOW *(Stelgidopteryx ruficollis)*
Seasonal status—transient and summer visitor, March to late September; *habitat*—for *breeding,* lowland areas with suitable soft banks and bluffs for digging nesting tunnels; otherwise, over open country or open water for foraging; *range in California*—length of state, west of southeastern deserts.

BARN SWALLOW *(Hirundo rustica)*
Seasonal status—transient and summer visitor, March to November; *habitat*—lowlands with suitable nest sites and water for creation of mud nests; otherwise,

over open country or open water for foraging; *range in California*—for *breeding,* almost length of state but scarcer in southern California; nests in sea caves on Channel Islands.

CLIFF SWALLOW *(Petrochelidon pyrrhonota)*
Seasonal status—transient and summer visitor, late February (in most southern portions of state) to October; *habitat*—for *breeding,* lowlands up through montane forests; open forests, farms, ranches, suburbs, cliff-faces; otherwise, forages over open country and open water; *range in California*—length of state during breeding season, except mountain areas and southeastern deserts.

PURPLE MARTIN *(Progne subis)*
Seasonal status—uncommon summer visitor, March to September; *habitat*—forested and woodland areas from sea level to about 6,000 feet in the montane forest; *range in California*—length of state, west of the deserts. *Breeds,* but does not inhabit "Martin houses" in California.

Purple Martin—male

Jays, Magpies, and Crows

GRAY JAY *(Perisoreus canadensis)*
Seasonal status—uncommon to rare resident; *habitat*—montane and subalpine forests of conifers; humid coniferous coastal forest of Coast Redwood and Douglas Fir; *range in California*—Coast Range south to Albion, Mendocino County, locally in Cascades of Siskiyou and Trinity counties, Klamath Mountains, Warner Mountains. *Breeds.*

STELLER'S JAY *(Cyanocitta stelleri)*
Seasonal status—common resident but some down-mountain movement in fall and return in spring; *habitat*—montane forest of conifers, humid coastal coniferous forest; *range in California*—in suitable habitat, almost length of state except lowlands of northeastern portion, Central Valley, eastern and southeastern deserts, and lowlands of southwestern portions. *Breeds.*

BLUE JAY *(Cyanocitta cristata)*
Seasonal status–accidental; *note*–two records: one at Chico, Butte County, Apr. 24, 1950; one at Mill Creek Canyon, San Bernardino County, Oct. 30, 1963–Apr. 20, 1964. Specimen.

SCRUB JAY *(Aphelocoma coerulescens)*
Seasonal status–common resident; *habitat*–mixed woodland and chaparral, groves of live oaks, chaparral, piñon-juniper woodland; *range in California*–length of state except deserts of eastern and southeastern portions; a race occurs east of the Sierra Nevada which is restricted to the piñon-juniper woodlands of Mono and Inyo Counties to extreme eastern San Bernardino County; *breeds. Note*–a distinctive race inhabits Santa Cruz Island.

Scrub Jay

BLACK-BILLED MAGPIE *(Pica pica)*
Seasonal status–resident; *habitat*–riparian woodland edges, open agricultural land, farms, ranches, edges of sagebrush flats with stands of trees; *range in California*– essentially east of the Sierra Nevada and Cascades from Modoc County south to as far as about Olancha, Inyo County. *Breeds.*

YELLOW-BILLED MAGPIE *(Pica nuttalli)*
Seasonal status–resident; *habitat*–broken woodland interspersed with open grasslands or agricultural lands, open riparian woodland, savannah; *range in California*–valleys and rolling foothills of Coast Range from about Santa Barbara County north to about San Francisco; Central Valley from about northern Kern County north to head of the Valley. *Breeds.*

COMMON RAVEN *(Corvus corax)*
Seasonal status–resident; *habitat*–varied; cities and suburbs, desert, rolling foothill grasslands and savannah, plains, portions of higher mountain areas; must have cliffs for breeding; *range in California*–length of state; has been found *nesting* from sea level to about 8,000 feet.

COMMON CROW *(Corvus brachyrhynchos)*
Seasonal status–common resident; *habitat*–savannah, agricultural lands–especially orchards; *range in California*–chiefly the Central Valley, the southwestern coastal region, and the northwest coastal region from Monterey County to Del Norte County. *Breeds.*

Common Crow

PINYON JAY *(Gymnorhinus cyanocephalus)*
Seasonal status–resident, but populations move from place to place depending upon local food conditions and weather; *habitat*–piñon-juniper woodland; lower portions of montane forest in Transition Life Zone; *range in California*–complex; Basin and Ranges Region south to about Walker Pass, Kern County; south along higher desert ranges to Providence Mountains, San Bernardino County; north side of San Gabriel and San Bernardino Mountains of the Transverse Ranges; Mt. San Jacinto area especially near Lake Hemet, Riverside County; south slopes of Mt. Pinos and north slopes of Frazier Mountain, Ventura County. *Breeds.*

CLARK'S NUTCRACKER *(Nucifraga columbiana)*
Seasonal status–resident, but flocks wander from year to year occasionally reaching lowlands and even the seacoast at long intervals; *habitat*–upper reaches of subalpine forest in the Canadian and Hudsonian Life Zones; often found feeding in the Arctic Alpine Zone; *range in California*–almost length of state in suitable mountain areas from Klamath Mountains in the north to the Laguna Mountains in the south. *Breeds.*

Titmice, Verdins, and Bushtits

BLACK-CAPPED CHICKADEE *(Parus atricapillus)*
Seasonal status–uncommon to rare resident; *habitat*–riparian woodland especially containing large willows; *range in California*–very local in Del Norte, Humboldt, and Siskiyou counties. *Breeds.*

MOUNTAIN CHICKADEE *(Parus gambeli)*

Seasonal status—common resident but small numbers descend to lowlands during fall and winter; *habitat*—montane forest and lower portions of the subalpine forest in the Transition and Canadian Life Zones; *range in California*—most mountainous areas of state except coastal mountains (except for Santa Lucia Mountains in Monterey County). *Breeds.*

CHESTNUT-BACKED CHICKADEE *(Parus rufescens)*

Seasonal status—resident; *habitat*—oak woodland, mixed deciduous and coniferous woodland, humid coastal coniferous forest, open pine forest; *range in California*—primarily coastal forests from San Luis Obispo north to Oregon border; also found eastward to Cascades of Siskiyou and Trinity counties; has been found as far south as Santa Barbara County and is spreading southward along western slope of Sierra Nevada; has reached Mariposa County. *Breeds.*

PLAIN TITMOUSE *(Parus inornatus)*

Seasonal status—common resident; *habitat*—oak woodlands, piñon-juniper woodlands; *range in California*—complex; length of state but mostly absent from northern portions of state except Modoc Plateau; absent from higher portions (coniferous forests) of Sierra Nevada; absent from San Joaquin Valley and eastern and southeastern desert region. *Breeds.*

Plain Titmouse

VERDIN *(Auriparus flaviceps)*

Seasonal status—resident; *habitat*—Colorado, Mojave, and Sonoran Deserts in areas of larger desert shrubs and small trees; *range in California*—southeastern portion of state. *Breeds.*

BUSHTIT *(Psaltriparus minimus)*

Seasonal status—common resident; *habitat*—lowland and coastal chaparral, open oak woodland, mixture of chaparral and oak, piñon-juniper woodland; *range in California*—length of state except absent from higher portions of Sierra Nevada (coniferous forests and above) and deserts of eastern and southeastern portions. *Breeds.*

Nuthatches

WHITE-BREASTED NUTHATCH *(Sitta carolinensis)*
Seasonal status—common resident but some down-mountain and southbound movement in fall and winter; *habitat*—riparian woodland, broken oak woodland, mixed coniferous and deciduous woodland, coniferous forest of montane or even subalpine types; *range in California*—for *breeding,* almost length of state, but absent from humid coniferous coastal forest, Central Valley, eastern and southeastern deserts, and southern California coastal lowlands.

White-breasted Nuthatch

RED-BREASTED NUTHATCH *(Sitta canadensis)*
Seasonal status—resident within state, but considerable down-mountain and southward movement in fall; *habitat*—for *breeding,* coniferous forests of higher montane and subalpine zones, notably Canadian Life Zone; *range in California*—length of state, breeding in the higher mountain areas from border to border.

PYGMY NUTHATCH *(Sitta pygmaea)*
Seasonal status—common resident; *habitat*—shows primary affinity for pines, either coastal forms or those of the Transition Life Zone of the montane forests; *range in California*—Sierra Nevada, Cascades, inner Coast Range of northern California, Transverse and Peninsular Ranges, coastal forests of pine intermittently scattered from San Luis Obispo County north to Mendocino County. *Breeds.*

Creepers

BROWN CREEPER *(Certhia familiaris)*
Seasonal status—resident, but there is some autumnal down-mountain movement; *habitat*—coniferous forests of the humid coastal type and the montane and subalpine types in the Transition and Canadian Life Zones; *range in California*—

mountains of the northern and northwestern portions; coast south to San Luis Obispo County; Sierra Nevada, Warner Mountains, and Transverse and Peninsular Ranges. *Breeds.*

Brown Creeper

Wrentits

WRENTIT *(Chamaea fasciata)*

Seasonal status–resident; *habitat*–coastal and lowland chaparral; *range in California*–length of state along coast from border to border and inland in areas of suitable chaparral habitat; absent from Central Valley and all areas east of Sierra-Cascade axis and from southeastern deserts. *Breeds.*

Wrentit

Dippers

DIPPER *(Cinclus mexicanus)*
  Seasonal status—resident; *habitat*—restricted to swift-flowing permanent streams and small lakes in these stream systems; some down-mountain movement as the higher streams freeze; *range in California*—from sea level to almost 12,000 feet; northern half of state in mountainous and coastal areas south to scattered suitable locations in southern California as far as San Diego County. *Breeds.*

Dipper

Wrens

HOUSE WREN *(Troglodytes aedon)*
  Seasonal status—resident in southern portion of state south of Tehachapis; elsewhere primarily a summer visitor, March to November; *habitat*—thickets and brush, edges of forest and woodland, chaparral—from sea level to over 9,000 feet where it occurs along borders of mountain meadows and where there are willows; *range in California*—for *breeding* almost entire state except humid coniferous forests of northwest, offshore islands, and eastern and southern deserts.

WINTER WREN *(Troglodytes troglodytes)*
  Seasonal status—most are resident but infiltrators from north enter state in winter and there is some southward dispersal in fall; *habitat*—dense coniferous forest or mixed coniferous forest with dense tangles of vegetation on or near the ground; *range in California*—for *breeding,* humid coastal coniferous forest south as far as Monterey County; also locally on western slope of Sierra Nevada.

BEWICK'S WREN *(Thryomanes bewickii)*

Seasonal status—primarily common resident but some altitudinal migration; *habitat*—thickets of vegetation as in riparian woodland, piñon-juniper woodland, willow thickets, lowland and coastal chaparral; *range in California*—for *breeding,* suitable habitat length of state except higher portions of Sierra Nevada and Cascades and southeastern deserts.

CACTUS WREN *(Campylorhynchus brunneicapillus)*

Seasonal status—common resident; *habitat*—deserts with suitable cacti, yuccas, and shrubs for nesting, arid coastal hillsides, arid interior valleys; *range in California*— southeastern deserts (Colorado, Mojave, Sonoran) and suitable arid habitats north coastally to Ventura County. *Breeds.*

LONG-BILLED MARSH WREN *(Telmatodytes palustris)*

Seasonal status—common resident but some withdrawal of birds from northeastern section during fall and winter; *habitat*—fresh-water marshes, ponds, streams, and lakes grown with cattail, tule, and bulrush; *range in California*—for *breeding,* coastally, length of state; also Central Valley, Imperial Valley, and Modoc Plateau.

CANYON WREN *(Catherpes mexicanus)*

Seasonal status—resident; *habitat*—rock walls, cliffs, boulder piles, deep canyons; *range in California*—scattered throughout state, chiefly in interior mountainous areas; coastally, not found north of Santa Cruz County and they are found in eastern desert mountains. *Note*—occurs from sea level to over 9,000 feet. *Breeds.*

Canyon Wren

ROCK WREN *(Salpinctes obsoletus)*

Seasonal status—resident; *habitat*—rocky slopes, talus, rocky outcrops, canyon walls, arroyos and other deep earth cuts and banks; *range in California*—for *breeding,* sea level to over 12,000 feet; length of state in suitable habitat.

Mockingbirds and Thrashers

MOCKINGBIRD *(Mimus polyglottos)*
Seasonal status—common resident, but individuals wander northward and westward in the fall; *habitat*—lowland gardens, cities, towns, suburbs, orchards, agricultural lands; edges of brushland and woodland; *range in California*—lowland regions of the state (sparser in the deserts) north to head of Central Valley; has *bred* as far north as Lassen County and Humboldt Bay, Humboldt County; *note*—range of breeding is expanding northwestward.

Mockingbird

GRAY CATBIRD *(Dumetella carolinensis)*
Seasonal status—accidental; *note*—four recent records: one at Oasis, Mono County, June 10, 1964; one at Deep Springs, Inyo County, June 10, 1964; one near Imperial Beach, San Diego County, Nov. 7-8, 1964; one at Pacific Grove, Monterey County, Sept. 30, 1968. Specimen.

BROWN THRASHER *(Toxostoma rufum)*
Seasonal status—casual visitor with most records occurring between September and April; *note*—most records are from the southern half of the state; inhabits thickets as is usual for thrashers.

BENDIRE'S THRASHER *(Toxostoma bendirei)*
Seasonal status—rare and very local summer visitor; *habitat*—desert with usual vegetation of cholla cactus, Creosote Bush, yuccas, and other shrubs; *range in California*—Colorado, Mojave, and Sonoran Deserts; *note*—a small *breeding* colony exists near Cima, San Bernardino County.

CURVE-BILLED THRASHER *(Toxostoma curvirostre)*
Seasonal status—accidental; eight records (all but one from southeastern deserts): 5 specimens collected near Bard, Imperial County (Dec. 31, 1916; Oct. 29, 1924; Jan. 14, 1925; Jan. 16, 1925; and Jan. 18, 1925); one near Havasu Lake, San Bernardino County, Dec. 26, 1952, one near Calipatria, Imperial County, Nov. 1, 1964-Jan. 25, 1965, and one near Imperial Beach, San Diego County, Sept. 6-19, 1965. Specimen.

Curve-billed Thrasher

CALIFORNIA THRASHER *(Toxostoma redivivum)*
Seasonal status—common resident; *habitat*—lowland and coastal chaparral, riparian woodland thickets; *range in California*—generally west of the Sierra-Cascade crest and west of the deserts; north to Humboldt and Shasta counties. *Breeds.*

LE CONTE'S THRASHER *(Toxostoma lecontei)*
Seasonal status—resident; *habitat*—desert scrub; *range in California*—disjunct; occurs in southwest portion of San Joaquin Valley Desert (which is its population metropolis) from about Maricopa, Kern County, north to about Coalinga, Fresno County; also occurs on east side of Sierra Nevada from southern Mono County and Panamint and Death Valleys, Inyo County, southward into northern Mojave Desert; also in Colorado Desert. *Breeds.*

CRISSAL THRASHER *(Toxostoma dorsale)*
Seasonal status—uncommon resident; *habitat*—dense desert scrub, especially of mesquite, arrowweed, desert "willows" and *Artemisia; range in California*—Colorado River Valley, Colorado Desert, southern and eastern Mojave Desert north to about Tecopa, Inyo County. *Breeds.*

SAGE THRASHER *(Oreoscoptes montanus)*
Seasonal status—summer visitor (on breeding grounds) and transient and winter visitor (September to April) elsewhere; *habitat*—for *breeding,* flat areas vegetated primarily with Great Basin Sagebrush in the Great Basin Desert; in winter, occurs in open country with sparse arid vegetation; *range in California*—breeds in Great Basin Desert south to northern edges of Mojave Desert and Walker Basin, Kern County; also very sparingly in southern end of San Joaquin Valley; winters south to southwestern part of state and in Mojave and Colorado Deserts.

Thrushes and Solitaires

AMERICAN ROBIN *(Turdus migratorius)*
Seasonal status—common summer visitor and resident in northern half of state; common winter visitor to lowlands throughout state; local resident in southern part of state; *habitat*—montane and subalpine coniferous forests, humid coastal coniferous forest, oak and riparian woodlands, agricultural lands with groves of

trees, orchards, savannah, gardens, suburbs, towns, parks; *range in California*—length of state but most of *nesting* occurs in northern half (both lowlands and mountains) and in the mountains of southern California where nesting American Robins also can be found in foothill and lowland suburbs and urban parks.

RUFOUS-BACKED ROBIN *(Turdus rufopalliatus)*
Seasonal status—accidental; *note*—one record, Imperial Dam, Imperial County, Dec. 17, 1973. Sight record.

VARIED THRUSH *(Ixoreus naevius)*
Seasonal status—resident and winter visitor; *habitat*—for breeding, dense, dark, humid coastal coniferous forest; elsewhere, cool shady canyons, oak woodlands with heavy shade, taller chaparral; *range in California*—*breeds* only in Del Norte and Humboldt counties; in winter (October to April) winter visitors from north of California move south through state, especially in Sacramento and San Joaquin (northern portion) valleys; coastal birds occur fairly commonly south to Monterey County and sparingly and erratically south of there; irregular winter visitors to southern California.

WOOD THRUSH *(Hylocichla mustelina)*
Seasonal status—accidental; *note*—two records: one near Imperial Beach, San Diego County, Nov. 18, 1967; one at Glendale, Los Angeles County, Aug. 1-10, 1968. Specimen.

HERMIT THRUSH *(Catharus guttatus)*
Seasonal status—complex: occurs as transient during spring and fall, summer visitor, and resident; *habitat*—for breeding, montane and subalpine forests, humid coniferous forests; otherwise, dense thickets of chaparral, willows, riparian woodland, desert scrub; *range in California*—for *breeding,* mountainous areas in coastal region (from Monterey County northward), Cascades, Warner Mountains, Sierra Nevada, higher mountains of Basin and Ranges Region, Mt. Pinos in Kern County, and San Bernardino Mountains; otherwise length of state.

SWAINSON'S THRUSH *(Catharus ustulatus)*
Seasonal status—transient and summer visitor, mid-April to late September; *habitat*—for breeding, thickets of willows and alders, riparian woodland, thickly vegetated moist slopes bordering meadows and streams; during migration, thick-

Hermit Thrush

ets and dense woodlands throughout lowlands; *range in California*—for *breeding,* length of state exclusive of higher portions of Sierra Nevada and eastern and southeastern deserts; common spring transient through deserts.

GRAY-CHEEKED THRUSH *(Catharus minimus)*

Seasonal status—accidental; *note*—two records: two on Farallon Islands Oct. 3, 1970; one on Farallon Islands May 28–June 8, 1971. Specimen.

WESTERN BLUEBIRD *(Sialia mexicana)*

Seasonal status—common resident; *habitat*—open forests of deciduous, coniferous, or mixed trees; savannah; edges of riparian woodland; *range in California*—for *breeding,* length of state exclusive of eastern and southeastern deserts; in winter, almost statewide.

MOUNTAIN BLUEBIRD *(Sialia currucoides)*

Seasonal status—summer visitor in mountains and northeastern plateau; winter visitor in some lowland areas; *habitat*—for breeding, subalpine forest of Canadian and Hudsonian Life Zones; frequently ranges upwards into Arctic Alpine Life Zone after nesting; in winter not uncommon in certain open plains and grasslands and more arid agricultural lands; *range in California*—for *breeding,* Sierra Nevada and Cascades, Warner Mountains, inner Coast Range south to Mendocino County, San Bernardino mountains; in winter sometimes common in San Joaquin Valley, Carrizo Plain in eastern San Luis Obispo County, Antelope Valley, and Imperial Valley.

WHEATEAR *(Oenanthe oenanthe)*

Seasonal status—accidental; *note*—one record: one at Farallon Islands, June 11, 1971. Specimen.

TOWNSEND'S SOLITAIRE *(Myadestes townsendi)*

Seasonal status—resident in state but summer visitor to higher mountain breeding grounds; *habitat*—for *breeding,* montane and subalpine forests in Transition, Canadian, and Hudsonian Life Zones; in winter descends to higher foothills and upper deserts and chaparral; *range in California*—Sierra Nevada, Cascades, Warner Mountains, inner Coast Range, Panamint Mountains, Mt. Pinos in Ventura County, and parts of the Transverse and Peninsular Ranges.

Townsend's Solitaire
(photo by Herb Clarke)

Gnatcatchers and Kinglets

BLUE-GRAY GNATCATCHER *(Polioptila caerulea)*
Seasonal status—for most of state, summer visitor, early April to October; resident in coastal southern California and winter visitor to lowlands in southern half of state; *habitat*—brushland and chaparral with nearby trees; *range in California*—for *breeding,* foothills surrounding Central Valley, interior coastal ranges of southern California, desert ranges north to White Mountains.

Blue-gray Gnatcatcher—male

BLACK-TAILED GNATCATCHER *(Polioptila melanura)*
Seasonal status—resident; *habitat*—desert and interior valley dry scrub; *range in California*—Colorado, Sonoran, and portions of eastern and southern Mojave Deserts; interior dry valleys of coastal southern California between Peninsular and Transverse Ranges. *Breeds.*

GOLDEN-CROWNED KINGLET *(Regulus satrapa)*
Seasonal status—summer visitor to higher mountains and northern coastal forest; spring and fall transient and winter visitor to lowlands; *habitat*—for breeding, humid coastal coniferous forest, montane forest, and subalpine forests especially in the Canadian Life Zone; *range in California*—for *breeding,* Coast Range south to Santa Cruz County and portions of Monterey County, inner Coast Range in northern portion, Klamath Mountains, Cascades, Sierra Nevada, Warner Mountains, Mt. Pinos in Ventura County, and portions of San Bernardino and San Jacinto Mountains.

RUBY-CROWNED KINGLET *(Regulus calendula)*
Seasonal status—common transient and winter visitor in lowlands; summer visitor in higher interior mountains; *habitat*—for breeding, higher montane but primarily coniferous forests of subalpine type in the Canadian Life Zone; *range in California*—for *breeding,* Klamath Mountains, Cascades, Sierra Nevada, Mt. Pinos in Ventura County, portions of Transverse and Peninsular Ranges; otherwise, length of state in transit and during winter.

Ruby-crowned Kinglet

Pipits and Wagtails

WATER PIPIT *(Anthus spinoletta)*
Seasonal status—common spring and fall transient and winter visitor, September to May; *habitat*—open country such as sea beaches, sparse grasslands, agricultural fields, river and lake margins; *range in California*—lowlands of length of state.

Water Pipit

RED-THROATED PIPIT *(Anthus cervinus)*
Seasonal status—accidental; *note*—four records: up to 15 near Imperial Beach, San Diego County, Oct. 12–27, 1964; up to ten near Imperial Beach, Oct. 9–29, 1966; up to ten near Imperial Beach, Oct. 22–Nov. 4, 1967; one at Farallon Islands, Nov. 3, 1968. Specimen.

Waxwings

CEDAR WAXWING *(Bombycilla cedrorum)*
Seasonal status—irregularly common winter visitor but small number are summer visitors to northwest coastal area; *habitat*—for breeding, riparian growths in humid coniferous forest; elsewhere distribution determined by availability of fruits, berries, buds, and other food sources which may be located in lowland or plateau environments such as orchards, agricultural lands, gardens, suburbs, towns, cities, desert edges, oases, chaparral; *range in California*—for *breeding,* only Del Norte and Humboldt counties; otherwise, length of state.

Cedar Waxwings

BOHEMIAN WAXWING *(Bombycilla garrulus)*

Seasonal status–irregular visitor both as to time and numbers; *habitat*–same as for Cedar Waxwings and often associates with them; *range in California*–almost length of state, but most occurrences are in northern half of state and especially east of Cascades and Sierra Nevada in the Modoc Plateau and Great Basin.

Silky Flycatchers

PHAINOPEPLA *(Phainopepla nitens)*

Seasonal status–resident in southeastern portion of state; elsewhere is a transient and summer visitor as major portion of California population withdraws to southeast in winter; *habitat*–lowlands and foothills of desert scrub with larger trees, orchards, oak woodlands bordering chaparral and open oak savannah–all these habitats must have trees bearing mistletoe; *range in California*–in winter, found in the southeastern deserts; summer birds range north to head of Central Valley and coastally to about San Francisco from San Diego County. *Breeds.*

Phainopepla–male

Shrikes

NORTHERN SHRIKE *(Lanius excubitor)*
Seasonal status—uncommon to rare winter visitor, October to March; *habitat*—open country with scattered trees and fenceposts in Great Basin Desert, ranches, agricultural land, farms, refuges; *range in California*—primarily northeastern section of Great Basin Desert and Modoc Plateau, but also Central Valley and central California coast; has reached Imperial Valley.

LOGGERHEAD SHRIKE *(Lanius ludovicianus)*
Seasonal status—mostly resident; *habitat*—open country such as desert, piñon-juniper woodland, savannah, grassland with fenceposts and scattered bushes, agricultural land, ranches, farms, refuges; *range in California*—length of state except for higher portions of mountains and northwest coastal and mountain forest areas. *Breeds.*

Loggerhead Shrike

Starlings

STARLING *(Sturnus vulgaris)*—INTRODUCED into United States
Seasonal status—common resident; *habitat*—open country, especially agricultural lands, ranches, farms, cultivated land, cities, towns, suburbs, parks; *range in California*—breeds throughout state in lowlands except in northwest coastal forests and southeastern open deserts; *note*—arrived in California about 1942 as winter visitors from Oregon; has undergone population explosion and threatens survival of such more timid hole-nesters as bluebirds, titmice, nuthatches, swallows, wrens, woodpeckers, and even American Kestrels.

Starling

Vireos

WHITE-EYED VIREO *(Vireo griseus)*
Seasonal status—accidental; *note*—one record: one at Farallon Islands, June 4–5, 1969. Photograph.

HUTTON'S VIREO *(Vireo huttoni)*
Seasonal status—resident; *habitat*—live oak woodland; *range in California*—length of state west of Sierra Nevada and other north-south ranges. *Breeds.*

BELL'S VIREO *(Vireo bellii)*
Seasonal status—summer visitor, late March to September; *habitat*—dense riparian growth, especially tangles of shrubs and vines; *range in California*—*breeds* in coastal and interior southern California (west of the deserts) and north through Central Valley to Tehama County; also breeds in Owens Valley and Death Valley and lower Colorado River Valley.

GRAY VIREO *(Vireo vicinior)*
Seasonal status—uncommon summer visitor, late March to August; *habitat*—dry chaparral particularly that associated with piñon-juniper woodland; *range in California*—very few known current *breeding* "colonies"; most frequently seen on north slope of San Bernardino Mountains and in the Mojave Desert from the Providence Mountains north to the Grapevine Mountains; *note*—occasionally seen in dry chaparral of interior valleys.

YELLOW-THROATED VIREO *(Vireo flavifrons)*
Seasonal status—accidental; *note*—four records: one at Wildrose, Inyo County, May 7, 1963; one at Cambria, San Luis Obispo County, May 24, 1966; one at Farallon Islands, June 12, 1969; one at Riverside, Riverside County, Dec. 5, 1969–March 19, 1970. Specimen.

SOLITARY VIREO *(Vireo solitarius)*
Seasonal status—transient and summer visitor, late March to October; *habitat*—for breeding, oak woodlands and mixtures of oaks and conifers; otherwise, lowlands in general where there are thickets, riparian woodlands, and other woodland and broken forest areas; *range in California*—for *breeding,* foothills and mountains of most of California east of the deserts and excluding the humid coniferous forest of the northwest coast; in migration, throughout state.

YELLOW-GREEN VIREO *(Vireo flavoviridis)*
Seasonal status—accidental; *note*—four records since 1900: one at Dana Point, Orange County, Sept. 22–27, 1964; one near Imperial Beach, San Diego County, Sept. 23, 1967; one at Costa Mesa, Orange County, Oct. 3, 1967; one at San Diego, San Diego County, Oct. 7, 1967. Specimen.

RED-EYED VIREO *(Vireo olivaceus)*
Seasonal status—very rare casual visitor; *note*—most records fall between May and October.

PHILADELPHIA VIREO *(Vireo philadelphicus)*
Seasonal status—accidental; *note*—seven records: one near Imperial Beach, San

Diego County, Oct. 9, 1965; one at Fairhaven, Humboldt County, Sept. 16, 1967; one at Point Loma, San Diego County, Nov. 9, 1969; one at Farallon Islands, Sept. 14, 1969; one at Point Reyes, Marin County, Sept. 26–Oct. 5, 1970; one at Kelso, San Bernardino County, Oct. 3, 1970; and one near Imperial Beach, San Diego County, Oct. 4–10, 1970. Specimen.

WARBLING VIREO *(Vireo gilvus)*
Seasonal status—transient and summer visitor, March to October; *habitat*—for breeding, riparian woodlands and other places where deciduous trees are found; otherwise, in migration may appear in any lowland area with suitable thickets and groves of trees; *range in California*—for *breeding,* in suitable habitat, length of state and west of deserts and Basin and Ranges Region; otherwise, any suitable lowland area.

Warbling Vireo

Wood Warblers

BLACK AND WHITE WARBLER *(Mniotitla varia)*
Seasonal status—rare but regular spring (mid-March to late June) and fall (mid-August to November) transient and rarer winter visitor; *habitat*—desert oases, riparian woodland, live-oak woodlands; *note*—more usual in eastern desert areas during spring and coastal areas during fall.

PROTHONOTARY WARBLER *(Protonotaria citrea)*
Seasonal status—accidental; *note*—ten records: 1953, 1963, 1965–2, 1967–2, 1969–2, 1970, 1971; three spring records (May 6–May 25) and seven fall records (Aug. 30–Dec. 7) of which seven are coastal and three from the interior including two records from east of the Sierra Nevada. Specimen.

WORM-EATING WARBLER *(Helmitheros vermivorus)*
Seasonal status—accidental; *note*—five records: one at Chula Vista, San Diego County, Sept. 18, 1960; one at Farallon Islands July 5, 1965; one at Carmel, Monterey County, Dec. 16, 1967; one at Pacific Grove, Monterey County, Oct. 25, 1969; one near Otay, San Diego County, Sept. 12, 1971. Specimen.

GOLDEN-WINGED WARBLER *(Vermivora chrysoptera)*
Seasonal status—accidental; *note*—six records: one at Montecito, Santa Barbara County, Oct. 23–24, 1960; one at Farallon Islands, May 26, 1963; one near San

Bernardino, San Bernardino County, Dec. 8, 1963; one at Deep Springs, Inyo County, June 5, 1972; one at Farallon Islands, July 1972; one at Deep Springs, Inyo County, May 20–21, 1973. Specimen.

BLUE-WINGED WARBLER *(Vermivora pinus)*

Seasonal status—accidental; *note*—four records: one in White Mountains, Inyo County, June 16, 1954; one at San Francisco, San Francisco County, Sept. 18, 1963; one at Point Loma, San Diego County, Sept. 9, 1964; one near Imperial Beach, San Diego County, Sept. 26, 1964. Specimen.

TENNESSEE WARBLER *(Vermivora peregrina)*

Seasonal status—very rare spring transient and uncommon fall transient; *note*— spring migrants are usually seen in eastern desert areas and fall transients are coastal.

ORANGE-CROWNED WARBLER *(Vermivora celata)*

Seasonal status—complex: common spring and fall transient, summer visitor, winter visitor, and resident; *habitat*—live oaks, chaparral, streamside thickets, riparian woodlands, undergrowth of forest and woodland; *range in California*—for *breeding,* in suitable habitat, length of state except primarily eastern and southeastern deserts, Central Valley, lowland portions of Modoc Plateau, and portions of coastal and interior southern California; a race breeds on most of the large off-shore islands in southern California.

NASHVILLE WARBLER *(Vermivora ruficapilla)*

Seasonal status—spring and fall transient and summer visitor, early April to October; *habitat*—for breeding, deciduous oaks and maples in montane forest of Transition Life Zone; otherwise, woodlands and thickets in migration; *range in California*—for *breeding,* west slope of Sierra Nevada north to Cascades; northern part of inner Coast Range; has been found in San Bernardino Mountains in summer.

VIRGINIA'S WARBLER *(Vermivora virginiae)*

Seasonal status—rare spring transient in eastern portion of state; uncommon fall (Sept.-Nov.) transient in coastal southern California; rare summer visitor to limited breeding grounds on Clark Mountain, eastern San Bernardino County and in the White Mountains of Inyo County; *habitat*—for *breeding,* arid coniferous forest of chaparral, White Fir, Piñon Pine, and juniper.

LUCY'S WARBLER *(Vermivora luciae)*

Seasonal status—uncommon summer visitor, mid-March to late August to breeding area; very rare fall transient along coast from Monterey County south; *habitat*—for breeding, mesquite thickets and nearby riparian woodland; *range in California*—breeds in lower Colorado River Valley, north in eastern Inyo County in suitable habitat along Amargosa River, and as far north as Scotty's Castle in Death Valley National Monument; westernmost breeding outpost is at Morongo Valley, San Bernardino County.

NORTHERN PARULA *(Parula americana)*

Seasonal status—very rare casual spring (late March to late June) transient and even rarer fall (late August to mid-November) transient; *note*—a male and two females built two *nests* and raised three young at Point Lobos Reserve, Monterey County, May 18–July 16, 1952.

YELLOW WARBLER *(Dendroica petechia)*

Seasonal status—transient and summer visitor, early April to mid-September; *habitat*—for breeding. riparian woodland in lowlands and lower mountain areas; *range in California*—for *breeding,* length of state except for southeastern deserts and higher mountain areas; also Colorado River Valley.

MAGNOLIA WARBLER *(Dendroica magnolia)*

Seasonal status—very rare spring (early May to late June) and rare fall (late August to mid-November) pure transient; *note*—most frequently seen at desert oases and coast.

CAPE MAY WARBLER *(Dendroica tigrina)*

Seasonal status—casual visitor; *note*—13 records: two in spring (very late May and very late June); 11 in fall (mid-September to late November); ten coastal fall records from Farallon Islands to San Diego County, one late spring record from Farallon Islands, and one late spring and one fall record from extreme eastern desert areas.

BLACK-THROATED BLUE WARBLER *(Dendroica caerulescens)*

Seasonal status—rare fall (early September to late November) pure transient; *note*—most records are coastal.

YELLOW-RUMPED WARBLER *(Dendroica coronata)*

"Myrtle" Warbler

Seasonal status—winter visitor, October to late April; *habitat*—broken forest and woodland, orchards, towns, suburbs, gardens; *range in California*—fairly common in northwest coastal region; less common to south and uncommon to rare in southern California.

"Audubon's" Warbler (formerly *Dendroica auduboni*)

Seasonal status—resident within state but common summer visitor, May to October, in mountains; transient and winter visitor in lowlands; *habitat*—for breeding, montane and subalpine forests of Transition, Canadian, and Hudsonian Life Zones; otherwise, woodlands, thickets, suburbs, towns, parks, in migration and winter; *range in California*—for *breeding,* virtually all mountainous regions of state except desert mountains of extreme eastern section in San Bernardino County; in Coast Range, south to Monterey County and in Peninsular Ranges, south to Santa Rosa Mountains; otherwise, length of state.

BLACK-THROATED GRAY WARBLER *(Dendroica nigrescens)*

Seasonal status—spring and fall transient and summer visitor, mid-April to October; *habitat*—for breeding, oak woodland, mixed oaks and coniferous forest, piñon-juniper woodland; otherwise, lowland thickets, woodlands, broken forest; *range in California*—for *breeding,* length of state in suitable habitat, preferring mountains, foothills, and mesas.

TOWNSEND'S WARBLER *(Dendroica townsendi)*

Seasonal status—spring (April and May) transient and fall (September to November) common transient; winter visitor in small numbers; *habitat*—live oak wood-

Townsend's Warbler—male

lands, mixed coniferous and deciduous woodland; *range in California*—during migration, length of state; during winter, chiefly found in coastal areas from central coast south.

BLACK-THROATED GREEN WARBLER *(Dendroica virens)*

Seasonal status—casual spring (early May to late June) and very rare fall (mid-September to early December) pure transient; *note*—most fall records are coastal.

GOLDEN-CHEEKED WARBLER *(Dendroica chrysoparia)*

Seasonal status—accidental; *note*—one record: one at Farallon Islands, Sept. 9, 1971. Specimen.

HERMIT WARBLER *(Dendroica occidentalis)*

Seasonal status—spring and fall transient and summer visitor, mid-April to early September; a few winter; *habitat*—for breeding, coniferous forests up to Canadian Life Zone; otherwise, oases, riparian woodlands, oak woodland, mixed coniferous and deciduous forest in migration; *range in California*—for *breeding,* Sierra Nevada, Cascades, Klamath Mountains, inner northern Coast Range; otherwise, length of state.

CERULEAN WARBLER *(Dendroica caerulea)*

Seasonal status—accidental; *note*—two records: one at Salton Sea, Imperial County, Oct. 1, 1947; one at Point Loma, San Diego County, Oct. 26, 1967. Specimen.

BLACKBURNIAN WARBLER *(Dendroica fusca)*

Seasonal status—very casual spring (late May) and rare to casual fall (early September to late October) pure transient; *note*—almost all records are coastal.

YELLOW-THROATED WARBLER *(Dendroica dominica)*

Seasonal status—accidental; *note*—five records: one on Farallon Islands, July 8, 1969; one at Carmel, Monterey County, Sept. 21–28, 1969; one at Point Loma, San Diego County, Oct. 15–Nov. 5, 1969; one at Scotty's Castle, Inyo County, May 30, 1971; one at San Pedro, Los Angeles County, Oct. 21, 1972. Photograph.

Yellow Warbler—male

GRACE'S WARBLER *(Dendroica graciae)*
Seasonal status—accidental; *note*—two records: one near Imperial Beach, San Diego County, Oct. 29, 1966; one near Point Loma, San Diego County, Sept. 8, 1968. Specimen.

CHESTNUT-SIDED WARBLER *(Dendroica pensylvanica)*
Seasonal status—very casual spring (early to late June) and casual fall (late August to early November) pure transient; *note*—almost all records are coastal.

BAY-BREASTED WARBLER *(Dendroica castanea)*
Seasonal status—very casual spring (late May to mid-June) and casual fall (late September to late November) pure transient; *note*—most records are coastal.

BLACKPOLL WARBLER *(Dendroica striata)*
Seasonal status—casual spring (mid-May to late June) and uncommon to rare fall (early August to mid-November) pure transient; *note*—almost all records are coastal.

PINE WARBLER *(Dendroica pinus)*
Seasonal status—accidental; *note*—at least four records: one near Imperial Beach, San Diego County, Oct. 22, 1966; one at Point Loma, San Diego County, Oct. 28, 1967; one at Point Reyes, Marin County, Oct. 5, 1970; one near Imperial Beach, San Diego County, Sept. 18, 1971. Specimen.

PRAIRIE WARBLER *(Dendroica discolor)*
Seasonal status—casual fall (early September to early November) pure transient; *note*—almost all records are from coastal areas.

PALM WARBLER *(Dendroica palmarum)*
Seasonal status—casual spring (early April to early June) and rare fall (mid-September to end of November) transient; a few winter records.

OVENBIRD *(Seiurus aurocapillus)*
Seasonal status—casual spring (mid-May to late June) and casual fall (mid-August to end of October) pure transient; *note*—most records are coastal.

NORTHERN WATERTHRUSH *(Seiurus noveboracensis)*
Seasonal status—casual spring (early April to late June) and very rare fall (mid-August to late November) pure transient; *habitat*—usually found near fresh-water pools, streams, and swamps with dense overhead or nearby cover.

LOUISIANA WATERTHRUSH *(Seiurus motacilla)*
Seasonal status—accidental; *note*—one record: one at Mecca, Riverside County, Aug. 17, 1908. Specimen.

KENTUCKY WARBLER *(Oporornis formosus)*
Seasonal status—accidental; *note*—three records: one at Point Loma, San Diego County, June 4, 1968; one on Farallon Islands, June 2, 1969; one on Farallon Islands, July 1972. Photograph.

CONNECTICUT WARBLER *(Oporornis agilis)*
Seasonal status—accidental; *note*—nine records: 1958, 1963, 1964, 1965–2, 1968–3, 1969; five were spring records (May 28–June 22) and four were fall records (Sept. 13–Oct. 3). *Note*—six records from Farallon Islands, two from San Diego, and one from Monterey. Specimen.

MOURNING WARBLER *(Oporornis philadelphia)*
Seasonal status—accidental; *note*—two records: one at Deep Springs, Inyo County, June 12, 1968; one at Point Loma, San Diego County, Oct. 3, 1968. Specimen.

MacGILLIVRAY'S WARBLER *(Oporornis tolmiei)*
Seasonal status—spring and fall transient and summer visitor, early April to mid-October; *habitat*—for breeding, soft and montane chaparral, streamside thickets, forest undergrowth; in migration, thickets in lowlands including deserts; *range in California*—for *breeding,* Sierra Nevada, Klamath Mountains, Cascades, Coast Range south to about San Francisco; males have been found in the San Gabriel and San Bernardino Mountains of southern California in summer.

COMMON YELLOWTHROAT *(Geothlypis trichas)*
Seasonal status—resident, spring and fall transient, summer visitor; *habitat*—thick tangles near fresh-water or brackish-water marshes, sloughs, ponds, streams, lakes; *range in California*—for *breeding,* length of state in suitable habitat including eastern and southeastern deserts and Sierra Nevada; *note*—resident in San Francisco Bay area and in southern California; elsewhere, transient and summer visitor.

YELLOW-BREASTED CHAT *(Icteria virens)*
Seasonal status—spring and fall transient and summer visitor, April to mid-September; *habitat*—for *breeding,* dense thickets in riparian woodland; otherwise, thickets in lowlands during migration; *range in California*—length of state in suitable habitat.

RED-FACED WARBLER *(Cardellina rubrifrons)*
Seasonal status—accidental; *note*—one record: one near Holtville, Imperial County, May 30, 1970. Specimen.

HOODED WARBLER *(Wilsonia citrina)*
Seasonal status—vary casual spring (early May to mid-June) and fall (late August to late November) pure transient.

WILSON'S WARBLER *(Wilsonia pusilla)*
Seasonal status—common spring and fall transient and summer visitor, late March to late October; *habitat*—for breeding—thickets of low vegetation in riparian woodlands or near water; otherwise, lowland thickets in migration; *range in California*—for *breeding,* length of state, irregularly distributed but absent from floor of Modoc Plateau, eastern and southeastern deserts, and floor of Central Valley; in migration, lowlands almost everywhere.

CANADA WARBLER *(Wilsonia canadensis)*
Seasonal status—very casual spring (late May to mid-June) and casual fall (late September to late November) pure transient; *note*—most fall records are coastal.

AMERICAN REDSTART *(Setophaga ruticilla)*
Seasonal status—very uncommon spring (mid-April to late June) and uncommon fall (early August to mid-December) transient; a few winter; *habitat*—riparian woodland, oak woodland, parks, open forest; *range in California*—length of state; *note*—this is the commonest of the "eastern" warblers to reach California; first found *nesting* in the state near Eureka, Humboldt County July 1972.

PAINTED REDSTART *(Myioborus pictus)*
  Seasonal status—casual visitor; *note*—most records are for fall and winter with only
  a few for spring and summer; northernmost station was in Kern County and all
  others from southern California. Unsuccessful nesting in Laguna Mountains, San
  Diego County, May 1974.

Weaver Finches

HOUSE SPARROW *(Passer domesticus)*—INTRODUCED into United States
  Seasonal status—common resident; *habitat*— cities, towns, suburbs, gardens, parks,
  farms, ranches, stables; *range in California*—length of state, in vicinity of human
  habitation. *Breeds; note*—reached California from adjacent states.

House Sparrow—male

Blackbirds and Orioles

BOBOLINK *(Dolichonyx oryzivorus)*
  Seasonal status—very rare spring (May) and very uncommon fall (September and
  October) transient; formerly and possibly still may be a rare summer visitor to
  the Modoc Plateau; *habitat*—in migration, oases, meadows, agricultural lands;
  range in California—spring birds occur in the extreme eastern-central portions;
  fall birds are coastal; *breeding* status today as in past is questionable.
WESTERN MEADOWLARK *(Sturnella neglecta)*
  Seasonal status—common resident; *habitat*—meadows, grassland, savannah, greenswards; *range in California*—length of state in suitable habitat. *Breeds.*
YELLOW-HEADED BLACKBIRD *(Xanthocephalus xanthocephalus)*
  Seasonal status—resident within state but some birds withdraw to south in September and return to breeding grounds in April and May; summer visitor to
  northern and central California breeding areas, April to September; *habitat*—for

breeding, fresh-water marshes of tules, cattails, and bulrushes; otherwise, lake shores, agricultural lands that have been freshly plowed or irrigated; *range in California*—for *breeding,* Modoc Plateau south to Owens Valley, marshy mountainous lakes, Central Valley, Imperial Valley, Colorado River Valley, and spottily along coast from Marin County south; otherwise, length of state except northwest coastal forest region.

*Yellow-headed Blackbird
—male*

RED-WINGED BLACKBIRD *(Agelaius phoeniceus)*
Seasonal status—common resident; *habitat*—fresh-water marshes, brackish-water marshes, grain and mustard fields, borders of lakes, rivers, ponds, and streams; commonly forages over agricultural lands; *range in California*—length of state in suitable habitat. *Breeds.*

TRICOLORED BLACKBIRD *(Agelaius tricolor)*
Seasonal status—resident within state but populations nomadic in fall and winter; they desert the breeding marshes and wander about agricultural lands in almost pure flocks but occasionally consort with other blackbirds; *habitat*—for breeding, fresh-water marshes of tules, cattails, bulrushes, sedges; *range in California*—for *breeding,* Central Valley, coastal areas from Sonoma County south, Modoc Plateau.

ORCHARD ORIOLE *(Icterus spurius)*
Seasonal status—casual visitor; *note*—most records are from fall and winter and a few from spring.

HOODED ORIOLE *(Icterus cucullatus)*
Seasonal status—primarily a summer visitor, late March to early September; *habitat*—for *breeding,* riparian woodland, palm oases, suburbs, parks, cities, towns, farms, ranches, and other places where palms and broad-leaved trees have been planted; *range in California*—lowland areas of southern half of state; numerous winter records.

Hooded Oriole—male

SCARLET-HEADED ORIOLE *(Icterus pustulatus)*

Seasonal status—accidental; *note*—five records: one at La Mesa, San Diego County, May 1, 1931; one near Imperial Beach, San Diego County, Sept. 22, 1962; one near Imperial Beach, San Diego County, Oct. 13, 1962; one near Imperial Beach, San Diego County, Oct. 8, 1963; one at Rancho Park, Los Angeles County, Jan. 2-5, 1966. Specimen.

SCOTT'S ORIOLE *(Icterus parisorum)*

Seasonal status—summer visitor, late March to late September; *habitat*—piñon-juniper woodland, high desert Joshua Tree "woodlands," palm oases; *range in California*—Colorado and Mojave Deserts north to Inyo County; a few birds winter in southern portions of state. *Breeds.*

NORTHERN ORIOLE *(Icterus galbula)*

"Baltimore" Oriole

Seasonal status—casual visitor, fall through spring; *note*—has occurred as far north as Marin County.

"Bullock's" Oriole (formerly *Icterus bullockii*)

Seasonal status—summer visitor, March to late September; *habitat*—riparian woodland, oak woodland, orchards, savannah; *range in California*—for *breeding,* length of state except humid coastal coniferous forest, mountain forests; some birds winter.

RUSTY BLACKBIRD *(Euphagus carolinus)*

Seasonal status—casual visitor but possibly a rare but regular fall transient in eastern portions of state; most records are fall and winter; very rare west of the Coast Range.

BREWER'S BLACKBIRD *(Euphagus cyanocephalus)*

Seasonal status—common resident; *habitat*—meadows, grasslands, agricultural lands, cities, towns, suburbs, parks; *range in California*—length of state in suitable habitat; *note*—birds of the mountain meadows and northeastern plateau move southward and to lower elevations for winter. *Breeds.*

GREAT-TAILED GRACKLE *(Cassidix mexicanus)*

Seasonal status—rare and local resident in lower Colorado River Valley; casual in Imperial Valley and accidental elsewhere; *note*—this species first was noted in the lower Colorado River Valley in 1964, was *nesting* by 1969, and slowly drifted west to the Imperial Valley in very small numbers.

BROWN-HEADED COWBIRD *(Molothrus ater)*

Seasonal status—resident within state but summer visitor to Modoc Plateau and Great Basin area; *habitat*—riparian woodland, meadows, pastures, ranches, agricultural land, suburbs, towns, parks, meadows; *range in California*—most of state except higher portions of Sierra Nevada, Cascades, Klamath Mountains, humid coastal coniferous forest, and parts of northern Coast Range. *Breeds.*

BRONZED COWBIRD *(Tangavius aeneus)*

Seasonal status—very rare summer visitor to lower Colorado River Valley; *note*—first noted in 1951; young birds have been seen so *breeding* is presumed.

Tanagers

WESTERN TANAGER *(Piranga ludoviciana)*

Seasonal status—complex transient and summer visitor, late April to late September; *habitat*—for breeding, open coniferous forests in mountains primarily in the Transition and Canadian Life Zones; otherwise, lowlands in general during migration; *range in California*—for *breeding,* length of state in suitable habitat.

Western Tanager—male

SCARLET TANAGER *(Piranga olivacea)*

Seasonal status—casual visitor spring (May 23–31) and fall (Sept. 26–Nov. 17); birds are presumably transients with nine fall records and three in spring.

HEPATIC TANAGER *(Piranga flava)*

Seasonal status—casual visitor; *note*—noted as far north as Monterey County and Oasis, Inyo County; records scattered throughout the year but suspected of nesting in the San Bernardino Mountains at Arrastre Creek, San Bernardino County, in 1971; definitely *nested* there (as newly fledged young were seen) in July 1972.

SUMMER TANAGER *(Piranga rubra)*

Seasonal status—rare summer visitor; *habitat*—riparian woodland; *range in California*—for *breeding,* lower Colorado River Valley; an isolated westernmost small group breeds at Morongo Valley, San Bernardino County each year; at other times ranges to coast as far north as Farallon Islands and various inland areas.

Finches and Sparrows

CARDINAL *(Cardinalis cardinalis)*

Seasonal status—uncommon and local resident; *habitat*—riparian woodland thickets; *range in California*—lower Colorado River near Parker Dam, Imperial County; *note*—this group was first noted in 1943 and has *nested;* these are native Cardinals of the Arizona race; a group of eastern Cardinals was INTRODUCED along the San Gabriel River, San Jose Creek, and Rio Hondo, Los Angeles County, prior to 1923 and a few pairs still persist.

PYRRHULOXIA *(Pyrrhuloxia sinuata)*

Seasonal status—accidental; *note*—one bird, probably constituting three records, was near Westmorland, Imperial County, Feb. 24–March 6, 1971, Dec. 31, 1971–March 27, 1972, and Jan. 27–Mar. 1, 1973; another male was at Calipatria, Imperial County, Jan. 20–Feb. 10, 1973. Photograph.

ROSE-BREASTED GROSBEAK *(Pheucticus ludovicianus)*

Seasonal status—casual visitor; *note*—seen throughout the year, length of the state.

Black-headed Grosbeak—female

BLACK-HEADED GROSBEAK *(Pheucticus melanocephalus)*
Seasonal status—transient and summer visitor, late March to mid-September; *habitat*—for breeding, open coniferous montane forest, riparian woodland, oak woodland in foothills and lower mountain slopes; otherwise, woodland patches and groves in lowlands; *range in California*—for *breeding,* length of state in suitable habitat.

BLUE GROSBEAK *(Guiraca caerulea)*
Seasonal status—summer visitor, mid-April to mid-September; *habitat*—thickets near riparian woodland and stream borders, mustard fields; *range in California*—Central Valley, Owens Valley, lower Colorado River Valley, Imperial Valley, southwestern lowlands west and south of the Transverse and Peninsular Ranges; *breeds; note*—in migration occurs in desert lowlands.

INDIGO BUNTING *(Passerina cyanea)*
Seasonal status—casual visitor, spring and fall; *note*—more common in spring than fall at desert oases in eastern California; may be a rare but regular transient.

LAZULI BUNTING *(Passerina amoena)*
Seasonal status—summer visitor, mid-April to early September; *habitat*—brushland and chaparral; *range in California*—length of state for *breeding* (except southeastern deserts).

VARIED BUNTING *(Passerina versicolor)*
Seasonal status—accidental; *note*—one substantiated record: 15 at Blythe, Riverside County, Feb. 8-9, 1914. Specimen.

PAINTED BUNTING *(Passerina ciris)*
Seasonal status—accidental; *note*—nine records: 1962–3; 1963–2; 1971; 1972–3; eight are fall records (Aug. 31–Nov. 10) with but one spring record (May 4); other birds have occurred at feeders near large metropolitan areas and it is questionable as to whether they are escapees or wild birds.

DICKCISSEL *(Spiza americana)*
Seasonal status—casual visitor; *note*—has appeared as far north as Humboldt County.

EVENING GROSBEAK *(Hesperiphona vespertina)*
Seasonal status—resident in mountains; casual winter visitor in lowlands; *habitat*—for breeding, coniferous forest of subalpine type in Canadian and Hudsonian Life Zones; *range in California*—for *breeding*—mountains in northern half of state—Sierra Nevada, Cascades, Klamath Mountains, Warner Mountains, coastal mountains in Humboldt County; irregularly appears in southern California mountains and lowland areas length of the state in winter and these incursions may be related to weather conditions and food supplies in the mountains.

PURPLE FINCH *(Carpodacus purpureus)*
Seasonal status—resident within state plus some winter visitors from north; vertical migration of mountain-nesting birds in fall and spring; *habitat*—for *breeding,* mixed coniferous and deciduous forest, oak woodlands; prefers shady, cool, humid canyons; *range in California*—western slopes of Sierra Nevada and Cascades;

mountains of southern California; Coast Range south to northern Ventura County; *note*–lowland areas in winter.

CASSIN'S FINCH *(Carpodacus cassinii)*

Seasonal status–common resident; *habitat*–primarily *breeds* in the subalpine forests of the Canadian and lower portions of the Hudsonian Life Zones; at lower levels sometimes overlaps with Purple Finch but this bird prefers the colder regions; *range in California*–Cascades, Sierra Nevada, higher Basin and Range mountains, Klamath Mountains and northern inner Coast Range, Mt. Pinos in Ventura County, and Transverse and northern Peninsular Ranges; *note*–some birds descend to lowlands in winter but not as many as Purple Finches.

HOUSE FINCH *(Carpodacus mexicanus)*

Seasonal status–common resident; *habitat*–open woodland, edges of forest, woodland, and chaparral; desert, cities, towns, suburbs, gardens, parks, farms, ranches, agricultural land, savannah; *range in California*–length of state. *Breeds.*

PINE GROSBEAK *(Pinicola enucleator)*

Seasonal status–uncommon resident; *habitat*–subalpine forests of Canadian and Hudsonian Life Zones; *range in California*–only in northern half of Sierra Nevada. *Breeds.*

GRAY-CROWNED ROSY FINCH *(Leucosticte tephrocotis)*

Seasonal status–resident; *habitat*–for *breeding,* Arctic Alpine Life Zone; *range in California*–higher portions of Sierra Nevada above 10,000 feet; also in the White Mountains and a different race (Hepburn's) occurs as resident on Mt. Shasta; *note*–in winter some of these birds move down-mountain and feed in the higher sagebrush valleys and on the talus slopes amidst piñon pine and juniper.

BLACK ROSY FINCH *(Leucosticte ater)*

Seasonal status–accidental; *note*–four records: one at Bodie, Mono County, Jan. 15, 1904; two near Hallelujah Junction, Lassen County, March 30, 1941; two near Deep Springs, Inyo County, Nov. 19, 1947; 3 near Deep Springs, Inyo County, Nov. 15, 1972. Specimen.

COMMON REDPOLL *(Acanthis flammea)*

Seasonal status–accidental; *note*–three records, but only one since 1900: "large flocks" around Eagle Lake, Lassen County, Nov. 30–Dec. 23, 1899; one in Plumas County, Dec. 23, 1899; one at Manila, Humboldt County, May 22, 1969. Specimen.

PINE SISKIN *(Spinus pinus)*

Seasonal status–resident within state but some mountain birds descend to lowlands for the winter; *habitat*–for breeding, coniferous forest; montane forest and subalpine forest from Transition to Hudsonian Life Zones; in lowlands during winter or away from coastal coniferous forests, riparian woodland, savannah, weedy fields, pastures–often in the company of goldfinches; *range in California*–northern mountain areas, Coast Range south to Monterey County, Sierra Nevada south to Peninsular Ranges (Mt. San Jacinto) for *breeding;* otherwise, length of state.

AMERICAN GOLDFINCH *(Spinus tristis)*
Seasonal status—resident; *habitat*—riparian woodland, orchards, savannah; *range in California*—primarily west of the Cascades, Sierra Nevada, and deserts. *Breeds.*

LESSER GOLDFINCH *(Spinus psaltria)*
Seasonal status—resident; *habitat*—riparian woodland, open forest, savannah, open areas with trees nearby; *range in California*—length of state. *Breeds.*

LAWRENCE'S GOLDFINCH *(Spinus lawrencei)*
Seasonal status—resident in southern half of state; summer visitor elsewhere; *habitat*—riparian woodland, oak woodland, open forest, montane forest of a more arid nature, piñon-juniper woodland; *range in California*—west of Cascades and Sierra Nevada and south of the northern mountains; coastwise (from about Sonoma County) and interiorly south through Central Valley to Mexican border. *Breeds.*

RED CROSSBILL *(Loxia curvirostra)*
Seasonal status—primarily resident but some influx of winter visitors from the north; *habitat*—primarily coniferous forests with pines but other types of coniferous forest as well; *range in California—breeds* in Coast Range south to Monterey County, Cascades, Sierra Nevada south through Mt. Pinos and San Bernardino and San Jacinto Mountains; *note*—flocks irregularly appear in lowland areas; has *bred* on Palos Verdes Peninsula, Los Angeles County.

GREEN-TAILED TOWHEE *(Chlorura chlorura)*
Seasonal status—transient and summer visitor, April to October; also winter visitor in small numbers in southern California; *habitat*—for breeding, mountain chaparral; otherwise, lowland thickets and oases; *range in California*—for *breeding,* Cascades, northern Coast Range south to Mendocino County, Sierra Nevada south through Mt. Pinos and Transverse Ranges to Mt. San Jacinto in Peninsular Ranges; Great Basin south through mountains of Inyo County.

RUFOUS-SIDED TOWHEE *(Pipilo erythrophthalmus)*
Seasonal status—primarily resident; *habitat*—chaparral and forest undergrowth, riparian thickets; *range in California*—extensive: absent only from higher mountain areas and southeastern deserts. *Breeds.*

BROWN TOWHEE *(Pipilo fuscus)*
Seasonal status—common resident; *habitat*—brushlands, chaparral of a more broken type, riparian thickets, thickets and edges in cities, towns, suburbs, parks, farms, ranches; *range in California*—absent from extreme northern, northeastern, eastern, and southeastern portions of state; not found on western edge of San Joaquin Valley; widespread elsewhere. *Breeds.*

ABERT'S TOWHEE *(Pipilo aberti)*
Seasonal status—resident; *habitat*—desert scrub of a thicker type, preferably with water nearby; *range in California*—lower Colorado River Valley; Imperial and Coachella Valleys of Colorado Desert. *Breeds.*

LARK BUNTING *(Calamospiza melanocorys)*
Seasonal status—rare and irregular visitor; *habitat*—open country such as desert,

grassland, agricultural land, arid brushland; *range in California*—in lowlands, length of state.

SAVANNAH SPARROW *(Passerculus sandwichensis)*
Seasonal status—complex: local resident, local summer visitor, local winter visitor, and widespread winter visitor, depending upon the subspecies; *habitat*—wide variety of grassland and meadows, grassy slopes; two subspecies breed in coastal salt-water marshes and one subspecies winters along edges of salt-water marshes and on coastal sand dunes; *range in California*—for *breeding,* coastal strip south to Monterey County and then interruptedly south to Mexican border; northeastern plateau region south through Owens Valley; otherwise, lowlands length of state west of deserts.

GRASSHOPPER SPARROW *(Ammodramus savannarum)*
Seasonal status—irregular local resident; northern and highland birds withdraw to south and west for the winter; *habitat*—grassland; *range in California*—erratic and irregular from one year to the next; west of Sierra Nevada and Cascades and southward from the head of the Sacramento Valley and northern mountains to San Diego County. *Breeds.*

BAIRD'S SPARROW *(Ammodramus bairdii)*
Seasonal status—accidental; *note*—one record: one at Farallon Islands Sept. 28, 1969. Specimen.

LE CONTE'S SPARROW *(Ammospiza leconteii)*
Seasonal status—accidental; *note*—one record: one at Farallon Islands, Oct. 13, 1970. Specimen.

SHARP-TAILED SPARROW *(Ammospiza caudacuta)*
Seasonal status—casual visitor with all post-1900 records falling between Oct. 17 and about April 1; *habitat*—salt-water marshes and fresh-water marshes near coast.

VESPER SPARROW *(Pooecetes gramineus)*
Seasonal status—winter visitor, and summer visitor to northeastern plateau and Great Basin region; *habitat*—for breeding, Great Basin desert; otherwise, short grass plains, meadows, sagebrush flats; *range in California*—for *breeding,* Basin and Ranges Region south to Inyo County; also in high mountain meadows along southern Sierran crest; otherwise lowlands west of Sierra Nevada and Cascades south.

LARK SPARROW *(Chondestes grammacus)*
Seasonal status—resident within state but summer visitor to northeastern plateau region; *habitat*—savannah, orchards, agricultural land with trees nearby, fields with brushy borders; *range in California*—*breeds* chiefly in lowland and foothill areas west of Sierra Nevada and Cascades; otherwise generally length of state.

RUFOUS-CROWNED SPARROW *(Aimophila ruficeps)*
Seasonal status—resident; *habitat*—arid brushy slopes with grassy patches; *range in California*—Coast Range from Sonoma County south; western foothills of Sierra Nevada south through Tehachapis to junction with Coast Range; drier portions of Transverse and Peninsular Ranges. *Breeds.*

CASSIN'S SPARROW *(Aimophila cassinii)*
Seasonal status—accidental; *note*—three records, all from Farallon Islands: July 11, 1969; Sept. 23, 1969; June 4, 1970. Specimen.

BLACK-THROATED SPARROW *(Amphispiza bilineata)*
Seasonal status—resident in deserts of southern California; summer visitor to northern portions of Great Basin; *habitat*—Colorado, Mojave, and Great Basin Deserts; *range in California*—generally east of Sierra Nevada and Cascades. *Breeds.*

SAGE SPARROW *(Amphizpiza belli)*
Seasonal status—complex: resident within state but summer visitor to northeastern plateau region and other local movements within breeding ranges; *habitat*—brushland, especially areas vegetated with Great Basin Sagebrush, Antelope Brush, and various species of salt bush—for the "Sage" Sparrow type; for the "Bell's" Sparrow type, the preferred habitat is "hard" chaparral with stands of not-too-dense Chamise not over five feet in height; *range in California*—complex: northeast plateau region; inner Coast Range south to San Francisco then south through entire Coast Range to Mexican border and eastward through Tehachapis to Great Basin and northern Mojave Desert; also in Transverse and Peninsular Ranges and foothills of western slope of central Sierra Nevada. *Breeds.*

DARK-EYED JUNCO *(Junco hyemalis)*
"Slate-colored" Junco
Seasonal status—rare winter visitor, October to April; *habitat*—open country with brush nearby or open forest; *range in California*—length of state.

"Oregon" Junco (formerly *Junco oreganus*)
Seasonal status—resident within state, breeding in mountains and wintering in lowlands; *habitat*—for breeding, piñon-juniper woodland, montane and subalpine forests from Transition to Hudsonian Life Zones, coastal humid coniferous forest, coastal pine forest, mixed deciduous and coniferous forest; otherwise, lowland areas with brush, forest understory, and thickets; *range in California*—for *breeding,* major mountainous areas, and Coast Range south to San Luis Obispo County.

GRAY-HEADED JUNCO *(Junco caniceps)*
Seasonal status—summer visitor to mountains of eastern portion; very rare winter visitor elsewhere; *habitat*—for breeding, piñon-juniper woodland, montane forests of White Fir; *range in California*—for *breeding,* Clark Mountain, San Bernardino County, and Grapevine Mountains, Inyo County.

TREE SPARROW *(Spizella arborea)*
Seasonal status—very rare winter visitor; *habitat*—open country with brushy borders and thickets; *range in California*—primarily the northeastern plateau portion and the Great Basin; has reached Imperial Valley.

CHIPPING SPARROW *(Spizella passerina)*
Seasonal status—resident within state but some are transient, some are summer visitors to the mountains, and birds from northern California move south and down-mountain for the winter; *habitat*—for breeding, varied: oak woodland, orchards, mixed coniferous and deciduous forest, montane and subalpine forest

from Transition to Hudsonian Life Zones; otherwise lowland areas with brush and open forest in winter; *range in California*—length of state for *breeding* except eastern and southeastern deserts.

CLAY-COLORED SPARROW *(Spizella pallida)*
Seasonal status—casual visitor, extremely rare in spring, less so in fall; *habitat*—brushy and weedy fields in association with Chipping Sparrows; *range in California*—coastal areas in fall; has occurred on Farallon Islands in June.

BREWER'S SPARROW *(Spizella breweri)*
Seasonal status—some are resident within state; summer visitor to breeding areas; others are transient; *habitat*—for breeding, brushland, particularly that which has extensive stands of Great Basin Sagebrush; *range in California*—for *breeding,* Basin and Ranges Region south to higher portions of Mojave Desert; portions of Transverse and Peninsular Ranges and near Mt. Pinos where open stands of sagebrush exist.

FIELD SPARROW *(Spizella pusilla)*
Seasonal status—accidental; *note*—one record; one bird at Farallon Islands, June 17 to July 9, 1969. Photograph.

BLACK-CHINNED SPARROW *(Spizella atrogularis)*
Seasonal status—summer visitor, late March to September; *habitat*—for *breeding,* arid chaparral and tall brushland with Great Basin Sagebrush; *range in California*—scattered localities in foothills and mountains of southern inner Coast Range, Coast Range around south end of San Joaquin Valley and Tehachapis north along western slope of southern Sierra Nevada; eastern slope of southern Sierra Nevada and across Owens Valley to mountains of Basin and Range Region and eastern San Bernardino County; Transverse and Peninsular Ranges to Mexican border.

HARRIS' SPARROW *(Zonotrichia querula)*
Seasonal status—rare but regular winter visitor, October to May; thickets interspersed with open or grassy ground; often in company with White-crowned and Golden-crowned Sparrows when they are present; *note*—most frequently seen east of Sierra Nevada in Modoc Plateau, Great Basin, and the northern desert oases such as at Furnace Creek, Inyo County.

WHITE-CROWNED SPARROW *(Zonotrichia leucophrys)*
Seasonal status—resident within state; breeding birds of mountains and northeastern plateau move south and down-mountain in winter; some northern birds are winter visitors; *habitat*—for breeding, mountain meadows and willow thickets, lake edges with thickets, coastal chaparral, coastal brushland; otherwise lowland areas of agricultural type with brush cover nearby, open forest understory, suburbs, gardens, farms, ranches; *range in California*—for *breeding,* Warner Mountains, Cascades, Sierra Nevada, Coast Range close to the seacoast south to Santa Barbara County; otherwise, lowlands length of state.

GOLDEN-CROWNED SPARROW *(Zonotrichia atricapilla)*
Seasonal status—winter visitor, October to May; *habitat*—brushland, broken chap-

arral, gardens, suburbs; prefers denser cover than that frequented by White-crowned Sparrows with which it frequently associates; *range in California*—length of state.

*Golden-crowned Sparrow
—winter plumage*

WHITE-THROATED SPARROW *(Zonotrichia albicollis)*
Seasonal status—rare winter visitor, October to May; *habitat*—open brushland, agricultural land, farms, chaparral edge; gardens, parks, suburbs; *range in California*—length of state.

FOX SPARROW *(Passerella iliaca)*
Seasonal status—resident within state; some are transients and winter visitors from north and northeast; *habitat*—for breeding, brushland and mountain chaparral, riparian woodland, streamside tangles, and open forests of mixed brush and coniferous trees in mountains in Transition and Canadian Life Zones; otherwise, lowland thickets and brushlands throughout state except open deserts; *range in California*—for *breeding,* Klamath Mountains, Cascades, Warner Mountains, Sierra Nevada, northern inner Coast Range, higher Basin and Ranges mountains, Mt. Pinos in Ventura County, Transverse and Peninsular Ranges to Mt. San Jacinto, Riverside County.

LINCOLN'S SPARROW *(Melospiza lincolnii)*
Seasonal status—winter visitor, transient, and summer visitor; *habitat*—for breeding, mountain meadows of subalpine forest in Canadian Life Zone; otherwise, lowland thickets, riparian woodland undergrowth, open forest understory in winter and migration; *range in California*—for *breeding,* Klamath Mountains, inner northern Coast Range, Cascades, Warner Mountains, Sierra Nevada, locally in San Bernardino and San Jacinto Mountains.

SWAMP SPARROW *(Melospiza georgiana)*
Seasonal status—casual visitor, most records in winter, October to April; *habitat*—fresh-water marshes; *range in California*—mostly coastal.

SONG SPARROW *(Melospiza melodia)*
Seasonal status—common resident but birds of mountains and Great Basin move to lowlands for winter; *habitat*—streamside thickets, tangles, weed thickets, thickets of willows and reeds at edges of watercourses, marshes and lake borders, brushpiles, gardens, suburbs, edges of salt-water marshes, salt-water marshes of *Salicornia* and *Grindelia* bushes; *range in California*—length of state except higher portions of Sierra Nevada, Great Basin, Mojave, and Colorado Deserts except for those birds along Mojave River, in the Imperial Valley, and along the lower Colorado River. *Breeds.*

McCOWN'S LONGSPUR *(Calcarius mccownii)*
Seasonal status—casual or very rare fall transient and winter visitor; *habitat*—sparse plains, cultivated open fields; *range in California*—chiefly east of Sierra Nevada and Tehachapis to Imperial Valley.

LAPLAND LONGSPUR *(Calcarius lapponicus)*
Seasonal status—uncommon but regular fall transient and winter visitor, October to March; *habitat*—sparse plains, cultivated open fields; *range in California*—length of state, chiefly east of Cascades and Sierra Nevada but they occur at Point Reyes, Carrizo Plain, San Joaquin Valley, Antelope Valley, and Imperial Valley with some regularity.

CHESTNUT-COLLARED LONGSPUR *(Calcarius ornatus)*
Seasonal status—rare fall transient and casual winter visitor, October to February; *habitat*—sparse plains, cultivated open fields; *range in California*—chiefly east of Cascades and Sierra Nevada and south to Imperial Valley.

SNOW BUNTING *(Plectrophenax nivalis)*
Seasonal status—accidental; *note*—13 records from 1945 to 1972 all occurring between Oct. 26 and Jan. 30; from Humboldt Bay, Humboldt County, to Saratoga Springs, San Bernardino County. Specimen.

The following birds, included in the North American avifauna by the 1957 A.O.U. *Checklist,* have appeared in California one way or another but have been excluded from the Annotated List of the Birds of California because of insufficient evidence regarding their wild status or because of sight records lacking sufficient details:

Falcated Teal *(Anas falcata)*

Baikal Teal *(Anas formosa)*

Spectacled Eider *(Somateria fischeri)*

Kiskadee Flycatcher *(Pitangus sulphuratus)*

American Flamingo *(Phoenicopterus ruber)*

Mute Swan *(Cygnus olor)*

Ruddy Sheld-duck *(Casarca ferruginea)*

Black Vulture *(Coragyps atratus)*

Whiskered Owl *(Otus trichopsis)*

Veery *(Catharus fuscescens)*

Eastern Bluebird *(Sialia sialis)*

Sprague's Pipit *(Anthus spragueii)*

Crested Myna *(Acrithoderes cristatellus)*

European Goldfinch *(Carduelis carduelis)*

Rustic Bunting *(Emberiza rustica)*

White Wagtail *(Motacilla alba)*

CHAPTER 4

California's Habitats for Birds

AT LEAST TWENTY-FIVE major habitats for birds can be recognized in California, all but three of which are natural habitats. After more than 200 years of European influence and settlement there are few areas remaining in California that still exist in the primeval state. However, despite the sometimes drastic changes rendered to the natural environment by man and his works, the adverse effects on California's wildlife and especially upon its bird life have been far less than in some other states and most other countries. As far as is known, no regular native breeding species other than the Sharp-tailed Grouse has been extirpated from or has become extinct in California since European settlement, although the Yellow Rail must now be considered extremely rare in the state and probably no longer breeds. In the case of the non-breeding Short-tailed Albatross which virtually disappeared from California's ocean waters after about 1900, the decline was due to the senseless and unremitting slaughter of the birds on their nesting islands near Japan. Certain species such as the California Condor, the California race of the Brown Pelican, the Peregrine Falcon, one race of the Bald Eagle, three races of the Clapper Rail in California, and the California race of the Least Tern have been so dangerously reduced in numbers as to have been declared by the California Fish and Game Commission to be "endangered or rare species" and therefore deserving of complete and special protection. The decline of at least some of these species is due to habitat alteration, destruction, or disappearance. For the White-tailed Kite, however, the reverse has been true in California and throughout the rest of its range in North America and South America as well. Earlier in the twentieth century, the White-tailed Kite was considered an endangered species in California and its rapid demise was predicted, especially in view of its shy habits and the anticipated urban and agricultural growth of the state. Yet despite these apparent handicaps, this kite has made a re-

markable recovery in recent years and its population and range expanded throughout suitable habitats in California. This may be due to expansion of agricultural
lands and the increase in meadow mice.

Other species formerly extremely casual or even unknown in California became
established as nesters within suitable habitats in recent years after having arrived in
enough numbers to colonize. Perhaps these suitable habitats did not exist in earlier
times or perhaps the species did not reach California in sufficient numbers to become firmly established in the past. For example, Cattle Egrets have a virtually un-
breakable foothold in the state and are expanding their range and numbers northward. Other recently discovered or recently arrived new breeders are Black
Skimmers, Whip-poor-wills, American Redstarts, and Hepatic Tanagers. Thus, despite the inevitable changes that have taken place in the natural landscape and
habitats of California, there has been a slight net gain of breeding birds and this is
probably due to the creation of new habitats in some cases. Also, changes in old
habitats and the creation of new habitats has had effects on the existing breeding
species as some have declined while others have expanded in range and population.
Although the Northern Parulas that nested in the grayish *Ramalina* lichens of
Point Lobos in the Monterey Peninsula in 1952 found suitable environmental conditions that closely approximated the Spanish Moss habitat of their traditional nesting areas in the southeastern United States, their population nucleus was too small
to sustain itself. A few Northern Parulas occur in California each year, but their
numbers are so few as to preclude the possibility of an adult pair meeting at the
right time or in the right habitat.

California's habitats for birds extend from the open sea and coastal islands on
the Pacific Coast to the searing deserts and arid plateaus in the east, and from the
humid coastal forests and deeply eroded mountains of the north to the Salton Sea
(whose surface waters are more than 200 feet below sea level) in the south. Between and among these extremes in topography, climate, precipitation, and elevation are to be found the multitude of California's wild and not-so-wild habitats for
birds. Some of the birds of California range over several habitat types during the
nesting season and may change to other habitat types during migration and in the
non-breeding season. For example, the MacGillivray's Warbler (a summer visitor)
occurs in the open desert and especially at desert oases during spring migration. As
it progresses further north it frequents cool foothill canyons and riparian woodlands before arriving at its preferred nesting habitat on the cool brushy and wooded
slopes of the coastal mountains and the northern Sierra Nevada. While in its winter range, which extends from southern Baja California and Sonora, Mexico, south
to Colombia, it inhabits an even greater variety of habitats. For this and other species as well, the *quality* of the *nesting* habitat is most critical. On the other hand, the
resident Nuttall's Woodpecker is confined to virtually a single habitat—interior and
coastal foothill belts containing extensive stands of oaks. However, another species,
the Common Raven, extends in its breeding range from sea level on the coastal islands, across the valleys, foothills, the high Sierras, to the deserts of the south-

eastern corner. Probably no other California bird nests in such a variety of habitats. In general, however, migratory land birds tend to seek similar habitats, en route, to their preferred nesting habitat.

THE SEA AND THE SEACOAST

California's extensive mainland and island seacoast, which totals almost 1,500 miles in length, includes some of the richest bird habitats to be found anywhere in North America. Because of the physical and biological nature of the ocean waters and the lagoons, beaches, bays, estuaries, salt-water marshes, and tidal flats that border them, the bird life along the seacoast is as diverse as it is plentiful. One factor that contributes to the uniqueness of the coastal avifauna is the open nature of the environment. The oceans being continuous, are literally open to the rest of the world, and offer broad unbroken avenues over which sea birds can travel. While there are real oceanic barriers to the dispersal of marine organisms including some sea birds, these barriers are more easily overcome by many of the pelagic birds. Virtually any true sea bird from any part of the world could conceivably appear off the California coast. That this does not occur with any frequency or regularity attests to the vastness of the oceans, the real barriers of sea temperatures and prevailing winds, and the deeply ingrained migratory habits of birds in general and sea birds in particular. The belts of tropical water, which in a very real sense isolate the northern hemisphere oceans from the southern, are effective barriers to the passage of southern ocean albatrosses. But even such high southern latitude species as Wandering, Black-browed, and Yellow-nosed Albatrosses, and Cape Petrels have at least once breached these barriers and reached the shores of the United States. Other species such as Sooty, Pink-footed, Short-tailed, and New Zealand Shearwaters routinely cross the tropical Pacific twice each year and pass along the California coast. The southern ocean albatrosses are no doubt inhibited by the relatively windless air masses of the doldrums near the equator and are thus thwarted from entering the northern oceans. Some albatrosses must have succeeded in crossing in sufficient numbers in the past, however, since there exist now three species of temperate Pacific albatrosses (Short-tailed, Laysan, and Black-footed) two of which, at one time at least, regularly visited the California coast. Today, only the Black-footed does. The Pacific Ocean, then, establishes California's contact with the farthest reaches of the earth and California's birders eagerly comb the seacoast for wanderers from far-off waters, searching for the world's greatest travelers, the sea birds.

For sea birds, the seacoast is not of itself a uniform habitat that is everywhere the same. At least five major subdivisions are recognizable. They are the open sea, the offshore islands and coastal sea cliffs, the sea beaches, reefs, and coastal waters, the lagoons, bays and estuaries, and the tidal salt-water marshes. These five habitats, while intimately involved with the sea itself, differ from one another in the nature of their physical and biological environments and the quality of their avifaunas.

The Open Sea

As the open sea habitat extends virtually unbroken completely around the globe, some limits must be established (for cataloging purposes only) to define the offshore boundaries of California. It would be useful and desirable to relate these arbitrary boundaries to some natural barrier or zoogeographic feature of the sea itself, i.e., the continental shelf or the California Current. Unfortunately the continental shelf along the California coast does not readily lend itself as such a natural boundary because of its complex nature, especially in southern California, but more importantly, it does not greatly influence the distribution of the birds of the open ocean. As for the feeble California Current, its unpredictable nature is well known as are its seasonal variations. Thus for no other reason than standardization and practicability, an offshore limit of 100 statute miles (measured perpendicularly from the nearest point of the mainland or offshore island, north of the Mexican border and south of the Oregon border, and extended 100 statute miles out to sea at the same latitude) is established as the statewide boundary of the Pacific coast of California and those birds that have occurred within these limits are considered to have occurred within the state. As for California's other aquatic border—the Colorado River in the southeast—the problem is much simpler as the bird need only be on the California side of the river or less than one-half the distance to the Arizona shore.

The habitat referred to here as the open sea is not easily defined, but is generally taken to mean the ocean waters out of sight of the mainland and inhabited by birds that do not come ashore on the mainland or on the islands to rest or feed, except during the breeding season when they come ashore for nesting activities only. It is inhabited by many birds whose complete home is the sea for as much as ten months of the year when they are not involved with courtship and breeding activities. For the first year of their lives some pelagic species such as shearwaters, storm-petrels, jaegers, many alcids, Sabine's Gulls, and Red Phalaropes spend the entire year on the open ocean. Some albatrosses, such as the Laysan, do not usually breed until their seventh year and the larger species (Wandering and Royal) even later. It is presumed that they spend these long years entirely at sea. During this time they do not come ashore to rest, sleep, feed, or even drink. All of these activities are accomplished on the open sea and often hundreds of miles from the nearest land. Occasionally these birds venture close to shore, especially when in pursuit of large schools of fish or squid and may even be seen feeding on garbage and refuse among the inshore waves. Even when this close to land, they do not come ashore except when sick or injured.

At first this open sea habitat appears monotonously uniform. Oceanographic measurements reveal real differences in depth, but in addition there are more subtle differences in temperature, salinity, dissolved gases, clarity, chemical quality, and other physical parameters which ultimately determine the quantity and quality of the marine microorganisms such as the phytoplankton and the zooplankton. These tiny plants and animals form the basis of the various food-chains that eventually lead to the pelagic birds themselves. Other factors such as ocean currents, sea mounts and banks, deep submarine canyons, and upwelling, coupled with the physical qualities of the sea water itself make for an extremely complex and dynamic environment that ultimately determines the distribution of the pelagic birds at any given moment. Some open ocean areas such as off Monterey Bay are consistently excellent for sea birds of all sorts. Other areas are exceptional for a few days and then the birds move on as their food supplies dwindle or shift.

The continental shelf off the California coast is more complex than on the Gulf or Atlantic coasts of the United States. In southern California, from the Mexican border to about Point Conception, the continental shelf is very narrow. Instead there is a series of submerged ranges and basins extending outward for about 160 miles and which is much more closely related in structure and topography to the land than to the deep ocean. This region of submarine banks and basins is termed the continental borderland and complicates the distribution of sea birds off southern California. In general, however, the greatest concentrations are often found close to the submarine banks where the deep cold water upwells to replace the warmer surface waters blown away by the prevailing winds. Sea bird concentrations are related to such biological events as surface concentrations of zooplankton, schools of surfacing anchovies, and spawning of squid. Large concentrations of Manx Shearwaters that occur sporadically have been attributed to this latter little-known phenomenon.

On either side of the three most pronounced breaks along the California coast at Point Conception, Monterey Peninsula, and Cape Mendocino are to be found the largest submarine canyons. Because of the upwelling of deep, nutrient-rich waters, these canyons, especially the one at Monterey Bay, attract hordes of pelagic birds throughout most of the year. Other large submarine canyons occur between Cape San Martin and Point Año Nuevo north of Monterey and are favored feeding areas for sea birds at certain times of the year. From San Francisco northward, the continental shelf is shallow and well defined, and in places extends outward for 25 miles, the greatest distance along the entire west coast of the United States.

Those birds which may be regarded as truly pelagic, that is, remain far at sea by day and night, rest and sleep on the sea surface, drink sea water, and feed on the animals of the open sea, are members of such groups as the albatrosses, the shearwaters, the storm-petrels, the tropicbirds, the phalaropes (Northern and Red), the gulls (Sabine's and Black-legged Kittiwake), the terns (Arctic), the jaegers and skuas, and most of the alcids. Other sea birds such as loons, grebes, Brown Pelicans, boobies, frigatebirds, cormorants, some of the sea ducks, and some of the gulls and terns are not truly pelagic species in that they frequent waters fairly close to the mainland and offshore islands and many of them roost on land during the night. Some of the gulls, terns, and the Brown Pelicans may venture well out of sight of land to feed with the pelagic species only to return to shore again that day.

None of the albatrosses, shearwaters, or fulmars nest on the California coast or its islands. Two albatrosses occur in California waters. The Laysan (occurring but rarely) and the Black-footed (occurring commonly) breed in the outer Hawaiian Islands during our winter season and are most numerous off the California coast during summer and fall. All of the shearwaters that frequent the California open-sea habitat breed somewhere to the south of the state. The Sooty and Short-tailed Shearwaters come from as far away as the waters off southern Australia. The New Zealand or Gray-backed Shearwater nests in distant New Zealand, but the Manx Shearwater breeds south of the Mexican border on islands off the west coast of Baja California. Of the eight species of storm-petrels that have occurred in California waters, only three species (Fork-tailed, Ashy, and the *beali* race of Leach's) nest in the state. A fourth species, the Black Storm-Petrel, nests on Los Coronados Islands just a few miles away from the U.S.–Mexico border. The Northern Fulmar is a high arctic breeder, as are both the Northern and Red Phalaropes, the three species of jaegers, the Arctic Tern, the Black-legged Kittiwake, and the Sabine's Gull. Of the thirteen species of alcids that have occurred in California, six species definitely breed in the state. They are the Common Murre, Pigeon Guillemot, Xantus' Murrelet (*scrippsi* race), Cassin's Auklet, Rhinoceros Auklet, and Tufted Puffin. The Marbled Murrelet, although its nest has not actually been found in North America, most certainly must nest in California. Other non-pelagic species that are frequently observed in migration over the open sea but rarely associate with the pelagic species as occasionally do the Brown Pelicans, cormorants, gulls, and terns, are loons of three species, scoters of three species, "Black" Brant, flocks of shorebirds of several species, and often such land birds as Mourning Doves, hummingbirds, swallows, Water Pipits, warblers, and sparrows.

None of the sea birds are herbivorous. The smaller ones such as the storm-petrels and phalaropes pick larger plankton organisms from the sea surface. The shearwaters chase surface-feeding fish, shrimp, and squid and may dive a short distance under the water in pursuit of prey. The alcids are active and vigorous surface divers, rapidly pursuing their prey by wing and foot propulsion under the water. Brown Pelicans, terns, and tropicbirds are plunge-divers, their prey being small fish that feed near the surface. The Skua, jaegers, and the Magnificent Frigatebirds are piratic birds of great maneuverability. They so aggressively pursue and harass gulls and terns that the frightened and confused birds regurgitate or drop the fish or other food that they have been carrying. So swift and agile are the pursuers that they can often seize the falling food before it splashes into the sea. Heermann's Gulls, which in flight strongly resemble jaegers, frequently chase terns for the latter's food. They also harass Brown Pelicans on the water and often succeed in snatching fish from the pelican's beak. The Black-footed Albatross scavenges for food on the sea surface, even feeding on garbage (they are persistent ship followers), offal, and dead organisms. In addition, they take small fish, squid, and larger crustaceans from the sea surface. The Laysan Albatrosses, on the other hand, feed almost exclusively on squid and other cephalopods that they obtain after dark and before dawn when these mollusks are known to come to the surface of the sea.

One of the most unique adaptations of some of the pelagic birds (notably the albatrosses, shearwaters, and storm-petrels, as well as some of the others) is their ability to drink sea water. No doubt this has been an essential contributing factor to their worldwide success. This remarkable feat is accomplished with the aid of a pair of special salt or "nasal" glands situated between the eyes and the beak. By means of this extra pair of "kidneys" these birds can distill the sea water they have drunk and concentrate the brine to almost twice the salinity of sea water. This brine is then expelled through the raised nostrils of the "tube-noses" where it either slides down a special groove at the side of the bill to drip off the tip as is the case of albatrosses or it may be forcibly expelled or "sneezed" into the air as in the case of the storm-petrels. Other seacoast birds possessed of this attribute include Brown Pelicans, cormorants, alcids, and gulls from which the brine is expelled by other means.

Some of the pelagic birds, notably the albatrosses and shearwaters, are among

Sooty Shearwaters on the open sea →

← Pink-footed Shearwater

Black-footed Albatross ↑

← Sooty Shearwater

Northern Fulmar—dark phase →

← Sabine's Gulls

↓ Black-legged Kittiwake—immature

← Red Phalarope—winter plumage

↑ New Zealand Shearwater

← Rhinoceros Auklet

← Pomarine Jaeger

the world's greatest travelers. One of the shearwaters, the Short-tailed, from its breeding islands off the south coast of Australia, completes an enormous figure-of-eight flight path that takes it into the north Pacific Ocean during which time it briefly skirts the California coast. By the time they return to their south temperate homes these birds will have completed a journey of more than 20,000 miles. Other California shearwaters come from as far away as New Zealand and Chile. The Short-tailed Albatross, formerly at least, came from Japan, and Laysan and Black-footed Albatrosses come from Midway Island in the outer Hawaiian chain. To traverse these vast distances across the open sea ordinarily would require a considerable expenditure of energy on the part of the birds. Dynamic soaring, a type of flight characteristic of these long-winged gliders, enables them to utilize even unfavorable prevailing winds to their advantage with a minimum of effort. This extraordinary type of gliding flight involves turning into the prevailing wind, gaining lift and some elevation, and then turning again and gliding "downhill" more or less in the preferred direction of migration. Additional lift is obtained from air deflected upward from the wave tops. During abnormally calm weather and flat seas, albatrosses and shearwaters become "becalmed" and have difficulty in rising from the sea surface. This is especially so after they have eaten heavily.

Birds of the open sea habitat may frequently be driven close to shore and even into open bays by strong onshore winds from the sea. At other times large feeding flocks may drift close to shore in pursuit of small fish or shrimp. The migratory flight paths of some sea birds, especially Sooty Shearwaters, may regularly bring them within viewing distance of the shore at such places as Point Loma, San Diego County; Point Fermin and Point Dume, Los Angeles County; Point Mugu, Ventura County; Point Sal, Santa Barbara County; Point Buchon, San Luis Obispo County; Point Sur and Point Pinos, Monterey County; Point Reyes, Marin County; Bodega Head, Sonoma County; Point Arena, Mendocino County; Cape Mendocino and Trinidad Head, Humboldt County; and Point St. George, Del Norte County. Excursions into the open sea from various ports along the California coast from San Diego to Eureka can be taken aboard sightseeing boats and sport-fishing boats. Specially chartered boats for birding are frequently engaged by bird clubs and other private natural history and hiking groups throughout the state. The open sea habitat can be visited any time of the year along the California coast with good results. During the spring migration of pelagic birds (May–June) great flocks of Sooty Shearwaters can be found along the entire length of the state. The open sea habitat in spring also includes Pink-footed Shearwaters, several species of storm-petrels, Black-footed Albatrosses, flocks of Arctic Terns, Sabine's Gulls in stunning plumage, Parasitic and Pomarine Jaegers, numbers of alcids of several species, and both Northern and Red Phalaropes. Fall brings additional shearwater species (notably Manx, New Zealand, and Flesh-footed), flocks of migrating Ashy and Black Storm-Petrels, Arctic Terns, Sabine's Gulls, Red and Northern Phalaropes, and such infrequently seen species as Skuas, Long-tailed Jaegers, Laysan Albatrosses, Fork-tailed Storm-Petrels, and in the southern part of the state, Magnificent Frigatebirds (close to the mainland), Red-billed Tropicbirds, Least Storm-Petrels, and Craveri's Murrelets. During the winter there is a southward movement of several species of alcids (Common Murres and Ancient and Marbled Murrelets), Northern Fulmars, and Black-legged Kittiwakes. Midsummer is the slack season for pelagic species although it is a rare day when no true oceanic bird can be seen offshore.

One of the more startling ornithological events observed on the open sea, especially during the spring migration, is the flight of small land birds (warblers, sparrows, blackbirds, tanagers, etc.) over the open ocean and heading in a more or less westerly or northwesterly direction. Unless these unfortunate waifs soon make a landfall or come aboard a vessel (which they frequently do when exhaustion finally overcomes their natural fear) they will fall exhausted into the sea and perish. The sea must claim many thousands of such birds each migratory season.

Most of these birds are nocturnal migrants which overshoot the coast before dawn and continue to fly in their "preferred" direction. This condition seems to be accentuated during overcast spring weather (especially during May) and those migrants are likely to be completely disoriented and far off course. This phenomenon may offer additional evidence for the theory that migratory birds of this type enter California from Mexico following a westerly or northwesterly flight path which eventually brings them to the coast at which time they normally swing northward and follow the coast. Southbound fall migrants encountered far at sea may have strayed over the open ocean as the north-south trending coast gradually swings to the southeast. That migratory small land birds populate the offshore islands of California indicates a considerable over-ocean flight of these birds.

The Offshore Islands and Coastal Sea Cliffs

California's largest offshore islands are well vegetated and are inhabited by animals and land birds that are identical or very similar to those found on the mainland and are of no special concern to an understanding of the birds of the seacoast. Migration of land birds does occur through the offshore islands in a time pattern similar to that of the mainland. The smaller offshore islands (Los Coronados, Santa Barbara Islands, Anacapa Island, the Farallon Islands, and the smaller islets and rocks) are largely devoid of significant vegetation for land birds, but are homes to tens of thousands of sea birds. However, South Farallon Island with its permanent bird-banding station operated by the Point Reyes Bird Observatory has proven to be an invaluable source of information regarding bird migration along the California coast. Also, a number of "first state records" have been obtained from there.

It is the sea cliffs of the mainland from about Morro Bay northward and the sea cliffs and other parts of the offshore islands where the various sea birds nest and roost that are of real importance to the birds of the California seacoast. The off-shore islands include about 290 miles of seacoast, the majority of which consists of precipitous sea cliffs and a lesser area of rocky beaches and sandy beaches. True sea cliffs extend for hundreds of miles along the mainland coast, but are broken here and there by sandy beaches, rocky beaches, bays, estuaries, lagoons, and river mouths. Probably because of human use and disturbance, the sea cliffs of California south of about Morro Bay no longer harbor many nesting sea birds. It is indeed for-tunate that most of California's offshore islands are relatively inaccessible to all ex-cept fishermen, skin divers, and yachtsmen because the nesting birds there are as-sured of little or no disturbance by the general public. Some islands are in private ownership while others are administered by the military. In both situations, tres-passing is prohibited and the birds remain undisturbed. Los Coronados Islands be-long to the Republic of Mexico but their avifauna is similar to that of other Cali-fornia offshore islands. San Clemente, San Nicolas, and San Miguel Islands are military property where no visiting is permitted. Santa Catalina, Santa Cruz, and Santa Rosa are almost entirely in private ownership and public entry is restricted on the private lands. Both Santa Barbara Island and the Anacapa Islands are included

Offshore island with Brown Pelicans and gulls

in Channel Islands National Monument and as a consequence are under the protection of the National Park Service. The Farallon Islands are a wildlife refuge formerly under the jurisdiction of the U.S. Coast Guard and contain the largest sea bird colonies in the contiguous United States. Eventually the Farallons may become a National Monument and receive the complete protection of the National Park Service.

The sea birds that utilize the islands and sea cliffs do so primarily for nesting and roosting purposes. During the non-breeding season many of the birds that nest on the offshore islands disperse somewhat along the coast of the mainland. Most of these birds are residents within the state and include such species as Brown Pelicans, Brandt's, Double-crested and Pelagic Cormorants, Common Murres, Pigeon Guillemots, and Western Gulls. Others, such as Fork-tailed Storm-Petrels, Marbled and Xantus' Murrelets, Cassin's Auklets, and Tufted Puffins, probably disperse widely over the open ocean well away from the mainland and become truly pelagic. Ashy Storm-Petrels, which may be residents in the state, probably follow this latter pattern as well, but the Beal's or white-rumped race of the Leach's Storm-Petrels is a summer visitor and probably leaves the state completely during the non-breeding season.

Those large sea birds that nest on ledges, cliff tops, and even on the island slopes include Brown Pelicans, the three species of cormorants, Common Murres, and Western Gulls. While not true sea birds, Black Oystercatchers nest and feed on rocky beaches, reefs, and shores at the bases of the island or mainland sea cliffs. Even during the nesting season, a few non-breeding Wandering Tattlers remain on these same rocky shores and beaches of the offshore islands. The large surface-nesting sea birds are active during the day and may travel scores of miles from their favored cliffs and islands in search of food. This often produces mixed flocks of truly pelagic species and those that are essentially coastal and island species. Other nesting sea birds of this habitat are the Fork-tailed, Leach's (*beali* race) and Ashy

Brown Pelican →

Brandt's Cormorant ↓

Pelagic Cormorant

Storm-Petrels, Xantus' Murrelets (*scrippsi* race), and Cassin's Auklets. This latter group of smaller birds includes those which are largely nocturnal at the nest burrows during the breeding season. These burrows have been tunnelled into the soft sod on top of the islands. Tufted Puffins are also burrow nesters but they are active at the nest site during daylight hours. Pigeon Guillemots, on the other hand, nest on ledges in sea caves, in crevices and rock crannies, and among the talus a little above high-water level on both islands and the mainland. Like the puffins, they too are active during the day at the nest site. Those species that today are island nesters exclusively are Brown Pelicans, Xantus' Murrelets, Cassin's Auklets, and Tufted Puffins. Common Murres nest primarily on offshore islets or islands. The following birds nest on both islands and on the mainland (principally from about Morro Bay northward) at secluded places: Brandt's and Pelagic Cormorants, Black Oyster-catchers, and Western Gulls. Double-crested Cormorants nest on some offshore islands and along the margins of lakes, sloughs, and large rivers inland. Marbled Murrelets no doubt nest on the heavily forested slopes on the mainland within the hu-

Black Oystercatchers

mid coast belt of the northwestern counties of Mendocino, Humboldt, and Del Norte.

Along the California coast, sea birds of all types find food plentiful. Frequently they must hunt over hundreds of square miles of ocean until they find the food resources they require, and this may take them many miles from their nesting and roosting cliffs. There is relatively little competition for food among the various types since the different species may seek different items of food. Where the same food item is sought (for example, shrimp, squid, or anchovies) it is usually so plentiful as to serve all those birds who hunt for it.

Natural hazards to sea birds are relatively unknown on ocean cliffs and offshore islands. Nesting as they do, they are relatively safe from predators. Instead, the chief threat to their survival stems from man himself. Human population expansion has

Wandering Tattler

already been cited as a major factor in the disappearance of many of California's mainland sea bird colonies. Ocean pollution by oil spillage or leakage resulting from ships discharging fuel oil at sea either deliberately or accidentally, oil tanker collisions, and leakage from undersea drill sites or wells is an ever-present menace. Once the sea birds become oil-soaked, the survival rate is very low even if the material can be removed from the feathers. Such oil pollution has resulted in the deaths of tens of thousands of sea birds along the California coast in recent years. A far more subtle and dangerous threat to sea bird survival along the California coast stems from the pollution of the ocean, particularly the southern coastal portion of it, by the pesticide DDT. DDT has been shown to interfere with the hormone production involved in the mobilization of calcium from the female bird's bones in order to produce a strong egg shell of a certain thickness. This phenomenon was first suspected among eggs of Peregrine Falcons in Great Britain in the early 1960's, but it was not until 1967 that enough incriminating evidence against the chlorinated hydrocarbon pesticides such as DDT was provided. The eggshell-thinning phenomenon was detected in the eggs of California Brown Pelicans in 1969 and surveys of the nesting colonies on Anacapa and Santa Barbara Islands that same year revealed almost total nonproduction of young pelicans due to eggshell breakage at the time of or soon after laying. Subsequently other studies revealed significant eggshell-thinning among cormorants, storm-petrels, alcids, and herons. DDT is essentially a nerve poison that results in tremors, convulsions, and ultimately death if taken in

Western Gulls

sufficient doses. However, among the sea birds of the California coast, the most obvious effect has been by eggshell-thinning and subsequent death of the embryo within. Thinning occurs in direct proportion to the amount of DDT (or DDE, a metabolic but no less dangerous product of DDT within the body) in the bird, and the breaking point seems to come when the eggs are 20 per cent thinner than normal. DDT and other chlorinated hydrocarbons contaminate the sea after having been applied to agricultural areas on the land. Rain washes it from plants and the soil into streams that ultimately empty into the Pacific Ocean. Much of it that was aerially sprayed by crop-dusters never reached the land surface but was carried aloft by air currents and later precipitated into the sea many miles from the source. DDT may be effective as a pesticide when applied in such extreme dilutions as 0.00003 parts per million. In such concentrations it is not injurious to birds. Unfortunately,

Pigeon Guillemots

DDT is a chemically tenacious and long-lived compound not easily broken down by chemical or biological agents in the sea. Also, being fat-soluble, it enters the bodies of tiny marine diatoms and deposits in the microscopic drops of oil which all living organisms have in their cells. As the diatoms are eaten by tiny marine animals (the zooplankton), the DDT is then transferred to the next higher level in the food-chain. Since it remains chemically unchanged during this time, it accumulates to a higher concentration at each feeding level of the food-chain. By the time it reaches the bodies of tiny fish, the concentration may have increased to 0.5 parts per million. When Brown Pelicans or cormorants feed on anchovy-sized fish with an accumulated DDT concentration of 10–20 parts per million in each fish, they receive a concentrated dose with each feeding. Ultimately the DDT concentration in an adult female Brown Pelican may reach almost 100 parts per million and the concentration of the DDT has been multiplied more than 1,000,000 times from the initial dilution sprayed on the crops far from the sea. It is impossible to determine how many tons of pure DDT have found their way to the oceans by this route and it is suspected that the industrial process for DDT production resulted in ocean contamination by more than 10,000,000 pounds of DDT off southern California alone.

Common Murre—winter plumage

Surveys have shown that nesting colonies of Brown Pelicans in the Gulf of California are relatively free of DDT contamination and continue to produce hundreds of young pelicans each year. Tagging of these young pelicans with colored streamers and markers revealed that many move northward into California waters in fall. It is to be hoped that the depleted California nesting colonies may eventually be naturally restocked by these Mexican birds.

The Sea Beaches, Reefs, and Coastal Waters

The sea beaches of California represent a sort of "hybrid" zone between the habitats of the immediate coastal waters on the one side and the tidal estuaries and salt-water marshes on the other in that it is frequented by representative birds from

Sea beach with gulls and shorebirds, Santa Barbara County

Pacific Loon—winter plumage

both sides of the strand. This habitat is a rather narrow strip of sparsely vegetated sand interrupted here and there by sea cliffs and rocky beaches of the intertidal zone. Its borders on the ocean side are constantly in a state of flux as the changing tides ebb and flow. The drier portions of the sea beach habitat offer very little nourishment for sea birds and relatively little cover among the Sand Verbena and Sand Strawberry plants. Consequently the number of breeding species in California is limited to just two on the sandy beaches—the Least Tern and the Snowy Plover. Black Oystercatchers nest along the rocky shores in secluded places on the mainland. Of the three species, the Least Tern of the California race has been classified as an endangered species by the California Fish and Game Commission. Fortunately some of the necessary habitat for Least Tern nesting colonies falls within the boundaries of large military installations such as those at the Seal Beach Naval

Red-throated Loon

Black Turnstone

Weapons Station and the huge United States Marine Base at Camp Pendleton near Oceanside. In the latter situation the Marines have made a special effort to restrict entry to and limit the use of the Least Terns' nesting areas so as to ensure the maximum production of young terns during the critical breeding season. Another Least Tern nesting sanctuary was established by the city of Long Beach.

Because this singular habitat is so narrow, its total area is not very great although in California the coastline extends for almost 1,200 miles. Sea beaches close to centers of human population invite considerable human traffic and use. As a result of this, the undisturbed areas of sea beach suitable for nesting within the Least Tern's breeding range from the Mexican border to Monterey have largely been usurped for human habitation and recreation. That the Snowy Plover has not declined in numbers as has the Least Tern is probably due to its more extensive breeding range in California (from Mexico to the Oregon border) which enables it to nest relatively undisturbed on the more secluded and less popular northern beaches. Another factor that probably contributes to its success is its willingness to inhabit busy sea beaches with people in close proximity. This is because it is less timid than the Least Tern, a colonial nester. For the colony nester, a single human intruder promptly puts the entire colony to flight and some time passes before calm once again settles in the tern colony. The Snowy Plovers, not being colonial nesters, are more tolerant of human intrusion. Additionally, the Snowy Plovers also nest away from ocean beaches on salt-pond dikes, and on shores of brackish or alkali lakes inland. The Least Tern, on the other hand, nests only close to the seacoast in the southern portion of the state.

During the summer months, the sea beach habitat is rather depauperate of bird life. However, during the spring, winter, and fall months migratory birds from other habitats near and far congregate on the sea beaches and although the Least Terns have departed, large flocks of other species of terns have replaced them. The resident Snowy Plovers remain throughout the year although there is some withdrawal southward of those inhabitants of the northern beaches. It is the tidal areas along the sea beaches rather than the dry upper beach zone that provide the abundant marine life for many of the sea, water, and shorebirds utilizing the beaches. This rich marine food resource consists primarily of animals such as sand crabs, marine worms, small bivalves, and various crustaceans that live in sand burrows at the water's edge. These must be probed for. Consequently such birds as Willets, Marbled Godwits, and Whimbrels, all of which are equipped with long probing beaks, are habitual visitors to the sea beaches. The much smaller Sanderlings with their short legs and relatively short bills pick their tiny food from the sand surface or just beneath it and are a familiar sight as they scurry back and forth in front of the breaking waves. The Snowy Plovers and the nonresident Black-bellied Plovers with their relatively short stubby bills are not really sand or mud probers. Their feeding habits are quite different from the probers. They stand quietly watching for some small movement on the surface of the sand. When an insect or a small crustacean such as an isopod scurries into the open the plovers make a sudden swift dash for their prey.

Rocky shores and reefs adjacent to sea beaches attract hordes of shorebirds and gulls especially during the winter months when their populations along the coast are high and when the daytime tidal changes are extreme for the year. The outgoing low tide exposes myriads of intertidal invertebrates that normally are exposed only rarely or during nocturnal low-tide periods at other times of the year. These rocks provide rich new sources of food for the shorebirds. Rocky reefs and man-made rocky breakwaters in the intertidal zone not only attract shorebirds and gulls from adjacent sea beaches, bays, and salt-water marshes when the usually submerged rock surfaces are exposed during low tides, but Surfbirds, Black Turnstones, Black Oystercatchers, Wandering Tattlers, and Rock Sandpipers are rarely found in any other habitat. Of these five species, only the Black Oystercatchers are residents. They occur on the offshore islands as far south as Los Coronados Islands, but on the mainland are rarely found south of Avila Beach, San Luis Obispo County. Of the other four species, the Rock Sandpiper is a rare but regular winter visitor. The other three are both transients and winter visitors. Black Turnstones and Surfbirds frequently occur together and are the most typical shorebirds to be found along California's rocky shores. The Wandering Tattler is a solitary species which is nowhere common. Sea beaches and rocky intertidal shores often occur in close proximity to tidal estuaries and salt-water marshes from which the gulls and shorebirds make regular forays to the seacoast during daytime low tides.

Besides providing additional fruitful feeding grounds for some birds, the sea beaches and reefs afford a convenient resting and loafing area for such typically coastal birds as Brown Pelicans, gulls of many species, cormorants, and terns of several species. Thus the sea beaches are really an ecotone where sea meets land and where birds of the sea mingle with birds of the shore.

The coastal waters adjacent to the shore are the feeding grounds of those water birds that are not truly pelagic. Nevertheless some birds of the open sea frequently occur well within the sight of land. The migration route of loons off the California coast brings them very close to the shore at Point Pinos, Monterey County, where tens of thousands have been counted as they passed the point during a single day in May. Sooty Shearwaters also pass close to the cliffs at Point Fermin, Los Angeles County, and numerous other headlands along the length of the state. Feeding flocks containing thousands of Sooty Shearwaters are occasionally observed feeding just behind the breakers within a stone's throw of the beach.

However, the most characteristic birds of the coastal waters fall into two broad categories. First, there are the Brown Pelicans, cormorants, gulls, and terns that usually roost on the offshore islands, cliffs, or mainland beaches at night but spend the daylight hours searching for fish in waters fairly close to land. These birds can swim well enough but prefer to come ashore each night. For the cormorants this is essential as their feathers are not very waterproof and they must spend hours drying out their plumage in the sun and air. The other group of birds that inhabits these coastal waters consists of birds that do not nest in California or along the immediate California coast. They are aquatic birds who are excellent swimmers and divers and do not need to come ashore at night. Indeed, if they do, it is usually because

← *Harlequin Duck—male*

Black Scoter—male, first winter →

Surf Scoter—male ↑

Snowy Plover →

← *Sanderlings*

Surfbird (larger) and Rock Sandpiper (smaller) ↑

Marbled Godwit →

← *Mew Gull*

Northern Phalarope—winter plumage ↑

← *Herring Gull—adult*

Glaucous-winged Gull →

Least Terns

they are ill or injured. It includes grebes, loons, scoters, and phalaropes—birds which are very much more at home on the water than on the land. During August, September, and October great flocks of both Northern and Red Phalaropes assemble in the coastal waters of California. In the southern part of the state the flocks consist primarily of Northern Phalaropes with a sprinkling of Reds. In northern California, flocks of up to 100,000 Red Phalaropes have been sighted close to shore in August. During May, northward-bound flocks of these two species are not quite so large. On the open sea these flocks gather where plankton is plentiful and these small swimming shorebirds daintily pick the organisms from the surface of the ocean. Flocks of feeding phalaropes are usually accompanied by gulls, terns, jaegers, and pelicans which feed on the small fish (primarily anchovies) also attracted to the concentrated plankton.

Heermann's Gull
—winter plumage

The Lagoons, Bays, and Estuaries

Some of California's largest concentrations of water and shorebirds are to be found during the winter months (November–March) on the various lagoons, estuaries, and bays that are spotted along the coast from San Diego to Crescent City. Frequently the bays and estuaries are associated or border on tidal salt-water marshes, a rather unique habitat for birds which deserves special attention. The bays and estuaries here considered are rather shallow bodies of water with muddy or sandy bottoms, and through which there is a twice daily tidal exchange. During the ebb tide, large expanses of mud and sand are exposed to the air and to the assault of hungry shorebirds and gulls. Monterey Bay and other similar embayments along the California coast do not properly fall within this section because of the nature of the sea bottom and the depth of the water. Listed in order from San Diego northward, the largest and most important lagoon, bay, and estuary habitats are to be found at San Diego and Mission Bays in San Diego County, Newport, Upper Newport, Bolsa, and Sunset Bays in Orange County, portions of Los Angeles—

Morro Bay, San Luis Obispo County

164

Common Loon—winter plumage ↑

←Lesser Scaup—male

Horned Grebe—winter plumage →

Common Goldeneye—male ↑

Barrow's Goldeneye—male→

←"Black" Brant

←*White-winged Scoter—male*

Bufflehead—male →

←*California Gull—adult*

↑*Thayer's Gull—adult (photo by Herb Clarke)*

←*Thayer's Gull—second winter plumage (photo by Gerald Maisel)*

Bufflehead—female →

Long Beach Harbors in Los Angeles County, Mugu Lagoon in Ventura County, Morro Bay in San Luis Obispo County, Moss Landing and Elkhorn Slough in Monterey County, various parts of San Francisco, Suisun and San Pablo Bays near San Francisco, Bolinas Lagoon, Drake's Estero, and Tomales Bay in Marin County, Bodega Harbor in Sonoma County, Humboldt Bay in Humboldt County, and near Pelican Bay, Del Norte County. In addition there are dozens of smaller bays, estuaries, river mouths, coastal lagoons, and large and small harbors throughout the length of the state that attract large numbers of aquatic birds. Unhappily many of the choice bays, lagoons, and estuaries are located close to large population centers. As a result of the demand for new artificial beaches, marinas, boat landings, water-skiing runs, and general waterside living and recreation facilities, some of these areas have been so altered (as at Mission Bay, San Diego County) as to support virtually no birds any more at all. Others are being encroached upon (as in San Francisco Bay) and the natural habitat nibbled away, while others are constantly under the threat of channelization, drainage, filling, or "improvement" for one purpose or another. The coastal wetlands of California are the most threatened and the fastest disappearing of all of the state's natural habitats and at the same time represent the

Bonaparte's Gull—immature

habitat that receives the most intensive use (for feeding and resting) by migratory aquatic birds.

There are a number of reasons why the bays and estuaries are such important concentration areas for migratory water birds like gulls, terns, cormorants, grebes, waterfowl, herons, and shorebirds. Millions of the migratory water and shorebirds that pass through or winter in California are birds that have nested inland, to the far north, or on the arctic tundra. A major route of their southward migration is along the Pacific coast of the United States and hence brings them to coastal California where tundra-like conditions no longer prevail. Thus as the birds desert their ancestral breeding grounds in the late summer their habitat requirements change somewhat. Many water birds that have spent the breeding season on inland lakes and marshes nesting, resting, and feeding in one kind of habitat, spend the rest of

Forster's Tern

the year resting and feeding on the salt-water bays, lagoons, and estuaries of the California coast. Western and Eared Grebes and Ring-billed Gulls are examples of this latter group. Therefore, this coastal habitat attracts hordes of birds from northern areas as well as those from inland areas and some of the gulls even come from as far away as lakes in the Great Basin. Many of the birds are winter visitors that arrive in the autumn, remain during the winter, and depart for the north again the following spring. Others are transients which pass through during the fall and pause only briefly for a day or so to feed and rest before traveling on. In the spring the pattern is reversed but the populations are never as great as they are during the fall and winter. Attrition has taken its toll so that by spring the northbound transient flocks are smaller. Also many of the winter visitors have already departed for their northern and inland breeding grounds.

Because of the steady diminution of the acreage available for feeding on these coastal estuaries, lagoons, and bays which are the ancestral stopping points and win-

Common Tern—adult

ter homes for these birds, the concentrations that yearly assemble during the fall and winter at such places as Upper Newport Bay in Orange County, Morro Bay in San Luis Obispo County, south San Francisco Bay, Bolinas Lagoon in Marin County, and Humboldt Bay in Humboldt County can be staggering. That such great concentrations of birds occur in these shrinking areas where decades ago they did not, attests to the high productivity of food in this habitat.

Most of these bodies of water are contiguous with the sea and the twice daily tidal exchange occurs. Some of the coastal salt-water lagoons are cut off from the sea by sand bars or some man-made structure such as a dike, a highway, or a railroad embankment. In these lagoons there is no significant tidal flow, but the water may be brackish because of seepage and accumulation of fresh water. Others may be very briny because of the input of sea water by seepage and a high rate of evaporation. Where there is an unimpeded tidal flow, the "flushing" effect of the tidal exchange serves several functions. The ebbing water from the bays and estuaries carries away with it noxious wastes that accumulate in the upper parts of the bays and channels. Some organic and mineral nutrients that are generated in the interior parts of the bay are brought to the bay itself to fertilize the phytoplankton there.

Red-breasted Merganser—male

The incoming tidal flow, fresh from the sea, brings with it more dissolved nutrients and oxygen-rich water. Because of the unique environmental conditions existing in such habitats, they are populated by myriads of invertebrate animals that ultimately become a plentiful source of nutritious food for fishes and birds alike. The larval forms of many of these intertidal invertebrates, as well as small adults of other types, thrive on the wealth of phytoplankton in the nutrient-rich waters. Thus, aquatic life ranges from the microscopic plants and animals up through thousands of species of invertebrates (adults and larvae) such as worms, snails, clams, oysters, shrimp and many other crustaceans, jellyfish, hydroids, sea slugs, and scores more. In addition, schools of small fish, which also feed upon the plentiful marine invertebrates, constitute a major source of food for many water birds. Consequently, the birds of the lagoons, bays, and estuaries are essentially swimming birds, some of which can plunge into the water after fish as do the Brown Pelicans and the many species of terns. The White Pelicans seize fish from the surface, and other diving birds such as loons, grebes, cormorants, and mergansers actively pursue small fish by swimming under water. Surf and White-winged Scoters dive to the bay bottoms in search of such bivalve mollusks as mussels, sea clams, scallops, and small razor clams. With their powerful bills they can crush the shells and sift and swallow the meat within. Buffleheads dive after shrimp, small fish, and bivalve mollusks when feeding in salt water. Goldeneyes dive for mussels, clams, and marine worms, while scaup and Canvasbacks consume considerable quantities of plant food in addition to the crustaceans, crabs, small starfish, and mollusks they relish. Other birds, such as American Coots and some of the ducks, dive for aquatic vegetation and at low tide the Coots graze on the delicate green algae growing on the surface of the mud. "Black" Brant, on the other hand, feed on eelgrass in the shallows near the surface. Occasionally, Bald Eagles and Ospreys may be seen in these areas as they too hunt for larger fish. Along the margins of the lagoons, bays, and estuaries occur the fish-stalkers, birds such as herons and egrets, that quietly wade through the shallower waters in search of their prey. During spring and fall, Northern and Wilson's Phalaropes gather briefly by the thousands to feed on the myriads of tiny organisms swimming near the surface or that can be stirred from the mud by the phalaropes' furious spinning and dabbling. Gulls, being primarily scavengers, feed on dead fish, dead birds, and other organic refuse to be found in a rich ecosystem such as this. Some of the gulls, notably the Heermann's, are aggressive pirates chasing and harassing Brown Pelicans and terns for their food.

This habitat is intimately associated with the intertidal mud flats, sandbars, and salt-water marshes but the avian inhabitants of those areas are primarily shorebirds that probe for their food. Consequently, a separate section is devoted to that habitat.

The Tidal Flats and Salt-Water Marshes

The several habitats of California's seacoast are integrated by the sea and salt water. All of these habitats border directly on the sea or are adjacent to it. Most of the water birds of the seacoast feed directly upon either invertebrate or vertebrate animals that live in salt water and a very few of the birds feed upon aquatic plants that grow in salt or brackish water. None of the aquatic birds of the seacoast feed upon each other at least while one of them is still alive. However, Western Gulls, in mixed breeding colonies with other birds, will eat chicks when they can. A reflection of the great productivity of the sea is the fact that within the various habitats of the seacoast at certain times of the year occur the highest concentrations of birds per acre that can be found in any of California's habitats for birds.

Adjacent to the coastal strand, around bays, and bordering on estuaries, occur two of the most monotonous of habitats, the salt-water marshes and the tidal mud flats. Since the bird life of each habitat is so intimately associated with the other

Tidal mud flats and salt-water marsh, San Luis Obispo County

Tidal flats and mixed shorebirds, Orange County

and since both habitats very frequently occur in very close proximity to each other with the birds shifting with the changing tides from one to the other and back again, they are treated here as a single unit. The monotony of the tidal mud flats is

Clapper Rail→

←*Black-bellied Plover—winter plumage*

clearly evident when the tide ebbs exposing the bare mud spotted here and there with some algal plants. As the tidal waters drain away through channels in the salt-water marsh, the mud borders of these 1- to 20-foot-wide avenues are exposed. If an adjacent bay or nearby estuary is shallow enough, much broader expanses of mud appear. The monotony of this habitat is deceiving, however, because the mud itself is teeming with invertebrate life of hundreds of types. Tiny fish are trapped in the shallowing waters and fall easy prey to the stalking waders and the terns. Succulent seaweeds of the tender green varieties are eagerly sought by Pintails, American Wi-

Ruddy Turnstone—winter plumage→

Semipalmated Plover ↑

Pectoral Sandpiper→

172

Marbled Godwit →

← Willets

Long-billed Dowitcher →

← Whimbrel

Long-billed Curlew ↓   Least Sandpiper →

← *Elegant Tern*

Savannah Sparrow ↑

Dunlin ↑

Little Blue Heron ↓

Short-eared Owl ↑

Greater Yellowlegs ↑

Reddish Egret

Franklin's Gull—subadult, winter plumage →

geons, "American" Green-winged Teal, and American Coots. But the primary food resources of this most productive habitat lie just beneath the surface of the mud and in the shallow waters. As the tide recedes, thousands of shorebirds, which have been resting and loafing in the depths and along the borders of the salt-water marsh, are galvanized into action and swarm onto the newly exposed mud. Vir-

←*Red Knot—winter plumage*

Louisiana Heron→

tually none of these birds nest locally near the salt-water marsh and most of them are transients and winter visitors that have come from the high arctic tundra, the sloughs and ponds of western Canada, and the lakes of the interior and the Great Basin. Despite obvious differences in size and general coloration, most of them are equipped with similar basic feeding adaptations that enable them to exploit these bountiful food resources. Most of them have long legs and relatively long bills and it would at first appear that the many shorebirds represented in one area are all competing for the same food animals. Close and careful observation reveals that some pick their food from the surface of the mud, others turn over shells and bits of seaweed, still others probe deeply into the mud with relatively longer bills, and still others skim tiny organisms from or near the surface of small pools of water. Most shorebirds can swim actively, but rarely do it. The phalaropes are an exception and they utilize their swimming and spinning behavior to stir up small invertebrates near the surface of the water so that they may quickly be seized by these frenetic birds. Northern Phalaropes are the commonest species of this family to be encountered during spring and fall in the bays and estuaries with Wilson's Phalaropes occurring in much smaller numbers. They feed primarily on mosquito larvae, brine shrimp, amphipods, and some seed material. Of the two species, the Wilson's Phalaropes are more prone to feed out of the water amongst other shorebirds. Red Phalaropes are only occasionally encountered in this habitat, and their numbers are few since they much prefer the open sea and coastal waters for feeding. Northern Phalaropes are equally at home at sea or in the bays and estuaries and Wilson's Phalaropes are almost never found at sea. The most numerous of the large shorebirds of the California coast is the Willet. Second in abundance is the Marbled Godwit, although in favored places the American Avocet is very numerous. Whimbrels never really occur in large flocks as occasionally do the Long-billed Curlews, especially in some of the grassy interior valleys. The long-legged American Avocet is a "skim-feeder" rather than a "mud-prober" and its food is made up almost entirely of swimming aquatic insects and crustaceans. Willets, Marbled Godwits, Whimbrels, and Long-billed Curlews with their very long legs and long bills tend to feed deeper in the water and are able to probe deeper into the mud for worms, small mollusks, crustaceans, and other similar food. The medium-sized shorebirds such as Red Knot, Long-billed and Short-billed Dowitchers, and Greater Yellowlegs feed closer to the margin of mud and water or upon the mud itself. In general the smaller sandpipers (Least and Western Sandpipers and Dunlin) tend to feed along the edges of the mud with the Dunlins generally found wading further out than the other two. These "peeps" also exploit the newly exposed mud at some distance from the water. Black-necked Stilts and Lesser Yellowlegs are very nervous active feeders that obtain their aquatic prey from the surface of fairly shallow waters. Feeding somewhat back from the water are usually the plovers—Semipalmated, Black-bellied, and Killdeer. With their short stubby bills, they are better adapted for seizing insects, isopods, small crabs, and spiders as they scurry across the drier parts of the mud flat. Pectoral and Baird's Sandpipers prefer the drier and grassier reaches and are often found far from salt-water habitats. Thus the shorebirds are well dispersed over this habitat and somewhat segregated into different feeding niches all of which reduces interspecific competition and makes for most efficient utilization of the food resources here.

The majority of the tidal mud flat area is frequently covered by a monotonous dense vegetation of which the most important plant type is *Salicornia* or pickleweed. It grows in dense stands to a height of about two feet above the mud. Other plants include *Spartina* grass, sedges, and *Grindelia* bushes. This vegetation is flooded, at least basally, by tidal waters. During periods of exceptionally high spring tides, most of the vegetation may disappear under the water for a while. At these times, the more elusive inhabitants of this salt-water marsh, notably Sora, Virginia, Clapper, and Black Rails, are exposed to view and knowledgeable birders make regular trips to the tidal salt-water marshes during these rare high tides.

Because of the lack of diversity of plant forms, the number of breeding birds of this habitat is limited in California to just four species. Clapper Rails of two races have such narrow habitat requirements and have declined so rapidly because of habitat destruction that they have been declared "rare and endangered species" by the California Fish and Game Commission. The rarely encountered Black Rail also nests in coastal salt-water marshes. During the fall and winter, Sora and Virginia Rails also inhabit these marshes, but do not remain to breed. The other two nesting species of the salt-water marsh habitat are Belding's race of the Savannah Sparrow and a race of the Song Sparrow *(samueli)* that occurs near San Francisco. Many nonbreeding shorebirds, gulls, and terns utilize the dense cover of the salt-water marsh to rest and sleep in relative safety while awaiting the ebbing of the tide. Other birds that feed along the margins of the hidden tidal channels include Black-crowned Night Herons, Great Blue Herons, Great and Snowy Egrets, American Coots, and a variety of ducks. Terns of several species and Belted Kingfishers find rewarding fishing in the shallow pools and channels, and Marsh Hawks and Short-eared Owls quarter over the marshes looking for mice and rats. During the summer months, however, this marsh is a quiet place as only the small resident population and a small number of nonbreeding water and shorebirds remain, but from October until May it is one of the busiest of all of California's bird habitats.

FRESH-WATER HABITATS

The salt-water marsh habitat frequently merges with fresh-water habitats especially at locations where streams and rivers reach the seacoast. Often there is a zone of brackish water that contains some vegetation representative of the two adjacent aquatic habitats. Many of the water and shorebirds of the salt-water marsh and tidal mud flats habitat may also be found in the fresh-water habitats. There is even a race of the Clapper Rail *(yumanensis)* that occurs in the marshes at the south end of the Salton Sea and along the southern portions of the Colorado River. The Black Rail also nests in fresh-water marshes. However, some species are limited almost exclusively to either fresh-water or salt-water habitats. Brown Pelicans, Pelagic and Brandt's Cormorants, and the more typical pelagic species of the open sea are not normally encountered in fresh water. The Double-crested Cormorant, however, occurs as a breeding bird in both. The Heermann's Gull, a very common coastal gull during late summer, fall, winter, and very early spring, is rarely found very far from salt water. A number of water birds, which breed on inland lakes ranging from fresh to strongly alkaline, move southward and westward in the late summer and fall only to spend the winter season in the salt-water habitats. Western, Eared, and Horned Grebes, Forster's Terns, and Ring-billed and California Gulls are some of the birds that make this change. Wilson's Phalaropes, on the other hand, nest on inland lakes that are almost always fresh water. In migration, they occur in large numbers on coastal lagoons and salt-water bays. However, on their wintering grounds in South America, they prefer those high Andean lakes that are not very alkaline. Many species of waterfowl that breed on fresh-water ponds, lakes, and marshes have no hesitation about utilizing salt-water habitats upon occasion. Pintails are frequently seen in coastal waters and American Coots not infrequently feed among the coastal beds of kelp. Obviously then, those aquatic birds whose food requirements are not too circumscribed can find enough of the proper food when they shift from their fresh-water breeding habitats to their salt-water wintering and transient habitats. The big shift, then, is from fresh to salt water in the fall with a reverse flight in the spring. However, numerous birds of fresh-water breeding grounds remain in the same habitat during the winter, although not necessarily in the same place, while others of their species move coastward. There is virtually no autumn shift from salt to fresh water as the number of breeding birds in salt-water marshes is very low, and other coastal species have a very high affinity for the sea.

The Fresh-Water Marshes

Only one other California bird habitat, the open sea, has a higher percentage of its avian inhabitants which show *exclusive* adherence to that habitat despite the shift of some species from fresh to salt water in the fall. The principal plants of this relatively dense marsh habitat are cattails, tules, sedges, and some grasses. The waters of the marsh itself contain numerous green and blue-green algae and microscopic dia-

Fresh-water marsh, Imperial County

toms. Invertebrate food-chains originating from this vegetational base include snails, fresh-water mussels, water fleas and other small crustaceans, crayfish, aquatic insects of all sorts (both adult and immature states), worms of many types, leeches, and many others. The fresh waters also host a myriad of microscopic forms whose principal food consists of the diatoms and other algae, and bacteria. Fishes of dozens of types, frogs, newts, turtles, and snakes are among the smaller vertebrates that are additional food for some of the aquatic birds. Thus this habitat affords its inhabitants an abundant source of food plus dense cover for nesting as well as hiding.

Birds such as American Coots, various species of ducks, Pied-billed, Western, and Eared Grebes, and Canada Geese which utilize the dense covers for refuge and nesting, swim into the more open waters for feeding. Other species, notably Least and American Bitterns, Common Gallinules, Virginia, Sora, Yellow, and Black Rails, Common Snipe, Long-billed Marsh Wrens, and Common Yellowthroats either remain within the dense vegetational cover or very close to it. These types can best be viewed at dawn and dusk when they venture forth to feed along the edges of the marsh. Other fresh-water marsh birds are far more conspicuous and spend much time perched high on the reeds or flying into and out of the marsh. Tricolored, Red-winged, and Yellow-headed Blackbirds nest and roost in the marsh vegetation and are very noisy and conspicuous, and swallows of several species routinely hawk for insects over the marsh vegetation and the open water, although they do not nest in the marsh proper.

The marsh plants serve as the chief source of nesting materials for the marsh birds. Tricolored, Red-winged, and Yellow-headed Blackbirds, Long-billed Marsh Wrens, and Common Yellowthroats suspend their woven nests from the higher levels of the cattails and tules. Rails, coots, and ducks build their nests on firmer

←*Great Egret*

Pied-billed Grebe ↑

areas in the marsh such as on matted vegetation or patches of mud. The grebes build their unique floating nests of aquatic vegetation so that changes in water level will neither flood the nest nor leave it perched too high for the grebes to reach it since they are too large and heavy-bodied for their small wings, and are awkward fliers.

Feeding relationships are such that little competition exists among members of the marsh community. Great Blue Herons, Great Egrets, and Green Herons stalk their food in the shallows along the edge of more open vegetation. The Great Blues seek larger prey such as small water snakes, crayfish, frogs, and small turtles, in ad-

Green Heron →

←*American Bittern*

← *Common Snipe*

Least Bittern →

Black Tern ↑

Red-winged Blackbird ↑

Virginia Rail →

← *Canada Goose*

←"American" Green-winged Teal—male

Common Yellowthroat—male ↓

←Long-billed Marsh Wren

Caspian Tern→

Tricolored Blackbird ↑

Cinnamon Teal—male →

dition to fish. Snowy Egrets and Green Herons seek smaller fish and some aquatic insects, and Great Egrets feed on small frogs, crayfish, and fish. American Coots feed primarily on submerged and floating aquatic vegetation and the ducks and geese relish seeds, bulbs, and tender shoots. The grebes are fish-eaters also, but they dive for their prey in deeper waters and they supplement their diet with aquatic insects such as dragonfly nymphs, water boatmen, and water beetles. The blackbirds usually forage for larger insects such as grasshoppers, beetles, and crickets at some distance from the marsh and this accounts for the constant streaming of blackbirds

Northern Shoveler—male

back and forth. During the breeding season this frenetic activity goes on all day. However, in the winter, the marsh is used only as a nighttime roost and the blackbirds spend the days far away in agricultural lands. Evening brings their return to the marsh and these flights are a spectacle to behold since they often involve hundreds of thousands of blackbirds of several species.

Because of the relatively dry nature of California's eastern, interior, and southern regions, this habitat does not involve as much area as do many of the others. Also, because of the drainage, flooding, and other alterations of natural marshes throughout Central Valley this habitat is constantly shrinking in this state. On the other hand, the establishment of a number of federal refuges and state wildlife areas along the length of the interior to replace the drained natural marshes, reduce crop depredation by waterfowl and blackbirds, and provide hunting facilities for some people, has added further acreage to fresh-water marsh habitats. The great primeval marshes of the Central Valley and the Modoc Plateau were annually visited by literally millions of ducks and geese, and although reduced in numbers today, great concentrations of millions of ducks and geese still build up during the winter on these federal and state lands. When the northern marshes at Tule, Lower Klamath, Eagle, and Honey Lakes freeze, the birds move southward and find open water and suitable marsh habitat at the Sacramento National Wildlife Refuge and other refuges near Willows, the various state wildlife areas near Marysville and the Sacramento River, refuges near Los Banos and Merced, the Salton Sea National Wildlife Refuge and various state wildlife areas near Brawley, and two federal refuges along

the Lower Colorado River. In addition, fresh-water marsh habitat (mostly of an intermittent nature) is to be found at various private shooting clubs up and down
the state.

Probably no other birding experience can equal that of a spring dawn in a
fresh-water marsh. The air is fresh and clear and the rich smells of growing things
and of pure life itself permeate the air. There is more to be heard than seen and the
chorus of amphibians and birds alike is a cacophony of wild noises. Were this not
enough, this is the best time of day to catch a glimpse of the shyer marsh birds
such as Least and American Bitterns, rails, and gallinules.

Lakes, Rivers, and Streams

This habitat is often intimately associated with fresh-water marshes because
lake, river, and stream borders frequently consist of marsh vegetation. No birds are
completely aquatic because their eggs must be incubated in air. Even such species as
grebes, loons, and Ruddy Ducks that cannot walk upright on land and almost
never leave the water except to nest, must at least do that. The grebes and a few

Fresh-water lake with waterfowl, Orange County

Fresh-water stream, Lassen County

others build nests of floating vegetation upon which they can "crawl," and loons nest on low muddy islands never very far from the water. Ruddy Ducks build their nests on matted vegetation some inches above the water and attached to marsh plants. They reach these nests via small ramps also constructed of marsh vegetation. No aquatic birds build their nests on the exposed open water of a lake or pond. Instead they select some cover in the form of a clump or stand of marsh grasses even if it is located at some distance from the shore or main body of the marsh. Occasionally Dippers build their nests on exposed boulders in the middle of fast-moving streams, but the nests are so well camouflaged by the mossy materials of their construction that they usually escape notice. Also the rushing waters are a deterrent to most predators. Usually however, Dippers build their oven-shaped nests under waterfalls, in deep rock crevices, and even under bridges where they are well hidden. Ospreys may build large conspicuous nests on dead trees in the middle of lakes, but the large size and the nature of this bird and the inaccessibility of the nest is enough to discourage most predators. Belted Kingfishers dig deep nest tunnels in the banks bordering lakes, rivers, and streams, but hunt for fish over the open waters. The lake, river, and stream habitat is also inhabited by birds that nest elsewhere, either nearby or in some distant habitat but utilize the open waters for feeding and resting.

Open-water areas are classified as lacustrine and fluviatile depending primarily upon whether the waters are moving or still. Lacustrine waters are still waters, relatively free of vegetation except for scattered tules or patches of floating vegetation, and may even be saline, but not tidal. Fluviatile waters are moving masses of water that are not saline. Lakes, ponds, and even desert lakes are included in the former group while rivers and streams are fluviatile. Although there are some significant differences in the aquatic vegetation and true aquatic organisms living beneath the surface of the waters, the differences in bird life for the most part are not sufficient enough for these two types of waters to be segregated here.

There are but few true aquatic birds on the streams of California. The Dipper or Water Ouzel is unique in that it is one of the very few aquatic Passerines in the world. Not only do they nest close to rushing waters, but the birds themselves can swim ducklike (although their toes are neither webbed nor lobed) and they can dive to the stream bottom and actually walk around looking for their food. The nictitating membranes cover their eyes while they are under water and their strong feet and relatively long claws enable them to hold on to the stream bottom as they search for their favorite food of caddisfly larvae, dragonfly nymphs, and other aquatic insects. Dippers are relatively nonmigratory but some move down to lower elevations when the streams in the higher mountain areas become covered with ice.

Harlequin Ducks formerly inhabited turbulent mountain streams on the western slopes of the Sierra Nevada during the breeding season. During the winter they are still found along the California coast in small numbers but they have not been recorded on their summer nesting streams in many years. Their ability to sustain themselves in the torrential streams they inhabit is legendary as is their ability to walk along the bottoms of these streams in search of fish, larvae, and aquatic insects. Another duck whose presence on its former breeding grounds in California has gone undetected for many years is the Barrow's Goldeneye, which like the Harlequin Duck occurs near the California coast during the winter, preferring however the sheltered lagoons and bays to the pounding waves enjoyed by the Harlequins. Barrow's Goldeneyes nested on small undisturbed, forest-bordered lakes in the high central and northern Sierra Nevada during the summer, and perhaps it has been the unparalleled increase in public use of the wilderness lakes in California that finally proved too disturbing for this species.

As a rule, California rivers do not harbor large numbers of waterfowl; however, Common Mergansers nest along some of the northern ones. The smaller rivers that flow westward out of the Sierra Nevada are too small and swift for most waterfowl. The same is true of the rivers that drain the Cascades and the Coast Range. California, south of the Tehachapis, has no rivers worthy of the name. The Colorado River between Needles and Yuma has some fine fresh-water marshes at Topock, Imperial Dam, and the Bill Williams Delta in Arizona, and these areas are important stopping places for transient and wintering waterfowl. The San Joaquin River, which drains the southern portion of the Central Valley, loses so much water to irrigation that it supports relatively few waterfowl today. The state's largest river, the Sacramento, supports some water birds, but not nearly as many as in the adjacent sloughs, ponds, and marshes created by the overflowing river during flood seasons.

Ruddy Duck ➤
—male

Black-crowned Night Heron ➤

Mallard—male ↑   Ring-necked Duck—male ➤

Wood Duck—male ↑

Eared Grebe—winter plumage ↑

← American Wigeons—male and female

 ← *Ring-billed Gull*

 *Osprey* →

Black Phoebe ↑

Hooded Mergansers—male and females ↑

← *Tufted Duck—male*

 ← *American Coots*

Wood Ducks still nest in the cavities in the large cottonwoods along its borders as do several species of herons. Black Phoebes and Rough-winged Swallows, although Passerine land birds, are almost invariably associated with fresh water. Black Phoebes almost always nest near water, preferably small lakes and streams, and make sorties for flying insects over the open water. Rough-winged Swallows nest in tunnels they have made or enlarged in the soft lake or river banks and spend much time hunting for insects over the water.

However, it is the lakes of California, both large and small, that attract unprecedented numbers of waterfowl during the winter. Artificial lakes such as at city parks and reservoirs are attractive to waterfowl also, especially the former, because of the intensive feeding carried on by the amused public. Such lakes as those in Golden Gate Park in San Francisco, Lake Merritt in Oakland, the Palo Alto Yacht Harbor, park lakes in Monterey and Santa Barbara, Fairmount Park in Riverside, and MacArthur Park in Los Angeles are just a few of the many city park lakes throughout California that are famous for their wintering waterfowl. Although 19 species of ducks (of the 33 species that have occurred) either nest or have nested in California, the millions of ducks that migrate through or winter in the state come from further north. The lakes and ponds of California produce such great quantities of fish, invertebrates, and plant life that millions of waterfowl spend the winter months in the state on unfrozen lakes. Some of the great Central Valley marshes no longer exist, and artificial feeding programs have been instituted by both the

Rough-winged Swallow

U.S. Fish and Wildlife Service and the California Department of Fish and Game on the various refuges to reduce waterfowl crop depredations on the rice, celery, and alfalfa fields of the Central and Imperial valleys. Hundreds of thousands of geese (of four principal species—Canada, White-fronted, Snow, and Ross') also spend the winter months on the refuges in the Central, Imperial, and Colorado River valleys and several thousand Whistling Swans winter in the northern half of the state. Even a few Trumpeter Swans are occasionally noted among them. Statewide, the most abundant "dabbling" or "puddle" ducks—those which can leap out of the water without a running takeoff and which feed at or near the surface, principally on vegetable food—are Pintails and Mallards in the northern half of the state, and Pintails and American Wigeon in the southern portion. Other abundant puddle ducks are "American" Green-winged Teal and Northern Shovelers, while Cinnamon Teal, Gadwall, and Wood Ducks are less numerous. The "bay" or "diving" ducks such

Dipper

as Lesser and Greater Scaup, Canvasbacks, Redheads, Common Goldeneyes, and Buffleheads prefer larger salt-water bays and estuaries, but large numbers do spend the winter on lakes. Ruddy Ducks and Common Mergansers are more at home in fresh water, and the striking but uncommon little Hooded Merganser prefers the wooded margins of lakes and rivers.

American Coots constitute one of the largest bird populations in California and they must number in the millions throughout the length and breadth of the state in suitable aquatic habitats. Although they nest in fresh-water marshes and on the suitable borders of lakes, and their populations there are very large indeed, there is a southward and coastward shift of much of the population in the fall, especially from the inland and northern lakes. There, as well as on bays and estuaries, they represent a very large segment of the aquatic bird life. White Pelicans formerly nested on larger lakes in the Central Valley, on the Modoc Plateau, and on the Salton Sea. They are essentially birds of large fresh-water lakes inhabited by fish large enough for them to eat and containing suitable well-sequestered islands for nesting. During the fall they migrate southward and coastward, and some spend the winter months on the larger bays and lakes and on the Salton Sea. In the spring they move northward and northeastward towards the lakes of the Great Basin. During the non-breeding season the gravel bars and exposed mud flats bordering lakes and rivers host many shorebirds, but only Killdeers and Spotted Sandpipers breed there. Killdeers prefer the drier portions of the lake or river margins and the Spotted Sandpipers choose the sandbars and gravel bars closer to the water's edge. The numbers and variety of wintering California waterfowl can be matched by no other state and provides a rare opportunity to view more than a million birds at one time on a prime day during the winter in the Sacramento Valley.

BRUSHLAND

Chaparral

Chaparral (a word of Spanish origin and referring to the *chaparro,* or Scrub Oak, which dominates some of the brushland or scrub communities) is a broad term generally applied to the scrub or brushland that extends southward in California from the Oregon border to the Mexican border through the coast mountains and from the Sierra Nevada foothills and higher montane habitats southward through the Transverse and Peninsular Ranges. It also occurs in southern Oregon and northern Baja California. On a worldwide scheme of habitats this biome is termed a Mediterranean Scrub Forest because of the predominance of this formation in some of the countries bordering the Mediterranean Sea. Similar formations also occur in South Africa, southern and western Australia, and coastal Chile. A feature shared by the brushlands in these far-removed regions of the world is the nature of the vegetation. It consists of forest dominated by shrubs and low bushes whose dense interlocking canopy of branches is seldom more than about 15 feet in height. These shrubs are primarily evergreen in nature with rather broad sclerophyll-type leaves, that is, the leaves are rather thick and waxy or in some other way protected from dessication during a prolonged summer dry season which is characteristic of a Mediterranean climate. These areas are also frost-free with climates that range from subtropical to mid-temperate. Most of the rainfall occurs during the winter season and ranges from about 10 inches to about 60 inches, but most Mediterranean Scrub areas receive from 15 to 30 inches of precipitation per year.

In California at least four distinctive chaparral vegetational types may be distinguished, but the bird life of all but one of them is principally the same. The *coastal*

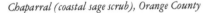

Chaparral (coastal sage scrub), Orange County

sage scrub is found near the sea on the foothills of the Coast Range from about San Luis Obispo County south through San Diego County. It also occurs on some of the south- and west-facing slopes of the Transverse Ranges. The plants are from 1 to 8 feet tall and are less dense and not as stiff-twigged as the dry or hard chaparral of the interior and the higher elevations. Rainfall averages from 10 to 20 inches per year and summer low clouds and fog keep the temperatures cooler than in the drier interior regions vegetated by the hard chaparral. Some common plants of this type of chaparral include California Sagebrush, Black Sage, White Sage, Purple Sage, California Buckwheat, Lemonade Bush, Poison Oak, Yerba Santa, Whipple Yucca, and in a few places the beautiful and delicate Red Shanks or Ribbonwood.

The *dry* or *hard chaparral* of the interior regions of California is often referred to as the true chaparral. The plants of this habitat are adapted to long rainless summers and grow between 1,000 and 4,000 feet on the slopes of the western foothills of the Sierra Nevada, the Transverse and Peninsular Ranges, and the coastal side of the Coast Range from San Luis Obispo County southward. It is found higher than the coastal sage scrub where both occur on the same slopes and the two types intergrade rather than interdigitate. On the desert side of the southern mountains it is found from 3,000 to 5,500 feet. The great diversity of evergreen shrubs of the dry chaparral, which have rather thick leathery leaves, produces a dense cover up to 15 feet high. The branches of these stiff-twigged shrubs interlock making passage through this habitat very difficult for large animals. Beneath the dense canopy is an impenetrable tangle of branches and trunks through which weave trails of smaller mammals. Typical plants of the true chaparral include Chamise, Ribbonwood (especially in the Peninsular Ranges), Scrub Oak, Foothill Ash, Mountain Mahogany, *Ceanothus* or wild lilac of several species, Hollyleaf Cherry, Bear Brush, manzanitas of several species, Sugarbush, Toyon, Whipple Yucca, Chaparral Pea, and California Fremontia.

Because of the dry and resinous nature of these two types of chaparral, and because of the prolonged dry season that extends from April until November, these habitats are frequently subjected to ravaging fires. Where natural forest fires have been prevented or thwarted, food productivity of the chaparral diminishes, and fuel, in the form of dead leaves, twigs, and branches beneath the canopy, accumulates. Ordinarily, fire does not kill chaparral shrubs but causes them to regenerate almost immediately after the first winter rains, and then to return to normal within ten years. Scorching stimulates the germination of seeds of certain chaparral shrubs such as *Ceanothus* or lilac. Fire usually favors the spread of chaparral into non-chaparral surrounding areas, especially sclerophyll forest because the chaparral plants in a sense thrive on fire in the long run. Fire prunes out the dead wood, causes rapid regrowth, permits the growth of annuals and herbs which were retarded by the thick canopy, and generally favors the bird and animal inhabitants by forcing the chaparral to produce more food. However, if chaparral is burned too frequently, it may die and be replaced by grassland. An ecological study in the Santa Monica Mountains revealed that chaparral stems were mostly about twenty-five years old, and chaparral without fire for fifty years was considered old.

Rufous-sided Towhee ↑

Wrentit →

←*Bewick's Wren*

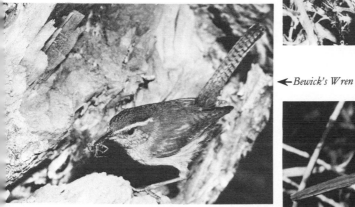

California Thrasher →

Orange-crowned Warbler ↑

←*Anna's Hummingbird—male*

Green-tailed Towhee →

← MacGillivray's Warbler—male

Mountain Quail ↓

Mountain chaparral, Los Angeles County ↑

Black-chinned Sparrow →

Lazuli Bunting—male

←Brown Towhee

Dusky Flycatcher ↓

Mountain chaparral, San Bernardino County ↑

←Fox Sparrow

The *humid coastal scrub* in California is found near the coast from Monterey County to the Oregon border and is not an uninterrupted stand. From Monterey County northward it is punctuated by stands of sclerophyll forest and humid coastal forest. Where soil and climatic conditions prevent forests to grow, this chaparral is a climax community, but where logging or fires have destroyed the forest, a subclimax community of humid coastal scrub may prevail for a number of years until natural plant succession has restored the original forest community. This region receives from 25 to 60 or more inches of precipitation annually in the form of rain or fog, and wind is a prevalent factor also. The shrubs, although superficially resembling other chaparral types elsewhere, have broader, thinner leaves and are softer-twigged. These shrubs tend to be smaller and fire is not a factor in this community because of the higher humidity, the less resinous nature of the shrubs, and the higher moisture content of the plants in general. Some typical plants of this humid coastal chaparral are Cow Parsnip, Wax Myrtle, California Blackberry, Salmonberry, Himalaya Berry, Toyon, *Ceanothus* of several species, Salal, Bear Brush, Black Twinberry, Cascara Sagrada, Hairy Manzanita, and Coyote Brush. This chaparral type has more distinctive plants of its own and contains fewer plant species which also occur in the other three chaparral types. However the birds are essentially the same basic chaparral species.

The *montane chaparral* occurs at higher elevations than other forms of chaparral and is principally found in the Sierra Nevada and the Transverse Ranges. It is a subclimax formation that springs up after forest fires or logging have eliminated the original montane forest. In areas unsuitable for forest growth because of slope-face, soil conditions, or other physical factors, this habitat is more or less permanent. In burned-over areas, this brushland may become so thick and persistent as to retard further succession back to the climax montane forest. This occurs because the conifer seedlings cannot compete with the dense established brush, particularly the manzanitas. This habitat is rarely contiguous with the hard chaparral, but most often is found in discontinuous patches, often of considerable acreage, interspersed among the stands of montane forest. It is found from about 4,000 feet to about 9,000 feet and receives much precipitation in the form of snow. Summer thunderstorms resulting from Sonora storms and Mexican cyclones account for about 20 percent of the annual precipitation which ranges from 20 to 40 inches. The chaparral plants of this region are somewhat shorter (usually under 5 feet) than in either coastal sage or hard chaparral, and the plant types are more similar to the ones in those formations than they are to those in the humid chaparral. Plant survival during the long, hot, dry summer months characteristic of parts of the Sierra Nevada and the Transverse Ranges requires xerophytic plants with drought-resistant sclerophyll characteristics. Of the four California chaparral habitats, the montane chaparral is inhabited by a number of birds which do not occur in the others. Plants of the montane chaparral include several species of manzanita, Deer Brush, Mountain Whitethorn, Sierra Chinquapin, High Sierra Sagebrush, Great Basin Sagebrush, Nude Buckwheat, and Fireweed.

As California bird habitats go, the chaparral harbors relatively few species. As a habitat, it is rather uniform and monotonous in nature despite the great diversity of plant types, but not plant forms. The brush is dense and birds of rather special habits occur there. A number of the birds are ground-foragers with good running ability and are able to dash about along the narrow avenues in the vegetation. Three species of towhees (Brown, Rufous-sided, and Green-tailed), California Thrashers, towhee-like Fox Sparrows, other sparrows such as White-crowned, Rufous-crowned, Black-chinned, Sage, and Song are all at home on the ground and in dense brush. Two other ground birds are California Quail, which occur at lower elevations, and the Mountain Quail found higher up. The common resident chaparral hummingbird is the Anna's, while the migratory Allen's occurs regularly from Santa Barbara northward along the coast. Other birds of this dense brush are Bewick's Wrens, Orange-crowned Warblers, Lazuli Buntings, MacGillivray's Warblers, and especially Wrentits. This latter species is so partial to dense chaparral that it will usually refuse to cross firebreaks and trails cut through the brush. Those birds which occur primarily in the montane chaparral during the nesting season are Mountain Quail, Green-tailed Towhees, Fox Sparrows, and MacGillivray's Warblers. Dusky Flycatchers breed in the higher brush of the mountains. The White-crowned Sparrow of the mountains prefer the meadows and brushy borders but another race *(nuttalli)* breeds in the coastal chaparral from Santa Barbara north to Mendocino County. Except for those in the montane chaparral, most chaparral birds are residents, but because of the snow and cold that prevail in the Sierra Nevada and Transverse Ranges during the winter months, such species as Black-chinned, Sage, and Fox Sparrows, Dusky Flycatchers, Green-tailed Towhees, and Orange-crowned and MacGillivray's Warblers migrate down the mountains in the fall. Mountain Quail also move down-mountain to escape the heavy winter snows, but only move to below the snow levels.

The chaparral habitats are abundant with bird and other animal life, even though the diversity is rather low. Chaparral plants produce vast quantities of food for birds and mammals as well as food for invertebrates, especially insects. Buds, berries, cherries and other fruits, nuts, seeds, bulbs, corms, flowers, and other vegetable parts are consumed by the birds and mammals. The insects and other invertebrate populations are very high, adding further to the rich diet afforded the birds by the chaparral. In the winter months swarms of American Robins and Cedar Waxwings, and small numbers of Townsend's Solitaires and Hermit Thrushes, gorge themselves on the ripened berries of the Toyon. In the spring, they descend upon the ripe fruits of the Hollyleaf Cherries in the same fashion. In the chaparral community, the primary flowering and growing season occurs between March and May and this season may be likened to summer elsewhere. June and July can be considered as "autumn" in the chaparral and the hot dry months of August, September, and early October when no new growth occurs is essentially like winter elsewhere. "Spring" really commences with the first rains of late November or early December and continues until the end of the rainy season in early April. Some new growth is put out during this time, but the warming temperatures of April and May force the most new growth of the year.

GRASSLAND AND SAVANNAH

Grassland

Grassland formerly constituted one of the largest unbroken expanses of pure habitat in California. In total area it was second only to desert, but when the extensive savannah country is totaled with it, the collective area was greater. Today, large stands of pure virgin grassland in California are almost nonexistent. That which has

Grassland, Kern County

Grassland, San Luis Obispo County

not been altered and converted to agriculture has been grazed by sheep and cattle, burned, or replaced with non-native grasses. Nevertheless, despite the extensive alterations to the native California grasslands, the changes in bird life have been far less than those effected on the mammals.

The largest single grassland region is on the floor of the great Central Valley, although it would be most difficult to recognize it as such today because of the extensive agriculture. The newly completed California Water Project has brought irrigation water south from the Feather River, and marginal grasslands in the western and southern portions of the San Joaquin Valley are being farmed for the first time. Where this has occurred, traditional grassland birds have disappeared and their places have been taken by more adaptable species better suited to farms and ranches. The phenomenal spread of the Starling in California south through the Central Valley can be attributed to the agricultural growth in that region. Other grassland areas are found in some of the river valleys such as the Salinas Valley, and on the foothills and mesas of the Pacific drainage. On the Modoc Plateau in northeastern California, some of the large lake basins are carpeted by grasslands which are interspersed here and there with sagebrush. An extensive savannah belt in the mountain foothills surrounds the Central Valley grasslands, and other savannah areas border the smaller areas of grassland. Ponds, sloughs, rivers, streams, reservoirs, irrigation canals, and fresh-water marshes are scattered among the valley grasslands adding to the total avifauna of these valleys.

Native plants of the grasslands are primarily annual or perennial grasses often mixed with low annual herbs, which, in the springtime, produce an unparalleled carpet of wildflowers making the grasslands a most attractive habitat during March and April. Typical native California grasses include Foxtail Brome, Sixweeks Fescue, Pine Bluegrass, Soft Cheat, Common Velvetgrass, California Oatgrass, and California Needlegrass. Three exceptionally successful imported grasses are Italian Ryegrass, Mouse Barley, and Wild Oat. Other grassland plants are California Goldenrod, Tidy Tips, Yellow Star Thistle, Yellow Mustard, Black Mustard, Owlclovers, California Buttercup, Red-stem Filaree, Grass-nut Brodiea, and Baby Blue Eyes.

California's grasslands receive from 6 to 20 inches of rain per year, most of it coming in winter and spring. The grasslands turn brown and golden during June and remain parched and dry through the long hot summer months of the interior

Mountain Plover ↑

←*Burrowing Owl*

valleys. It is not until late in the winter (January and February) that the grasslands once again become green. Thus the growing season in this habitat is relatively short.

Because of the highly specialized nature of the grassland habitat, the number of nesting bird species is rather low but the density is high, reflecting the exceptional food productivity of this habitat. The breeding birds of the grasslands must necessarily make their homes on, near, or under the ground. Ground-nesters are very vulnerable to predators such as snakes, weasels, foxes, badgers, and skunks and it is not surprising that their nests are so well concealed among the grasses. Even the Horned Larks, which nest at the edge of very short grasses or even in the open, are expert at hiding their nests. The stealth with which the Western Meadowlarks approach their nests is matched only by the excellent camouflage of the domed grassy nests themselves. Instead of flying directly to the nest site and thus revealing its location, the Meadowlark lands conspicuously at some distance from it and then proceeds to sneak through the grass to its nest via a circuitous route. The success of these maneuvers is attested to by the high populations of Meadowlarks in the grasslands. Burrowing Owls live in long underground burrows excavated by California Ground Squirrels and perhaps enlarge the tunnels somewhat themselves, but this is not known for certain. From here they forage over the grasslands at dusk hunting for large beetles and grasshoppers and an occasional small rodent or shrew. Grasshopper and Savannah Sparrows complete the short list of nesting grassland species. In the winter the ranks of birds foraging in the grasslands are swelled by the transient and visiting Horned Larks, the uncommon Lapland, Chestnut-collared, and rare McCown's Longspurs, Long-billed Curlews, Mountain Plovers, blackbirds, Starlings, and in favored parts of the San Joaquin and adjacent valleys, Sandhill Cranes. Winter also brings Rough-legged and Ferruginous Hawks to add to the local raptors which hunt and forage over the open grasslands throughout the year. These include Golden Eagles, Prairie Falcons, American Kestrels, Turkey Vultures, California Condors, White-tailed Kites and, during spring and fall migrations, flocks of Swainson's Hawks. Many other birds from interdigitated and bordering habitats also come into the grasslands to search for food. These include Mourning Doves, Western Bluebirds (and in the winter, Mountain Bluebirds), Yellow-billed Magpies, Loggerhead Shrikes, and Western and Cassin's Kingbirds.

This extensive use of the grasslands for foraging by birds from other habitats

Western Meadowlark ↑

← *Bobolink—female*

attests to the abundance of food to be found there. Grass seeds form a most important staple for the larks and sparrows. Insects, especially grasshoppers and beetles abound in the grasses, and hordes of flying insects above the grasses attract flycatchers, bluebirds, and swallows. The lizards and snakes, but especially the rodents and rabbits, provide food for the larger predatory birds.

Savannah

Savannah being an "edge" situation of sorts is inhabited by some birds of both the adjacent grasslands and the oak woodlands. Savannah is fundamentally a combination of grassland with widely scattered trees. These trees are primarily oaks such as Valley, Blue, Mesa, Coast Live, and Interior Live. The habitat takes on a rather parklike aspect because of the open spacing of the trees. The presence of trees among the grasses provides additional nesting opportunities for many more species than the few that nest on the ground. The savannah, therefore, is inhabited by a larger number of nesting species than is the grassland. However, as a foraging area,

Oak savannah, San Benito County

← *Turkey Vulture*

←*Loggerhead Shrike*

Swainson's Hawk—dark phase ↑

Golden Eagle ↑

Yellow-billed Magpie ↑

Mourning Dove ↑

Lark Sparrow →

the savannah falls far short of the adjacent grassland, to which in fact, go many of its inhabitants to hunt. Artificial savannahs such as occur on ranches and farms where windbreaks and orchards have been planted, are considered in the section devoted to all artificial bird habitats. The savannah affords retreats and nest sites for White-tailed Kites, Red-tailed Hawks, Swainson's Hawks, Golden Eagles, American Kestrels, Barn Owls, Great Horned Owls, Western and Cassin's Kingbirds, Yellow-billed Magpies, Common Ravens, Common Crows, Western Bluebirds, and Loggerhead Shrikes, all of which forage in the open, either in the savannah proper, but more likely, as in the case of the larger species, over the adjacent grasslands. Acorn and Lewis' Woodpeckers, "Red-shafted" Flickers, Plain Titmice, Warbling Vireos, and "Bullock's" Orioles forage among the trunks and leaves of the savannah trees proper and do not venture very far from this cover.

WOODLANDS

California's woodlands are of two general types—oak woodlands and riparian woodlands. Of the two types, the oak woodlands are much more extensive in California. In contrast to forests, woodlands are rather more open and not as dense as forests. Also, woodland trees are not as compact as are the evergreen conifers of the forests. This structure allows more light to reach the forest floor to stimulate the growth of herbs, shrubs, and grasses. The trees of California's woodlands are primarily broadleaved angiosperms (flowering trees), most of which are oaks of a number of species that are either evergreen or deciduous. Riparian woodlands occur along or near watercourses and are much more restricted in distribution. Riparian woodlands are somewhat denser than oak woodlands because of the denser nature of the undergrowth induced by greater light penetration as a result of the transluscence of the canopy leaves. Most of the trees of this habitat are deciduous and are such types as alders, cottonwoods, poplars, sycamores, some maples, redbuds, birches, and willows. Because of the less uniform nature of these habitats, the diversity of the tree types and the intermixing with other habitats, the woodlands of California have a very rich and varied avifauna.

Oak Woodland

The oak woodland in California occurs from about sea level to about 5,000 feet in the Coast Range, Sierra Nevada, Cascades, and the other higher ranges of the state. It is found the entire length of California west of the deserts and the Sierra Nevada-Cascade divides but is not found amid the humid coastal forests of the extreme northwest corner. This woodland commonly occurs throughout the entire Coast Range from border to border but is almost absent on slopes actually facing the ocean. It is found in broad expanses in the foothills surrounding the grassy valleys and in many areas interdigitates or intergrades with grasslands, chaparral, savannah, and even coniferous forests.

The quality of the California oak woodland is not everywhere the same. Differences in precipitation, soils, species of oaks, and understory plants prevail, but in general, the differences in the quality of bird life are not as great. Annual precipitation, mostly in the form of rain at the lower elevations, but occasionally snow at higher levels, ranges from 15 inches in the southern coastal oak woodlands to 30 inches and even higher in the central and northern coastal ranges. At the higher elevations where the Black Oak association occurs, 40 inches, mostly in the form of winter snow, is not unusual. The Black Oak association is usually encountered between 4,000 and 5,000 feet in conjunction with the Yellow Pine lower montane forest with which it intermixes and intergrades freely. Here and there in dry valley floors and on small mesas relatively pure stands may be found and the birds are a mixture of the primary oak woodland species such as Plain Titmice, White-breasted Nuthatches, and Western Bluebirds and the Steller's Jays, White-headed and Hairy Woodpeckers, Brown Creepers, and Mountain Chickadees so characteristic of the montane forest. The broad-sclerophyll or live oak association is found in the hotter, drier regions where the thick, tough evergreen leaves retard dessication during the long, hot, rainless summers. Dominant plants of this association include California Laurel, Golden-cup Oak, Interior Live Oak, Tan Oak, Madrone, Wax Myrtle, Poison "Oak," Western Bracken Fern, Chinquapin, and the largest of them—the Coast Live Oak. North of Santa Barbara in the Coast Range, these stately oaks are usually draped with the grayish *Ramalina* lichen. This association is frequently mixed with grass or chaparral or has some chaparral components (*Ceanothus* and manzanita as an understory) and the two habitats are often found in alternating patches in almost any part of their overlapping ranges. To the south, this woodland intergrades frequently into pure chaparral or grass and becomes isolated in canyons in the southern part. To the north, it intergrades with coniferous forest. Where this oak woodland and chaparral alternate, the chaparral is found on the drier, hotter south-facing slopes while the broad-sclerophyll forest is on the cooler, moister, north-facing slopes and in the sheltered valleys. Red-shouldered Hawks, Great Horned Owls, Acorn and Nuttall's Woodpeckers, Band-tailed Pigeons, Scrub Jays, Hutton's Vireos, Plain Titmice, and Bushtits are common resident species in this association, as are some other birds of lower altitudinal range. Band-tailed Pigeons, however, range up-mountain and are very abundant in montane forests containing stands of Black Oaks. Summer visitors to this association include Western Wood

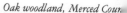

Oak woodland, Merced Coun.

Pewees, Ash-throated Flycatchers, Purple Martins, Blue-gray Gnatcatchers, Warbling Vireos, Orange-crowned Warblers, Black-throated Gray Warblers, Black-headed Grosbeaks, and Lawrence's Goldfinches.

The Blue Oak-Digger Pine association occurs in the drier regions of the foothills, particularly those bordering the Central Valley and other hot, dry valleys of the interior. The Digger Pines are rather diffuse trees with fine needles and hence do not cast much shade during the hot summer months when it is most needed. Consequently, bird life among these pines is rather sparse. The deciduous Blue Oaks attract many flying insects during their period of flowering in early spring. Often they are badly infested with caterpillars when leafed out and many insectivorous birds find good foraging there. The pine seeds and acorns provide food for the Band-tailed Pigeons, Scrub Jays, and Acorn and Lewis' Woodpeckers and the grassy understory of this savannah-like association provides food and cover for California Quail, Western Meadowlarks, and Lark Sparrows. During the winter months this association receives a down-mountain influx of White-breasted Nuthatches, Dark-eyed Juncos, White-crowned Sparrows, Purple Finches, Mountain Quail, and other montane species from the higher slopes and forests. In places, the dominant understory is manzanita-dominated chaparral with its complement of Brown and Rufous-sided Towhees, Wrentits, and California Thrashers.

The oak woodlands characterized by the large and picturesque Valley Oaks are closely associated with the grasslands and savannahs. This association is found on the floors of the higher interior valleys, the foothills of the Coast Range away from the influence of the seacoast, and in the foothills surrounding the northern portions of the Central Valley where it frequently merges with Ponderosa Pine, Coulter Pine, and Douglas Fir. The birds of this association are not distinctly different from those of the savannah habitat since grasses flourish even among the oaks of this woodland which is somewhat denser than typical open savannah. Woodpeckers, particularly Flickers (of the "Red-shafted" type), Lewis' Woodpeckers, and in the higher foothills of the Sacramento Valley, Pileated Woodpeckers are conspicuous inhabitants here. Acorn Woodpeckers also occur, but they are more at home in the thicker broad-sclerophyll oak woodlands of the coastal and southern ranges. As with typical savannah, Turkey Vultures, Golden Eagles, Red-tailed Hawks, and American Kestrels utilize the big oaks for roosting, nesting, and watching for prey or carrion.

Other smaller, less well-defined, and more restricted California woodlands are the Golden-cup Oak association which is found chiefly in canyons and on shaded slopes and often grades into a mountain chaparral. The Garry Oak association is found chiefly in the less humid portions of interior coastal mountains of the northwest portion of California. This habitat is an intermixture of woodland and prairie and the trees are all deciduous hardwoods such as Garry Oak, Black Oak, and Bigleaf Maple. The coastal hardwood association is frequently found interspersed among the coastal coniferous forests of Redwood and Douglas Fir. In areas of fire and logging, this hardwood forest is a subclimax formation ultimately replacing the

← *Scrub Jay*

Common Flicker ("Red-shafted" type) ↓

Nuttall's Woodpecker—male ↑

Band-tailed Pigeon →

Great Horned Owl ↑

Acorn Woodpecker →

Lawrence's Goldfinch—male ↑

Broad-billed Hummingbird—male ↑

Bushtit (photo by Herb Clarke) ↓

Western Bluebird—female ↑

k-headed Grosbeak—male ↓　　*House Wren* →

grass and chaparral, but in time will be replaced by the climax coniferous forest. Evergreen broad-leaved trees such as Golden-cup Oak, Tan Oak, Madrone, and California Laurel dominate this association.

Riparian Woodlands and Oases

In California, the habitat that most closely approximates the eastern broad-leaved hardwood forests is the riparian woodland. This is so because of the nature of the trees in this woodland, their denseness, and the unparalleled diversity of the bird life. Riparian woodlands are really small in area and are restricted to places where abundant and constant water occurs at or very near the surface of the ground such as in the bottomlands of rivers, streams, and lakes. If the floodplain is broad (as at Mojave Narrows on the Mojave River or along the Sacramento River) then the woodland can be quite broad and extensive. More often, however, it occupies a rather narrow belt along lake shores and river and stream margins.

Palm and cottonwood oasis, Riverside County

Streamside alder woodland, Los Angeles County

Cooper's Hawk—immature
(photo by Herb Clarke)

The riparian woodland in places approaches the denseness of a true forest and indeed where the undergrowth of herbs, shrubs, and vines is very dense, it is actually junglelike. The denseness of the undergrowth is due to the extreme light penetration through the light green canopy to the forest floor. Some of the riparian woodland trees exceed 100 feet in height, but most range from 15 to 90 feet. These trees are primarily broad-leaved hardwoods whose leaves are rather thin and light green thus giving a translucent effect to the foliage when viewed from below. Because of the nature of the leaves, which tend to lose much water to the atmosphere by transpiration, and the extreme height of the trees themselves, this woodland must be supplied with a plentiful and easily available source of subsurface water. Trees such as the cottonwoods and alders can only grow to such great heights if they have the ability to raise large volumes of water against gravity. They can do

Ground Doves

this by "transpiration-tension" when they have a large leaf surface for evaporation and a root system capable of absorbing large quantities of water from an abundant source. Because of the large leaf surface for photosynthesis and the deciduous nature of the trees themselves, growth is rapid. Fast growth, spring flowering, and the deciduous nature of this woodland results in a preponderance of insect food for birds. The annual leaf fall produces a thick carpet of leaf litter which is home to snails, worms, centipedes, spiders, beetles, crickets, and myriads of other invertebrates, as well as toads, salamanders, snakes, lizards, shrews, and mice, all of which generate a complex food-web of which some of the birds (those living on or near the ground or those that hunt near the ground) are a part. The tree trunks, limbs, flowers, and foliage are inhabited by a different fauna of insects that serve as food for birds. In addition, the herbs, shrubs, vines, and trees produce flowers, fruits, and seeds, thus adding to the plethora of bird food in this woodland. Con-

Long-eared Owl

Downy Woodpecker—male ↑

Vermilion Flycatcher—female ↑

Yellow-breasted Chat ↑

Eastern Phoebe ↑

← *Black-chinned Hummingbird—male*

Bell's Vireo →

Yellow Warbler (female) and young Brown-headed Cowbird ↑

Tree Swallow—male ↓

Northern Oriole ("Bullock's" type)—male ↑

versely, however, food production drops off sharply during the winter months when this woodland goes dormant (which it does paradoxically during the *rainy* season) and the leaves fall to the ground. Consequently a high percentage of the breeding birds of this habitat are summer visitors that must migrate south in the fall.

The dominant riparian woodland trees are the cottonwoods (Fremont and Black) and the alders (White and Red). Western Sycamores are broad stately trees

*Blue Grosbeak
—male and young*

prone to broken branches which result in numerous ready-made nest holes and cavities much used by White-breasted Nuthatches, Plain Titmice, Screech Owls, and Violet-green and Tree Swallows. Because of the spreading nature of these trees, they produce a more open woodland than do the often dense stands of cottonwoods and Quaking Aspens. The understory when present is an interlocking tangle of California Blackberry, willows of several species, Mule-fat, California Laurel, California Wild Rose, Creek Dogwood, Redbud, Blueberry Elder, California Wild Grape, nettles, and Mugwort Wormwood, not all necessarily growing in the same association.

In California the range of this habitat roughly coincides with that of the various lakes, rivers, and streams of the state. There is a fairly broad expanse of it at the junction of the Colorado and Sonoran Deserts bordering the Colorado River from about Yuma to about Needles, but it is not continuous and much has been cleared for homesites and recreational development. Extensive patches are still extant along the San Joaquin River and larger strips are to be found along the Sacramento River. All of the rivers draining the Sierra Nevada and the Cascades have extensive borders of riparian woodland as do most of the other streams and rivers of the state. In the deserts of the southeastern corner it occurs sparsely as scattered oases sometimes containing Washington Palm trees. Because of the special requirement of abundant surface or subsurface water, riparian woodland extends in California through a broad altitudinal range from sea level to above 9,000 feet, thereby coming into contact with at least five "life zones" which include a number of different habitats for birds.

Turkey Vultures are fond of roosting among the dense tall cottonwoods at night and will occasionally nest in hollow sections of the fallen trees. Stratification of nesting bird life is fairly well developed in this woodland. Long-eared Owls nest in abandoned hawks' nests (usually of Cooper's Hawks) which are located high up under the canopy. Yellow Warblers, Warbling Vireos, and "Bullock's" Orioles are primarily high-canopy nesters and feeders. Black-headed Grosbeaks occur about midway between the canopy and the floor of the forest. "Red-shafted" Flickers nest and forage on the trunks of the larger trees while the smaller Downy Woodpeckers select small trees. Willow Flycatchers, American Goldfinches, and Bell's Vireos pre-

Cardinal—male

fer the denser taller shrubs and small trees for nesting. Tree Swallows are hole-nesters, utilizing abandoned woodpecker holes in moderate-sized trees. The low dense brushy tangles afford cover and concealment for the nests of Yellow-breasted Chats, Song Sparrows, Swainson's Thrushes, and Wilson's Warblers. Blue Grosbeaks utilize taller herbs and small bushes in more open areas. Introduced Cardinals (of the eastern race) nest sparingly in bushes along the San Gabriel River and the Rio Hondo in Los Angeles County, and native Cardinals of the Arizona race (*superba*) occur in the riparian woodlands along the Colorado River near Parker Dam.

The great diversity and abundance of birds in this habitat is the result of at least three factors acting in concert. Because the riparian woodland extends through such a great life-zonal range, birds of the adjacent areas utilize the riverine woodland for foraging all along its route from the high mountains to the sea. Thus some of the birds of the riparian woodland proper may themselves extend through a great altitudinal range. The different regions of riparian habitat are in contact with a large number of adjacent habitats of diverse types quite different from the "island" of isolated riparian vegetation. Thus birds from a variety of habitats may utilize the riparian woodlands for foraging and even nesting at times. This well-known "edge" effect in which inhabitants of two dissimilar habitats meet and inter-mingle in a habitat suitable for each thus swells the list of riparian species. In addi-tion, there are those birds such as Song Sparrows and House Wrens whose primary habitat affinity is the "edge" itself. Finally, in California most of the other bird habitats are essentially dry (xeric) or near dry. The riparian woodlands represent a small area of shady "wet" woodland of broad-leaved trees whose area elsewhere in the United States is much more extensive. Thus is provided in California a suitable habitat for a large avifauna which in other regions is widespread.

Desert oases are of particular importance to migrant birds entering California from the southeast. The riparian woodland along the Colorado River is in effect a protracted desert oasis and thus an important feeding, watering, and resting area for migrants. Its long and sinuous nature and north-south orientation invites migrants to utilize it as an avenue for many miles through the inhospitable desert. Other oases are scattered throughout the Colorado, Mojave, and Great Basin Deserts. Many of the oases in the Colorado Desert have groves of native Washington Palms in addition to the usual cottonwoods and willows so characteristic of California oases. In the Coachella Valley the palm oases occur along the San Andreas Fault, an area of important earthquake movements in California. Other palm oases are found along lesser faults to the east of the Coast Range in San Diego County. At these locations, ground water is able to reach the surface along the fissures and enable plants requiring relatively large amounts of water to flourish in an otherwise alien environment. Not only do the transients take advantage of the water, food, shade, and cover, but resident desert birds such as Gambel's Quail, Cactus Wrens, Road-runners, and Black-chinned Sparrows make regular visits to drink. Mammals and other animals also find these desert springs, pools, and oases essential for survival.

Important oases for birds in California are located at Agua Caliente Springs, Borrego Springs, Bow Willow Springs, and Dos Cabezas Spring in eastern San Diego County; Palm Springs, Cottonwood Spring, and Thousand Palms Oasis in Riverside County; Morongo Valley, Twentynine Palms, Box S Spring, Old Woman Spring, and Saratoga Springs in San Bernardino County; Amargosa River, Furnace Creek Ranch, Deep Springs, and Scotty's Castle in Inyo County, and Oasis in Mono County. These areas and many others of similar type are thoroughly searched by knowledgeable birders for migrants, especially unusual ones, during the latter part of the spring migration (end of May and early June) and the latter part of the fall migration (mid-October to November).

Certain of the riparian oases are responsible for the westward range extensions of a number of species that ordinarily are not commonly found west of central Arizona. These outposts of proper habitat support only a small number of these population outriders. Within their range Elf Owls are birds of the giant Saguaro cacti of the Sonoran Desert, the riparian woodlands, and the canyon oak woodlands. In California a very small population exists in the extensive riparian woodlands bordering the southern Colorado River north of Yuma. A few birds may also exist in the small stands of Saguaro cacti representing the Sonoran Desert habitat on the California side of the Colorado River. A few desert oases in the southern Mojave Desert, such as the one at Cottonwood Spring in Joshua Tree National Monument, are inhabited by a pair or two of these diminutive owls at the extreme limits of their range. Wied's Crested Flycatchers, Lucy's Warblers, and Summer Tanagers are birds whose real westward range limit is in the patches of riparian forest of the lower Colorado River Valley. However, they have succeeded in colonizing an extreme western outpost at Morongo Valley, San Bernardino County, but because of the small acreage of this oasis, their populations are limited to but a few pairs.

Song Sparrow

Although the Vermilion Flycatchers have nested sporadically at a few places in southern California (Mojave River, San Diego, etc.) a small persistent population of no more than two or three pairs at a time exists at the Morongo Valley oasis. This population fluctuates but never disappears entirely. It presents a rare opportunity to relate some environmental factors to the limitation of a population. The Vermilion Flycatchers are early nesters (April) and were they in optimum habitat in Sonora or southern Arizona, their reproductive success would be assured. Unfortunately for them April in the California desert is an extremely windy month and because of this their reproductive success is very low. Each year nests are toppled by the strong winds or the young are blown out of the nests. Thus their survival as a nesting species is tenuous at best, yet they just manage to persist probably because of immigrants from the east constantly replenishing the population.

THE CALIFORNIA DESERTS

Almost one-third of the land area of California is desert. This region, totaling almost 50,000 square miles, occupies the northeastern, eastern, and southeastern portions of the state and a small portion of the southern San Joaquin Valley. This vast area of little rain, sparse thorny vegetation, driving winds, and at times almost intolerable heat, supports a surprising number and variety of birds at certain times of the year. During the summer months the desert is at its worst and little stirs during the heat of the day. The birds seek the shade, some of the mammals and reptiles are estivating and others are lying low in crevices, under shrubs, and underground. The plants are sere. Many of them are leafless and appear lifeless. There are no flowers and very few insects. Strong winds blow and raise clouds of dust and sand. Occasionally a severe thunderstorm bursts over the mountains, briefly flooding the ravines, arroyos, and washes, but after the storm dissipates, the water vanishes into the sand almost as quickly as it appeared. During the fall some brief flowering may follow the late summer showers and later on, winter rains drench the land sporadically. Winter days are pleasantly cool, and in the high deserts snow may fall and the nights are freezing. Most of the birds have withdrawn to the south, the reptiles and some of the mammals are hibernating, and very few insects are active.

Spring in the desert is the most delightful of all seasons. The early morning hours are sweet and cool. Birds, both residents and transients, are everywhere, and many are in full song. Flowers carpet the washes and the dunes and the flowering trees, shrubs, and bushes are humming with insects. Lizards flash across the sand or sun themselves on the rocks. Midday is pleasantly warm and the bird activity continues but at a somewhat abated pace. The oases swarm with migrants which remain for just one day before continuing their northward journey and each night brings a new flood of birds from the south. Unstable spring weather brings strong winds that generate dust storms and sand storms, sometimes grounding the migrants for a short time. By early May the spring tide has flowed through the deserts and the long summer season begins.

Desert climates are not the same everywhere in California. The low hot deserts of the extreme south and southeast are much warmer than are the Mojave Desert and the cool, high, more northerly steppe deserts of the Great Basin and the Modoc Plateau. The latter deserts, especially to the north, are snow covered during part of the winter. Yet despite these important differences in climate, terrain, and vegetation, the deserts of California share a number of essential physical and biological characteristics in common, the most important of which is the amount of annual precipitation. Deserts the world over are formed when the annual precipitation, whether it be fog, rain, or snow, totals less than about 10 inches. In California most of it comes in the form of winter rain in the south and snow in the north. Precipitation may vary from 1 to 12 inches of water annually but it averages from 5 to 10 inches. Flash floods usually occur during the short, violent storms of late summer, especially in the eastern portions of the southern deserts. Strong winds are also characteristic of deserts and are generated by a number of climatic factors. These winds start to blow when air rushes in to replace rising warm air over the relatively barren desert terrain so easily heated by the intense solar radiation. Very strong local winds are frequent in the western and southern deserts because of the usual high-pressure system associated with desert latitudes. The unstable weather of early spring brings weak cyclonic storms and low pressure to the coastal regions of southern California, and in areas where the two systems closely approach each other such as in the Antelope Valley of the Mojave Desert and the Coachella Valley of the northern Colorado Desert (especially at San Gorgonio Pass), the desert winds are more severe than anywhere in the state. Dust and sand storms are a constant menace to birds during March and April.

In the high desert (essentially the Mojave Desert north of the Transverse Ranges), the mean temperature in January is below 50°F. and in July it is below 90°F. Precipitation here averages higher (between 5 and 10 inches annually) than in the low deserts to the south. The high desert merges gradually with the low deserts (the Colorado to the south and the Sonoran to the east) as the terrain of the Mojave Desert gradually descends towards the Salton Sink to the south and towards the Colorado River to the east. The climate of the low deserts is the warmest, driest, and sunniest of California's climates. Annual precipitation averages about 50 per cent of that of the high desert and unlike the high desert, late summer thunderstorms produce about 30 to 40 per cent of the year's total. In the low deserts the sun shines more than 90 per cent of the time it is above the horizon. Daily temperatures during the summer regularly exceed 100°F. and frequently reach 120°F.

Because of the low relative humidity of the desert air, the visibility often exceeds 50 miles. Solar radiation is intense for the same reason and reflection by the hot desert terrain heats the air above it during the daytime, rapidly raising the temperature. At night the desert cools quickly because of the lack of moisture in the air and temperatures may drop to 60°F., a change of 50 to 60 degrees within 24 hours. Desert rocks absorb the heat of the intense sunlight and become hot at their surfaces. At night they cool slightly but retain much of the warmth acquired during the day and thus slowly accumulate heat. A sudden chilling thunderstorm cools the expanded rocks causing them to fracture and fragment. Wind-blown sand, daily expansion and contraction, rain, and chemical erosion gradually wear down the desert mountains. Winter rains and summer thunderstorms transport this eroded material to the bases of the parent mountains and gradually they become buried in their own debris. These desert lithosoils, which were formed from the parent rock and not transported very far from it, are thin and rocky residual soils not suited to holding much water.

Only because of the paucity of water, can the desert landscape take on such a striking character. There is little vegetation to protect the soil, and gullies, arroyos, and canyons are easily carved into the soft unprotected ground. Because rains are infrequent and severe, the landscape has no opportunity to become softly rounded and gently contoured. Instead it is rugged, deeply eroded, and beautifully sculptured into infinite forms. Here and there, especially in the Mojave Desert and the Great Basin, temporary alkali lakes form in the basins and sinks after heavy rains, but most of the time these playas are dry. Desert washes and arroyos, despite their sandy and gravelly soils, support fairly dense stands of larger desert vegetation such as Palo Verde trees, mesquite, Desert Ironwood, and Desert "Willows." In sharp contrast, where sand has blown in from the surrounding desert and accumulated into dunes because of the peculiar nature of the terrain and the winds, vegetation is very sparse or even nonexistent.

Over the desert flats and mesas, vegetation is rather monotonous and evenly spaced, with conspicuous areas of bare ground between the widely separated plants. There is virtually no understory although patches of grass grow here and there. The shrubs, bushes, and trees are xerophilous or dry-adapted. Those that are evergreen have thickened waxy or "hairy" leaves to retard evaporation of water by the dry desert winds. Others have very small leaves for the same reason, while still others put out leaves only during the rainy season when they can afford to lose water by transpiration. Most of the desert vegetation is from 3 to 6 feet in height although some of the trees, notably Desert Ironwood, often reach 20 feet. Creosote Bush is the most extensive plant association in the California deserts south of the shadscale and sagebrush of the Great Basin Desert. It carpets thousands of square miles of lower slopes, alluvial fans, and valleys of low desert country from below sea level to about 3,000 feet. In pure extensive stands it harbors relatively few birds but produces large numbers of seeds essential to the survival of many desert rodents which form the primary food source for Ravens, Prairie Falcons, American Kestrels, Swainson's Hawks, Red-tailed Hawks, Great Horned Owls, and Barn Owls.

Other common desert plants include mesquites, Catclaw, Palo Verde, Smoke Tree, Desert "Willow," Desert Ironwood, Agave, chollas, yuccas, nolinas, ephedras, Ocotillo, saltbushes (especially bordering the desert sinks), and Saguaros (on the mesas bordering the Colorado River). When these plants are in bloom during the spring, they attract clouds of insects, which in turn lure birds, especially transients, to them. Particularly attractive to birds are the blooming Desert "Willows," Palo Verdes, mesquites, Smoke Trees, and Desert Ironwoods which tend to grow in rather dense stands along the desert washes where intermittent water is more plentiful. The blossoms themselves, as well as the fruits and seeds produced by the desert plants, provide a rich and abundant source of food for desert animals and birds and it is in the washes and oases, where the vegetation is densest and most varied, that most of the transient desert birds tend to congregate. The resident desert species are rather more evenly distributed although for nesting purposes the washes have a higher density of breeders because of the concentration of plants for food, cover, shade, and nest sites.

The transient birds are not especially well adapted to desert life, but they pass through it when conditions are optimum and thus can safely make the transit. However, it is the residents and summer visitors among the desert species that display the types of adaptations that enable them to survive after the transients have departed for wetter and greener country to the north and west. After the blooming season has ended, the true desert birds must rely upon fruits and nuts for food and upon those crawling and climbing insects that were not attracted to the now-withered blossoms. Phainopeplas feast primarily on small flying insects and on the berries of the Desert Mistletoe. Many of the numerous clumps of this plant, so prevalent and widely scattered among the larger desert trees and shrubs, represent the sites of old Phainopepla nests where the quantities of the voided sticky seeds have clung to the branches and trunks and germinated there. White-winged Doves feed on drupes and berries as well as seeds of many desert plants. Those birds which feed on fallen seeds include Gambel's Quail, Black-throated Sparrows, Abert's Towhees, Cactus Wrens, Le Conte's and Crissal Thrashers, and Sage Sparrows. Roadrunners catch small snakes, lizards, and insects from the desert floor. The thrashers with their long sickle-shaped beaks so well suited to probing beneath rocks, twigs, and leaves also search for insects among the leaf litter beneath the desert shrubs. The wide avenues among the desert shrubs are suitable pathways for escape and foraging for such strong runners as Crissal, Bendire's, and Le Conte's Thrashers, Cactus Wrens, Roadrunners, Gambel's Quail, and Sage Sparrows. Ladder-backed Woodpeckers drill into the larger desert trees for nest cavities and for wood-boring insects. The "Gilded" Flickers and Gila Woodpeckers obtain their food by drilling into the pulp of the Saguaro cacti near the Colorado River. They also use excavated cavities in these giant cacti for nest chambers. Small insects are gleaned from leaves and twigs by the Verdins and Black-tailed Gnatcatchers and the Rock Wrens clamber about cliffs and boulder piles hunting insects in the crevices. Cliff-nesting Ravens feast on road-killed animals (actually "patrolling" the desert roads for such carcasses), carrion in general, and snatch eggs and young birds from the nests of smaller species. Those species which build their nests in the dense shrubs, cacti, and trees are well guarded from predators by the thorns. spines, and sharp twigs and leaves of these plants.

Water for drinking and bathing is more critical for the transients than for the residents. There are very few summer visitors to the desert. Oases are essential for the transients as they cross the southeastern California deserts from Mexico. They must drink and bathe almost every day and therefore do not linger long in the hostile desert habitat. White-winged Doves and Costa's Hummingbirds are summer visitors to the desert, and of the two, the White-winged Dove drinks frequently and must therefore nest in the vicinity of an oasis. The hummingbirds obtain their liquids in the form of flower nectar and will bathe when they have the opportunity. Of the desert residents, those that must drink daily are the Gambel's Quail and the Mourning Doves. They will travel many miles for water, but their "bathing" is done in the dust. Cactus Wrens, thrashers, Black-throated and Sage Sparrows, and even Roadrunners will occasionally drink water, but they rarely bathe in water. The food of these birds provides them with sufficient moisture for enduring several days without actually drinking water. The predatory habits of the Roadrunner ensures this species liquid provided by the body fluids of its prey. Those desert birds not known to drink or bathe regularly or not at all include Ravens, Phainopeplas, Verdins, Barn, Elf, and Great Horned Owls, Lesser Nighthawks, Poor-wills, Black-tailed Gnatcatchers, "Gilded" Flickers, and Gila and Ladder-backed Woodpeckers. These birds probably obtain enough moisture from the foods they consume.

Despite its vast size and formidable aspects, the desert is in reality a very fragile environment and all of its inhabitants live in perfect harmony with it. The very slow rate of decay and lack of rain enables materials and scars to endure for many years. Because of its remote nature, people for years have used the desert as repository for unwanted rubbish and because of the slow rate of decay and weathering, this material persists and the desert beauty is blighted. An even more serious threat to the desert habitat is manifested by the ORV's (off-road vehicles) that crush the fragile desert vegetation, destroy Indian artifacts, and leave permanent scars on the landscape. Because of its remoteness and inhospitable nature, the desert has long been safe from the ravages of man, but now, with modern technology producing new gadgetry for camping comfort and for crossing roadless terrain, even this seemingly safe sanctuary is seriously threatened.

California's desert habitat consists of four contiguous desert associations plus a fifth isolated association—the San Joaquin Valley Desert. Birds of the contiguous associations show far more overlap among them as well. There are subtle climatic and soil factors at work which result in differences in vegetation among the several desert associations.

The San Joaquin Valley Desert

The San Joaquin Valley Desert is isolated from the other four desert associations by the Tehachapi Mountains and the Sierra Nevada. It occupies the drier southern and southwestern portion of the San Joaquin Valley centered around the former lake bed of Buena Vista Lake and extends on the west side of the valley as

San Joaquin Valley desert, Kern County

Barn Owl

far north as Coalinga in Fresno County. Portions of Kern, Fresno, Kings, and San Luis Obispo counties are encompassed by this desert association. It continues westward over the lower reaches of the Temblor Range in western Kern County to the Elkhorn Valley, the Carrizo Plain, and a few other small inland valleys and hills of the inner Coast Ranges of eastern San Luis Obispo County. Unlike the other deserts it is entirely devoid of cacti and yuccas. The soil is largely alkaline. It was formed under conditions of poor drainage coupled with high temperatures. As the water accumulated in low places (such as at Soda Lake in San Luis Obispo County) it carried with it in solution the salts leached from the soils of the surrounding hills. Evaporation of the shallow waters left behind the accumulated salts which the meager rainfall could not leach away. The plants of this desert then are those necessarily adapted to soils of extreme alkalinity and include Many-fruited Saltbush,

Lesser Nighthawk

Roadrunner

Spinescale, Bush Pickleweed, Torrey Alkali Blight, and Alkali Heath. They are all small bushes not exceeding 4 feet in height, grayish or whitish green in color, and widely and fairly uniformly spaced. In the arroyos where water infrequently flows, the vegetation is densest. Annual precipitation averages less than 5 inches, summer temperatures often reach 110°F., and dense "tule" fogs settle in for weeks at a time during the chilly winter months.

Because of the monotony and uniformity of the vegetation, bird life is relatively sparse and not very diverse but small mammal life and reptile life abound. American Kestrels which nest in the few trees around habitation and Prairie Falcons, Red-tailed Hawks, and Golden Eagles from eyries on nearby cliffs find enough of their preferred food for more than adequate sustenance—Black-tailed Jackrabbits and San Joaquin Antelope Squirrels for the Red-tails and the eagles, small birds and rodents for the Prairie Falcons, and grasshoppers, crickets, and small rodents for the

Rock Wren

Le Conte's Thrasher

kestrels. Barn Owls, which roost in the deep arroyos, find kangaroo rats, woodrats, and pocket mice plentiful and Burrowing Owls survive on large beetles, crickets, locusts, centipedes, scorpions, and small rodents. Roadrunners nest in the densest clumps of brush and find lizards, snakes, and nestling birds in plentiful supply. At dusk Lesser Nighthawks skim the ground in pursuit of moths and beetles and are quite at home nesting on the open rocky ground, so well camouflaged are they and their nestlings. Other nesting species include Mockingbirds, House Finches, Rock Wrens, Loggerhead Shrikes, Say's Phoebes, Sage Sparrows, and Le Conte's Thrashers. Although this thrasher also occurs sparingly in the Owens Valley, Mojave Desert, Death Valley, and portions of the Colorado Desert, its population center of highest density is the San Joaquin Valley Desert. It is perfectly suited by coloration, form, and habits for dashing through the runways amongst the alkali bushes, probing for insects and seeds among the leaf litter under bushes, and nesting among the prickly saltbushes. It is the most characteristic bird of this desert.

The Sonoran Desert

The Sonoran Desert association is strongly influenced by the riparian woodland of the lower Colorado River Valley adjacent to it. Vermilion Flycatchers, Lucy's Warblers, Gila Woodpeckers, Harris' Hawks, Crissal Thrashers, Cardinals, and Abert's Towhees occur on the fringes of and occasionally within this desert but in California are more attached to the riparian association. However, in Arizona and northern Sonora, where the Sonoran Desert prevails, Gila Woodpeckers, Harris' Hawks, and Cardinals are typical birds of this desert. Almost always associated with riparian situations in the desert are the Vermilion Flycatchers, Lucy's Warblers, and

Sonoran Desert with Saguaro cacti ↑

Harris' Hawk ↑

← *Common Flicker ("Gilded" type)—male*

Gila Woodpecker—male

Abert's Towhees. This Sonoran Desert association is characterized by the giant Saguaro cacti so prominent in the deserts of southern Arizona and northern Sonora.
In California, from about Needles to Yuma, there exist a few scattered stands on the
mesa bordering the Colorado River above the riparian woodland of the river margin. The Common Flicker (of the "Gilded" type) and the Elf Owl, both of which
occur in very small numbers, plus the aforementioned species from the riparian association, make up the avifauna of the Sonoran Desert association in California.
The Sonoran Desert is effectively isolated from the Colorado Desert in the Salton
Basin by the sterile Algodones Sand Dunes, but Crissal Thrashers, Abert's Towhees, and, formerly at least, Harris' Hawks and Gila Woodpeckers have been able to
disperse westward. The Mojave Desert gradually intergrades with the Sonoran
Desert in the vicinity of Needles and the Bendire's Thrasher, a bird typical of the
Sonoran Desert in south central Arizona, has established a viable isolated popu-
lation in the Joshua Tree forests south of Cima in northeastern San Bernardino
County although they do not occur in California's intervening Sonoran Desert or
in the riparian woodlands of the lower Colorado River.

Black-tailed Gnatcatcher—male

The Colorado Desert

The Colorado Desert is contained within portions of Riverside, San Diego, and Imperial counties and includes some of the hottest and driest regions in the world. It includes such important geologic features as the Salton Sea, the Imperial and Coachella valleys, the 45-mile-long Algodones Dunes, and Palm Springs. On the west it is bordered by the Santa Rosa and Vallecito Mountains of the Peninsular Ranges but includes important desert valleys such as Borrego and Clark valleys. To the north it is bordered by the Little San Bernardino Mountains and Eagle Mountains but it includes such smaller desert ranges as the Orocopia, Chuckwalla, Chocolate, Palo Verde, and Cargo Muchacho Mountains to the east and northeast. Much of the Colorado Desert lies in the Salton Trough, a northwest-oriented landward extension of the Gulf of California reaching 140 miles to San Gorgonio Pass. More than 2,000 square miles of this trough is below sea level, the largest such area in the Western Hemisphere.

The Imperial Valley region is one of the hottest in the world and is the hottest part of the United States. The highest recorded temperature was 130°F. and the

Colorado Desert, Riverside County

Colorado Desert, San Diego County

White-winged Dove

lowest was 22°F. Annual rainfall ranges from 1.1 inches at Ogilby, Imperial County, to about 3.5 inches at Palm Springs, Riverside County. Because of the Salton Sea the relative humidity in its immediate vicinity is often quite high making conditions there most uncomfortable at times.

Elf Owl

Ornithologically the natural portions of the Colorado Desert are not significantly different from the larger Mojave Desert to the north. The extreme western edge of the Colorado Desert is dotted with palm oases. A number of them also occur along the south slopes of the Little San Bernardino Mountains in the northwest corner. This is an area where the San Andreas Fault enables ground water to flow to the surface. Native desert vegetation includes Washington Palms, cottonwoods, and willows at the oases, Screwbean Mesquite, Creosote Bush, Indigo Bush, Brittlebush, chollas and various other cacti, Burrobush, Palo Verde, Smoke Tree, Desert Ironwood, and several species of *Atriplex* (saltbush), the latter bordering the Salton Sea and the few playas. Yuccas are conspicuous by their absence. The Desert Agave grows only in the southwestern portions as do the very local Elephant Trees.

Ladder-backed Woodpecker—male

Verdin

Smoke Trees, Desert Ironwoods, Desert Lavender, Sandpaper Plant, Cheese Bush, Bandegea, Palo Verde, Desert Mistletoe, and Desert "Willows" flourish in the desert washes near the bases of the mountains.

No specific desert bird species are confined exclusively to this desert. Verdins, Phainopeplas, and Gambel's Quail are conspicuous where the brush is taller and denser, as along washes and arroyos. The alluvial fans dominated by Creosote Bush are largely devoid of birds except for the occasional Raven coursing overhead. The dense patches of mesquite and saltbush at the north and south ends of the Salton Sea are the population centers for Abert's Towhees and Crissal Thrashers in California. In the far west, Mockingbirds are not a conspicuous part of the desert avifauna as they are in west Texas, but in this Salton Basin scrub they are very numerous.

Of the five California deserts, the Colorado Desert figures most importantly in the spring migratory patterns of small land birds into California from Mexico. Lying as it does in the natural valley of the Salton Trough, the Colorado Desert receives most of the land bird migrants from Mexico that are funneled into it by the

Pyrrhuloxia—female

Costa's Hummingbird—male

surrounding mountains. To the east, those migrants following the valley and riparian woodlands along the Colorado River tend to remain in that attractive habitat for as long as possible. They therefore follow the river northward for some distance before once more crossing the inhospitable open Mojave Desert. The Salton Sea itself is a powerful attraction for migratory waterfowl and shorebirds. It is such a unique component of the Colorado Desert that a special section is devoted to it.

The New and Alamo rivers carrying irrigation waters into the Salton Sea are bordered by thick stands of brush, both native and introduced. The growth of exotic alkali-loving Tamarisk or Salt Cedar near the Salton Sea itself and along the irrigation canals, the two rivers, and the several lakes in the Coachella and Imperial valleys has been extensive. When in bloom it attracts hordes of flying insects which likewise lure the migrants to feed upon them. The dense groves and rows of Tamarisk also provide welcome cover and shade for the birds.

Agriculture in both the Coachella and Imperial Valleys is so extensive and intense that these two large portions within the heart of the Colorado Desert are in effect huge artificial oases populated by such plants as Date Palms, Chinese Elms, Oleanders, Cottonwoods, Tamarisks, Grapefruit, Lemon, Grape, Alfalfa, Lettuce, Barley, Sugar Beet, Onion, Tomato, Cotton, Watermelon, and Cantaloupe. During the spring migration, these fields, groves, and orchards swarm with migrants which are often pinned down for several days by the driving spring desert winds. Warblers, orioles, vireos, grosbeaks, tanagers, flycatchers, and gnatcatchers search and glean the dense foliage for small climbing insects while the doves, blackbirds, sparrows, and towhees comb the ground in search of seeds and insects. Over the fields rove flocks of swallows and swifts feasting on the hosts of aerial insects.

Because of the development of this artificial and relatively recent new habitat in the midst of one of the most difficult of the desert environments, the population of transients through this part of the desert has undoubtedly increased and the survival rate of some of these transients has also increased in recent years. Migrants entering California flying at perhaps an elevation of 1,500 to 2,000 feet can easily spy the inviting greenery of the Imperial Valley even if many miles away to one side or the other. After a long night of travel and fasting these migrants could be expected to alter course and make for lush greenery in the distance.

The Mojave Desert

The Mojave Desert is situated almost entirely within California and in area is slightly smaller than the Great Basin Desert complex which borders it on the north. Like the Colorado Desert to the south it includes mesas, low desert mountains, washes, alluvial fans, and playas. Compared with the Colorado Desert there are significant geological differences, slight differences in vegetation, real differences in average elevation, temperature, and precipitation, slight differences in soils, and a few small differences in bird life. It is a "high" desert when again compared with the Colorado Desert but in its eastern extremities, as its elevation diminishes towards the Sonoran Desert and the Colorado River, it imperceptibly changes to a "low hot" desert and in that respect is indistinguishable from the bordering Colorado Desert with which it intergrades.

On the northwest it is bounded by the Sierra Nevada and the Tehachapi Mountains. The southwestern border consists of the San Gabriel, Sawmill, and

Mojave Desert, San Bernardino County—Creosote Bush formation

Mojave Desert, Los Angeles County—Joshua Tree "woodland"

Liebre Mountains and its southern border is the San Bernardino Mountains, Little San Bernardino Mountains, and the Colorado Desert. Its northern border is less precisely defined. In general, the mountain ranges of the Great Basin are high parallel ranges running in a north-south direction. Those of the Mojave Desert lack parallel arrangement and are lower. Where geological distinction exists, a northern boundary has been established in northern San Bernardino County along a line

Gambel's Quail—male

Cactus Wren

running eastward from the El Paso Mountains, passing just to the north of Rands-burg and Johannesburg, and reaching the Nevada border just east of the valley be-tween the Nopah and Kingston Ranges. The elevation of this "high" desert aver-ages about 3,000 feet. Although hot enough in the summer, the Mojave rarely reaches the searing heat of the low Colorado Desert and its winters are somewhat cooler. Precipitation, occasionally in the form of snow, is slightly greater also. Both precipitation and air temperature vary with elevation, the former increasing with higher altitude and the latter decreasing.

The basin margins, alluvial fans, and especially the southern and southeastern

Common Raven

portions of the Mojave Desert are dominated by the ubiquitous Creosote Bush wherever the terrain is relatively flat. This shrub, together with Burrobush, Indigo Bush, Dye Bush, Brittlebush, and various smaller cacti, comprise the vegetation of the lower reaches of this desert. In the eastern portion, the lower foothills also contain Ocotillo. Birds are scarce and their population is not very diverse. Roadrunners hunt for lizards before the heat of the day drives the reptiles to cover and the Mojave Desert's most conspicuous birds, the Ravens, soar out from their cliff eyries in search of prey and carrion. Cactus Wrens nest in the formidable chollas and are not found among pure stands of Creosote Bush as are the Black-throated Sparrows. Le Conte's Thrashers occur sparingly among the Creosote Bushes, preferring denser stands of saltbushes, Palo Verde trees, and mesquite. Costa's Hummingbirds, the only nesting hummingbirds of the California deserts, are present from about late February to September, and are very partial to the scarlet blossoms of the Ocotillo.

Phainopepla—female and young

The sand dunes at Kelso and the Dunlop Dunes south of Tecopa as well as smaller scattered sand dunes elsewhere are among the most birdless areas in the United States. The dunes are devoid of vegetation except for patches of Spanish Needle, Dune Evening Primrose, and a few grasses but are bordered by scattered shrubs from which Roadrunners occasionally sally forth onto the dunes in pursuit of Zebra-tailed and Fringe-toed Lizards. The loose footing on the dunes, however, discourages most Roadrunners from long pursuits of their prey. Also, Zebra-tailed Lizards are among the fastest of terrestrial reptiles and the Fringe-toed Lizards are quick to bury themselves in the loose sand when a predator approaches. .

As in the Colorado and Sonoran Deserts, bird life is most plentiful in the desert washes where the vegetation is most profuse. These same desert washes frequently retain water in pools or rock basins for short periods after rains and are therefore doubly attractive to the birds. Catclaw, Desert Ironwood, Palo Verde, and Desert "Willow" are the largest plants found in the washes. All are infested with Desert

Scott's Oriole—male

Mistletoe, whose berries are a favorite food of the Phainopeplas. Other smaller plants include Desert Apricot, Desert Almond, Woolly Brickellia, and Bebbia. These form an irregular broken carpet on the floors of the washes. During spring migration, the migrants tend to follow the greenery of these desert washes because of the food, cover, and shade they provide. Verdins prefer to build their conspicuous but almost impregnable, hollow, twiggy nests in the denser Palo Verdes and Black-tailed Gnatcatchers construct and camouflage their beautiful little nests so well that they easily escape recognition by predators. Gambel's Quail assemble at the water holes early each morning and spend the rest of the daylight hours feeding and resting nearby. In the evenings they go to roost, preferably in the trees with the thickest foliage—the Palo Verdes.

The alkali sinks contain the playas or dry lakes vegetated at the margins with several species of saltbushes and Iodine Bush, and they, like the sand dunes, are relatively free of bird life in contrast to the few scattered riparian oases whose cottonwoods, willows, and mesquites abound with birds during the spring migration.

Black-throated Sparrow

In the higher reaches of the Mojave Desert, from 4,000 to 6,000 feet, are mesas and gravel slopes vegetated with sagebrush scrub which intergrades with the piñon-juniper woodlands higher up and yields to the low desert scrub lower down. The preponderant plant here is the Great Basin Sagebrush intermixed with Blackbush, Rabbitbrush, Purple Sage, and Four-wing Saltbush. To the north, in the Great Basin Desert, the sagebrush is even more prominent. Sage Sparrows and Brewer's Sparrows replace the Black-throated Sparrows in this plant association. In the northern Mojave Desert, growing on soils that are somewhat alkaline and located on mesas and other flat areas between 3,000 and 6,000 feet, are large expanses of grayish-green shrubs dominated by Shadscale. This vegetation is not very disparate and consequently bird life is not particularly distinct or interesting except for the Black-throated Sparrows.

Ornithologically the most interesting and unique plant association of the Mojave Desert is the Joshua Tree "woodland." In addition to these tree yuccas which predominate, a variety of other desert plants including Mojave Yuccas, Antelope Bush, chollas, Desert Apricot, Desert Almond, ephedras, Rabbitbrush, Paperbag Bush, Galleta, and junipers are found in this association. This higher portion of the Mojave Desert frequently receives snow in winter and most winter days are chilly. At its upper fringes this plant association merges with the Pygmy Conifer woodland of piñon pines and junipers. Extensive stands of Joshua Trees exist in Joshua Tree National Monument (in the northern portions), on the desert slopes of the Tehachapi, San Gabriel, and San Bernardino Mountains, and in the high valleys and mesas of eastern San Bernardino County. The Joshua Trees and Mojave Yuccas are preferred homes for Scott's Orioles who weave their nests among the dagger-like leaves. Cactus Wrens prefer the protection of the yuccas and chollas for their nests. Ash-throated Flycatchers nest in the rotted cavities in the yuccas or in the abandoned nest-cavities carved by Ladder-backed Woodpeckers. American Kestrels require cavities and also utilize chambers in the tree yuccas. Loggerhead Shrikes nest in the hearts of the densest shrubs and find a plethora of lizards to eat in this part of the desert. House Finches are abundant, especially if open water is nearby. Their nests are often placed well within the protective branches and spines of the formidable chollas. Gambel's Quail are found where water is readily available and if cliffs are nearby, Ravens, Red-tailed Hawks, Golden Eagles, and Prairie Falcons establish their eyries high upon them and forage over the desert for reptiles, rabbits, rodents, and carrion. Other nesting birds of this diverse "woodland" include Scrub Jays, Gray Vireos, Green-tailed Towhees, Mourning Doves, Roadrunners, Poorwills, Lesser Nighthawks, Mockingbirds, California Thrashers, Black-tailed Gnatcatchers, and in a few scattered colonies in eastern San Bernardino County, Bendire's Thrashers. During the non-breeding season Pinyon Jays and Mountain Quail from the adjacent but higher piñon-juniper woodland move down to lower elevations. Because of the winter snows and frost in this environment most of the birds either migrate far to the south or withdraw slightly to the milder winter climate of the low deserts to the south and southeast.

THE GREAT BASIN

The Great Basin Desert is an integral part of the Basin and Ranges landform province or Great Basin. Like the Sonoran Desert, the greater part of this desert lies somewhere to the east of California and the western extremity of both desert associations terminates, at least in part, somewhere in the state. The geologic history of the Basin and Ranges Region is dissimilar to that of the adjacent Modoc Plateau and Sierra Nevada to the west and the Mojave Desert to the south. The Basin and Ranges Region extends roughly from the Sierra Nevada east to the Rocky Mountains and includes most of Nevada, most of Utah, southeastern Oregon, and southern Idaho. It consists of numerous mountain ranges, large and small, aligned in a north-south direction. Between the parallel ranges are depressed basins or troughs called grabens with an average elevation of about 4,000 feet. Surprise Valley in

Modoc County, Death Valley, and Owens Valley are grabens. Many of the basins contain lakes, some of which are permanent, while others contain water only part of the year or after irregular intervals determined by the local precipitation. Most of the lakes are either alkaline or saline. In extreme northeastern California to the east of the Warner Mountains lies the large basin of Surprise Valley. It contains the large basin lake called Middle Lake. Upper Lake to the north of it and Lower Lake to the south are smaller. Goose Lake is situated just to the west of the Warner Mountains. Eagle Lake and Honey Lake (usually dry in the summer) in Lassen County are part of the Great Basin lake system as is Mono Lake in Mono County just east of Tioga Pass at the eastern base of the Sierra Nevada. Owens Lake in the southern part of Owens Valley in Inyo County was formerly a fairly large lake but the Los Angeles Aqueduct takes so much water from its feeder, the Owens River, that this lake rarely contains much water. Some of the mountains of this Basin and Ranges Region are quite high and support dense stands of conifers above which are alpine meadows and fell-fields. In California, White Mountain Peak in the White Mountains reaches 14,242 feet and a number of other peaks surpass 11,000 feet in both the White Mountains and the Panamint Mountains to the south.

Great Basin desert, Inyo County

In California there are three areas of the Great Basin that fall within its boundaries. In the extreme northeast, Surprise Valley east of the Warner Mountains, is a
Great Basin valley as is the smaller valley of Honey Lake to the south. The largest

Sage Grouse—male

area of Great Basin Desert in California forms a rough triangle bounded on the east
and northeast by the Nevada border, on the west and southwest by the Sierra
Nevada, and on the south by the Mojave Desert. The Great Basin Desert association occupies the troughs, lake borders, and lower mountain slopes vegetated by
Great Basin Sagebrush and Shadscale.

The Great Basin Desert is a cold desert. Killing frosts may occur any month of
the year. The frost-free season is very short and there are frosts almost every night,
often accompanied by bitter cold temperatures during fall, winter, and spring. The
growing season is short and the region is very arid, averaging only from 4 to 12
inches of precipitation annually. This is greatest during the winter, increases with
altitude, and often occurs in the form of snow. Dryness increases from north to
south and is intense in the lower basins. Death Valley receives about 1.4 inches of
precipitation annually. Independence in northwestern Inyo County averages 4.8
inches, and Bishop which is slightly higher, receives about 6.0 inches. The bordering high ranges receive much snow in the winter. Despite the relatively high average elevation (about 4,000 feet) of the basins of the Great Basin Desert, the climate
is extremely arid. This is due to a number of factors not the least important of
which is the fact that the latitude of this area places it at the belt of the subtropical
"high," a region of persistent high atmospheric pressure and consequent fair
weather. Another and more dramatic factor in the formation of this desert is the
close proximity of the Cascades and the Sierra Nevada whose massive presence between the Great Basin and the Pacific Ocean obstructs the moisture-bearing westerly winds as they blow landward from the sea. The moist cyclonic winds, so prevalent during the winter months, are forced to rise as they cross the western front of

the Sierra Nevada and the Cascades. Upon cooling, they precipitate most of their moisture on the western side and upon the crest of the mountains and most of this water drains westward into the Central Valley via numerous westward-flowing rivers. Bitter cold dry winds then race down the valleys on the eastern slope of these mountains creating this coldest of California deserts. By the time these air masses have moved eastward and been forced once again to rise over the Inyo, White, and Panamint Mountains, the last bit of moisture is wrung from them as they once again dust the higher ranges with snow. This effect, called a "rain shadow," is responsible for the formation of deserts in other regions of the world as well. All of the other California deserts are the result of this phenomenon to some degree.

Because the climatic conditions of this region are so distinctive, the desert vegetation is a distinct formation, separate from the scrub types of the deserts to the south. Two major plant communities are prevalent and often extend monotonously unbroken for miles. The sagebrush association dominated by Great Basin Sagebrush is the climax vegetation at higher elevations in the southern portion of this desert and covers vast areas of basin flats in the northern portion. The shadscale association, consisting primarily of Shadscale and Bud Sage, occurs at lower elevations and ranges to the southern portions of this desert. Other shrubs with similar growth forms that give this desert a grayish-green look include saltbushes, Rabbit-

Poorwill

brush, Antelope Brush, Iodine Bush, and pickleweed (where soil salt content is high), Hop Sage, Mormon Tea, Winterfat, and several other species of *Artemesia*.

The several distinctive plant formations result in a rather unique assemblage of birds in the Great Basin Desert. Resident raptors include Turkey Vultures, Golden Eagles, Red-tailed Hawks, Prairie Falcons, and American Kestrels. Winter brings an influx of Ferruginous Hawks down from the Canadian Great Plains. Most of them move south out of the snow country, but the Rough legged Hawks from the arctic tundra prefer the snow-covered flats of this northern desert. Small numbers of Bald Eagles from Canada and Alaska remain near the basin lakes as long as they are unfrozen, but after they freeze the eagles continue south.

The Sage Grouse is probably the most characteristic bird of this special desert country. Being strong runners, they are perfectly at home among the avenues between the bushes through which they can dash when a Golden Eagle, Bobcat, or Coyote appears. Their plumage pattern of browns, grays, and black affords them excellent camouflage in this habitat. Early in the spring, even while snow is still on the flats, the male grouse assemble well before dawn at special clearings in the sagebrush where their kind have gathered for untold generations. Here, even before it is light, the cock grouse commence a most unusual courtship display. Each male selects a territory, sometimes with a very small hillock in it. Here he displays his plumage by erecting his magnificent white ruff, erecting and fanning his tail, drooping his wings, and alternately inflating and deflating his bright yellow pectoral air sacs to the accompaniment of various cackles, pops, and deep bubbling notes. Shortly after dawn, the females emerge from the brush where they have been observing, and mating may take place nearby. Usually this display terminates with the appearance of the sun but the birds may return to the dancing grounds in the late afternoon for a shorter performance.

Great Horned Owls hunt the flats at night from their roosts in the nearby cliffs

Say's Phoebe

and groves of trees and Burrowing Owls inhabit the tunnels abandoned by the ubiquitous ground squirrels. The only hummingbird of this habitat is the Blackchinned and it occurs where there is some riparian woodland along the streams. The Gray Flycatcher nests only in this habitat, preferring the taller sagebrush bushes of the northern half of this desert. The Sage Thrasher is another characteristic breeding bird of this sagebrush environment. Ravens are the only large Corvids found here except for the Black-billed Magpies whose range in California conforms almost exactly to the western boundaries of the Great Basin and the Modoc Plateau. These magpies prefer stream and lake valleys where the taller denser vegetation provides them with proper nesting habitat but they forage over the sagebrush flats and are plentiful about farms and ranches whose groves of trees provide additional nest sites. Loggerhead Shrikes occur commonly and in the winter the larger

Sage Sparrow

whiter Northern Shrikes come south from the arctic and, especially in northern portions of this desert, may outnumber the Loggerheads. Rufous-sided Towhees inhabit the higher slopes and mesas, the dense shrubbery with runways between the plants and dense overhead cover being exactly to their liking as ground-foragers. The Green-tailed Towhee occurs higher up on the slopes and its range extends into the piñon-juniper woodlands. House Finches are numerous and Sage and Brewer's Sparrows are the most common sparrows with Vesper Sparrows somewhat less numerous and preferring grassy openings among the sagebrush.

As a bird habitat, the Great Basin Desert itself does not attract a profusion of species but the greater region of the Great Basin itself does. This is because of its complex nature and the variety of habitats contained within it. In addition to the desert proper, there are lakes, streams, riparian woodlands, oases, piñon-juniper woodlands, montane and subalpine forests, alpine tundra and alpine fell-fields, and rocky cliffs and talus slopes. The northern lakes—Goose, Upper, Middle, Lower, Eagle, and Honey—accommodate tens of thousands of waterfowl during their fall migration. After these shallow lakes freeze over in the winter, the birds move south probably as far as the marshes of the lower Colorado River Valley and the Colorado River Delta in Baja California. Mono Lake is inhabited by many thousands of Eared Grebes during the winter and at times of spring and fall migration these numbers are swelled by additional thousands of Wilson's Phalaropes also pausing to feed on the rich harvest of brine shrimp in the lake. The oases at Furnace Creek Ranch,

Scotty's Castle, and Saratoga Springs in Death Valley National Monument, Deep
Springs Valley, Oasis, and other choice localities throughout the Great Basin in
California attract large numbers of migrants during spring and fall. Extensive
stands of riparian woodland along the Owens River, Amargosa River, and other
north-south oriented troughs are situated along the flight paths of the migrants. In
addition, such man-made habitats as windbreaks, golfcourses, gardens, reservoirs,
lakes, crop fields, meadows, and orchards are scattered throughout the Great Basin
and offer food, shelter, shade, and water for birds.

In some respects winter is the most exciting season of the year in California's
Great Basin. Thousands of Gray-crowned Rosy Finches from the northern Rocky
Mountains migrate south and they are joined by a small number of local Gray-

Brewer's Sparrow

crowned Rosy Finches which have moved down the mountains from their summer
alpine homes to feed on the sagebrush flats. Lapland Longspurs in flocks of hundreds feed on weed seeds on the more open snow-covered plains. Occasionally the
accidental Snow Bunting occurs with them. Small groups of Chestnut-collared
Longspurs may also linger into the winter and among them may be a few casual
McCown's Longspurs. Unfrozen openings in the basin lakes attract Whistling
Swans until these freeze and among them occasionally may be the casual Trumpeter
Swan, probably down from Malheur Refuge in Oregon. Flocks of Evening Grosbeaks roam the farms seeking alder, birch, and other tree seeds. Sometimes large
flocks of such irregular visitors as Bohemian Waxwings make their way south from
Canada in search of juniper berries, and almost every winter brings at least a few to
the Great Basin. Tree Sparrows are very rare winter visitors to California, but a few
can always be found in the brush along the margins of the fields near Honey Lake
and other places as can the rare Harris' Sparrow. Northern Shrikes and Rough-
legged Hawks occur here in greater numbers than anywhere else in California.
Winter also brings the promise of such ultra-rarities as Snowy Owls, Gyrfalcons,
and Common Redpolls to this sparsely populated part of the state.

THE MOUNTAINS
AND MOUNTAIN FORESTS

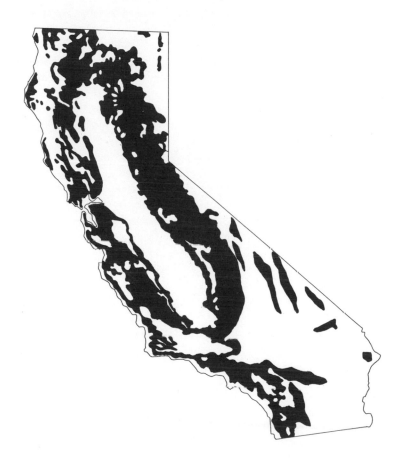

The mountain ranges of California constitute a most prominent geological and ecological complex. Because of the nature of the terrain, gradations in altitude, local climatic conditions, slope-faces in relation to sun or prevailing winds, the effects of standing or running water, and various other physical environmental factors, the distribution of bird life in mountainous regions depends most directly upon vegetational associations which in turn are directly related to these physical environmental factors. Mountain bird life is also very strongly influenced by seasonal climatic changes, which, in high mountainous areas, are rigorous. Distinctive

vegetational associations may occur in localized patches or stands or may be strati-
fied altitudinally in broad bands as "life zones."

The California "life zones" are best expressed in the Sierra Nevada, and although the concept itself, which is based upon increasing precipitation and decreasing temperatures with increasing altitude and/or latitude, is somewhat out of date,
it still provides a useful system for understanding the distribution of plant and animal life in temperate mountainous regions, particularly in the western United
States where mountain ranges thrust so abruptly out of the surrounding flatlands.
The north-south axis of the Sierra Nevada lies across the path of the prevailing
westerly winds sweeping moistly landward from the Pacific Ocean. The climate of
the entire region is strongly influenced by these winds which bring the winter precipitation, accounting for 80-85 per cent of the total annual precipitation. Most of
this falls on the gentle western slope that rises to more than 14,000 feet at the Sierran crest. The steep eastern slope drops sharply to the floor of the arid Great Basin,
situated as it does in the Sierran "rain shadow" at about 4,000 feet. This arid side
receives only 10 to 15 inches of precipitation annually and there is a long unbroken
summer dry season. This dry summer season shortens and moistens with increasing
altitude and a larger proportion of the precipitation is in the form of snow.

The Lower Sonoran Zone encompasses the low desert regions and the Joshua
Tree "woodlands" of the higher deserts from about sea level (or below in a few
places) to about 3,000 feet (depending upon local geomorphic and climatic conditions) and receives 0 to 10 inches of precipitation annually. The Upper Sonoran
Zone which extends from about 2,000 to 4,000 feet receives about 10 to 20 inches
of precipitation annually, and includes such habitats as interior grasslands, chaparral, "high" desert associations of sagebrush, piñon pine and juniper, foothill oak
woodlands, and the valleys and basins of the Great Basin region. The Transition
Zone, as its name implies, represents a zone in which both "southern" and "northern" plant and animal elements are present. On the western slopes of the Sierra
Nevada it would be found between 4,000 and 6,000 feet, receives about 30 to 45
inches of precipitation (mostly in the form of snow) annually, and is a region of
open Ponderosa Pine and Black Oak, pure pine (mostly Ponderosa), pine and some
White Fir, and mixed pines, firs, and Giant Sequoias. On the eastern slopes of the
Sierra Nevada, because of the "rain shadow" effect, the various "zones" occur at
slightly higher elevations. For example, on the eastern slopes of the southern Sierras
an Upper Sonoran Zone formation of piñon pine and juniper containing much
sagebrush is found as high as the 5,000 to 6,000 foot level, which, on the opposite
Sierran slope at the same altitude, is vegetated with Transition Zone pine forest.
The Canadian Zone, from 6,000 to 8,000 feet, receives between 40 and 50 inches of
precipitation annually, most of which is snow. On the western slope of the Sierra
Nevada it consists primarily of Red Fir and Lodgepole Pine; on the eastern slope it
is mostly Jeffrey Pine. Numerous mountain meadows occur in the denser forests of
this life zone. Still higher in the mountains, above the Canadian Zone and extending from 8,000 feet to timberline at about 10,000 feet, is the Hudsonian Zone. This

is a zone of smaller more widely scattered coniferous trees such as Mountain Hemlock, Lodgepole Pine, and such five-needled pines as Whitebark Pine, Limber Pine, Foxtail Pine, and in the White Mountains, Bristlecone Pine. Here the soil is thinner, winds are stronger, and snow piles deeper. Annual precipitation in the form of snow averages from 50 to 60 inches and more. Above the timberline is a rocky, wind-swept, treeless arctic-like zone—the Arctic Alpine Zone. In this zone winter lasts from October to July and the brief growing season and other difficult environmental conditions permit only the hardiest lichens, mosses, grasses, and small shrubs to exist. Above the vegetated tundra-like portions of this highest zone are permanent snow fields, a few small glaciers, talus slopes, and bare rocky cliffs which harbor no vegetation.

As there are well-defined vegetational zones on the far western mountainsides, the vertical distribution of birds follows a similar pattern but with considerably more overlap than with the plants. Also, many mountain-nesting birds are migratory, leaving the inhospitable regions well before their food supply disappears. Those species that remain in the mountains can survive the winter season on seeds, berries, insect eggs, and buds. Those that must depart for the lowlands or for tropical regions do so because they cannot find the necessary insect and plant food for survival. A few species such as Mountain Quail, Steller's Jays, and Mountain Chickadees move a short distance down-mountain in the late fall only to return to their higher breeding grounds the following spring. Southbound Rufous Hummingbirds, on the other hand, move up-mountain in the late summer to feed in the mountain meadows still in bloom. Their migrational movements are leisurely as they slowly drift southward from meadow to meadow along the mountain chains. As they reach the southern limit of the mountains they descend to lower elevations and move more rapidly away from a region in the grip of hot summer weather.

Vertical distribution of bird life is nicely illustrated by a number of closely related species. The three California red finches—House, Purple, and Cassin's; the three California nuthatches—White-breasted, Pygmy, and Red-breasted; the three California quail—Gambel's, California, and Mountain; and the four California grosbeaks—Blue, Black-headed, Evening, and Pine, illustrate the principle of vertical zonation of birds, primarily during the breeding season. Among the red finches, House Finches are mainly lowland inhabitants of well-watered desert areas, sagebrush scrub, savannah, and farmlands; Purple Finches prefer oak woodlands and shaded mountain canyons from 2,000 to 5,000 feet; and Cassin's Finches are most frequently found in the pine and fir forests from 5,000 to 8,000 feet. There is some overlap, seasonal shifting of populations, and in certain mountain canyons all three species may occasionally be found together during the breeding season. White-breasted Nuthatches are birds of the riparian woodlands, oak woodlands, and the lower mixed reaches of the montane pine forests; Pygmy Nuthatches are almost never found away from Transition Zone pine forests; and the Red-breasted Nuthatches favor the higher fir forests of the Canadian Zone. Gambel's Quail are of the Lower Sonoran Deserts; California Quail prefer the Upper Sonoran chaparral, oak

woodlands, and to a lesser extent, the savannahs; and Mountain Quail most frequently inhabit the Transition Zone. Blue Grosbeaks breed only in the Upper
Sonoran Zone, remaining close to the edge of grasslands and shrubs with water
nearby; Black-headed Grosbeaks build their nests among the thick foliage of the
Upper Sonoran oak woodlands and the lower portions of the Transition Zone; Evening Grosbeaks select the pines and firs of the Canadian Zone for feeding and nesting; and the Pine Grosbeaks occur in the higher forests of the upper Canadian and
the Hudsonian Zones. Vertical distribution occurs among all mountain-dwelling
bird species and this distribution pattern ultimately devolves upon the nature of
the habitat for breeding and feeding. Among some species with broader habitat tol-
erances, a wider zone of distribution exists. Scrub Jays, for example, nest in fairly
dense shrubbery on the desert edge, in the chaparral, the oak woodlands, and in the
mixed oak and pine forests of the lower Transition Zone, but Gray-crowned Rosy
Finches with much narrower habitat requirements for foraging and nesting require
the extreme conditions that prevail in the Arctic Alpine Zone.

Because the specific habitat for birds is more important than the elevation at
which it occurs (while recognizing that there are particular relationships not only
between habitat quality and temperature-precipitation factors, but with soils,
winds, exposure, substrate, proximity to large bodies of water, and other such physical parameters) bird distribution in mountains during the nesting season is determined chiefly by habitat distribution. The complex nature of California's mountains coupled with the directions of their axes has resulted in a number of diverse
habitats for birds. On the drier southerly eastern slopes of the Sierra Nevada and on
other desert or desert-facing ranges are found the Pygmy Conifer Woodlands consisting mostly of junipers, piñon pines, and sagebrush. The Montane Forests consist
of dry open stands of pine trees, primarily Ponderosa Pines. Subalpine Forests occur
higher on the mountains. These Lodgepole Pine and Red Fir forests are denser and
moister, and mountain meadows are interspersed among them. This forest type
continues upward, becoming more open with gains in altitude until timberline is
reached. Above the tree line are found the alpine tundra, alpine fell-fields, talus
slopes, rocky cliffs, snow banks, and even a few small glaciers in the Sierra Nevada.
In the mountain valleys and basins are more meadows, lakes, small marshes, rivers,
streams, and riparian woodlands. The foothills and lower slopes on the wetter side
are vegetated with oak woodland, oak and pine woodland, savannah, chaparral, and
combinations of these habitats. On the dry desert slopes, drought-tolerant vegetation may extend upward to an altitude of 5,000 feet. Thus the mountains of California encompass a diversity of habitats and birds found nowhere else in the United
States.

Piñon-Juniper Woodland

The open stands of piñon pine and juniper that constitute the pygmy coniferous forests of the far western United States are more properly designated as

woodlands rather than forests because of the open nature of the tree growth. The piñon pines, junipers, and in the southern portions, the Joshua Trees, are essentially plants of relatively dry regions of the edges of deserts where precipitation is only 10 to 20 inches per year. Because of this paucity of water the larger plants cannot grow in dense stands since the root system of each tree extends outward from it for a considerable distance in order to obtain maximum moisture from the soil. In favorably sloped canyons and hillsides where snow accumulates and does not melt and evaporate as fast as on south-facing slopes, dense stands of piñon pines occur which take on the aspects of a true coniferous forest. Interspersed among the trees of this woodland are shrubs, principally Great Basin Sagebrush, most of which are derived from the desert formations lower down. Both the trees and the shrubs are well adapted to the near-drought conditions that prevail in these regions of scanty rainfall. The needles of the piñon pines are short, rather stout, and somewhat tough and the scalelike leaves of the juniper, so tightly bound to their twigs as to be hardly recognizable as leaves at all, reflect the need to conserve water and reduce water loss by transpiration. The Joshua Trees and the various drought-resistant shrubs show other modifications for dryness and heat.

Piñon-juniper woodland, Inyo County

In California this open woodland of widely spaced, small trees (10 to 30 feet) consists primarily of Single-leaf Piñon Pine and California Juniper. In the eastern desert ranges of the Mojave and Great Basin Deserts occur Utah Junipers. Joshua Trees derived from the high desert formations occur in the lower portions of this woodland, especially on the southwestern and southern edges of the Mojave Desert

Broad-tailed Hummingbird—male

and on the desert ranges of the eastern Mojave. Grasses are scarce, and herbs are mostly lacking because of the limited shade beneath the trees. The shrubs include Great Basin Sagebrush, Antelope Bush, Scrub Oak, and Desert Mint. The coniferous evergreen trees relate this woodland to the taller, denser, true coniferous forests while the Joshua Trees and Mojave Yuccas relate to the southern desert scrub indicating that this pygmy coniferous woodland represents a reasonable transition from scrub to forest.

In California this essentially Great Basin habitat occurs on the east side of the Sierra Nevada-Cascade axis but is completely lacking in the northern Sierra zonation which changes directly from Great Basin Sagebrush and Antelope Bush on the lower slopes to Jeffrey Pine on the higher slopes—omitting the Transition Zone altogether. The piñon-juniper woodlands occur broadly on the Modoc Plateau and on the desert side of the Transverse Ranges from 3,500 to 6,000 feet. In the Mojave Desert it occurs on the crests of the New York, Old Woman, Grapevine, Providence, Granite, Kingston, Clark, and Ivanpah Mountains. In the Inyo, Panamint, and White Mountains it forms a broad belt between the high desert scrub and the open pine forests of the Transition Zone above. It also occurs on the desert slopes of the Peninsular Ranges bordering the western edge of the Colorado Desert. In its northern reaches on the Modoc Plateau, this woodland receives little rain, but considerable amounts of snow. Much snow also falls in this woodland belt of the Inyo, Panamint, and White Mountains. Some snow falls in this habitat on the fringes of the southern Mojave Desert on the Transverse Ranges, but almost none occurs on the lower Mojave Desert ranges or in the woodlands bordering the western Colorado Desert. Here, precipitation comes in the form of winter rains and the Sonoran storms and tropical cyclones of late summer.

As a bird habitat, the piñon-juniper woodland seems almost impoverished when compared with oak woodland or montane forest. In food production for birds, however, it ranks very high. During the winter months hordes of American Robins and Cedar Waxwings and lesser numbers of Bohemian Waxwings and Townsend's Solitaires descend upon the fruitful junipers and quickly strip them of the ripened "berries." The piñon pine nuts are eagerly sought by the Pinyon Jays, and in winter the Clark's Nutcrackers from the subalpine forests high above fly down to feast on the ripened pine nuts. Despite the few birds which show a primary nesting preference for this habitat, a subspecies of each of six bird species, which are more prominent in other habitats, shows a primary affinity for the piñon-juniper woodland. They are the Screech Owl, Scrub Jay, Plain Titmouse, Bushtit, Bewick's Wren, and the Loggerhead Shrike. It is possible that the "plumbeous" race of the Solitary Vireo from the Rocky Mountains and Great Basin may also breed sparingly somewhere in this habitat in California. The most typical birds of this habitat are the Pinyon Jays, whose noisy flocks roam the woodlands in search of piñon nuts, and the Gray Vireos, whose elusive little colonies seem to appear one year only to disappear the next. Gray Vireos require dense patches of chaparral within or very near the stands of piñon pine and juniper. In the White, Inyo, and Grapevine Mountains and on Clark Mountain, Broad-tailed Hummingbirds, al-

Black-throated Gray Warbler—male

though uncommon and whose westward limits occur there, are the summer resident hummingbirds of this habitat. Ladder-backed Woodpeckers are equally at home here or in the desert scrub. In eastern San Bernardino County, Cassin's Kingbirds are the summer resident kingbirds of this habitat. Ash-throated Flycatchers are the most numerous members of this tribe and frequently utilize the holes left by broken branches of Joshua Trees and Mojave Yuccas for nesting sites. Gray Flycatchers are the only summer resident *Empidonax* flycatchers of the northern portions of this habitat, but Willow Flycatchers occur along the strips of riparian growth within it as do other riparian species. Other fairly common birds of this

Pinyon Jay

type of woodland include Mountain Chickadees (towards the higher reaches), Cactus Wrens (towards the lower reaches), Mockingbirds, Blue-gray Gnatcatchers, and Black-throated Gray Warblers. Where Joshua Trees occur among the stands of piñon pines and junipers, Scott's Orioles build their well-concealed nests among the protective spiny leaves of those tree yuccas. An isolated population of Mountain Quail lives in the piñon-juniper belt of the Little San Bernardino Mountains in the western part of Joshua Tree National Monument, although elsewhere this species is confined to the montane forests from which it descends, even as far as to the upper deserts, in late fall.

The piñon-juniper woodland, as with other arid habitats, yields the most intense bird activity during the spring when the breeding birds are territorial and the transients are flooding through. Activity diminishes as summer wears on and the fall season continues hot. Winter, however, brings renewed activity with the arrival of Robins, Cedar Waxwings, Western Bluebirds, and even Evening Grosbeaks from the north. Pinyon Jays, many of which move up-mountain to the cooler montane pine forests during late summer, return to their accustomed habitat for the winter.

Ash-throated Flycatcher

Montane Forest

In the far west, the most extensive forests are the montane forests. As the name implies, they are situated in mountainous areas of sufficient elevation and precipitation. In terms of life zonation, they conform to the Transition and lower Canadian Life Zones. This is an open and rather dry forest dominated primarily, but not exclusively, by White Firs, Incense Cedars, and Ponderosa Pines. In appearance it seems almost parklike with tall scattered trees among which are open areas, many of which are virtually bare of vegetation. Here and there are scattered bushes, grasses, and herbs and in some more exposed places, dense, almost impenetrable stands of mountain chaparral of which manzanita and Mountain Mahogany form a substantial part. These chaparral patches may represent burned over forest areas and are a predictable stage in the successional regeneration of the montane forest. Sometimes the dense chaparral persists for many years because its compactness smothers

Montane forest, San Bernardino County

the germinating pine seedlings. The trees of this forest are from 50 to 120 feet tall. At its lower levels the forest may be suffused with Black Oaks, sometimes in pure stands. Elsewhere, rather pure stands of Golden Cup Oaks from the oak woodlands of lower elevations may intrude into this habitat.

Within this montane forest, which is broad in both range and elevation, there is some consistency in the intrinsic distribution of its major tree types. In the Cascades this forest occurs between 2,000 and 6,000 feet; in the central Sierra Nevada

Blue Grouse—female (photo by Herb Clarke)

between 4,000 and 7,000 feet; and in the more southerly ranges between 5,000 and 8,000 feet. At the higher elevations of this forest, White Fir, sometimes in pure stands, is the dominant tree. Its numbers decline with decreasing elevation where it intermixes with Sugar Pine first, and lower still with Incense Cedar and especially Ponderosa and Jeffrey Pines. To the north, Douglas Fir becomes more abundant, especially in deeply shaded valleys and on the north-facing mountain slopes. In the ranges of southern California the "Big-cone Spruce" type of Douglas Fir is found at the lower elevations. In deeply shaded canyons and on north-facing slopes they even extend down into the Sonoran Zone of the chaparral. On the western slopes of the central and southern Sierras are isolated stands of Giant Sequoias between 4,500 and 6,000 feet. Their range is not expanding and is only a fragment of its former extent. Because they are a subclimax tree which depends upon forest fires to periodically eliminate some of the surface humus of the forest floor so that their seeds can better germinate, they are gradually being supplanted by the climax White Fir in areas where natural fires have for years been prevented or quenched.

Because of the annual summer drought, this montane forest is very susceptible to fires especially when the relative humidity is low and the temperature is in the 80's or 90's as it frequently is. Winter temperatures are, of course, well below freezing every night. Precipitation occurs primarily during the winter months (from about November to late March) and varies somewhat with elevation and proximity to the coast as well as latitude within the state. The more northerly forests and the

Saw-whet Owl →

Red-breasted Sapsucker

higher forests receive greater amounts of snow than do the more southerly forests and the lower forests. In general this habitat receives 35 to 50 inches annually, most of it in the form of winter snow, but extremes of 25 to 80 inches occur. In fact, parts of the central Sierra Nevada are subjected to fiercer blizzards with more snow and driving winds and lower temperatures than any other place in the contiguous United States. Consequently the birds of this area must be attuned to a shorter growing season and briefer summer than in the lowlands. Those that spend the winters must be able to forage successfully for food with the ground covered by snow in some places as much as 30 feet deep. In these forests, spring arrives late and winter comes close upon the heels of the brief autumn season.

In California this bird habitat extends throughout the lower middle levels of

Hairy Woodpecker—male

the Sierra Nevada, the Siskiyou, Trinity, and Cascade Mountains, and the inner portions of the northern Coast Range to about Clear Lake in Lake County. There are smaller developments in the inner central Coastal Range and in the higher mountains of Santa Barbara County as at Figueroa Mountain. Other areas of considerable extent occur in the San Gabriel and San Bernardino Mountains of the Transverse Ranges and in the Mount San Jacinto and Santa Rosa and Laguna Mountains of the Peninsular Ranges further south. In northeastern California, it is found on the higher regions of the Modoc Plateau and in the Warner Mountains. It occurs sparingly in the eastern desert ranges as in the White Mountains but is absent from the Panamints and the Clark and Kingston Mountains of Death Valley. On the desert or eastern slopes of the Sierra Nevada this forest occurs at higher elevations and is poorly developed. The almost pure open stands of the lower Canadian Zone Jeffrey

White-headed Woodpecker—female

Pines on these precipitous slopes bear little resemblance to the lush green forests on the western side.

The montane forests support a large variety of birds, larger than either of the other three coniferous forests—the Pygmy Conifer Forest, the Subalpine Forest, and the Coastal Coniferous Forest. The birds of the montane forest can be grouped according to their seasonal status into three broad categories. Since available bird food is drastically reduced in the winter, only those species that can avail themselves of it remain. Pine and fir seeds, berries, nuts and fruits, buds, insect larvae, insect eggs— this is the fare available to the resident birds of the montane forest in the winter. Those birds that feed upon nectar, blossoms, live insects and other invertebrates, seeds, corms, bulbs, and other terrestrial plant foods must move away from the mountains. Some predatory birds such as Goshawks and Great Gray, Spotted, and Pygmy Owls remain as they are able to sustain themselves upon live prey.

The avian summer visitors to the montane forest include Common Night-

← *American Robin*

Western Wood Pewee ↓

Steller's Jay →

Violet-green Swallow—female ↓

Olive-sided Flycatcher ↑

← *Pygmy Nuthatch*

Nashville Warbler ↓

Hermit Warbler–female ↑

Hepatic Tanager–female ↓

Western Tanager–female ↑

← Solitary Vireo

Mountain Chickadee →

hawks, Western Wood Pewees, Olive-sided Flycatchers, Violet-green Swallows, American Robins, Solitary Vireos, Nashville and Hermit Warblers, Western Tanagers, and Chipping Sparrows. Most of these species not only abandon the mountains in the fall, they leave the country for tropical climes. The American Robins are an exception. They descend into the lowland valleys, orchards, farms, and suburbs where they find juniper "berries," seeds, and fruits plentiful, in addition to an

Chipping Sparrow

assortment of insects. Sharp-shinned Hawks are migratory as are probably at least some of the Flammulated and Saw-whet Owls. Red-breasted Sapsuckers move into the lowlands and Mexico but many of the Williamson's Sapsuckers from the higher subalpine forests remain through the winter. Resident species such as Blue Grouse, Mountain Quail, Band-tailed Pigeons, Hairy, White-headed, and Pileated Woodpeckers, Steller's Jays, Gray Jays, White-breasted Nuthatches, Pygmy Nuthatches, and Dark-eyed Juncos (primarily of the "Oregon" type) can remain in the montane forests in considerable numbers if the winters are mild or not too severe. Blue Grouse move to lower elevations but the Pygmy Nuthatches remain through the severest winters feeding upon dormant insects and insect eggs. Only rarely do they venture into the lowlands. Mountain Quail, Band-tailed Pigeons, some Steller's Jays, many White-breasted Nuthatches, and many "Oregon" Juncos move into the lowlands each fall but the Mountain Quail only walk down to the lower limits of the snow while the others descend all the way to the seacoast at times. When winters are unusually severe or when a particular food substance fails them, these birds come down to the lowlands in large numbers and among them are occasionally some of the more durable mountain residents such as Goshawks, Hairy, and White-headed Woodpeckers, Williamson's Sapsuckers, Clark's Nutcrackers, and other species from the subalpine forest above.

Winters in the montane forest are long and quiet times. The migrant birds have long since departed, many of the mammals and all of the reptiles and amphibians are hibernating. Most of the insects are either dormant or dead, but the eggs deposited the previous summer will survive the winter if not eaten by the Pygmy Nuthatches, Mountain Chickadees, and Brown Creepers. As spring ascends the mountainsides it brings with it a flood of migrants almost all of which are summer visitors. The winter silence is broken by the songs of birds, chirping of crickets, and the croakings of frogs. As sometimes happens, a late spring snowstorm or even a blizzard will sweep through the mountains killing most of the exposed insects and blossoms. The newly arrived birds do not retreat down-mountain but stay to endure the onslaught of the weather. Many of the insectivorous species may die, not as much from starvation as from exposure since they cannot long maintain the high body temperature necessary to stave off chilling. However, it is usually the vanguard of the summer visitors which are thus affected and the main party usually arrives after the last snows have fallen.

Nesting commences soon after arrival because of the brevity of the summer season. June and early July constitute the main nesting months and by mid-July the forests are alive with family bird parties. A few species attempt a second nesting in July. In August the ratio of juveniles to adults is about 1:1 and the total population of each species has more than doubled. However, by the following spring, predators, disease, accidents, the hazards of migration, food shortages, and weather factors will have taken their toll with about 50 per cent mortality. The summer visitors depart the montane forests in August, well before the abundant summer food supply has diminished to critical levels. The migratory habit then takes them away from a potentially deadly environment well before the habitat becomes unendurable. It takes them to a more agreeable and productive environment for the winter and returns them again to their ancestral breeding grounds when conditions there are once again tolerable.

Subalpine Forest

The cool, dark, dense, Red Fir forests of the Central Sierra Nevada represents the main dense forest of the Canadian Life Zone. Higher still, the Subalpine Forest of the Hudsonian Life Zone thins out, the meadows disappear, and the trees are smaller, until timberline is reached at about 10,000 feet above which is the Arctic Alpine Life Zone with its snow banks, glaciers, alpine meadows and fell-fields, talus slopes, and barren cliffs and peaks. In the Sierra Nevada of central California the Subalpine Forest commences at about 6,000 feet. To the north in the Cascades it may begin as low as 4,000 feet and in the mountains of southern California, not only is it found at higher elevations (7,000 to 10,000 feet) but the types of trees contained therein are different.

The Subalpine Forest coincides with the elevations of greatest snowfall and the precipitation averages 40 to 65 inches annually. This forest is cool in summer because of the altitude, the shading caused by the denseness of the trees, or both. In winter, daytime temperatures hover between 26° and 10°F. The growing season is short and snow banks last well into summer, melting slowly, and providing breeding pools for hordes of mountain mosquitoes, the only bane in an otherwise idyllic habitat.

Subalpine forest (Canadian Life Zone), Tuolumne County

Subalpine forest (Hudsonian Life Zone), Mariposa County

In its lower reaches in the Sierra Nevada and Cascades, the Subalpine Forest consists primarily of magnificent Red Firs with a smattering of Western White Pines and Lodgepole Pines. The Red Firs are the largest trees of this forest, often exceeding 100 feet in height. Where the forest floor is sunless and cool, little in the way of undergrowth occurs. Lodgepole Pines occur in densely packed pure stands where they have invaded after fires have consumed the climax Red Fir forests. However, in these situations these tall, slender, almost birdless, forests will in time revert to Red Fir once again. Lodgepole Pines occur as successional stages bordering the numerous mountain meadows that interrupt the almost continuous stands of Red Fir. These tall stately trees are shallow-rooted and easily toppled by strong winds. Matchrows of downed timber are characteristic of these forests. Because of their shallow-rootedness, the Red Firs tend to grow in very dense stands for mutual protection, usually in fairly well-protected valleys and glades.

Because of the excessive amounts of winter snow in this forest, it is dissected by numerous lakes, streams, seeps, and meadows. These in turn provide suitable homes for meadow mice, shrews, Belding's Ground Squirrels, and other smaller rodents. Goshawks and the rare Great Gray Owls patrol the meadow borders in search of these rodents. The larger Yellow-bellied Marmots frequent the rocky meadow edges where downed timber and rock piles afford safe haven from these aggressive predators. The ferocious Goshawks will also take larger birds, even Blue Grouse, when they can. This uncommon accipiter is widely distributed in this forest habitat throughout the Cascades and the Sierra Nevada and its southern limit of range is about Greenhorn Mountain in Kern County. The very rare Great Gray Owl is confined to a few forest-bordered meadows such as those at Crane Flats, Peregoy, and Bridalveil Creek in Yosemite National Park. These mountain meadows, seeps, streams, and lakes are frequently bordered by Quaking Aspens and small willows in addition to the Lodgepole Pines. Where beavers have dammed a stream and created a pond, dense stands of aspens grow and other trees of the original forest are killed by the pond waters which immerse their roots. The meadows are favorite nesting places for White-crowned and Lincoln's Sparrows. Water Ouzels or Dippers may occur along the tumbling streams and Tree Swallows, Mountain Bluebirds, and House Wrens occupy the abandoned nest holes in the aspens and drowned trees. These chambers were excavated by the Red-breasted Sapsuckers and Hairy Woodpeckers.

Pileated Woodpeckers are scarce residents in the denser portions of this forest and the resident sapsucker is the stunning Williamson's whose males and females are so different in appearance that they were at first thought to be of different species. The uncommon Black-backed Three-toed Woodpecker also inhabits these dense forests but they occur with greater regularity among the Lodgepole Pines at the meadow edges or higher up. Here they successfully flake away the scaly bark of the Lodgepole Pines in their diligent search for wood-boring beetles. In summer the flutelike and ventriloquial notes of the Hermit Thrush float through the forest making it difficult to locate the singer. Such acoustically pure notes as those seem

← Great Gray Owl

Yellow-rumped Warbler ("Audubon's" type)—male ↑

Calliope Hummingbird—male ↑

Red-breasted Nuthatch ↑

← Hermit Thrush

Dark-eyed Junco ("Oregon" type)—male ↑

Cassin's Finch—male ↑

Pine Siskin ↑

Red Crossbill—male →

← *Lincoln's Sparrow*

to be reserved for inhabitants of dense forests in which they probably carry further and are thus more effective for locating mates and establishing territories. The Ruby-crowned Kinglet's song of unexpected exhuberance from a bird so small may serve the same function, but the thin lisping notes of the Golden-crowned Kinglet seem to belie this theory. Bell-like notes are also rendered by the Townsend's Solitaires, a bird from a group of renowned singers throughout the American tropics. Generally, this is a quiet forest, sheltered from the winds, and punctuated by the occasional nasal "tooting" of the Red-breasted Nuthatches, the melodious warble of the Yellow-rumped Warblers ("Audubon's" type), the nasal "dee-dee-dee" of the Mountain Chickadees, and the breezy notes of the Cassin's Finches. In the winter, when the snow lies deep, only the Mountain Chickadees remain vocal in this forest.

Resident birds of this forest include Goshawks, Blue Grouse, Great Gray Owls, Pileated Woodpeckers, Williamson's Sapsuckers, Black-backed Three-toed Woodpeckers, Mountain Chickadees, Evening Grosbeaks, Pine Grosbeaks, and Red Crossbills although in very severe winters some of these birds will descend to more favorable elevations. The breeding summer visitors include Calliope Hummingbirds, Hammond's Flycatchers, Western Wood Pewees, Olive-sided Flycatchers, American Robins, Hermit Thrushes, Ruby-crowned Kinglets, Yellow-rumped ("Audubon's" type) and Hermit Warblers, Western Tanagers, and Dark-eyed Juncos ("Oregon" type). In autumn the resident Townsend's Solitaires move down to lower elevations as do the Pine Siskins.

In California the Subalpine Forest of the Canadian Zone type occurs in the Cascades, the Sierra Nevada, a few high parts of the Trinity and Siskiyou Mountains west to South Fork Mountain, and south as far as the northern part of Lake County. In southern California a Canadian Zone forest of a different type occurs generally above 8,000 feet near the summits of the San Gabriel and San Bernardino Mountains in the Transverse Ranges and in the San Jacinto Mountains of the Peninsular Ranges. These drier forests of the high southern California mountains consist primarily of White Fir, Lodgepole Pine, Jeffrey Pine, and Limber Pine. A very small patch of it consisting only of Jeffrey and Limber Pines occurs on the summits of Sawmill Mountain and Mt. Pinos in the southern Tehachapis and a forest of only White Firs occurs near the summit of Clark Mountain in eastern San Bernardino County. The usual Sierra Nevada birds such as Blue Grouse, Goshawks, Evening Grosbeaks, and Pine Grosbeaks are normally absent from these southern subalpine forests.

In the higher Hudsonian Life Zone, the character of the forest changes dramatically. The trees are smaller, are of different types, and are more widely spaced. At the lower reaches of this zone the forest consists of Lodgepole Pines and Mountain Hemlocks in relatively dense stands which become more diffuse with gains in elevation. At the upper levels of the Hudsonian Zone many of the trees are sculptured, twisted, and bent by the howling gales of winter into beautiful and grotesque shapes. Foxtail, Limber, and Whitebark Pines, which grow near timberline, can be found creeping along the ground as shrubs, so heavy is the winter snowpack and so severe are the winds. Trees of this type are called *Krummholz* trees. The seemingly ageless Bristlecone Pines occur in the higher portions of the White Mountains as components of the forest. The Mountain Hemlocks and other trees develop broad "skirts" of low branches which are covered by winter snows and thus are protected from the pruning effects of the winter winds.

Few birds inhabit these high lonely forests. Occasional Golden Eagles and Ravens course over the open areas in summer searching for the unwary rodents. Red Crossbills and Pine Grosbeaks extract seeds from the ripened pine cones and the occasional Black-backed Three-toed Woodpecker scales the bark of the Lodgepole Pines lower down. The proper "owners" of these inhospitable heights are the flashy Clark's Nutcrackers. These small, black, gray, and white crows (named for Capt. William Clark of the famed Lewis and Clark Expedition) predominate in this highest of California's forests. Their raucous calls resound from the mountainsides as they noisily search among the pine tops for open ripened pine cones from which they expertly extract the seeds. Clark's Nutcrackers are bold inquisitive birds who quickly learn that human campsites invariably provide them with tidbits of food. In some of the parks they have become remarkably tame. They descend to lower elevations during the worst part of the winter and very infrequently come all the way down to the seacoast. When they do, it is usually a sign that winter in the high country is very severe or that the pine nut crop is poor that year. In very late summer before the first killing frosts of autumn, some birds from the lower forests ascend to this Hudsonian Zone to feed on the last of the flowers, fruits, berries, and insects of the summer season. Here can be found Blue Grouse, Dark-eyed Juncos, Fox Sparrows, Green-tailed Towhees, Hermit Thrushes, American Robins, and Mountain Bluebirds for a short while before the first sign of approaching winter drives them back downhill.

Alpine Zone

In the California mountains, the Alpine Zone is the least habitable for bird or beast. This highest and most inhospitable of bird habitats commences at about timberline, which in California's Sierra Nevada occurs at about 10,500 feet. The upper reaches of the Hudsonian Zone Subalpine Forest are sparsely populated with conifers that have been subjected to driving winds and in places, deep snow packs. These bent, twisted, and matted trees, called *Krummholz* by ecologists, mark the beginning of the true Alpine Zone. From here it extends upwards to the summits of the highest California mountains which are slightly less than 15,000 feet. Above and within the *Krummholz* zone are found alpine meadows, alpine fell-fields, alpine lakes, and higher still are permanent snow banks, a few live glaciers, talus slopes, and barren cliffs and peaks.

The physical enviroment of the Alpine Zone is in many ways the most trying of all of California's habitats for birds with the possible exception of the desert dry lakes in mid-summer. On these high mountain peaks, winter is reluctant to loosen

Alpine meadows, Tuolumne County

"*Krummholz*" *vegetation, Siskiyou County*

its grip until late June and is quick to return in September. The soil is thin and rocky because it forms slowly, has little chance to accumulate in the face of the howling winds, and because of the paucity of the vegetation, contains relatively little organic material. What plants there are tend to be found where soil has had a chance to form and accumulate in hollows, valleys, or even crevices or behind boulders. The more open and exposed slopes are barren of vegetation. Summer snow-banks occur where the winds have driven the winter snows into more sheltered locations and on north-facing slopes. During the brief growing season of summer, freezing temperatures occur almost every night and there are very few frost-free days. Because of the severity of the almost constant winds, seeds and flying insects are blown away. The relatively small numbers of birds can be found where such foods have been deposited or are sheltered from the winds.

Above the *Krummholz* trees the Life Zone is Artic-Alpine and in California the total area of this Alpine Zone is relatively small. It occurs along the summits of the Sierra Nevada and in the Cascades. Much smaller patches of this zone are found in the highest portions of the San Jacinto, San Bernardino, White, and Warner Mountains. However, at the summits of the southern ranges, many of the more typical plant and animal components of the Arctic-Alpine Life Zone are lacking and it would be an exaggeration to so designate the summits of Mt. San Gorgonio, Mt. San Antonio, and Mt. San Jacinto.

As expected, bird life in these high alpine regions is scanty. Food, in the form of seeds, blossoms, and insects is present in the vegetated areas only for a short period during the year. Diversity of nest sites is low and the unfavorable climate discourages post-nesting wanderers from the lower zones. There are no permanent bird residents in this zone although a number of mammals remain here throughout the year. All of them but one, the Pika, hibernate. This little rabbit-like animal stores enough grasses, forbs, and other plants through the short summer to last him through the long winter months. The Pikas don't actually emerge from the snow during the winter, but scurry about from storehouse to storehouse through the labyrinth of passageways in the snow-covered talus. The White-tailed Ptarmigan of the Alpine Zone of the northern Cascades and the Rocky Mountains does remain in this habitat throughout the year, enduring the frigid winter season by burrowing into the snow for warmth and feeding on the buds of willows and other plants that protrude from the snow. These birds, however, do not occur in the Alpine Zone of California.

The *Krummholz* region of the Alpine Zone contains the largest vegetation in the form of Whitebark, Limber, Foxtail, and Bristlecone Pines although not all in the same association. Clark's Nutcrackers and Red Crossbills extract seeds from the cones of these pines. Occasionally Ravens and Golden Eagles soar over the open areas in search of prey or carrion and the Ravens alone may nest on the craggy cliff faces. A race of the White-crowned Sparrow nests in the low vegetation of the alpine tundra. The tundra vegetation consists of compact perennial herbs such as Mountain Sorrel, Mountain Fleabane, and Alpine Buttercup. Grasses and sedges are abundant and the only "tree" is the Alpine Willow whose prostrate stems creep over the ground, usually rising only about four inches above it. This tundra vegetation, so similar in many ways to arctic tundra of the far north, is a relict habitat reflecting a time when continental glaciers advanced into the northern United States. At that time, the arctic tundra must have extended far south of its present limits. As the last continental glaciers withdrew to the north, the tundra vegetation followed the ice as it receded. Today only these small areas of tundra vegetation still survive in places where the climate approximates what this vegetation required at sea level at those latitudes thousands of years ago. As the ice retreated then, the tundra not only moved northward, but upward as well. In the mountains of Southern Canada the alpine tundra is found as low as 6,000 feet, but southward its lowest elevation increases at the rate of about 360 feet for each degree of latitude. This rate continues southward until about latitude 30° north and then gradually declines to the equator.

The alpine fell-fields are boulder-strewn areas with patches of tundra vegetation. Rock Wrens are occasionally found nesting in this environment and the Gray-crowned Rosy Finches, which hide their nests in cracks and crevices of the higher cliffs and peaks, forage for seeds and insects here. They also spend much time at the edges of melting snowpacks, lakes, and glaciers searching for frozen insects as they are released from their icy tombs. In the winter some of the Gray-crowned Rosy Finches, truly the most alpine of California birds, must move to lower elevations to

↑*Gray-crowned Rosy Finch—male*

←*Mountain Bluebird—male*

find enough food. They descend from the barren summits of the Sierra Nevada and the White Mountains to the higher portions of the sagebrush valleys of the Great Basin there to be joined by other races of Gray-crowned Rosy Finches from the Northern Cascades and Rocky Mountains. Occasionally a few Black Rosy Finches may be found among them. While these flats are snow-covered in the winter, the rosy finches find weed and shrub seeds in abundance and they especially favor the seeds of Russian Thistle that grows on the disturbed margins of roadsides. A small isolated race of the Gray-crowned Rosy Finch—Hepburn's—breeds on the slopes of Mt. Shasta, descending in winter to the adjacent lowlands. In late summer, Mountain Bluebirds from the higher portions of the Hudsonian Life Zone move upwards into the Alpine Zone to feed on the insects then available. Dark-eyed Juncos, Fox Sparrows, and Green-tailed Towhees from the lower mountain chaparral may also be found here briefly in the late summer.

The high alpine lakes harbor neither waterfowl nor shorebirds, although formerly, small families of Barrow's Goldeneyes were occasionally seen on some of the high Sierra Nevada lakes. Rock Wrens creep about the talus slopes and cliff bases but are much more common in the lowlands. White-throated Swifts infrequently streak across the barren cliffs and peaks but they nest no higher than the cliffs in the Transition Zone. Often the only signs of life above the snow line are the brightly colored lichens defying the elements on the bare granite and lava.

White-crowned Sparrow↑

Clark's Nutcracker →

THE COASTAL CONIFEROUS FORESTS

The grandest forest in all of North America is the inimitable Pacific coastal coniferous forest extending southward from Alaska to central California. Within it are some of the largest trees in the world exceeded in girth only by the Giant Sequoias of the central Sierra Nevada and approached in height only by the "mountain ash" (really a species of eucalyptus) forests of southeastern Australia. This is a dense forest of extremely tall trees many of which surpass 300 feet. Possibly the tallest tree in the world, a magnificent Coast Redwood in Humboldt County, has been measured at 367.8 feet. The crowns of the great trees of this forest are broad enough to form a fairly close canopy overhead through which only filtered sunlight passes. Hence the forest floor is in everlasting shadow and is carpeted with shade-tolerant plants. When one of the forest giants falls because of age, disease, wind, flood, or lightning, the newly illuminated space is quickly filled in with fast growing smaller trees and shrubs which in turn eventually give way by secondary plant succession to mature coniferous forest once again.

Five types of large coniferous trees constitute the basic elements of this forest in California and all depend upon considerable amounts of annual precipitation and high atmospheric humidity for optimum growth. The climate in this relatively narrow coastal region is moderated by the adjacent Pacific Ocean. Annual precipitation may exceed 100 inches per year in some places and elsewhere it may be as little as 40 inches. Frosts almost never occur except in the higher portions of the Coast Range. Summers are hot with temperatures frequently in the 90's and the lack of summer rain is somewhat compensated for by the prevalence of summer fog. The Coast Redwoods extend southward in a coastal belt rarely more than 20 miles inland, from southern Oregon to about San Francisco. South of there to Monterey County they occur in isolated groves near the coast. The pure stands of redwoods coincide closely with the fog belt which also fades out somewhat south of San Francisco. Douglas Fir occurs in fairly pure stands further inland and these trees can tolerate

Coast Redwood forest, Humboldt County

Spotted Owl (photo by Herb Clarke) ↑

Pygmy Owl ↓

Western Flycatcher ➜

Chestnut-backed Chickadee (photo by Herb Clarke) ↘

Rufous Hummingbird—male (photo by Herb Clarke) ↑

Allen's Hummingbird—male ↓

somewhat drier conditions than the other four types. Closer to the ocean it is found in mixed stands with the Coast Redwoods. Sitka Spruce and Lowland Fir occur in dense stands on the seaward slopes and on the higher drier portions of the Coast Range is found the Western Hemlock. Non-evergreen trees of the coastal coniferous forest include Tan Oak, Laurel, Madrone, and Red Alders. California Rhododendron, Western Azalea, and ferns of many species, are major components of the forest understory.

The forests of Monterey and Bishop Pines and the very local groves of the picturesque Monterey Cypress on the Monterey Peninsula may represent a transitional form between the coastal coniferous forest and the montane forest and the birds found therein represent both habitats in California. Groves of redwoods and Douglas Firs occur in isolated humid pockets south of Monterey and the largest southern stand of significance is the one at Big Sur in Monterey County.

Bird life in the coastal coniferous forest is fairly rich and consists of many species which also occur in the montane forest habitat. Where the continuous stands of tall conifers are interrupted by streams, riparian growth occurs. Savannahs, grasslands, oak woodlands, and coastal chaparral are also found interspersed among the redwood forests. The diversity of plant types naturally increases and this accounts for the richness of the avifauna. Where the forests are thick, pure, and extensive, the number of bird species sharply declines.

In California only six species of birds nest primarily in this forest. The Ruffed Grouse occurs as a resident very sparingly only among the dense streamside trees

Wilson's Warbler—male ↑

Purple Finch—male ↑

Swainson's Thrush →

and deeper coastal canyons near Prairie Creek Redwoods State Park in Humboldt County. The Vaux Swift, a summer visitor and transient, nests in burned and hollowed conifers—almost always Coast Redwoods—in the northwest coastal forests. The migratory race of the Allen's Hummingbird is a summer visitor and transient in this forest and for nesting chooses the more open areas at the edges of the forest. Chestnut-backed Chickadees occur as residents from the Oregon border south to about Morro Bay in San Luis Obispo County but they are not necessarily restricted to the coniferous forest habitat as they are frequently encountered in the adjacent coastal oak woodlands and even the Sierra Nevada. In California, Rufous Hummingbirds nest only in the coastal forests of Del Norte County. Probably the most characteristic bird of the coastal coniferous forest is the Varied Thrush. It nests deep in the dark forest glades where it is resident the year around although in winter there is some movement to the south and towards less dense stands of forest. Six species of birds—Blue Grouse, Steller's Jay, Pygmy Nuthatch, Hermit Thrush, Hairy Woodpecker, and Red Crossbill—occur in montane forest as well but have a local subspecies confined only to the coastal coniferous forest. The Screech Owl also has a race confined to this forest as does the Gray Jay which occurs spottily in this habitat. Another race lives in the subalpine forests of the northern Cascades and in the Warner Mountains far to the east near the Nevada border. In California, Black-capped Chickadees occur only in small colonies in riparian woodlands set among the coastal forests in the northwestern corner of the state. Other important residents of this habitat include Pygmy and Spotted Owls, Pileated Woodpeckers, Pygmy Nuthatches, Brown Creepers, Golden-crowned Kinglets, and Purple Finches, all of which occur in the montane forests as well.

The ethereal notes of the resident Winter Wrens can be heard emanating from the dark depths of these forests during May and June but the mouselike skulking singers are difficult to locate as they scurry about on the forest floor beneath a cover of ferns and mosses. Most of this species is confined to this habitat but small numbers occur locally in the Sierra Nevada as well. Additional important summer visitors and transients in this habitat include Western Flycatchers, American Robins, Hermit and Swainson's Thrushes, Cedar Waxwings, Wilson's Warblers, Western Tanagers, and Dark-eyed Juncos of the "Oregon" type.

Much of this forest remains in private ownership by large lumber companies. Already great tracts of virgin redwood forests have fallen to the axe and saw and a pitifully small remnant has been incorporated into the disjunct and narrow Redwoods National Park. Unfortunately some of the finest stands of virgin redwood forest and the forests on the upper watersheds of the several rivers flowing through the national park still remain in private hands. Some forest areas cut as long as 50 years ago still show no signs of regeneration because of the lack of nearby "seed" forests and the severe damage substained by the soil and the streams during the "cut-out and get-out" logging days. And, as the forests go, so go the birds and other wildlife.

MAN-CREATED HABITATS

Perhaps 40 to 50 per cent of the land area of California has been changed by man from the original virgin native habitat to something unnatural. Virgin forests have been cut down and in some cases have been allowed to revert back to the original habitat through the stages of natural secondary plant succession during which time temporary habitats replaced each other in predictable sequences. Some forested areas have been converted to agriculture, ranching, urban developments, and even industrial sites. Man-caused forest fires have destroyed tens of thousands of acres of brush and forest, which in time may have reverted to dense chaparral or grassland. Valley grasslands have been grazed and overgrazed and virgin stands of oak woodland have been opened up and converted to savannah for cattle and sheep. Other natural grasslands, chaparral, and oak woodlands have been cleared for farming. The extensive natural fresh-water tule and cattail marshes of the San Joaquin and Sacramento valleys have been drained for agriculture, industry, and urbanization and today only about 10 per cent of these natural wetlands remain. Much of this acreage is now used for commercial rice farming and totals about 350,000 acres. Elsewhere in the state smaller marshlands have been obliterated and some natural valley lakes such as Tulare Lake in Kings County and Buena Vista Lake in Kern County no longer exist in a natural state as they did formerly because so much of the water is now diverted for irrigation. Coastal salt-water marshes and tidal flats and lagoons have fared no better, but their conversion to an unnatural state has been the result of spreading urbanization and the development of coastal recreation facilities. Marshes and small natural lakes have been drained or filled for mosquito abatement. The great salt-water marshes of south San Francisco Bay have been drastically depleted by rubbish-filling followed by industrial and urban development on top of it. Along watercourses scheduled for channelization, the riparian forests have been removed. After this, channelization proceeded to straighten the courses of the rivers; dikes on the margins prevent periodic overflowing into the adjacent natural flood plain, and lining the channel itself with concrete prevents plant growth and erosion. Elsewhere, rivers have been diverted from their natural courses, water has been removed for irrigation purposes, and larger rivers and streams have been dammed for flood control, irrigation, water projects, and generation of hydroelectric power. Water pollution by phosphates, pesticides, and industrial and urban wastes has contaminated lakes, rivers, and streams to the detriment of wildlife—both fish and fowl. Mining, particularly strip-mining, radically alters the landscape by removing or destroying all of the surface material including topsoil and vegetation. Air pollution has been known to kill natural vegetation as well as certain farm crops. Thousands of Ponderosa Pines east of Los Angeles have been killed by smog. Water is brought into arid areas for irrigation of farmlands where virgin desert existed before. Prime examples of this are to be found in the Imperial, Coachella, San Joaquin, and Colorado River valleys. Freeway and highway construction gobbles up thousands of virgin acres as well as agricultural land every year. Newly constructed water impoundments have been created throughout the state as part of the California Water Project, and for irrigation programs, domestic water sources, recreational lakes, small farm ponds, and waterfowl refuges and wildlife areas. Each year thousands more acres of wild California land are converted to unnatural habitats of one kind or another.

Californians have created an artificial environment which sprawls and threads its way over the length and breadth of the state. Yet despite these extensive changes to the natural habitats, birds continue to exist and in some cases to flourish in these man-created environments. In most cases the original avian inhabitants disappeared with the vanished original habitat, but their places were taken by other birds better suited to the new environments. The upsurge in the population of the

White-tailed Kite reflects spreading agriculture and the increase in the population of meadow mice which results. The population explosion of Starlings is most certainly attributable to the type of monoculture agriculture practiced in California wherein large fields of a single cereal crop or other crop attract and support many thousands of these birds which feed upon the grains or upon the insects in the fields. By contrast, in Europe this Starling has never reached the pest proportions it has in the United States because of the nature of small farm European agriculture. Thus man-created habitats in California have been both a blessing and a curse.

Farms, Ranches, and Refuges

California's primary industry is agriculture and the hundreds of thousands of acres of land converted to this use are not ornithological deserts. The net result of this change has been the increase in populations and range expansions of some birds of the grasslands, savannahs, lakes, and marshes, and an overall decrease in the absolute populations of the scrub, woodland, and forest birds. To somewhat offset

Farmland, Imperial County

Ranchland, Inyo County

Waterfowl refuge, Sutter County

the depletion of the marshland habitats, federal and state waterfowl refuges and wildlife areas have been established in key locations in an attempt to restore some of the wetlands and to restrain the ducks from depredations upon nearby crop fields.

The extensive fruit orchards in and bordering the Central Valley and elsewhere in the interior valleys formerly were heavily sprayed with DDT and other pesticides. The reduction and eventual elimination of this practice should ultimately lead to the increased use of these habitats by birds, thereby rendering effective natural biological controls over some of the insect pests. The orchard trees provide food, shelter, and nest sites for a variety of birds. Hummingbirds and orioles obtain nectar from the blossoms. The orchard insects attract kingbirds, swallows, warblers, bluebirds, and tanagers. Woodpeckers nest in the larger trees and Screech Owls and Pygmy Owls utilize the abandoned cavities for roosting and nesting. The surplus rotting fruit, with its inevitable hordes of flies, attracts American Robins, sparrows, House Finches (which unfortunately also attack the ripened fruits still upon the trees), and Scrub Jays. Fallen seeds and weeds growing among the rows provide food for sparrows, goldfinches, doves, and quail. Freshly plowed fields provide gulls with newly unearthed terrestrial insects such as crickets, grubs, and grasshoppers and it is not unusual to see gulls far from water following a tractor and plow. Mountain Plovers, Horned Larks, Water Pipits, and occasional flocks of longspurs also gather in these fields during fall and winter. Waste grain in freshly harvested fields attracts large numbers of Mourning Doves, blackbirds of several species, Starlings, goldfinches, and numerous sparrows. Cattle Egrets by the hundreds gravitate to herds of grazing cattle in the Imperial Valley and feast upon the insects flushed from the grasses by these large herbivores. Cattle feeding pens provide waste grain for hundreds of thousands of Starlings, Brown-headed Cowbirds, and Red-winged, Tricolored, Brewer's, and Yellow-headed Blackbirds. Grain stubble from wheat and barley crops are eagerly sought by Ring-necked Pheasants, Sandhill Cranes, and by geese of several species. Other waterfowl, particularly American Wigeon, are fond of young lettuce, rice, and other growing crops and would cause considerable damage were they not lured away from those fields by attractive plantings of grain on nearby refuges and wildlife areas. The open pastures are not unlike native grasslands and thus invite such grassland types as Western Meadowlarks, Horned Larks, and Lark Sparrows to nest.

Farms and ranches frequently contain windbreaks of tall trees such as eucalyptus, pine, cypress, cottonwood, or tamarisk. In this regard farms and ranches are not unlike savannah since these groves of large trees provide cover and nest and roost sites for Barn and Great Horned Owls, Turkey Vultures, Red-tailed Hawks, White-tailed Kites, Western and Cassin's Kingbirds, and other species which forage for food over open grasslands. Some other nesting birds of these artificial "savannah" trees are "Red-shafted" Flickers, American Kestrels, "Bullock's" Orioles, Brewer's Blackbirds, Black-billed Magpies, and Common Crows. Barns and stables provide suitable nesting sites for Barn and Cliff Swallows and House Sparrows, as well as occasional Barn Owls. Brown-headed Cowbirds, Red-winged Blackbirds, and House Sparrows find much spilled grain to eat around the barnyards and stables. Many farms and ranches have irrigation and drainage canals along which grow strips of fresh-water marsh vegetation. A few rails may be found in these together with Red-winged Blackbirds and Common Snipe although the latter birds prefer wet pastures with tussocks of grass. Barn Swallows commonly nest under bridges spanning these canals and Cliff Swallows choose the larger bridges, but both find plentiful flying insect food over the surface of the canal waters. Black Phoebes are almost always associated with small bodies of fresh water and are regularly found nesting and foraging near these canals. Ranch lakes and ponds with grassy, marshy, or tule-cattail borders harbor many of the birds typical of the fresh-water marsh habitat. Nesting water birds include American Coots, Common Gallinules, Ruddy Ducks, Pied-billed Grebes, Cinnamon Teal, Wood Ducks, and Sora and Virginia Rails. Common Yellowthroats and Long-billed Marsh Wrens flit through the taller marsh vegetation and colonies of Tricolored, Red-winged, and Yellow-headed Blackbirds add color and action to the marsh scene. During the winter months additional waterfowl species from the north appear and several types of geese may find good forage in the fields. Wintering upland shorebirds of the pastures include Killdeers, Long-billed Curlews, and Mountain Plovers. Farms and ranches, then, with perhaps as many as six or seven habitats of varying extent and in close proximity to one another, are attractive places for birds.

Western Kingbird ↑

White-tailed Kites ↑

Canada Geese
← *("Cackling")*

Cliff Swallow ↓

Barn Swallow →

Brown-headed Cowbird—male ↓

Lesser Goldfinch—male ↑

American Kestrel—female →

Great-tailed Grackle—male →

The twenty-five state and federal wetlands refuges and wildlife areas in California were established to control crop damage by waterfowl, Starlings, and blackbirds in addition to providing wetlands habitat for feeding, nesting, and resting of waterfowl. The most extensive refuge system is found in the Sacramento Valley because this traditionally received the largest number of wintering waterfowl on the original native marshes which today are 90 per cent gone because of land leveling and drainage. Other important waterfowl refuges are located in the Tule-Klamath Basin of northern California and southern Oregon, the Imperial Valley of extreme southern California, and along the Colorado River near Needles and near Yuma. The Sacramento Valley string of refuges accommodates more than five million waterfowl each year. The refuges and wildlife areas are in reality large farms with the same variety of habitats as other typical cereal and grain farms but with a very strong emphasis on the creation and maintenance of wetlands habitat. In fact, most of the remaining good wetlands in the Sacramento Valley are to be found only on the federal and state lands and on private duck club lands.

These federal and state refuges and wildlife areas provide diverse and attractive waterfowl and marshland environments which serve not only the waterfowl themselves but also herons, bitterns, rails, marsh wrens, blackbirds and other marsh-dwelling birds as well. In addition to the creation and preservation of wetlands habitats by diking, dredging, ditching and otherwise creating water impoundments both open and marshy, these lands provide native food plants and cereal crops to help reduce crop depredation. As many as 30 species of waterfowl utilize the Sacramento Valley refuges alone and many have different food preferences. For this reason, a large variety of food plants must be grown. Milo or gypcorn is grown on upland areas primarily for the control of Starling and blackbird depredations but sparrows, Mourning Doves, California Quail, Ring-necked Pheasants, and Sandhill Cranes also relish it. Millet and other marsh aquatics are grown and left for the waterfowl to harvest to reduce crop damage to the neighboring rice fields. Wheat, barley, safflower, Sudan grass, field corn, and sunflower are planted to augment the other plants as a multispecies wildlife food. The native alkali bulrush, which is highly relished by waterfowl, is also encouraged to grow in the diked ponds. All of these lands contain special sanctuary areas on which the waterfowl can remain undisturbed. The birds quickly learn where these areas are because these sanctuaries are invariably surrounded by either public or private shooting areas and often both. Both the federal and state refuges and waterfowl management areas permit public hunting on parts of their lands.

Fresh-water wetlands in California total about 425,000 acres, of which some 175,000 acres are on lands owned and operated for waterfowl shooting by about 1,000 private hunting clubs. The California State Department of Fish and Game manages nine wetlands areas totaling about 50,000 acres, the first of which, the Los Banos Wildlife Area in Merced County, was established in 1929. Other state wildlife areas are the Imperial Wildlife Area in Imperial County, Mendota Wildlife Area in Fresno County, San Luis Wasteway Wildlife Area in Merced County, Napa Marshes Wildlife Area in Napa County, Lower Sherman Island and Grizzly Island Wildlife Areas in Solano County, Gray Lodge Wildlife Area in Butte County, and Honey Lake Wildlife Area in Lassen County. The sixteen national wildlife refuges in California total more than 200,000 acres and are strategically located so as to accommodate the waterfowl in the so-called Pacific Flyway. They are the Lower Klamath and Tule Lake National Wildlife Refuges in Siskiyou County, Clear Lake and Modoc National Wildlife Refuges in Modoc County, Sacramento National Wildlife Refuge in Glenn County, Delevan and Colusa National Wildlife Refuges in Colusa County, Sutter National Wildlife Refuge in Sutter County, San Luis, Kesterson, and Merced National Wildlife Refuges in Merced County, Pixley National Wildlife Refuge in Tulare County, Kern National Wildlife Refuge in Kern County, Salton Sea and Imperial National Wildlife Refuges in Imperial County, and the Havasu National Wildlife Refuge in San Bernardino County. In addition to the lake and marsh habitats to be found on these wildlife areas and refuges, there are riparian woodlands, open fields, meadows, croplands, irrigation canals, mud flats, and brushy areas all of which provide food, cover, and shelter for a variety of birds and wildlife other than waterfowl.

Cities, Towns, and Suburbs

The urban areas of California are not without their birds. In fact, there are often more birds to be seen within or near cities than there are in many parts of wild California. Of all the kinds of wild animals that inhabit California, birds are en-

Suburb, Los Angeles County

countered by more people than any other, except for some insects (both beneficial and undesirable). Virtually everyone in California comes in close contact with some wild birds every day of his life, but of course, most people take no notice of them and yet the birds represent a very real contact with the wild world. Even the ghetto-bound inner city dweller may enrich his life somewhat by feeding a few wild Rock Doves, House Sparrows, and Starlings. But the cities and towns of California attract and offer food and shelter to many more species than the three just mentioned. During the winter coastal cities throughout the length of California are visited by sea gulls. They can almost always be seen overhead as they make their way from their coastal nightly roosts to feed somewhere in the interior. Garbage and rubbish dumps and sanitary landfills attract thousands of gulls from the seacoast. They stream inland during the morning hours and return to the coast in the evening and as long as man continues to generate the mountains of garbage and rubbish that he does, the future of these birds is secure.

Gulls like to drink and bathe in fresh water and often they may be seen resting on freshly watered lawns, wet parking lots, and city lakes, ponds, and reservoirs. These bodies of fresh water within or near cities also attract American Coots and waterfowl of many sorts. The lakes in public parks are inevitably inhabited by domesticated ducks and geese of many bizarre hybrid types. These domestic hybrid ducks usually are mixtures of wild Mallard and Pekin types. Often too there are strange-looking hybrids involving Muscovy Duck strains. Citizens bring gift Easter ducks to these places and release them, thereby swelling the numbers further. Truly wild ducks are attracted to these lakes by these live decoys and during the winter large duck lists can be tabulated at such places. In Oakland's Lake Merritt, one of

City Park, Santa Barbara County

the finest city waterfowl lakes in the United States, wintering wild ducks may include Mallards, Pintails, Northern Shovelers, American and European Wigeons, Canvasbacks, Redheads, Ring-necked Ducks, Ruddy Ducks, Buffleheads, Hooded Mergansers, Common Mergansers, Greater and Lesser Scaup, and both the Common and Barrow's Goldeneyes. In fact, Lake Merritt remains the most reliable place to observe the Barrow's Goldeneye in California. Golf course ponds and city reservoirs are also suitable for waterfowl and gulls, but here they never become as tame as they do in the city parks because of the inevitable feeding activities of the public. Some of the better park lakes in California include the various lakes within the zoos at San Francisco, Los Angeles, and San Diego. Here, the exotic waterfowl collections also act as live decoys and attract the wild waterfowl. The lake at Los Angeles State and County Arboretum is good as are Harbor and MacArthur Park Lakes in Los Angeles, Lt. Maxton Brown Sanctuary Lake near Carlsbad, in San Diego County, the Bird Refuge Lake in Santa Barbara, various park lakes in Monterey, Fairmount Park Lake in Riverside, and Stow Lake in Golden Gate Park, San Francisco.

In addition to the lakes proper, the city parks, cemeteries, golf courses, and parkways are luxuriantly landscaped with trees, shrubs, and extensive lawns. The greenswards attract gulls, Killdeers, Brewer's Blackbirds, Starlings, Western Meadowlarks, Rock Doves, Mourning Doves, and even an occasional Cattle Egret has been known to drop in. In spring, but especially during the fall migration, trees and shrubs in even some of the smallest city parks, particularly those situated near the coast, lure large numbers of migrating warblers and sparrows. Some of the best rare warbler finds have been made at parks such as these. Other birds to be found regularly in city parks include House Finches, American Robins, Mockingbirds, Common Flickers (mostly of the "Red-shafted" type but in winter a few of the "Yellow-shafted" type), White-crowned Sparrows, Dark-eyed Juncos (commonly of the "Oregon" type with the odd "Slate-colored") and the casual Gray-headed Juncos.

Although boat harbors and marinas have replaced many of the natural coastal salt-water marshes and lagoons, they do attract good numbers of coastal birds. The bait tanks and bait boats that service the sport-fishing fleets are always surrounded by crowds of gulls and Brown Pelicans. During the winter Bonaparte's Gulls are among the most abundant birds in these harbors. The commonest terns are the small Forster's Terns and the cormorants include both Double-crested and Brandt's with an occasional Pelagic. Surf Scoters and White-winged Scoters with the occasional Black Scoter like the protection of the quiet harbors and they relish the mussels that cling to the piers and wharves. Small fish abound in the harbors also and Common, Red-throated, and Pacific Loons may all be seen there in addition to Western, Eared, Horned, and the rare Red-necked Grebes. Ocean piers and artificial breakwaters outside of the harbors also attract coastal and shorebirds. The scoters dive close to the piers to find the mussels they want. Sometimes they are joined by a few Oldsquaws, uncommon coastal ducks in California. Breakwaters offer resting places for Brown Pelicans, cormorants, and gulls and the algae and invertebrate-

Spotted Dove ↓

Brewer's Blackbird—male ↑

Rock Dove ↓

Mockingbird ↑

House Sparrow ↑

Ringed Turtle Dove ↓

covered rocks provide food for such rock-loving shorebirds as Black Turnstones, Surfbirds, Wandering Tattlers, and the rare Rock Sandpipers.

Possibly the most ubiquitous birds the world over are the Park Pigeons or Rock Doves. They have prospered through the centuries at the hands of a generous and sympathetic public. The pigeons of London, New York, Paris, Rome, and Florence are well known. They are hardy, prolific, and have little difficulty in adapting

House Finch—male

to the artificial "cliffs" of the cities' tall buildings for nesting. They have also adapted well to freeway and expressway overpasses, nesting fearlessly upon the ledges overlooking the onrushing traffic. In fact, they have expanded their range somewhat by following along the courses of these new roadways.

In addition to the usual city parks, large urban areas have created arboretums, zoos, animal parks, and botanical gardens. These are excellent places for birds because of the dense shrubbery, tall trees, lakes, marshes, and lawns that may have been included in the landscaping plans. They are really extensions of home gardens in that they are planted primarily with non-native exotic trees, and shrubs that produce edible fruits, nuts, seeds, and berries. Suburbanites have a better opportunity than city-dwellers to observe a greater variety of wild birds close to home because of the more extensive and varied plantings found in the home gardens of the suburbs, the closer proximity of suburbs to native scrub, desert, and forest, and the usual buffer zone of small agricultural areas surrounding cities and towns and into which the suburbs inevitably spread. The common resident and transient birds of the surrounding habitats don't find the suburban gardens too different from the natural vegetation, and in many ways they are more productive. Cedar Waxwings and American Robins descend upon berry-bearing trees and shrubs, especially Pyracanthas, like plagues of locusts and strip them clean in a twinkling. In some communities situated close to oak woodlands and pine forests, Band-tailed Pigeons congregate in the oaks to gorge upon the acorns.

Many suburbanites have discovered that wild birds add song, color, and animation to any garden, and while these people may not necessarily be bird watchers, they enjoy the pleasure of the birds' company. Birds respond quickly to scraps of food left over from outdoor picnics and barbeques and learn to frequent the garden in search of these tidbits. Simple bird-feeders placed near suitable cover and supplied with cracked corn, chick scratch, bread crumbs, sunflower seeds, raisins, and even peanut butter quickly attract a variety of birds. Hummingbirds and orioles can be lured to special artificial feeders filled with sugar water colored red and soon prefer these to the flowers in the garden. The attraction of formal bird baths is well known and their effectiveness can be enhanced by the addition of *dripping* water either from a tap or a special slow dripping device which is easy enough to construct or purchase.

Home gardeners can enhance the effectiveness of their gardens for attracting birds by planting shrubs and trees that produce edible fruits, nuts, and berries or even by building a garden of native California plants. Advice as to the best plants for this purpose can be obtained from publications of the U.S. Department of Agriculture and the National Audubon Society as well as from special books on the subject. Gardens in California's desert communities would probably contain plants best suited to an arid environment and would then lure birds from the surrounding desert. In addition to some of the resident species, seasonal changes would bring different species to gardens in different regions of the state. For example, a desert garden in Palm Springs would attract Gambel's Quail, Mourning and White-winged Doves, Costa's Hummingbirds, Cactus Wrens, and Mockingbirds. A mountain garden near Donner Pass in the high Sierra Nevada could have Mountain Quail, Calliope Hummingbirds, White-headed and Hairy Woodpeckers, Mountain Chickadees, Evening Grosbeaks, Cassin's Finches, and "Oregon" Juncos during the summer. In winter, when feeding programs become critical to the birds in such areas, those birds that remain might include the woodpeckers, chickadees, Steller's Jays, grosbeaks, and finches. In coastal northern California, lowland gardens would attract Allen's Hummingbirds, Mountain Chickadees (in winter), Chestnut-backed Chickadees, American Robins (especially in winter), Varied Thrushes (also in winter), Hermit Thrushes, and White-crowned Sparrows. A southern California garden located near the chaparral and oak canyons would in summer lure California Quail, Band-tailed Pigeons, Mourning Doves, Black-chinned and Anna's Hummingbirds, Plain Titmice, Scrub Jays, Brown and Rufous-sided Towhees, and House Finches. Clearly then, if a person wishes to introduce wild birds into his life for pleasure, it can be done virtually anywhere in California and at any time.

The Salton Sea

The man-created Salton Sea in southeastern California must be one of the most unique bird habitats in the United States. This salt-water lake lies mostly within Imperial County, is about 35 miles long, ranges from 9 to 16 miles in width, occupies an area of about 370 square miles, and its depth averages 8–12 feet with its deepest point at 45 feet. It lies within the Colorado Desert in the trough of the Imperial-Coachella graben, the bottom of which is about 250 feet below the level of the sea. The elevation of the surface waters of the Salton Sea is about 235 to 240 feet below sea level. The climate of this region is the hottest and driest in the United States and one of the hottest in the world. The hottest temperature recorded there was 130°F. and the lowest 22°F. Annual precipitation averages about 2.3 inches, most of it coming between December and February. Because of the large surface-to-depth ratio of this lake and the extremely hot dry climate, the rate of evaporation is very high. Yet despite the enormous daily water loss the Salton Sea continued to rise until just a few years ago, submerging some of the famous thermal "mud pots" at the south end near the Obsidian Buttes. Much of the marsh and pond area of the Salton Sea National Wildlife Refuge near Westmorland was also claimed by the rising waters as were a few small sandy islands upon which were located California's only nesting colonies of Laughing Gulls and Gull-billed Terns. However, today the Sea seems to have been stabilized by the incoming irrigation

South end of Salton Sea, Imperial County

waters through the Whitewater River at the north end, the Alamo and New rivers at the south end, and various minor irrigation canals leading to the Salton Sea itself. Despite the constant inflow of irrigation water the Salton Sea with a salinity of 38–39 parts per thousand or 3.8 to 3.9 per cent is actually saltier than the ocean.

During fairly recent geologic time the Gulf of California extended about 125 miles north of its present limit and one arm of it projected into the Coachella-Imperial trough. The Colorado River eventually deposited a huge delta across the upper end of the Gulf of California cutting this trough off from the rest of the Gulf. Evidence of this is the ancient beach line still visible some 40 to 50 feet above sea level and more than 300 feet above the present level of the Sea. At about the same time, the climate in southern California became increasingly more arid causing the "stranded" arm of the Gulf to dry up leaving behind the great amounts of salt originally dissolved in the sea water. The entire Salton Trough then became a very dry desert. The Colorado River continued to discharge some of its water into the drying basin and the trapped water became fresher. Gradually a fresh-water lake, Lake Cahuilla, formed which was some 450 miles long. Its fresh-water nature is evident from the quality of the shells that have been found along its ancient borders. Indians inhabited its shores and the lake may have retained its waters until as recently as 300 to 400 years ago. However, from the time of the earliest Spanish incursions into interior California more than 200 years ago, it is known to have been dry. From 1904 to 1907 the great floods of the lower Colorado River partially filled the Salton Basin once again.

In the very early part of the twentieth century the potential of agriculture in the fertile Imperial Valley was being realized and more irrigation water was needed. In 1900 work commenced on a canal project to bring much needed water from the nearby Colorado River. Flood waters from the Colorado River periodically discharged into the Salton Basin through the Alamo and New rivers, but this was never sufficient to create a lake in the basin. In the spring of 1905 unusual floods on the Gila River, an Arizona tributary of the Colorado River, caused a breach in the canal dikes and water began pouring into the then dry Salton Basin along the old courses of the Alamo and New rivers whose gorges were widened and deepened by the flood waters. After much travail in 1905 and 1906, during which time several other floods washed away repairs to the breaks in the dikes, the breach was finally closed in 1907, but not before the Salton Sea had formed, dissolved the salts from the soil, and reached about its present configurations. Today the All American Canal continues to bring regulated Colorado River water to the Imperial Valley and its tributary, the Coachella Canal, carries water northwards to irrigate the Coachella Valley. Hoover Dam further upstream on the Colorado River precludes the possibility of further flooding into the Salton Basin by the river and today only irrigation water flowing in along the Alamo, New and Whitewater rivers replaces that lost by evaporation. The incoming irrigation waters carry leached salts from the surrounding agriculture lands and as a result the saltiness of the Sea is increasing and at certain times of the year reaches 40 parts per thousand. Also, the Colorado

River water used for irrigation in the Imperial and Coachella Valleys is about 12 parts per thousand of salt and this also contributes to the Sea's increasing salinity.

The California State Department of Fish and Game succeeded some years ago in establishing a successful sport fishery in the Salton Sea. Planktonic organisms exist in the Sea and barnacles, probably carried as eggs or larvae on the hulls of sea planes, are well established in the Sea. They, together with the plankton, form the basic food of the smaller fish—mollies, bairdiellas (Gulf Croakers), and Sargo, which in turn feed the game fish, the Corvinas. Some of the birds that utilize the Salton Sea for feeding, notably the diving ducks, terns, Black Skimmers, White Pelicans, grebes, and boobies, relish the smaller fish which they catch beneath the water's surface. The mud flats surrounding the north and south ends of the sea have been created by the silt carried in by the Whitewater, Alamo, and New rivers and are rich in aquatic invertebrates. Such areas attract large numbers of shorebirds during migration and thousands spend the winter harvesting these nutritious resources. Resident breeding shorebirds include Killdeers, Snowy Plovers, American Avocets, and Black-necked Stilts. The adjacent agricultural fields and orchards of the Imperial and Coachella Valleys form an integral part of the Salton Sea avifaunal system. Gulls which roost on the sea spend their days feeding in the nearby fields. Gull-billed Terns leave their nests near the mouth of the New River to forage for grasshoppers and crickets over the open fields. Cattle Egrets, Snowy Plovers, and White-faced Ibis, all of which nest near the delta of the New River, search for food in the farms of the Imperial Valley. During the fall, winter, and early spring, tens of thousands of ducks and geese roost on the Sea by day during the hunting season only to venture inland to the refuges and wildlife areas at night to feed on the grains and stubble planted for them. The Salton Sea National Wildlife Refuge and the Imperial Wildlife Area were created for this purpose to help reduce crop depredations, to provide sanctuary for the birds, and to provide sport for the hunters.

Exclusive of the birds of the Colorado Desert proper and most of those of the agricultural areas of the Coachella and Imperial Valleys, some of the resident birds of the Salton Sea environs include Cattle Egrets (first discovered nesting off the delta of the New River in July 1971), Snowy Egrets, Least Bitterns, Black-crowned Night Herons, White-faced Ibis, Clapper Rails (Yuma race), Virginia Rails, Sora Rails, Common Gallinules, American Coots, Snowy Plovers, Killdeers, American Avocets, Black-necked Stilts, Yellow-headed Blackbirds, Long-billed Marsh Wrens, and Common Yellowthroats. In light of the small number of resident species, the large majority of birds that occur at the Salton Sea at different times of the year are clearly visitors of one sort or another. The usual pure and complex transients utilizing the borders, waters, and marshes of the Salton Sea are primarily waterfowl, White Pelicans, some terns, and many shorebirds. During the winter months the populations of birds in and around the Salton Sea reaches its peak and the total number of birds utilizing it must be in the millions. Eared Grebes dot the water from end to end and their numbers are probably equalled only by the Ruddy Ducks. More than 15 species of ducks occur, most abundant of which besides the

Ruddy Ducks are the American Wigeon, Pintail, and Northern Shovelers. These and other "dabbling" ducks frequent the waterfowl refuges and wildlife areas near the south end of the sea for feeding and try to escape the hunters' guns by flying out to the sea where the hunting pressure is less severe. The diving ducks (scaup, Canvasbacks, Redheads, Buffleheads, Ruddy Ducks, and Common Goldeneyes) remain on the Sea most of the time and feed by diving for the aquatic life. Some 20,000 Snow Geese (of the Lesser race) plus a few hundred large-type Canada Geese are the most prominent of the geese. Small numbers of White-fronted Geese and a few Ross' and "Blue" Geese also regularly occur. The geese use the Sea only as a refuge from the hunters and return to the grain fields of the refuges after sundown. The long skeins of trumpeting geese winging in from the Sea just at sunset provides one of the most inspiring sights to be found anywhere in wild California. Little wonder that the numbers of bird watchers visiting the Salton Sea at this time of year is beginning to outnumber those who come to hunt the birds.

A relatively small number of summer visitors arrives at the Salton Sea in late spring, breeds, and then returns south again in the fall. Although many Yellow-headed Blackbirds remain through the winter (or probably have come south from more northern nesting areas), large numbers of them breed near the south end of the Sea and include many birds that have arrived from southerly wintering grounds in Mexico. Black Terns may be seen near the south end of the Sea from April through August and yet there is no indication that they nest there as they do further to the north in the Great Basin and in the Central Valley. Small numbers of

Snowy Egret →

Cattle Egret ↓

Blue-footed (two on left) and Brown Boobies →

Snow Geese with a single Ross' Goose →

American Avocet ↓

Little Gull—winter plumage →

White-faced Ibis ↑

Black-necked Stilt ↑

← *Roseate Spoonbills*

Fulvous Tree Ducks nest in the fresh-water marshes at Finney Lake a short distance south of the Sea and a small colony of Gull-billed Terns, numbering no more than a few dozens, arrives in late March to nest on sandbars off the mouth of the New River. Formerly they nested on small sandy islands near the west side of the sea but the steadily rising waters eroded these in time. Only in the summer of 1972 were Black Skimmers first detected nesting on the delta of the New River and hopefully in time will become established as regular summer visitors. Prior to this, they were accidental post-breeding visitors in late summer and fall. Laughing Gulls formerly nested on sandy islands near the west side of the Sea but have not done so for years. Recently, however, hundreds of post-breeding birds from Mexico have appeared at the south end and may in time become regular fall (or post-breeding) visitors. Wood Storks are regular post-breeding visitors to the south end of the Sea, normally arriving in mid-July, reaching a peak of 150 to 200 in August, and dwindling to none by the end of September. On a few occasions small numbers of Roseate Spoonbills have been with them but these must still be considered accidentals in California. Western Gulls of the "Yellow-legged" race from the Gulf of California regularly visit the Salton Sea in small numbers after their breeding season in Mexico is completed by August. Other casual post-breeding visitors to the Salton Sea in summer and whose appearances are at best irregular are Blue-footed Boobies, Brown Boobies, and Magnificent Frigatebirds.

Some of the birds recorded from the Salton Sea are very unusual for that region only and elsewhere in California they may be expected regularly. Still other species considered as extremely casual visitors or accidentals in California have appeared at or near the Salton Sea and at no or very few other places in the state. Some of the birds that more or less regularly appear at the Salton Sea during the summer months are post-breeding visitors from Mexico. In a sense they are fall visitors since they have come north after their breeding season. Normally they arrive in the Imperial Valley in July and remain until about October. All of them are rather large water birds and it is the habit of some members of this group to disperse to the north after the breeding season. A large percentage of those that come north are young birds of the year. This dispersal to the north accomplishes several things for the species. First, it alleviates some of the competition in the immediate area of the nesting colonies and sends the birds into a region where their species does not normally breed and therefore would encounter minimum competition from their own kind. Second, it sometimes results in the extension of the species' breeding range into an area where it can but does not breed. Third, since many of these post-breeding visitors are young birds of the year, their chances of survival once they have successfully completed the journey into "alien" territory is fairly good because of the lack of competition from experienced adults of their own kind. However, often times these northward thrusts by a species are met with disaster because of lack of food, intolerable conditions of the environment, and the like. This "pulsating" type of expansion and withdrawal is not without its advantages to the species which can afford to sacrifice some of its kind in range expansion. It is by processes such as these that animal and plant dispersal and distribution is accomplished.

Black Skimmers at the Salton Sea are a case in point. They first appeared there in 1968 and small numbers reached the Sea each year until 1972 when more than 20 birds occurred and this was enough for the nucleus of a nesting colony at the mouth of the New River which resulted in five nests. It remains to be seen whether the increasing salinity of the Sea and the eventual possible depletion of the small fish will be a limiting factor to the northward spread of this species. Young Brown Pelicans reared in the Gulf of California move northward in summer and some of them come directly north out of the Gulf and arrive safely at the Salton Sea, a distance of only 115 miles. This northward journey by these water birds is made over some of the driest and hottest desert in the world, a most alien habitat for these birds. If, however, the migrating birds gain but 2,500 feet of elevation over the northern Gulf they might then be able to see the sun shimmering on the distant waters of the Salton Sea and the journey would not be so fearsome. Other post-breeding visitors that make this northward summer flight from Mexico are Blue-footed and Brown Boobies, both of which nest on islands in the Gulf of California. These booby incursions are sporadic and flights involving dozens of birds occurred in 1969, 1971, and 1972. In 1969 the ratio of Blue-footed Boobies to Brown Boobies was 4:1 but in subsequent years it was 20:1. Roseate Spoonbills appeared at the south end of the Salton Sea during seven years between 1927 and 1972 so their incursions cannot be considered as regular. Reddish Egrets and Little Blue Herons have appeared only twice although records for other parts of California are numerous. Almost all of the post-breeding Magnificent Frigatebirds seen at the Salton Sea are immatures. Only one or two appear every year or so, but 1968 accounted for eight sightings at the Salton Sea, mostly at the north end. The "Yellow-legged" race of the Western Gull from the Gulf of California occurs with some regularity after its breeding season ends in Mexico. The Laughing Gull, which formerly

Laughing Gull ➜

←*Gull-billed Tern*

nested in the Salton Sea near the south end, has occurred by the hundreds as a post-breeding visitor in recent years. The most consistent post-breeding Mexican water birds to the Salton Sea have been the Wood Storks.

Part of the excitement of birding in the Imperial Valley and the Salton Sea area, besides the fact that there are always large numbers of birds to be seen there at any time of the year, is the ever-present possibility of the discovery of a bird that is either uncommon, rare, casual, or accidental in either the Imperial Valley-Salton Sea area proper or in California. Some of the species that have occurred in this interior region and that are rare or casual there but not elsewhere in California include Common Loons, Horned Grebes, New Zealand and Sooty Shearwaters (!), "Black" Brant, Surf Scoters, Oldsquaws, Bald Eagles, Ferruginous Hawks, Peregrine Falcons, Sandhill Cranes, Black Turnstones, Wandering Tattlers, Sanderlings, Red Phalaropes, Least and Common Terns, Parasitic Jaegers, Saw-whet Owls, Common Crows, and Golden-crowned Kinglets.

It remains the only place in California where Gull-billed Terns nest and the only place where Stilt Sandpipers occur with some regularity and in reasonably good numbers during fall, winter, and spring. Franklin's Gulls, rare everywhere in the state, occur with some regularity there as do three species of longspurs. Small flocks of Lapland Longspurs winter on the fields in the Imperial Valley and among them may be a few of the very rare McCown's. During fall these flocks also contain a small number of Chestnut-collared Longspurs which leave for Mexico before the winter season.

The real prizes, however, are the accidentals such as the Roseate Spoonbills, whose appearances in California number less than ten times since 1900. Among this list of accidentals are the Black-bellied Tree Ducks (1912, 1951, 1972), Zone-tailed Hawk (1960), White-rumped Sandpiper (1969), Semipalmated Sandpiper (1960, 1967–1973), Little Gull (1968), Red-headed Woodpecker (1968), Coues' Flycatcher (1962), Curve-billed Thrasher (1964), and Pyrrhuloxia (1971-1973).

Gila Woodpeckers, more typical of the Sonoran Desert of southern Arizona, occasionally occur in the scattered palms about farml. ouses. The very rare Eastern Phoebe has occurred there and Harris' Hawks formerly nested but have not been seen alive there since 1952. A badly decomposed Harris' Hawk corpse was located in 1972. Great-tailed Grackles occur regularly in California in small numbers near Imperial Dam. Spreading slowly westward from Arizona they reached the Salton Sea area in 1970 and 1971.

Birding in the Imperial Valley-Salton Sea area is exciting any time of the year. Spring migrants, both land birds and water birds, flood northward through the valley. Fall brings interesting migrants from the north, shorebirds, and vast flocks of waterfowl. Winter produces great concentrations of ducks and geese, large flocks of sparrows, Mountain Bluebirds, and Mountain Plovers, but in many ways summer, with its almost intolerable climatic conditions including consistent daytime temperatures of almost 120°F. and relative humidity of 60 to 80 per cent, best rewards those who would be persistent enough to enter this inferno.

INDEX

Note–the following species, first sighted in California in 1974, subsequent to the first printing of *Birds of California,* do not appear in the index but are listed on p. xxii: Dotterel *(Eudromias morinellus);* Groove-billed Ani *(Crotophaga sulcirostris);* Rufous-necked Sandpiper *(Calidris ruficollis);* Sprague's Pipit *(Anthus spragueii);* Sulphur-bellied Flycatcher *(Myiodynastes luteiventris);* Veery *(Catharus fuscescens);* White Wagtail *(Motacilla alba).*

The index includes both the common English and the scientific names of the birds only. All text page references are in either ordinary or italic type. These references in italics refer to Chapter 3, Annotated List of the Birds of California, in which the seasonal status, habitat preferences, and range in California are given.

Page references to photographic illustrations are in boldface type. They are listed following the common English bird names only.

Acanthis flammea, 132
Accipiter cooperii, 58
　gentilis, 58
　striatus, 58
Acridotheres cristatellus, 138
Actitis macularia, 72
Aechmophorus occidentalis, 37
Aegolius acadicus, 91
Aeronautes saxatalis, 93
Agelaius phoeniceus, 127
　tricolor, 127
Aimophila cassinii, 53
　ruficeps, 134
Aix sponsa, 53
Ajaia ajaja, 48
Albatross, Black-browed, 142
　Black-footed, 20, 25, *38,* **38,** *142,* 145, **146,** 148
　Laysan, 21, 25, *38, 142-45,* 148
　Royal, 143
　Short-tailed, *38,* 139, 142, 148
　Wandering, 21, *37, 142-43*
　Yellow-nosed, 142
Alectoris chukar, 64
Ammodramus bairdii, 134
　savannarum, 134

Ammospiza caudacuta, 134
　leconteii, 134
Amphispiza belli, 135
　bilineata, 135
Anas acuta, 51
　americana, 52
　carolinensis, 51
　clypeata, 52
　crecca, 51
　cyanoptera, 52
　discors, 52
　falcata, 138
　formosa, 138
　penelope, 52
　platyrhynchos, 51
　rubripes, 51
　strepera, 51
Anser albifrons, 50
Anthus cervinus, 116
　spinoletta, 116
　spragueii, 138
Aphelocoma coerulescens, 104
Aphriza virgata, 70
Aquila chrysaëtos, 60
Archilochus alexandri, 93
Ardea herodias, 45

Arenaria interpres, 71
　melanocephala, 71
Asio flammeus, 91
　otus, 90
Asyndesmus lewis, 96
Auklet, Cassin's, *86,* 145, 151-52
　Parakeet, 86
　Rhinoceros, *86,* 145, 147
Auriparus flaviceps, 106
Avocet, American, 76, 77, *175,* 297, **299**
Aythya affinis, 54
　americana, 53
　collaris, 53
　fuligula, 54
　marila, 54
　valisneria, 53

Bartramia longicauda, 72
Bishop, African, 33
Bittern, American, *47, 178,* **179,** 183
　Least, *47, 178,* **180,** 183, 297
Blackbird, Brewer's, *128-29,* 285, 291, **292**
　Red-winged, 11, 12, *127, 178-79,* **180,** 285-86
　Rusty, *128*
　Tricolored, *127, 178-79,* **181,** 285-86

Yellow-headed, *126-27*, **127**, 178-79, 285-86, 297-98
Bluebird, Eastern, 138
  Mountain, *114*, 201, 267, 271, **274**, 275, 302
  Western, *114*, 201, 204, 205, **209**, 256
Bobolink, 19, *126*, **201**
Bobwhite, 33
Bombycilla cedrorum, 116
  garrulus, 117
Bonasa umbellus, 63
Booby, Blue-footed, 18, *43*, **43**, **298**, 300-01
  Brown, 18, *43-44*, **298**, 300-01
Botaurus lentiginosus, 47
Brachyramphus brevirostris, 85
  marmoratus, 85
Brant, 21, 33, *49-50*, **164**
  "American", 49
  "Black", *49-50*, 145, *164*, 169, 302
Branta bernicla, 49-50
  canadensis, 49
Bubo virginianus, 89
Bubulcus ibis, 46
Bucephala albeola, 54
  clangula, 54
  islandica, 54
Budgerigar, 33
Bufflehead, *54*, **165**, 169, 189, 291, 298
Bulbul, Red-whiskered, 33
Bunting, Indigo, *131*
  Lark, *133-34*
  Lazuli, *131*, **195**, 197
  Painted, *131*
  Rustic, 138
  Snow, 26, *138*, 248
  Varied, *131*
Bushtit, *106*, 206, **209**, 255
Buteo albonotatus, 59
  harlani, 58
  jamaicensis, 58
  lagopus, 60
  lineatus, 59
  platypterus, 59
  regalis, 60
  swainsoni, 59
Butorides virescens, 45

Calamospiza melanocorys, 133-34
Calcarius lapponicus, 138
  mccownii, 138
  ornatus, 138
Calidris acuminata, 73
  alba, 74
  alpina, 73
  bairdii, 73
  canutus, 72
  ferruginea, 73
  fuscicollis, 73

  mauri, 74
  melanotos, 73
  minutilla, 73
  ptilocnemis, 73
  pusillus, 73-74
Calypte anna, 93
  costae, 93
Campylorhynchus brunneicapillus, 110
Canvasback, *53*, **53**, 189, 291, 298
Capella gallinago, 71
Caprimulgus vociferus, 91
Caracara, 34
Cardellina rubifrons, 125
Cardinal, 26, *130*, 217, **217**, 228
  Brazilian, 33
Cardinalis cardinalis, 130
Carduelis carduelis, 138
Carpodacus cassinii, 132
  mexicanus, 132
  purpureus, 131-32
Casmerodius albus, 46
Cassarca ferruginea, 138
Cassidix mexicanus, 129
Catbird, Gray, *111*
Catharacta skua, 79
Cathartes aura, 56
Catharus fuscescens, 138
  guttatus, 113
  minimus, 114
  ustulatus, 113-14
Catherpes mexicanus, 110
Catoptrophorus semipalmatus, 72
Centrocercus urophasianus, 63
Centurus uropygialis, 96
Cepphus columba, 85
Cerorhinca monocerata, 86
Certhia familiaris, 107-08
Chaetura pelagica, 92
  vauxi, 92
Chamaea fasciata, 108
Charadrius alexandrinus, 69
  melodus, 69
  montanus, 70
  semipalmatus, 69
  vociferus, 70
  wilsonia, 69
Chat, Yellow-breasted, *125*, **214**, 217
Chen caerulescens, 50
  hyperborea, 50
  rossii, 51
Chickadee, Black-capped, 26, 105, 280
  Chestnut-backed 18, *106*, **278**, 280, 294
  Mountain, *106*, 205, 251, 256, **263**, 264, 270, 294
Chlidonias niger, 84
Chlorura chlorura, 133
Chondestes grammacus, 134
Chordeiles acutipennis, 92
  minor, 92
Chukar, 33, 64

Cinclus mexicanus, 109
Circus cyaneus, 61
Clangula hyemalis, 54
Coccyzus americanus, 88
  erythrophthalmus, 88
Colaptes auratus, 95
  cafer, 95
  chrysoides, 95
Columba fasciata, 86
  livia, 86
Columbina passerina, 87
Condor, California, 1, 2, 12, 18, *57*, **57**, 139, 201
Contopus pertinax, 101
  sordidulus, 101
Coot, American, 12, 68, **68**, 169, 174, 176-79, 182, **187**, 189, 286, 297
Coragyps atratus, 138
Cormorant, Brandt's, *25*, 44, 151-52, **151**, 177, 291
  Double-crested, *44*, **44**, 151-52, 177, 291
  Olivaceus, 44
  Pelagic, *25*, *44*, 151-52, **152**, 177, 291
Corvus brachyrhynchos, 105
  corax, 104
Coturnicops noveboracensis, 66-67
Cowbird, Bronzed, 26, *129*
  Brown-headed, *129*, **214**, 287, **287**
Crane, Sandhill, *65*, *66*, 201, 287-88, 302
Creeper, Brown, *107-08*, **108**, 205, 264, 280
Crossbill, Red, 12, *133*, **269**, 270-71, 273, 280
Crow, Common, *105*, **105**, 204, 287, 302
Cuckoo, Black-billed, 21, *88*, **88**
  Yellow-billed, 26, *88*
Curlew, Long-billed, *71*, *172*, 201, 286
Cyanocitta cristata, 104
  stelleri, 103
Cyclorrhynchus psittacula, 86
Cygnus olor, 138
Cyanthus latirostris, 94
Cypseloides niger, 92

Daption capense, 38
Dendragapus obscurus, 62
Dendrocopos albolarvatus, 98
  nuttallii, 97-98
  pubescens, 97
  scalaris, 97
  villosus, 97
Dendrocygna autumnalis, 51
  bicolor, 51
Dendroica auduboni, 122
  caerulea, 123
  caerulescens, 122
  castanea, 124
  chrysoparia, 123
  coronata, 122

discolor, 124
dominica, 123
fusca, 123
graciae, 124
magnolia, 122
nigrescens, 122
occidentalis, 123
palmarum, 124
pensylvanica, 124
petechia, 122
pinus, 124
striata, 124
tigrina, 122
townsendi, 122
virens, 123
Dichromonassa rufescens, 46
Dickcissel, 131
Diomedea albatrus, 38
exulans, 37
immutabilis, 38
nigripes, 38
Dipper, 109, **109**, 184-85, **189**, 267
Dolichonyx oryzivorous, 126
Dove, Ground, 87, **212**
Inca, 26, 87
Mourning, 11, 87, **87**, 145, 201, **203**, 224, 241, 285, 288, 291, 294
Ringed Turtle, 87, **292**
Rock, 33, 86, 290-91, **292**, 293
Spotted, 33, 87, **292**
White-winged, 33, 87, 233-24, **232**, 294
Dowitcher, Long-billed, 74, **172**, 175
Short-billed, 74, 175
Dryocopus pileatus, 95-96
Duck, Black, 51
Black-bellied Tree, 51, 302
Fulvous Tree, 20, 51, 300
Harlequin, 26, 54, **160**, 185
Muscovy, 290
Ring-necked, 53, **186**, 291
Ruddy, 55, 183-84, **186**, 189, 286, 291, 297-98
Tufted, 34, 54, **187**
Wood, 53, **183**, 188-89, 286
Dumetella carolinensis, 111
Dunlin, 73, **173**, 175

Eagle, Bald, 26, 60, 139, 169, 246, 302
Golden, 60, 201, **203**, 204, 207, 227, 241, 245, 271, 273
Egret, Cattle, 46, 140, 287, 291, 297, **298**
Great, 46, 176, **179**, 182
Reddish, 46, **172**, 301
Snowy, 46, 176, 182, 297, **298**
Egretta thula, 46
Eider, King, 54-55
Spectacled, 138
Elanus leucurus, 57
Emberiza rustica, 138

Empidonax difficilis, 101
hammondii, 100
minimus, 100
oberholseri, 100
traillii, 100
wrightii, 100-01
Endomychura craveri, 86
hypoleuca, 85
Eremophila alpestris, 101
Eudocimus albus, 48
Euphagus carolinus, 128
cyanocephalus, 128-29

Falco columbarius, 62
mexicanus, 61
peregrinus, 62
rusticolus, 61
sparverius, 62
Falcon, Peregrine, 62, 139, 153, 302
Prairie, 61, **62**, 201, 227, 241, 245
Finch, Black Rosy, 132, 275
Cassin's, 12, **132**, 251, **269**, 270, 294
Gray-crowned Rosy, 132, 248, 252, **274**, 274-75
Hepburn's Rosy, 275
House, 11, **132**, 228, 241, 247, 251, 285, 291, **293**, 294
Java, 33
Purple, 131-32, 207, 251, **279**, 280
Flamingo, American, 138
Flicker, Common, 95, 204, 207, **208**, 217, 224, **229**, 230, 285, 291
"Gilded", 95, 224, **229**, 230
"Red-shafted", 95, 204, **206**, 207, 217, 285, 291
"Yellow-shafted", 95, 291
Florida caerulea, 45
Flycatcher, Ash-throated, 99, 207, 241, 255, **256**
Coues', 101, 302
Dusky, 100, **195**, 197
Gray, 100-01, 246, 255
Great Crested, 99
Hammond's, 100, 270
Kiskadee, 138
Least, 100
Olivaceous, 99
Olive-sided, 101, **262**, 264, 270
Scissor-tailed, 99, **99**
Traill's, see Willow
Vermilion, 101, **214**, 219, 228
Western, 101, **278**, 280
Wied's Crested, 99, 219
Willow, 100, 217, 255
Fratercula corniculata, 86
Fregata magnificens, 45
Frigatebird, Magnificent, 10, 26, 45, **45**, 145, 148-49, 300
Fulica americana, 68
Fulmar, Northern, 25, 38, **39**, 144, 146,

149
Fulmarus glacialis, 38

Gadwall, 51, 189
Gallinula chloropus, 68
Gallinule, Common, 67, 68, 178, 286, 297
Purple, 67
Gavia adamsii, 36
arctica, 36
immer, 36
pacifica, 36
stellata, 36
Gelochelidon nilotica, 82
Geococcyx californianus, 88
Geothlypis trichas, 125
Glaucidium gnoma, 89
Gnatcatcher, Black-tailed, 115, 224, **230**, 240-41
Blue-gray, 115, **115**, 207, 256
Godwit, Bar-tailed, 75
Hudsonian, 75
Marbled, 75, **75**, 158, **161**, **172**, 175
Goldeneye, Barrow's, 54, 164, 169, 185, 275, 291
Common, 54, 164, 169, 189, 291, 298
Goldfinch, American, 133, 217
European, 33, 138
Lawrence's, 133, 207, **209**
Lesser, 133, **287**
Goose, "Blue", 50, 298
"Cackling", see Goose, Canada
Canada, 49, 178, **180**, 188, **286**, 298
Emperor, 21, 26, 50
Red-breasted, 34
Ross', 51, 188, 298, **299**
Snow, 33, 34, 50, 188, 298, **299**
White-fronted, 50, **50**, 188, 298
Goshawk, 58, 261, 267, 270
Grackle, Great-tailed, 26, **129**, **287**, 302
Grebe, Eared, 37, 167, 177-78, **186**, 247, 291, 297
Horned, 36, **164**, 177, 291, 302
Least, 37
Pied-billed, 12, 37, 178, **179**, 288
Red-necked, 36, 391
Western, 37, **37**, 167, 177-78, 291
Grosbeak, Black-headed, **130**, **131**, 207, **209**, 217, 251-52
Blue, 131, **216**, 217, 251-52
Evening, 131, 248, 251-52, 256, 270, 294
Pine, 132, 251-52, 270-71
Rose-breasted, 130
Grouse, Blue, 62-63, **258**, 264, 267, 270-71, 280
Ruffed, 26, 63, 279
Sage, 63, **63**, **244**, 246
Sharp-tailed, 63, 319
Grus canadensis, 65
Guillemot, Pigeon, 85, 145, 151-52, **155**

Guiraca caerulea, 131
Gull, Black-headed, *81*
  Black-tailed, *81*
  Bonaparte's, *82,* **166,** 291
  California, *81,* **165,** 177
  Franklin's, *81,* **173,** 302
  Glaucous, *80*
  Glaucous-winged, *80,* **161**
  Gray, 20
  Heermann's, 17, 20, *82,* 145, **162,** 169, 177
  Herring, *80,* **161**
  Laughing, 26, *81,* 295, 300-01, **301**
  Little, *82,* **299,** 302
  Mew, *81,* **161**
  Ring-billed, *81,* 167, 177, **187**
  Sabine's, 25, *82,* 143-44, **147,** 148
  Thayer's, *80,* **165**
  Western, 18, 20-21, 25, *80,* **80,** 151-52, **154,** 169, 300-01
  "Yellow-legged", 18, 20, *80,* 300-01
Gymnogyps californianus, 57
Gymnorhinus cyanocephalus, 105
Gyrfalcon, 26, *61,* 248

Haematopus bachmani, 69
  palliatus, 68
Haliaeetus leucocephalus, 60
Halocyptena microsoma, 41
Hawk, Broad-winged, *59*
  Cooper's, *58,* **212,** 217
  Duck, see Falcon, Peregrine,
  Ferruginous, *60,* 201, 245, 302
  Harlan's, *58-59*
  Harris', 26, 34, *60,* 228, **229,** 230, 302
  Marsh, **60,** *61,* 176
  Pigeon, see Merlin,
  Red-shouldered, *59,* 206
  Red-tailed, *58-59,* **59,** 204, 207, 227, 241, 245, 285
  Roadside, 34
  Rough-legged, 20, *62,* **60,** 201, 245, 248
  Sharp-shinned, *58,* 264
  Sparrow, see Kestrel, American,
  Swainson's, *59,* 201, **203,** 204, 245-46
  Zone-tailed, *59,* 302
Helmintheros vermivorous, 120
Heron, Black-crowned Night, 46-47, 176, **186,** 297
  Great Blue, *45,* **46,** 176, 179
  Green, *45,* 179, **179,** 182
  Little Blue, 21, *45,* **173,** 301
  Louisiana, *46,* **174**
  Yellow-crowned Night, 47
Hesperiphona vespertina, 131
Heteroscelus incanus, 72
Himantopus mexicanus, 76
Hirundo rustica, 102-03
Histrionicus histrionicus, 54

Hummingbird, Allen's, 14, *94,* 197, **278,** 280, 294
  Anna's, 93, **193,** 197, 294
  Black-chinned, *93,* **93,** **214,** 246, 294
  Broad-billed, *94,* **209,** 255
  Broad-tailed, *94,* **254**
  Calliope, 1, *94,* **268,** 270, 294
  Costa's, *93,* 224, **235,** 239, 294
  Rufous, 14, 15, 19, *94,* 251, **278,** 280
Hydranassa tricolor, 46
Hydroprogne caspia, 83
Hylocichla mustellina, 113

Ibis, White, *48,* **48**
  White-faced, *48,* 297, **299**
Icteria virens, 125
Icterus bullockii, 128
  cucullatus, 127
  galbula, 128
  parisorum, 128
  pustulatus, 128
  spurius, 127
Ictinia mississippiensis, 57
Iridoprocne bicolor, 102
Ixobrychus exilis, 47
Ixoreus naevius, 113

Jacksnipe, European, *71*
Jaeger, Long-tailed, 21, 25, *79,* 144, 148
  Parasitic, *79,* 144, 148, 302
  Pomarine, *79,* **79,** 144, **147,** 148
Jay, Blue, 21, *104*
  Gray, 26, *103,* 264, 280
  Pinyon, *105,* 241, 255-56, **256**
  Scrub, *104,* **104,** 206–07, **208,** 241, 252, 255, 294
  Steller's, *103,* 205, 251, **262,** 264, 280, 294
Junco, Dark-eyed, 18, *135,* 207, 264, **269,** 270-71, 275, 280, 291, 294
  Gray-headed, *135,* 291
  "Oregon", 18, *135,* 264, **269,** 270, 280, 291, 294
  "Slate-colored", *135,* 291
Junco caniceps, 135
  hyemalis, 135
  oreganus, 135

Kestrel, American, *62,* 201, 204, 207, 227, 241, 245, 285, **287**
Killdeer, *70,* **70,** 175, 189, 291, 297
Kingbird, Cassin's, *98-99,* 201, 204, 255, 285
  Eastern, *98*
  Thick-billed, *98*
  Tropical, 18, 20, *98*
  Western, *98,* 201, 204, 285, **286**
Kingfisher, Belted, 12, *95,* **95,** 176, 184
Kinglet, Golden-crowned, *115,* 270, 280, 302
  Ruby-crowned, 19, *115,* **116,** 270
Kite, Mississippi, *57*
  White-tailed, *57,* **58,** 139-40, 201, 204, 283, 285, **286**
Kittiwake, Black-legged, 25, *82,* 144, **147,** 149
Knot, Red, *72,* **174,** 175

Lanius excubitor, 118
  ludovicianus, 118
Lark, Horned, *101,* **102,** 201, 285
Larus argentatus, 80
  atricilla, 81
  californicus, 81
  canus, 81
  crassirostris, 81
  delawarensis, 81
  glaucescens, 80
  heermanni, 82
  hyperboreus, 80
  minutus, 82
  occidentalis, 80
  philadelphia, 82
  pipixcan, 81
  ridibundus, 81
  thayeri, 80
Laterallus jamaicensis, 67
Leucosticte ater, 132
  tephrocotis, 132
Limnodromus griseus, 74
  scolopaceus, 74
Limosa fedoa, 75
  haemastica, 75
  lapponica, 75
Lobipes lobatus, 78
Longspur, Chestnut-collared, *138,* 201, 248, 302
  Lapland, *138,* 201, 248, 302
  McGown's, *138,* 201, 248, 302
Loon, Arctic, see Loon, Pacific
  Common, *35-36,* 145, **164,** 291, 302
  Pacific, *36,* 145, **157,** 291
  Red-throated, *36,* 145, **157,** 291
  Yellow-billed, *36,* **36**
Lophodytes cucullatus, 55
Lophortyx californicus, 63
  gambelii, 64
Loxia curvirostra, 133
Lunda cirrhata, 86
Lymnocryptes minimus, 71

Magpie, Black-billed, *104,* 247, 285
  Yellow-billed, 2, *104,* 201, **203,** 204
Mallard, *51,* **186,** 189, 291
Martin, Purple, *103,* **103,** 209
Meadowlark, Western, 12, *126,* 201, **201,** 207, 285, 291
Megaceryle alcyon, 95
Melanerpes erythrocephalus, 96

formicivorus, 96
Melanitta deglandi, 55
  nigra, 55
  perspicillata, 55
Meleagris gallopavo, 65
Melospiza georgiana, 138
  lincolnii, 137
  melodia, 138
Merganser, Common, *56*, 185, 189, 291
  Hooded, *55*, **187**, 189, 291
  Red-breasted, **55**, *56*, **168**
Mergus merganser, 56
  serrator, 56
Merlin, *62*
Micrathene whitneyi, 90
Micropalma himantopus, 75
Mimus polyglottos, 111
Minotilta varia, 120
Mockingbird, *111*, **111**, 228, 234, 241, 256, 291, **291**, 294
Molothrus ater, 124
Motacilla alba, 138
Murre, Common, *84-85*, 145, 149, 151-52, **155**
  Thick-billed, *85*, **85**
Murrelet, Ancient, *86*, 149
  Craveri's, 10, 17, 20, 25, *86*, 149
  Kittlitz's, 21, *85*
  Marbled, 33, *85*, 145, 149, 151-52
  Xantus', 2, *85*, 145, 151-52
Muscivora forficata, 99
Myadestes townsendi, 114
Mycteria americana, 47
Myiarchus cinerascens, 99
  crinitus, 99
  tuberculifer, 99
  tyrannulus, 99
Myioborus pictus, 126
Myna, Crested, 138

Nighthawk, Common, **91**, *92*, 261
  Lesser, *92*, 224, **226**, 228, 241
Nucifraga columbiana, 105
Numenius americanus, 71
  phaeopus, 71
Nutcracker, Clark's, *105*, 255, 264, 271, 273, **275**
Nuthatch, Pygmy, *107*, 251, **262**, 264, 280
  Red-breasted, 12, *107*, 251, **268**, 270
  White-breasted, *107*, **107**, 205-07, 216, 251, 264
Nuttallornis borealis, 101
Nyctanassa violacea, 47
Nyctea scandiaca, 89
Nycticorax nycticorax, 46-47

Oceanites oceanicus, 41
Oceanodroma castro, 40
  furcata, 40
  homochroa, 40
  leucorhoa, 40

  melania, 41
  tethys, 40
Oenanthe oenanthe, 114
Oldsquaw, *54*, 291, 302
Olor buccinator, 49
  columbianus, 49
Oporornis agilis, 124
  formosus, 124
  philadelphia, 125
  tolmiei, 125
Oreortyx pictus, 64
Oreoscoptes montanus, 112
Oriole, "Baltimore", *128*
  "Bullock's", *128*, 204, **215**, 217, 285
  Hooded, *127*, **128**
  Orchard, *127*
  Northern, *128*, 204, **215**, 217, 285
  Scarlet-headed, *128*
  Scott's, *128*, **240**, 241, 256
Osprey, *61*, **61**, 169, 184, **187**
Otus asio, 89
  flammeolus, 89
  trichopsis, 138
Ovenbird, *124*
Owl, Barn, *88*, **89**, 204, 224, **226**, 228, 285
  Burrowing, *90*, **200**, 201, 228, 246
  Elf, *90*, 219, 224, 230, **233**
  Flammulated, *89*, 264
  Great Gray, 26, *90*, 261, 264, **268**, 270
  Great Horned, *89*, 204, 206, **208**, 224, 246, 285
  Long-eared, *90*, **90**, **213**, 217
  Pygmy, *89*, 261, **278**, 280, 285
  Saw-whet, *91*, **259**, 264, 302
  Screech, *89*, 216, 255, 280, 285
  Short-eared, *91*, **173**, 176
  Snowy, 26, *89*, 248
  Spotted, *90*, 261, **278**, 280
  Whiskered, 138
Oxyura jamaicensis, 55
Oystercatcher, American, *68*, **69**
  Black, 12, 25, *69*, 151-52, **152**, 159

Pandion haliaetus, 61
Parabuteo unicinctus, 60
Parakeet, Canary-winged, 33
Parrot, Yellow-headed, 33
Parrotlet, Blue-rumped, 33
Partridge, Gray, 33, *64*
Parula americana, 121-22
Parula, Northern, 121-22, 140
Parus atricapillus, 105
  gambeli, 106
  inornatus, 106
  rufescens, 106
Passer domesticus, 126
Passerculus sandwichensis, 134
Passerella iliaca, 137
Passerina amoena, 131
  ciris, 131

  cyanea, 131
  versicolor, 131
Peafowl, 33
Pedioecetes phasianellus, 63
Pelecanus erythrorhynchos, 42
  occidentalis, 43
Pelican, Brown, 17, 20, 25, *43*, 139, 144-45, **150**, **151**, 151-56, 159, 168-69, 177, 291, 301
  White, *42*, **42**, 169, 189, 297
Perdix perdix, 64
Perisoreus canadensis, 103
Petrel, Cape, 21, 25, *38*, 142
Petrochelidon pyrrhonota, 103
Pewee, Western Wood, *101*, 206-07, **262**, 264, 270
Phaethon aethereus, 41
  lepturus, 41
Phainopepla, *117*, **117**, 223-24, 234, **239**, 240
Phainopepla nitens, 117
Phalacrocorax auritus, 44
  olivaceus, 44
  pelagicus, 44
  penicillatus, 44
Phalaenoptilus nuttallii, 91
Phalarope, Northern, 25, *78*, 144, 148, **161**, 162, 169, 174-75
  Red, 25, *78*, 143-44, **147**, 148, 162, 174, 302
  Wilson's, 21, *78*, **78**, 169, 174-75, 177, 247
Phalaropus fulicarius, 78
Phasianus colchicus, 64
Pheasant, Ring-necked, 33, *64*, 285, 288
Pheucticus ludovicianus, 130
  melanocephalus, 131
Philacte canagica, 50
Philomachus pugnax, 76
Phoebe, Black, *99-100*, **187**, 188, 286
  Eastern, 21, *99*, **214**, 302
  Say's, *100*, 288, **246**
Phoenicopterus ruber, 138
Pica nuttallii, 104
  pica, 104
Picoides arcticus, 98
Pigeon, Band-tailed, *86*, 206-07, **208**, 264, 293-94
Pinicola enucleator, 132
Pintail, 19, 20-21, *51*, **52**, 171, 177, 189, 291, 298
Pipilo aberti, 133
  erythrophthalmus, 133
  fuscus, 133
Pipit, Red-throated, *116*
  Sprague's, 138
  Water, *116*, **116**, 145, 285
Piranga flava, 130
  ludoviciana, 129
  olivacea, 129
  rubra, 130

Pitangus sulphuratus, 138
Plectrophenax nivalis, 138
Plegadis chihi, 48
Plover, American Golden, 70
    Black-bellied, *70, 158,* **171,** 175
    Mountain, *70,* **200,** 201, 285-86, 30
    Piping, 12, 69
    Semipalmated, *69,* **171,** 175
    Snowy, *69,* 157-58, **160,** 297
    Upland, see Sandpiper, Upland,
      Wilson's, 69
Pluvialis dominica, 70
    squatarola, 70
Podiceps auritus, 36
    dominicus, 37
    grisegena, 36
    nigricollis, 37
Podilymbus podiceps, 37
Polioptila caerulea, 115
    melanura, 115
Pooecetes gramineus, 134
Poor-will, *91,* 224, 241, **245**
Porphyrula martinica, 67
Porzana carolina, 66
Progne subis, 103
Protonotaria citrea, 120
Psaltriparus minimus, 106
Ptarmigan, White-tailed, 273
Ptychoramphus aleuticus, 86
Puffin, Horned, 86
    Tufted, *86,* 145, 151-52
Puffinus bulleri, 39
    carneipes, 39
    creatopus, 39
    griseus, 40
    puffinus, 40
    tenuirostris, 40
Pyrocephalus rubinus, 101
Pyrrhuloxia, *130,* **234,** 302
Pyrrhuloxia sinuata, 130

Quail, California, 18, *63,* **64,** 197, 207, 251,
    288, 294
    Gambel's, *64,* 218, 223-24, 234, **237,**
      240-41, 251, 294
    Mountain, *64,* **194,** 197, 207, 241,
      251-52, 256, 264, 294

Rail, Black, 12, 26, 67, 175, 177-78
    Clapper, *66,* 139, **171,** 175, 177, 297
    Virginia, *66,* 175, 178, **180,** 286, 297
    Yellow, 12, 66-67, 139, 178
Rallus limicola, 66
    longirostris, 66
Raven, Common, 12, *104,* 140-41, 204,
    224, 234, **238,** 239, 241, 247, 271, 273
Recurvirostra americana, 76
Redhead, *53,* 189, 291, 298
Redpoll, Common, 26, *132,* 248
Redstart, American, *125,* 140
    Painted, *126*

Regulus calendula, 115
    satrapa, 115
Riparia riparia, 102
Rissa tridactyla, 82
Roadrunner, *88,* 218, 223-24, **227,** 228,
    239, 241
Robin, American, 18, *112-13,* 197, 255-56,
    262, 264, 270-71, 280, 285, 291, 293-94
    Rufous-backed, 113
Ruff, 76
Rynchops niger, 84

Salpinctes obsoletus, 110
Sanderling, 21, *74,* 158, **160,** 302
Sandpiper, Baird's, 19, 21, *73,* 175
    Buff-breasted, 75
    Curlew, 73
    Least, *73,* **172,** 175
    Pectoral, *73,* **171,** 175
    Rock, 20, 26, *73,* 159, **161,** 293
    Semipalmated, *73-74*
    Sharp-tailed, 73
    Solitary, 72
    Spotted, 19, *72,* 189
    Stilt, *75,* 302
    Upland, 72
    Western, 21, *74,* **74,** 175
    White-rumped, *73,* 302
Sapsucker, Red-breasted, 12, 96-97, **260,**
    264, 267
    Red-naped, 96, **97**
    Yellow-bellied, 96
    Williamson's, *97,* 264, 267, 270
Sayornis nigricans, 99-100
    phoebe, 99
    saya, 100
Scardafella inca, 87
Scaup, Greater, *54,* 169, 189, 291
    Lesser, *54,* **164,** 169, 189, 291
Scoter, Black, *55,* 145, **160,** 291
    Surf, *55,* 145, **160,** 291, 301
    White-winged, *55,* 145, **165,** 169, 291
Seiurus aurocapillus, 124
    motacilla, 124
    noveboracensis, 124
Selasphorus platycercus, 94
    rufus, 94
    sasin, 94
Setophaga ruticilla, 125
Shearwater, Flesh-footed, 21, 25, *39,* 148
    Manx, 25, *40,* 144, 148
    New Zealand, 25, *39,* 142, 144, 147,
      148, 302
    Pink-footed, 25, *39,* **39,** 142, **146,**
      148
    Short-tailed, 25, *40,* 142, 144, 148
    Sooty, 10, 11, 20, 25, *40,* 142, 144,
      146, 148, 159, 302
    Wedge-tailed, 25
Sheld-duck, Ruddy, 34, 138
Shoveler, Northern, *52-53,* **182,** 189, 291,

    298
Shrike, Loggerhead, *118,* **118,** 201, **203,**
    204, 228, 241, 247, 255
    Northern, *118,* 247-48
Sialia currucoides, 114
    mexicana, 114
    sialis, 138
Siskin, Pine, *132,* **269**
Sitta canadensis, 107
    carolinensis, 107
    pygmaea, 107
Skimmer, Black, *84,* **84,** 140, 297, 300-01
Skua, 79, 144-45, 148
Snipe, Common, *71,* 178, **180,** 288
Solitaire, Townsend's, *114,* **114,** 197, 255, 270
Somateria fischeri, 138
    spectabilis, 54
Sora, 66, **67,** 175, 178, 288, 297
Sparrow, Baird's, *134*
    Bell's, *134*
    Black-chinned, 136, 144
    Black-throated, *134,* 223-24, 239,
      240, 241
    Brewer's *136,* 241, 247, **248**
    Cassin's, *134*
    Chipping, *135-36,* 264, **264**
    Clay-colored, *136*
    English, see Sparrow, House,
    Field, *136*
    Fox, *137,* **195,** 197, 271, 275
    Golden-crowned, *136-37,* 137
    Grasshopper, *134*
    Harris', *136,* 248
    House (English), 11, 33, *126,* **126,**
      285-86, 290, **292**
    Lark, *134,* **203,** 207, 285
    Le Conte's, *134*
    Lincoln's, 12, *137,* 267, **269**
    Rufous-crowned, *134,* 197
    Sage, *134,* 197, 223-24, 228, 241, 247,
      247
    Savannah, *134,* **173,** 176
    Sharp-tailed, *134*
    Song, *138,* 176, 197, 217-18, **219**
    Swamp, *138*
    Tree, 26, *134,* 248
    Vesper, *134,* 247
    White-crowned, 18, *136,* 197, 207,
      267, 273, **275,** 291, 294
    White-throated, *137*
Speotyto cunicularia, 90
Sphyrapicus nuchalis, 96
    ruber, 96-97
    thyroideus, 97
    varius, 96
Spinus lawrencei, 133
    pinus, 132
    psaltria, 133
    tristis, 133
Spiza americana, 131
Spizella arborea, 135

atrogularis, 136
breweri, 136
pallida, 136
passerina, 135-36
pusilla, 136
Spoonbill, Roseate, 26, *48,* **299,** 300-01
Starling, 11, 33, *118,* **118,** 200-01, 283, 285, 288, 290-91
Steganopus tricolor, 78
Stelgidopteryx ruficollis, 102
Stellula calliope, 94
Stercorarius longicaudus, 79
parasiticus, 79
pomarinus, 79
Sterna albifrons, 83
forsteri, 82
hirundo, 82
paradisaea, 82-83
Stilt, Black-necked, *76,* **76,** 175, 297, **299**
Stork, Wood, 17, 26, 47, *47,* 300, 302
Storm-Petrel, Ashy, 2, *40,* 144, 148, 151-52
Black, 20, 25, 28, *41,* 144, 148
Fork-tailed, *40,* 144, 148, 151
Galapagos, 25, *40*
Harcourt's, 25, *40*
Leach's, *40,* 144, 151
Least, 10, 18, 20, 25, *41,* 149
Wilson's, 25, *41,* **41**
Streptopelia chinensis, 87
risoria, 87
Strix nebulosa, 90
occidentalis, 90
Sturnella neglecta, 126
Sturnus vulgaris, 118
Sula leucogaster, 43-44
nebouxii, 43
Surfbird, *70,* 159, **161,** 293
Swallow, Bank, *102*
Barn, *102-03,* 285-86, **287**
Cliff, 14, *103,* 285-86, **287**
Rough-winged, *102,* 188, **188**
Tree, 12, *102,* **215,** 216-17, 267
Violet-green, *102,* 216, **262,** 264

Swan, Mute, 138
Trumpeter, *49,* 188, 248
Whistling, 20, *49,* **49,** 188, 248
Swift, Black, *92*
Chimney, *92*
Vaux's, *92,* 280
White-throated, *92, 93,* 275
Synthliboramphus antiquus, 86

Tachycineta thalassina, 102
Tanager, Blue-gray, 33
Hepatic, *130,* 140, **263**
Scarlet, *129*
Summer, 20, 26, *130,* 219
Western, 19, 20, *129,* **129,** **263,** 264, 270,·280
Tangavius aeneus, 129

Tattler, Wandering, 25, *72,* 151, **153,** 193, 302
Teal, "American" Green-winged, *51,* 174, 181, 189
Baikal, 34, 138
Blue-winged, *52*
Cinnamon, *52,* **181,** 189, 286
"Eurasian" Green-winged, 26, *52*
Falcated, 34, 138
Green-winged, *51-52,* **181**
Telematodytes palustris, 110
Tern, Arctic, 25, *82-83,* 144, 148
Black, 28, *84,* **180,** 298
Caspian, *83,* **83,** 181
Common, *82,* **167,** 302
Elegant, 2, 10, 17, 20, *83,* **173**
Forster's, *82,* **167,** 177, 291
Gull-billed, 26, *82,* 295, 297, 300, **301,** 302
Least, *83,* 139, 157-58, **162,** 302
Royal, *83*
Thalasseus elegans, 83
maximus, 83
Thrasher, Bendire's, *111,* 224, 230, 241
Brown, *111*
California, 2, *112,* **193,** 197, 207, 241
Crissal, *112,* 223-24, 228, 230, 234
Curve-billed, *111,* **112,** 302
Le Conte's, *112,* 223-24, **228,** 228, 239
Sage, *112,* 246-47
Thrush, Gray-cheeked, *114*
Hermit, *12, 113,* **113,** 197, 267, **268,** 271, 280, 294
Swainson's, *113-14,* 217, **279,** 280
Varied, 18, *113,* 280, 294
Wood, *113*
Thryomanes bewickii, 110
Titmouse, Plain, *106,* **106,** 204, 205, 206, 216, 255, 294
Towhee, Abert's, *133,* 223, 228, 230, 234
Brown, *133,* **195,** 197, 207, 247, 294
Green-tailed, *133,* **194,** 197, 241, 247, 271, 275
Rufous-sided, *133,* **193,** 197, 207, 247, 294
Toxostoma bendirei, 111
curvirostre, 111
dorsale, 112
lecontei, 112
redivivum, 112
rufum, 111
Tringa flavipes, 72
melanoleuca, 72
solitaria, 72
Troglodytes aedon, 109
troglodytes, 109
Tropicbird, Red-billed, 10, 18, 25, *41,* 42, 149
White-tailed, 21, *41*
Tryngites subruficollis, 75

Turdus migratorius, 112-113
rufopalliatus, 113
Turkey, 33, *65,* **65**
Turnstone, Black, *71,* **157,** 159, 293, 302
Ruddy, *71,* **171**
Tyrannus crassirostris, 98
melancholicus, 98
tyrannus, 98
verticalis, 98
vociferans, 98-99
Tyto alba, 88

Uria aalge, 84-85
lomvia, 85

Veery, 138
Verdin, *106,* 224, 234, **234,** 240
Vermivora celata, 121
chrysoptera, 120-21
luciae, 121
peregrina, 121
pinus, 121
ruficapilla, 121
virginiae, 121
Vireo, Bell's, *119,* **215,** 217
Gray, *119,* 241, 255
Hutton's, *119,* 206
Philadelphia, *119-20*
Red-eyed, *119*
Solitary, *119,* 255, **263,** 264
Warbling, *120,* **120,** 204, 207, 217
White-eyed, 12, *119*
Yellow-green, *119*
Yellow-throated, *119*
Vireo bellii, 119
flavifrons, 119
flavoviridis, 119
gilvus, 120
griseus, 119
huttoni, 119
olivaceus, 119
philadelphicus, 119-20
soilitarius, 119
vicinior, 119
Vulture, Black, 138
Turkey, 14, *56,* **56,** 201, **203,** 207, 217, 245, 285

Wagtail, White, 138
Warbler, "Audubon's", *122,* **268,** 270
Bay-breasted, *124*
Black and White, *120*
Blackburnian, *123*
Blackpoll, *124*
Black-throated Blue, *122*
Black-throated Gray, *122,* 207, **255,** 256
Black-throated Green, *123*
Blue-winged, *121*
Canada, *125*
Cape May, *122*
Cerulean, *123*

Chestnut-sided, *124*
Connecticut, *124*
Golden-cheeked, 12, *123*
Golden-winged, *120-21*
Grace's, *124*
Hermit, *123*, **263**, 264, 270
Hooded, *125*
Kentucky, *124*
Lucy's, 26, *121*, 219, 228
MacGillivray's, *125*, 140, **194**, 197
Magnolia, *122*
Mourning, *125*
"Myrtle", *122*
Nashville, *121*, **263**, 264
Orange-crowned, *121*, **193**, 197, 207
Palm, *124*
Pine, *124*
Prairie, *124*
Prothonotary, *120*
Red-faced, 21, *125*
Tennessee, *121*
Townsend's, *122*, **123**
Virginia's, *121*
Wilson's, *125*, 217, **279**, 280
Worm-eating, *120*
Yellow, *122*, **123**, **215**, 217
Yellow-rumped, 12, *122*, **268**, 270
Yellow-throated, *123*

Waterthrush, Louisiana, *124*
    Northern, *124*
Waxwing, Bohemian, 21, 26, *117*, 248,
    255
    Cedar, *116*, **117**, 197, 255-56, 280,
    293
Wheatear, 12, *114*
Whimbrel, *19, 71*, **71**, 158, **172**, 175
Whip-poor-will, 12, *91*, 140
Wigeon, American, *52*, 171, **186**, 189,
    285, 291, 298
    European, *52*, 291
Willet, *72*, 158, **172**, 175
Wilsonia canadensis, *125*
    citrina, 125
    pusilla, 125
Woodcock, American, 33
Woodpecker, Acorn, 18, *96*, 204, 206-07,
    208
    Black-backed Three-toed, 18, 26, *98*,
    267, 270-71
    Downy, *97*, **214**, 217
    Gila, *96*, 224, 228, 230, **230**, 302
    Hairy, *97*, 205, **260**, 264, 267, 280,
    294
    Ladder-backed, *97*, 224, **233**, 241, 255
    Lewis', 18, *96*, 204, 207
    Nuttall's, *97-98*, 140, 206, **208**

Pileated, *95-96*, 207, 264, 267, 270,
    280
    Red-headed, 21, *96*, 302
    White-headed, *98*, 205, **261**, 264, 294
Wren, Bewick's, *110*, **193**, 197, 255
    Cactus, *110*, 218, 224-24, **238**, 239,
    241, 256, 294
    Canyon, *110*, **110**,
    House, 12, *109*, **209**, 218, 267
    Long-billed Marsh, 12, *110*, 178-79,
    181, 286, 297
    Rock, *110*, **227**, 228, 274-65
    Winter, *109*, 280
Wrentit, 12, 18, *108*, **108**, **193**, 197, 207

Xanthocephalus xanthocephalus, 126-27
Xema sabinii, 82

Yellowlegs, Greater, 21, *72*, **173**, 175
    Lesser, 21, *72*, 175
Yellowthroat, Common, *124*, 178-79, **181**,
    286, 297

Zenaida asiatica, 87
    macroura, 87
Zonotrichia albicollis, 137
    atricapilla, 136-37
    leucophrys, 136
    querula, 136